HAMPTON SIDES

Americana

A native of Memphis, Hampton Sides is editor-at-large for *Outside* magazine, and the author of *Ghost Soldiers*. He won the 2002 PEN USA award for nonfiction, and in 2003 he was nominated for a National Magazine Award. He lives in New Mexico with his wife, Anne, and their three sons. He is at work on a narrative history about the conquest and exile of the Navajos.

Americana

Americana

Dispatches from the New Frontier

HAMPTON SIDES

ANCHOR BOOKS
A Division of Random House, Inc.
New York

Some of the essays in this book have been previously published in different form in the
following magazines: *DoubleTake, Icon, Memphis Magazine, Men's Journal, Mid-Atlantic
Country, Modern Maturity, The New Republic, The New Yorker, Outside, Penthouse,
Preservation Magazine, The Washington Post, The Washington Post Magazine,
The Washingtonian,* and *Worth.*

In addition, some of the essays in this book were originally published in *Stomping Grounds,*
published by William Morrow, New York, in 1992.

In the piece "A Murder in Falkner," several names have been changed to protect
the privacy of persons involved in the case.

Library of Congress Cataloging-in-Publication Data
Sides, Hampton.
Americana : dispatches from the new frontier / Hampton Sides.—1st Anchor Books ed.
p.   cm.
ISBN 1-4000-3355-1
1. United States—Description and travel—Anecdotes.   2. United States—Social life
and customs—1971- —Anecdotes.   3. United States—Biography—Anecdotes.
4. National characteristics, American—Anecdotes.
5. Sides, Hampton—Travel—United States—Anecdotes.   I. Title.
E169.04S564 2004
973.929—dc22   2003066439

Book design by Anne Scatto / Pixel Press

www.anchorbooks.com

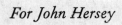

For John Hersey

Contents

Introduction

A FEW YEARS AGO, I was passing through Marrakech on my way to the Sahara for a magazine assignment. One afternoon, outside Le Mamounia Hotel, I was accosted, as all tourists inevitably are, by a "guide." He was an intense young Berber with penetrating eyes and a brisk stride, one of those canny creatures of the bazaar. He wore a slick black suit.

"Hello, American?" he said, instantly sizing me up.

"No, no American," I replied and walked on as fast as I could. Not that I'm embarrassed by my nationality, but I'd been told the guides assume all Americans are loaded. Besides, I didn't want a guide that day, and this guy really seemed like an operator.

He looked puzzled. "American, yes? You need guide for the souk. We buy rugs now."

I shook my head vigorously and picked up my step, but he persisted. "British, German, yes? Canadian?" I could almost hear his brain racing.

"I am Finnish," I said. Someone had told me this always throws the guides.

"Finished?"

"No, I from Helsinki, Finland. *Fin*-land. I speak a Finnish, no understand you."

He walked alongside me a hundred yards toward the market without saying a word, thinking so hard that he seemed on the verge of a massive aneurysm. At last he made a pronouncement: "No Finland. You are American. You need a guide."

I was beaten down by his relentlessness. "You're right," I said. "I'm American, and I need a guide. Let's go buy lots of rugs!"

And so we walked deep into the hot, loud maze of the Marrakech souk. He took me to shops and stalls that were doubtless owned by his various cousins. We haggled over cups of mint tea. Of course, I bought rugs.

Over the next few days, we became friends. His name was (what else?) Muhammad, and he was originally from a small village in the Atlas Mountains. After dinner one night, we went over to his tiny apartment, and he put on a Queen eight-track. We smoked a variety of hand-rolled cigarettes, talking far into the night. We argued about politics—he didn't understand why America was so intent on running the planet, why we singled out Saddam Hussein, why we were always dropping bombs on countries we didn't like. Still, he was fascinated by America, dazzled by its freedoms and its energy. "I will go there, some-day," he declared.

"Muhammad," I said, zoning out (the cigarettes were good). "Right from the start, how did you know I was American?"

I had thought, stupidly, that Americans passed under the stylistic radar screen. That being American wasn't so much a look or a man-ner as it was an absence of one. That we were a mutt race of people whose only real defining characteristic was our lack of defining charac-teristics.

But Muhammad had made a career of assessing people of all nationalities, and his instincts were razor sharp. "It's in the eyes," he said. "In the walk. The way you hold your mouth. Your hands, clothes. It's everything."

"But what is it?" I wanted to know. "What does an American look like?"

"Confident," Muhammad answered. "Confident like you own the world. But open."

THE OLDER I GET, the surer I am that I have no idea what America "means." The more I read and travel, the more jaundiced I grow toward anyone who claims to have "found" this country. The United States of America is such a glorious mess of contradiction, such a crazy quilt of competing themes, such a fecund mishmash of people and ideas, that defining us is pretty much pointless. There is, of course, a kind of faded notion of "Americana," one that concerns Route 66, din-ers, freak rock formations, and the like—but even in its halcyon days this "roadside attraction" version of America was never an accurate or nuanced distillation of our massively complicated culture.

On the other hand, there are stories out there, contemporary stories, that have a certain quality of "American-ness." There are scenes and places, wattages and personages, that belong—inextricably, unmistakably—to this country and this country alone. There is an American quality, a tone, an energy as instantly recognizable as I was to Muhammad. "Confident but open" may be as good as any description I've heard for it.

We're a supremely confident people, sure of our ways, proud of our machines, swaggering with our guns—a people confident enough to wage preemptive war on sovereign nations in defiance of world opinion. This confidence, perhaps rooted in our frontier past and in the licenses of our Constitution, scares the crap out of other countries, especially now that the United States has achieved a cultural and military hegemony without parallel in the history of the world.

But it's a confidence that, more often than not, is also cut with an extraordinary openness to change, a youthful embrace of new ideas and new people and indeed, anything new. The two qualities feed off each other, I think: More than anything else, our confidence comes from our openness.

We're still a country living on the frontier, it seems to me, only the frontier today is less geographical than it is social. Having pushed our physical borders, we're now pushing the boundaries of how we live and organize our lives, lighting out for uncharted territory.

This tendency is best seen in our knack for spawning subcultures of every strain and stripe. I love traveling around America and falling in with various tribes: Harley bikers, Grand Canyon dorymen, Mormon archaeologists, high-end audiophiles, World War II veterans, ravers, cavers, spelling bee champions, Tupperware sales ladies, skateboarders. I love losing myself in group gatherings, tribal hideouts and places of pilgrimage. Ours is a land of refined fanaticism. Anything we might dream of doing, we can find a society of Americans who are already doing it, and doing it so intensely that they've organized their lives around it. They buy the tools and toys. They build up a circle of friends in the group. They spend their vacations doing whatever the group does. They slip into the subcultural lagoon, and by degrees of emotional and financial investment, they become submerged.

Over the past fifteen years or so, I've worked this vein of subject matter with a consistency of fascination that, looking back on it now, surprises me. Most of the thirty pieces in this book came about in the haphazard, give-and-take way in which magazine assignments usually evolve. The idea of collecting them in one place didn't occur to me until last year, when I looked back and realized that I'd reached a kind of critical mass of material touching on the same broad theme—a theme that works and plays with a more modern notion of "Americana."

I hope this collection captures something real and true about who we are, even if who we are is always changing. I hope also that in the final section of the book I've managed to convey some of the daunting challenges our country has faced, sometimes heroically, since September 11, 2001. If these thirty pieces have a consistent theme and voice, I hope it can be said that they're "confident but open."

As a writer and a citizen, I'm grateful to be living in this vast protean hulk of a country during these times—these scary, strenuous, intensely interesting times. Whatever we are, whatever we "mean," there's never been a country like us.

No offense to Finland, but I'm an American.

SANTA FE, NOVEMBER 2003

AMERICAN ORIGINALS

The Birdman Drops In

Las Vegas, Nevada

THE GROMS PRESS FORWARD, inching eagerly toward the arena entrance. Mullet-haired rampheads, bescabbed halfpipe urchins, scuffling along in their clompy skate shoes, their laces tied with a precise looseness. Eight thousand zitty faces lit with incipient testosterone, waiting to be shown revolutionary ways in which Newtonian physics can be warped, postponed, and dicked with.

They've come to the Mandalay Bay Area in Las Vegas for a new kind of entertainment, a show that pumps the raw crude of male adolescence, a hormonic convergence of phatness and sweetness and straight-out sickness. These young acolytes have come for amplitude, for stunts and biffs, for grinds and grabs and serious air, for loud music and fumy motorcycle farts.

They've come for the Boom Boom HuckJam.

Once through the doors, the grommets come face-to-face with the thing itself. Behind a scrim of netting lies a baroque installation of giant stages, jumps, and ramps glinting in a swirl of strobe lights. Soon the chanting begins—*toe-KNEE, toe-KNEE, toe-KNEE*—the whole arena surging with raw skate-kid wattage.

Tony Hawk is the mind and wallet behind this unprecedented show. It's his private experiment, designed as a two-hour adrenaline extravaganza, a busy amalgam of motocross, BMX, and live music, with vertical skateboarding taking center stage. Tonight is the live debut of the HuckJam. It represents a huge financial gamble for the thirty-four-year-old skateboarding venture capitalist; nearly $1 million of Hawk's own money is invested in this modern vaudeville act, which he will take on the road.

Toe-KNEE, toe-KNEE!

To my immediate left, sitting with his dad in the VIP section, is Jonathan Lipnicki, the bespectacled twelve-year-old child star of *Stuart Little* and *Jerry Maguire*. Lipnicki has been a Hawk fan for as long as he can remember. "Oh yeah, Tony's, like, the *greatest!*" he says.

Now the circus-barking announcer starts whipping up the crowd: *Las Vegas! We need a little thunder!*

A few aisles over sit Hawk's mom, Nancy, his wife, Erin, and his sister Pat, who manages the business that is Tony Hawk Inc. Near them is Sarah Hall, Hawk's publicist, who used to work as a tour assistant for the singer Michael Bolton back when he had long, curly hair and lived at the top of the charts. "Tony's bigger now than Michael ever was," she confided to me earlier at the rehearsal. "Even at his peak, even with 'When a Man Loves a Woman.' He's *that* huge."

C'mon Vegas—we're not with you yet!

In front of me sits an executive from Hansen's, the beverage company. They're poised to inflict a new energy drink on American youth called Monster. The exec says she's been negotiating with Hawk's people to strike up a sponsorship deal. "Tony's hard to walk away from," she says over the roar.

Energy drink? Like ginseng, ginkgo—that sort of thing?

"Caffeine, mostly," she shouts. "And sugar. We use *lots* of sugar."

Las Vegas, let's hear some more noise!

Now the houselights go out and a bevy of fembots—jiggy young models in silver lamé body stockings, white Lone Ranger masks, and platinum-blond wigs—come out holding signs that signal the start of the HuckJam. From the far stage, swaddled in a dry-ice haze, the punk band Social Distortion cranks up.

C'mon, people, let's DO this!

Here come the skateboarders—zipping down, one by one, from a thirty-foot-high perch in the scaffolding. Like buzzy, looping electrons, Bob Burnquist, Andy Macdonald, Lincoln Ueda, Bucky Lasek, and Shaun White—five of the preeminent vert skaters in the world—power through the massive bronze bowl of the halfpipe and launch high over the lip in a dervish of spins and kickflips, ollies and McTwists. And then—

Ladies and gentulmennnnnnnnn . . .

The man we've all been waiting for dives down the ramp, lanky and tough-sinewed and—true to his name—curiously avian, with a beaky nose and flailing arms and big, alert eyes. He soars through the air and lands effortlessly on the platform with the other skaters, Quetzalcoatl among mere mortals: *the Birdman.*

Calmly drinking in the adulation, Hawk hoists his board over his helmeted head and tips it toward the roaring crowd in a ritual gesture of beneficence, as if to say, "Welcome, children of the pipe, your sins are forgiven!"

Now let's hear some Las Vegas thunder for TOE-KNEEEEEEE HAWWWWWWWWWWK!!!!!!!!!!!!!!

A FEW DAYS BEFORE I FIRST MET Tony Hawk, I was skiing down a chute on California's Mammoth Mountain when I hit a patch of ice. The next instant I was pinwheeling, out of control, for three hundred terrifying yards. I ended up in the hospital with a broken humerus and a messed-up shoulder socket. Alex, the ski-patrol guy who sledded me down to the clinic, kept asking me questions. "Who is the president? What do you do for a living?"

I'm a writer, I said. I'm working on a story about a skateboarder named Tony Hawk.

"The *Birdman?*" Alex's expression changed completely: no longer was I just another boring casualty. I'd seen the same look of reverence on the face of my nine-year-old son, whose room is pretty much wallpapered with Hawk posters. "Growing up, I worshiped him," Alex told me. "I still do. He's like a god."

Three days later, I'm at the Four Seasons Resort in Carlsbad, California, my arm in a sling, and I'm trying to interview the god himself through a fog of Vicodin. The Four Seasons seems like a weird lunch spot for a skateboarder, a very staid, adult establishment with Haydn pomp-and-circumstancing in the background and, in one corner, a bridge game in full swing. But Hawk suggested the place and raved about its buffet. As we settle into lunch, I have a hard time cutting my prime rib with my slinged arm, and there comes an awkward moment when Hawk is clearly thinking, *Should I help the poor wretch?* He decides against it.

Maybe he doesn't want to seem patronizing. Just as likely, he's unimpressed by my puny injury. Here's a guy, a professional human projectile, basically, who is intimately acquainted with words like *meniscus* and *arthroscopic*. A guy who's knocked himself out a half dozen times, fractured his ribs, broken his elbow, sustained several concussions, had his front teeth bashed in twice, all while collecting stitches too numerous to count. *You broke your arm—so what?*

But as we sit there, Hawk's initial reserve wears off, and he projects an endearing, youthful innocence. Though he's the father of three boys, though he has three stockbrokers and two agents and rakes in eight digits a year, he still somehow carries himself like a kid, a manteen in the promised land.

Hawk seems bright in the same way a bright sixteen-year-old does—sharp, watchful, with quick reflexes but little use for introspection. His dirty-blond hair is neat and clipped short, almost to the point of spikiness. His voice still has an adolescent crack to it, and he speaks in a *Ridgemont High* dialect, the stoner-surfer vernacular of Southern California, in which declaratives are haphazardly turned into interrogatives with a little last-second inflection. ("I don't know why, but I've always had, like, a fetish *for watches?*") His taste in movies is refreshingly juvenile. (Favorites: *Caddyshack* and *Aliens*.) He has a young person's radar for musical infractions by artists he views as "lame" and a hypervigilance for the cool currency of brand names (just now he's down on Swatch, a former sponsor).

After lunch, Hawk tips the valet and we hop into his Lexus sports car. As we glide onto Interstate 5, he steers with one hand and recalibrates his driving environment with the other, his long, bony fingers floating over the dials and buttons in the wooden inlay of his $70,000 ride. He adjusts his Arnette sunglasses, checks his Nixon sports watch, plugs in his Apple iPod, and scrolls through tunes until he finds one he likes, by the White Stripes.

"I can fit eighteen hundred songs on a single disk," he says, with a geek's pure faith in the righteousness of electronics. As we head north, the console's navigational screen charts our blipping progress, as if we're trapped in our own private Game Boy.

The Lexus—an SC430 in a metallic plum color that the sales brochure calls "amethyst pearl"—is a recent acquisition, a product of the phenomenal success Hawk has enjoyed since rising to the status of Zeus (or is it Seuss?) in the pantheon of kids' idols. Nowadays, Hawk regularly commands up to $25,000 per skating appearance and has reportedly earned $10 million in personal income in each of the last two years. Hawk owns Tony Hawk Inc.—a San Juan Capistrano–based company that employs fifteen people—and co-owns Birdhouse Skateboards, 900 Films, Blitz Distribution, and SLAM, an action-sports management firm. Through these he markets clothes, shoes, films, skateboards, gear, events, and even a slightly scary-looking remote-control action figure. Hawk's got a foothold in retail, too, with new Hawk Skate stores in Salt Lake City, Los Angeles, and Paramus, New Jersey. Combined with the licensing deals he's made—lending his name to "signature products"—his mini-empire pulled in $314 million in 2001.

Looming over it all is the astonishing success of Activision's three-game series *Tony Hawk's Pro Skater,* to which Hawk licenses his name, likeness, and expertise. Since hitting the shelves in 1999, *Pro Skater* has become one of the most popular video games of all time, generating $473 million, with more than 12 million copies sold. The game's impact has helped make Hawk a fixture on every cable channel aimed at kids. Recent TV triumphs have included stints doing color commentary for skateboarding competitions; an ESPN2 reality-based show, *Tony Hawk's Gigantic Skatepark Tour;* and a guest appearance on Nickelodeon's hit cartoon *Rocket Power.* His autobiography, *HAWK—Occupation: Skateboarder,* which came out in 2000, was a best seller and has been optioned, perhaps inevitably, by Disney.

Thus the toys have increased in quantity and quality. Cartier watches, plasma screens, Armani suits. Over the summer, Hawk surprised Erin with a new BMW sport-utility vehicle. And then there's the house, practically a zip code unto itself, on a lagoon in Carlsbad. The bodacious five-thousand-square-foot gated mansion has been duly featured on MTV's *Cribs*. Things have actually reached the point where Hawk has started buying cars for his friends, like Elvis used to do. Because he's a nice guy. Because he can.

HAWK AND I SPEED PAST SIGNS for Legoland, past the cancerous climb of pink mission-style apartment complexes, past a billboard for a house of worship that says GOT CHURCH? This is Hawk's native turf, a place of beautiful weather, beautiful ocean, and not-so-beautiful suburban sprawl webbed by traffic-snarled highways. Though he travels constantly, Hawk feels at home only here, along this ribbon of coastal enclaves stretching north from San Diego to San Juan Capistrano—the land where he was born and raised.

"Australia's pretty cool," he says, citing a favorite foreign locale. "But I can't imagine living anywhere else but here."

Hawk's Nokia chirps for the third time in five minutes, but the liquid crystal display on the phone reads CALLER UNKNOWN, so he elects not to answer it. "Always suspect," he says, the mild scowl on his face implying that too many strangers have gotten hold of his private cell number.

Hawk, a neatnik, keeps his Lexus immaculate. The only bit of clutter is a stash of DVD games and a PlayStation, which Riley, his nine-year-old son from a previous marriage, uses to occupy himself on long trips. "Those games are awesome," Hawk says. "He never gets bored. He flew with me to South Africa recently, and he was engrossed the whole way. That's like a twenty-hour flight."

One of Riley's favorite games, naturally, is *Tony Hawk's Pro Skater*. At the outset, players can scroll down a roster of real-life professional skaters and choose to "be" any one of them—Rodney Mullen, or Chad Muska, or whoever. Each one looks strikingly like the real person and has a special arsenal of skating tricks. Riley likes to be his dad.

Riley, as it happens, is our next errand. It's nearly three o'clock, and Hawk has to pick him up at elementary school. But not in this tiny roadster. So we dash by the house and exchange the SC430 for the pickin'-up-the-kids Lexus, this one a roomy sedan. In a few minutes we're idling in the train of waiting moms, some of whom turn away from their cell phones to throw Hawk a smile of recognition. *Oh, yeah, there's the millionaire skateboard dad.*

Soon the bell rings, and the building exhales a stream of laughing kids carrying backpacks. The traffic is bad— "Cars come through here *way* too fast," Hawk says—but once there's a gap, Riley crosses over and hops in, a good-looking third-grader with blond hair.

"Hey, buddy," Hawk says, smiling in the rearview mirror.

"Hey, Dad," Riley replies. Then, under his breath: "Who's *this?*"

Once Hawk introduces me, Riley seems satisfied, if thoroughly bored. He's understandably suspicious of the stream of people vying for his father's time. I make matters worse by telling him that I have a nine-year-old boy who's into skateboarding, too.

"Oh," he says, trying to be polite.

There can be little doubt that Riley Hawk will grow up with one of the most discerning bullshit detectors on the planet. As Hawk informs me later: "Riley's gotten good at telling who really wants to be his friend, and who just wants to come over and skate with his dad. He can weed 'em out real fast."

WAY BACK IN THE MISTS of Southern California history, back when the surfboard first sprouted wheels and rolled onto the kelp-strewn shores, in the dark time of teen endeavor that's come to be known as B.E. (Before Extreme), the youth dwelled in a world that was, we now realize, pitifully dull. Gravity was a despot, feared and respected. During these primordial years—the late sixties and early seventies—the skateboard was a pale derivative of its aquatic parent. Skaters, by and large, were surfers who wanted something to do when the waves were flat and junky. They skated like surfers, too, with a hang-five style that was sinuous and cool but fundamentally uneventful.

Then one summer, during an even darker period known as the Late

Jimmy Carter Administration, the swimming pools of Southern California went dry. A historic drought was on, and cement ponds were deemed a frivolous waste. In one of those crucial moments of Darwinian advance, packs of kids started sneaking into empty backyard pools to experiment with their skateboards. They discovered that, in a pool with a nicely curved bowl, they could go up and down and up again, almost endlessly, like human pendulums. If they gathered enough momentum, they could soar over the pool's lip, do a little flippety trick in the air, and safely land to do it all over again—in one continuous splooge of adrenaline. And so the board, having shed its fins for wheels, developed wings and broke gravity's tyranny. It could *fly*.

Tony Hawk was growing up in San Diego when all this was taking shape. At the time, his father, Frank, was the president of the local Little League, and naturally he wanted his son to play baseball. But Tony hated America's pastime, hated it to the core. He hated the rules, the funny pants, the yelling parents, the peer pressure. And the truth was, he wasn't very good. As his older brother, Steve Hawk, fondly recalls: "Tony wasn't what you'd call a natural athlete. He kind of throws like a girl."

One afternoon, after striking out in a game, seven-year-old Tony leaped into a nearby ravine and hid. Frank peered over the edge and implored him to come out. Tony wouldn't budge, so Frank had to go down and drag him back up. Shortly thereafter, Tony worked up the nerve to tell his dad he was quitting baseball forever. At which point, Frank did a curious thing. Instead of getting angry, he quit baseball, too. And then he devoted much of the rest of his life to facilitating Tony's growing love affair with skateboards.

Team Hawk eventually became an unbeatable combination, but Tony's rise to prominence was far from preordained. To begin with, there was the fact that Frank and Nancy Hawk were not trying to have a fourth child when Tony came along. Frank, a champion swing dancer in Montana in his younger days, had flown torpedo bombers in the Pacific during World War II, winning the Distinguished Flying Cross. After the war, he and Nancy settled down in California and started a family—two girls (Lenore and Patricia) and then Steve. Twelve long years passed before Tony was born. Nancy, who was forty-three when she had him, says he was "a complete surprise."

Tony was a vexatious kid, full of what his mother calls a "ferocious determination" that was primarily directed at driving his parents crazy. "We said, 'Wow, how can he fight two grown adults like this?'"

That all changed when Tony turned nine. Steve, an accomplished surfer who would later become editor of *Surfer* magazine, gave his little brother an old Bahne fiberglass skateboard. Tony took to it fast, and his mood became sunnier. He'd practice for hours at a time, never tiring of the endless repetition, until he nailed a trick that had taken root in his mind.

Frank aided the cause by building Tony a series of increasingly elaborate ramps. He was a salesman by profession, but his real love was carpentry; when a Home Depot opened in Oceanside, it became his tabernacle. After Frank learned, to his dismay, that skateboarding had no formal sanctioning body to oversee competition, he created one—the National Skateboard Association—and became its first president and guiding force. Many kids are drawn to skateboarding as a means of rebelling against their parents—and authority in general. In Tony's case, his father *was* the sport's ultimate authority figure, the original skateboard dad.

In the early days, Tony was considerably handicapped by his pipe-stem physique. "People didn't take him seriously at first, because he looked like a puppet," recalls Stacy Peralta, a famous promoter who in the 1980s tapped Hawk to join the Bones Brigade, a troupe of young skaters who traveled all over the world and appeared in Peralta-produced skater documentaries like *Future Primitive* and *The Search for Animal Chin*. "He was so fine-boned and brittle-looking, we thought, If he ever falls he's going to break apart like porcelain."

"The guy was just a stick man," agrees Grant Brittain, the photo editor of *Transworld Skateboarding* magazine. Brittain ran the Del Mar Skate Ranch when Tony first started skating there in 1981. "People called him 'Bony Cock' and made fun of him because his skating wasn't very cool," says Brittain. "It wasn't surfer's style, and getting that fluid style was all that mattered back then."

Tony compensated for his gangly style by concentrating almost exclusively on tricks, perfecting a kind of human origami on the skateboard, torquing and compressing his body while launching himself in the air. These were viewed by the surfer-influenced skating establishment as technically impressive but seriously dweeby. "He became a very brainy skater," Brittain says. "He was always a bit of a geek, anyway. He took that love for technicality and applied it to his sport."

Gradually, however, Tony's twisty-spinny contrivances were accepted as the norm in halfpipe competitions, and as that happened, his career took off. He turned pro at fourteen. By seventeen, he had moved out of the house and bought his own place. Three years later, he acquired a four-and-a-half-acre property out in the desert hills of Fallbrook, California, where his dad built him a "monster skate ramp."

Rodney Mullen, a fellow conscript in the Bones Brigade who is generally regarded as the most accomplished street skater around, recalls how he watched Hawk with admiration and awe back then. "He was never satisfied with himself," Mullen says. "He's got this nagging for perfection. It has nothing to do with money or external praises or even the push of his father. It's something inside of himself—a duty he feels to his gifts."

That sense of duty sustained Hawk through the ups and downs of his early career, and even now helps him deal with the maelstrom of fame. His father, however, never got to see that part of the story; he died of cancer in 1995. After he passed away, Tony and Steve decided to honor him in quintessentially Hawkian style: they swam out to a little cove and dumped their father's ashes into the Pacific. But something about the ceremony seemed . . . off. Fortunately, Tony had saved a reserve baggie of his father's cremains. So a few days later, he and Steve did it right. They went to Home Depot, sneaked down Frank's favorite aisles, and when no one was looking, sprinkled him around.

SKATEDOM IS A POLYGLOT subculture in which tribes and alliances are constantly metamorphosing according to genre (street versus vert), modes of protection (helmet and pads versus none at all), and music (punk versus hip-hop), among other things. Hawk's rise through this world was not meteoric, but it was relentless. Bob Burnquist, a twenty-six-year-old vert champion and friend of Hawk's, has a phrase for what he brought to the party: tricks on command. "The dude invented half the moves everyone else uses," Burnquist says.

Indeed, over the years, Hawk has created eighty-five new tricks (and counting), strange contortionist maneuvers with names like the Stalefish, the Kickflip McTwist, the Nosegrind, and the Gay Twist Heelflip Body Varial—loose variations of which have also infiltrated snowboarding and surfing.

Hawk has been something else, too: a leading economic indicator of skateboarding's broader national appeal. By the time he hit twenty, he had won twenty-seven pro competitions and was without question the greatest vert skater in creation. But all the tricks in the world couldn't help him when skateboarding experienced a precipitous drop in popularity in the late eighties and early nineties, owing largely to a sketchy economy and a suddenly fickle teen market. Hawk, who had gotten used to owning a Lexus and constantly upgrading his computers and gadgets, was forced to sell the house, get rid of the car, and put himself on a five-dollar-a-day "Taco Bell allowance." Things got so bad that he briefly contemplated taking a job as a computer programmer.

What turned things around was the arrival in 1995 of a curious spectacle: ESPN's Extreme Games. Looking for a way to capitalize on kids' growing fascination with edgy sports fare, the X Games introduced a halfpipe skateboard competition. It quickly became the marquee event, the perfect distillation of what the producers were driving at—totally senseless danger in a controlled environment. And there was Hawk, the leading man in the main act, the pied halfpiper primed for prime time.

It was at the 1999 X Games in San Francisco that Hawk reached the height of his skateboarding career thus far. After eleven grueling tries, he landed a trick called the 900. The maneuver, which involves launching off the lip of a halfpipe, executing two and a half aerial rotations, and landing on the downslope without biffing, was a kind of Holy Grail of skating, a trick that many of the best practitioners had tried to master but had given up on. Hawk had obsessed over the 900 for six years, working on it during his financial doldrums and through his ascendancy to household fame. He endlessly analyzed the physics of the thing, and practiced until he knocked himself silly. When he finally nailed it that night in San Francisco, he told the media, "This is the best day of my life, I swear to God!"

Since landing the 900 and officially retiring from competition in 2000, Hawk has transcended his sport to become a pop-culture superstar, crossing a threshold of celebrity from which there is no turning back. Whatever "extreme" really is—flash, speed, exhilaration, freedom, the high likelihood of spinal-cord injury, all tied up in an aggressively marketable box—the name Tony Hawk is shorthand for it. He's the voice and look of a niche that's grown so big that nobody calls it a niche anymore.

Stacy Peralta sees Hawk as "the walking icon of all action sports. He has this bit of magic inside of him, and everybody wants a piece of it." Part of that magic is Hawk's very name. "Mattel couldn't have invented a better one," Peralta says. "It's like a toy name, a name for a cartoon hero. It sounds cool. And—this is important—it gives you the idea of soaring."

Hawk despises the term "extreme" and much of what it implies, and he's ambivalent about the role he has assumed as its leading oracle. "The term's a little condescending to us skateboarders who've been doing our thing for more than twenty years," he says. "Really, I'm doing the same thing I was doing when I was twelve."

It seems to make sense that a master of suspended animation would have a quality of arrested development, as if he freeze-framed the person he was when he perfected the thing that made him famous. People who know Hawk well talk about this strange quality he has. Peralta likens him to Peter Pan: "He's shown kids they can be kids the rest of their lives."

During an after-party at the Boom Boom HuckJam, I met a twelve-year-old named Phil Jennings who had just wangled a free Birdhouse skateboard with Hawk's signature on it. Grinning fiendishly as he clutched his new swag, Phil put it this way: "I don't even think of Tony as an adult. He doesn't act like the big man. He's one of us."

★　　★　　★

HAWK IS SITTING at his computer, talking to himself while he reads his e-mail. "They can really *do* that?" he murmurs. *"Cool."*

His wife, Erin, a former competitive ice skater, is about to turn thirty, and Hawk wants to surprise her with an ice-skating party so she can do some triple lutzes, just like old times. "It's amazing what this company can do," he says. "I looked into renting out a public ice rink, but it turns out that for twelve grand they can just come over here with Zambonis and stuff and turn our tennis court into a rink for a day."

"The sanctuary," as Hawk calls his office, is a big, bright room off the back of his house, pin-neat and stuffed with a carefully arranged assemblage of computer equipment. This is where he edits his skate videos for 900 Films, test-drives the newer versions of *Pro Skater*, and replies to e-mails from fans. He gets about three thousand a month, and he's diligent about responding, no matter how mundane or inane the message:

Hey, Tony. What's your favorite pizza topping?
—Artichoke hearts, sun-dried tomatoes.
Favorite interstate highway?
—The 5 leads me to most necessary destinations.
Hi—I am looking for information on Tony Hawk. My nephew loves him! However, as I am trying to research this name on the Web, I am gathering that he is not, in fact, an actual skater but the name of a character in a video game. Is this correct? Is there a real Tony Hawk? Thanks.

Standing in one corner is a Marvin the Martian gumball machine. Along the wall there's a framed Snoopy poster signed by Charles Schulz, and a photograph of Hawk straddling a motorcycle with his boyhood hero, Evel Knievel. Above his computer there's a signed basketball jersey under glass: Chicago Bulls No. 23. I ask him how he came by this little gem.

"One night I was ahead at the blackjack table at Mandalay Bay, so I went over to this sports memorabilia place," he says. "The jersey cost almost exactly the same as my take, so—what the hell—I bought it."

Over the years, media people have compared Hawk to Michael Jordan with such frequency that his handlers have taken to reversing the analogy: Jordan, they like to say, is the Tony Hawk of basketball. Yet the comparison falls short. Hawk will be the first to tell you that skateboarding is vastly different from basketball or any other team sport. It's unrealistic to expect any one person to represent all skatedom—let alone dominate it. "Who's the best skateboarder in the world?" Hawk asks. "That's all a matter of personal opinion."

Certainly Hawk's skating MO isn't for everyone. Some old-school skaters tend to view him as a sellout, a circus act, or worse. Hard-core street skaters—renegades in extra-baggy pants who aggressively trail-blaze urban obstacles and tend to flirt with the illicit thrill of getting arrested—could care less about the Tony Hawks of the world. If they think about him at all, they're inclined to blame him for commodifying, and therefore dorkifying, their pure underground pursuit.

Hawk has been hearing such gripes since he was sixteen, and dismisses them. "Pro skaters have always had ties to the skate companies, since the beginning," he says. "So what? You could call me a sellout only in this sense: My stuff actually *sells out*."

Not that many skaters seem to begrudge his success. "Even the most hard-core noncommercial skater says, 'Tony Hawk deserves what he gets,'" notes Grant Brittain. "We all remember the guy when he was destitute and eating at Taco Bell."

Rodney Mullen concurs. "You can say that skateboarding has been sold out to some extent, and Tony's been part of that, but at the same time he's got so much integrity. Skating's the only thing he knows. It's his expression. It's the pen with which he writes his verse."

Hawk gives me a tour of the house, which is a fair workout. The place looks like a sumptuous cross between Pier 1 and Circuit City. There are walls of speakers and big-screen TVs, with remotes and joysticks neatly stashed everywhere. He leads me to the great room, where the oversize couches are piled high with throw pillows. "You can't really *sit* in here," he says. "Erin has a bit of a pillow obsession."

He shows me the command center for all his electronics. Discreetly lodged in a massive piece of distressed furniture, it connects every imaginable system—VHS, DVD, a hundred-disc CD changer, laserdisc, Dreamcast, and a few generations of PlayStation, all wired to high-end preamps and equalizers and sliding control switches for each room in the house.

At one point, Erin comes dashing in with their one-year-old son,

Keegan, and their three-year-old son, Spencer. Keegan's smelling pretty ripe, so Erin tells Hawk to go change him. As he dashes down the hall, the baby tucked under one arm, Erin says, "Honey, you're not going to *belieeeeve* what happened today." She has a prom queen's effervescence, but she's clearly had a tough day in the child-rearing trenches. Spencer apparently *bit* one of his playmates. Erin says she spanked him, which she'd never done before.

Meanwhile, all afternoon, Riley's been out by the garage, feverishly skateboarding. I'd seen his room earlier; it's a gilt forest of skating trophies. "I really don't pressure him," Hawk says. "It's just that he's been at it since he was three." Riley's practicing up for a little stunt that will involve jumping over the Lexus SC430 in an upcoming advertisement for Hawk Shoes, Tony's own line of Adio skate footwear.

"You're not going to be mad at me if I scratch up your car, are you, Dad?" Riley asks.

"Don't worry about it," Hawk deadpans. "If anything happens, we'll just take it out of your college fund."

LATE ONE AFTERNOON, Hawk exits the highway on the outskirts of Oceanside and noses into the drive of a modest ranch house shaded by eucalyptus trees. There's a cluster of cars wedged into the yard, and next to the house a high fence guards what appears to be a large vacant lot. "Only a few of us have the key to this place," Hawk says with a grin as he cuts the engine. "We've tried to keep the location a secret." Then he gives me a look that says, *Whatever you do, don't disclose it*.

Today he's wearing baggy skater's shorts that come down almost to his knees and a T-shirt touting a sponsor, Quiksilver. His shoes are white-white, with a red H on them: a pair of Hawks, fresh from the box.

We get out, and Hawk opens the trunk and grabs an assortment of skating paraphernalia, along with a brand-new board made by his own gear company, Birdhouse. On the board's underside there's a skeletal hawk, its skull and beak sharply etched, its long talons stretching hideously as if to pluck its prey. "Rad graphics, huh?" he says, semi-facetiously. Hawk has to change boards every few weeks, he says, because the old ones quickly grow spongy and lose their pop. He tightens the trucks with an Allen wrench and lays a fresh sheet of grip tape on top of the deck.

He unfastens the gate and we file down a sandy path to behold a neighbor's worst nightmare: a stark new edifice risen from the brambles, a mountain of plywood. Call it the Hawk's Nest, his own private skate ramp, the test laboratory where he invents and perfects his latest tricks.

Last year, Hawk's celebrity grew to such a degree that he could no longer skate at his local ramp at the Encinitas YMCA without being interrupted by strangers pestering him for autographs. So he designed this leviathan of lumber and had it built for about $100,000. Even bigger than his old ramp in Fallbrook—untold truckloads of two-by-fours, metal pipes and rails, and Skatelite, a smooth, bronze, polymerized plywood, went into the construction—it would have made his father's eyes water.

As I watch, Hawk's movements take on a crisp new deliberateness, a tight gathering of energy that I haven't seen before. It reminds me of something Bob Burnquist said: "One minute Tony can be all teenager-like, and the next he's all business. He can flip the switch just like that."

He's all business now, and the clock is ticking. He's aware that everything—the companies, the sponsorships, his house and cars—is built around what he cooks up here. Like Houdini, like Knievel, Hawk acutely realizes that as far as the demanding public is concerned, he's only as good as his latest trick.

And so, in "retirement," he's had to concoct increasingly bold and sometimes cheesy stunts to catch the public's eye. Over the past few years, he has, among other things: vaulted between two six-story buildings in downtown Los Angeles; ollied over recumbent *Today* show host Ann Curry; and launched himself across the "Murrietta Fat Gap," a huge set of ramps separated by a hair-raising gap that grew from twelve to eighteen to twenty-four feet wide as Tony ratcheted up the pucker factor. The ramp was built just so the feat could be documented by the drooling photographers of *Transworld Skateboarding*. And now there's the Boom Boom HuckJam, which he's taking on a twenty-four-city tour.

Hawk has fun coming up with these projects, but he's clearly under an enormous amount of pressure. Kids pepper his Web site (clubtony hawk.com) with e-mails beseeching him to try the next obvious permutation of the 900: a 1,080, three full rotations in the air. 1,080 OR BUST! they write. Hawk's response: "I'm gonna have to go with 'bust' at this point."

Walking beneath the halfpipe's ribbed underbelly, we hear the scratch and smack of urethane wheels on the upper lip. "Sounds like a good session," Hawk says. He hasn't had a chance to skate in days, and he's itchy and restless. A small group of his buddies are already on the ramp. Chris and Jesse, Matt and Andy. A few hangers-on click pictures and hoot praise—*ooooooooh yeah, sick*—whenever someone lands a nice one. Hawk and his crew greet one another with a series of inscrutable salutations—various yodeling noises, Hawaiian-style bruddah handshakes, catcalls of *sweeeeeeit, dooood*—the preverbal patois of the skating fraternity. To his friends, Hawk is known simply as T, as though more than one syllable would break the linguistic bank.

Hawk grew up with many of these guys, and partied with them when his ramp in Fallbrook was the place to skate and hang. Now he employs many of them. They travel with him, promote him, shield him. And, of course, they skate with him. Hawk would no more want to skate alone than an improv saxophonist would want to jam by himself in a phone booth. A good skate session is a social event, with each athlete bringing something to the party and feeding off the spontaneity of the group.

Hawk is visibly impatient to skate, but first things first—the tunes could stand some improvement. He patches his iPod into the boom box that's set up beside the massive floor of the halfpipe. A minute later the place is throbbing to "Terrible Life," by Nine Inch Nails.

Satisfied with the mood music, Hawk ascends the stairs to the ramp's forty-five-foot summit and, in a flurry of scritching Velcro, dons his exoskeleton of elbow guards and knee pads. I take a seat on the platform behind him and watch as he girds himself. It's then, for the first time, that I notice his shins. They look like they're covered in barnacles, twenty unforgiving years of scars and stitches and scabs layered in endless combinations: a palimpsest of injury, a wound that never heals.

"You're overrotating, dude," he says, dispensing advice to a younger skater who's having trouble landing an aerial. Then he stands back, surveying the scene below with a magisterial aloofness.

Hawk straps on his helmet and brings his board to the metal coping that defines the brink, nudging the nose over the precipice. He's looking across the halfpipe now, at a rail set high over the lip. For the past week he's been obsessing on a new trick that involves hitting this rail in a certain glancing way he's never done before.

"You could call it a Frontside Overturn Grind, or you could call it a Frontside to Switch Crooks," he explains, opaquely.

This is the way he skates, even among friends. This is the "nagging for perfection" that Mullen speaks of, the delicious little problem that's turned like a worm in his imagination. Now he gets to solve it.

Hawk glances west, where the sun is lowering into the Pacific, whence all boards sprang. He composes his lanky frame, tenses his stringy arms. His bulging blue eyes intensify. He looks suddenly serious, sober-minded, fiercely adult.

The bronze swell is clear for takeoff. Someone yells out, *"T!"*

And then, with all eyes watching in fresh admiration, the Birdman drops in.

—2002

Waiting for Liddy

Santa Ana, California

WARHOL SAID everyone would get his fifteen minutes of celebrity, but some people sure know how to stretch it out.

Back in 1987, I read that G. Gordon Liddy, the guy who botched the Watergate break-in, had founded, of all things, an academy of corporate security. "Since my name was associated with an ability to break into places," Liddy reasoned, "I made the corollary assumption that people would think I could *prevent* break-ins."

Thus was born the G. Gordon Liddy Academy of Corporate Security and Private Investigation, a traveling school for aspiring private eyes and macho men *manqué*. For $1,500 (ammo included) I could take a five-day "advanced-training seminar" featuring classes in hostage negotiation, electronic surveillance, and—my favorite—intrusion. The only criterion for enrollment in the school was a clean police record, an irony in itself: Liddy couldn't take his own course. I paused over the first blank of the application—*I will ( ) will not ( ) be bringing my own weapon*—and decided I'd rely instead on the Uzis that Liddy & Associates promised to provide at the shooting range. I received police clearance and made reservations for the next class.

*   *   *

THE COURSE WAS HELD in Southern California's Orange County, an hour south of Los Angeles.

"I'm here for the . . . uh . . . terrorist camp," I whispered to the reservations clerk at the hotel.

"Oh, you mean you're with the Liddy group!" she said. She was struggling to keep a straight face. "You're scheduled to meet in the seminar room in fifteen minutes."

I tossed my luggage in my room, made a cursory sweep for bugging devices, and wandered down to greet Gordon Liddy and my fellow classmates.

The brochure for the academy had warned us that the selection process would be rigorous. Liddy had to know exactly who we were and what our purpose was in taking the course. In an earlier class, only ten of fifty-six applicants had been accepted. (Graduates of the second class included Ron Reagan Jr. and *Rambo* author David Morrell.) No one with a history of mental illness would be accepted. "One bad applicant can jeopardize the program," the literature said. Our references would be contacted, our credit ratings checked, our résumés scrutinized. The result of this winnowing process: an elite corps of future Liddys who might one day serve as a kind of alternative intelligence network to rival the FBI and the CIA. Liddy wanted to form what he called a "post-graduate fraternal link." An alumnus of the Liddy school would have a "professional association to call upon in every corner of the nation."

Given all the talk about security, I was surprised when I learned that not one of my references had been contacted by Liddy & Associates.

I slipped into the seminar room and confronted my classmates hunkered over a long, U-shaped Formica table. G. Gordon Liddy wasn't there, but there were fifteen G. Gordon Liddy notebooks, fifteen G. Gordon Liddy sport shirts, and fifteen G. Gordon Liddy baseball caps to wear on the firing range.

The Liddy people had neatly arranged our name tags on the table, and we began to study each other's faces under the fluorescent lights.

There was Paul, a weight lifter and "business professional" from Greenville, Kentucky, who said he was ready for a career change.

There was Matt from Massachusetts, a veterinarian who said he moonlighted as a dealer of automatic weapons and countersurveillance equipment. Matt said he could relate to Gordon Liddy. "We both had to conquer our own fears," he said. "When I was afraid of water, I became a scuba diver."

There was Frank, a dapper Beverly Hills stockbroker who said he was one of Liddy's old buddies. "Every man still has some boy in him," Frank said, "and as a boy I wanted to be a policeman."

There was a thin, pale, brainy San Francisco "customs broker" named James who already seemed to know an awful lot about wiretapping.

There were Paxton and Mannix, a strange, stylish couple from Ketchum, Idaho. We all presumed they were married, though they claimed they were just partners writing a book about women and guns.

There were three homicide cops, an ex-FBI agent, a former starting lineman for UCLA, a criminal-justice student from Missouri, and a dentist/fisherman from Alaska who looked a bit like Grizzly Adams.

All told, we were one white woman and fourteen white men, united in a desire to learn at the knee of the Watergate mastermind—and to fire an Uzi.

I WAS JUST A KID WHEN the Watergate scandal broke, more interested in Pop-Tarts than in what the president knew and when he knew it. But even then the man they called G. Gordon Liddy stood out. Liddy just looked mean to me, and he had an evil-sounding name that clung to my imagination like some cartoon villain. Unlike his sniveling coconspirators, Liddy never sang. I might not have understood all the constitutional shadings of Watergate, but I could appreciate a guy who refused to be a snitch.

By the time I got to college, Watergate occupied a chapter in our history textbooks, and Gordon Liddy was a cult figure on America's increasingly conservative campuses. He seemed to travel in a *film noir* netherworld that quickened our sense of the bizarre.

Liddy knew about guns, jails, fast cars, bugging devices, J. Edgar Hoover. He could talk convincingly about cops and robbers because he'd been both. He claimed he could kill a man with a pencil. None of us had ever eaten a rat. We'd never scorched the palms of our hands to prove a point. Few of us had ever believed in the rightness of anything so intensely that we'd plot the deaths of our enemies.

Of course, we could never know for sure whether Gordon Liddy had actually done these things, but that was beside the point. What was important was that he said he had done them, and said it without a flicker of remorse. What was important was the consistency of his act, the inner logic of his principles, the way his cloak-and-dagger world challenged conventional morality. As Liddy once said, "Obviously crime pays, or there'd be no crime. What would be the point?"

LESSON 1: COUNTERTERRORISM

Our first instructor was not Gordon Liddy, but one Steven Shai Goldrat, a security expert with El Al Airlines, and before that an intelligence officer with the Israeli Defense Forces. Goldrat was a barrel-chested dandy with a thick red beard and an even thicker Middle Eastern accent. He eyed us all suspiciously, then asked us to produce positive identification.

El Al is supposed to be the safest airline in the world, and, listening to Goldrat, I could understand why. He kept talking about "*methodes,*" as in "There are many *methodes* for dealing with terrorists." He made it sound like science.

"Counterterrorism," Goldrat said, "is the art of controlling as many factors as you can. You want to have what we call an 'onion system'—layer upon layer of increasingly rigid security *methodes*. A terrorist will have to peel back the layers one at a time."

Onion system or no, Goldrat made it clear that if a terrorist really wants to blow up your airplane or take you hostage, there's not much you can do about it—except stay home.

But he did offer a few "practical *methodes*":

- It's not a bad idea to affix a maple leaf to your baggage. Everybody likes Canadians.
- At the airport, beware of the "three-day Arafat beard."
- When staying in a hotel in a foreign country, don't reserve a penthouse suite. Get a lower-floor room by a staircase.

- Above all, "realize that the American government is not there for you. You are on your own."

We adjourned for the day and regrouped that night at a hopping Santa Ana singles bar called the Red Onion, which we took to calling the Red Onion System, after Professor Goldrat's metaphor about pulling back the layers. We drank long-neck Corona beers and kept our eyes peeled for characters sporting the three-day Arafat beard.

Our first day at the academy had drawn to a close without an appearance by Gordon Liddy, but we were hopeful we'd catch him for breakfast the next morning.

THE ACADEMY OF CORPORATE SECURITY, I later learned, is only the latest in a long line of services offered by G. Gordon Liddy & Associates, the Miami operation that calls itself "a full-service corporate-security company."

Apart from its traveling academy, G. Gordon Liddy & Associates manages a bodyguard service, a polygraph company, a security consulting firm, and a private-investigation agency with a list of clients that has reportedly included Sergio Valente, Ralph Lauren, and Citicorp. The people at Liddy & Associates claim they cracked a multimillion-dollar ring of bogus-trademark garment manufacturers in Miami a few years ago.

The company can also offer clients a ten-man "strike team" made up of Israeli, British, and Cuban commandos. Hurricane Force, as it's called, is billed as the only private antiterrorist unit in the world. Liddy has said his A-team can rescue a loved one or business executive held hostage in a foreign country for $500,000 to $1 million.

The United States armed forces have their own specially trained commandos for such rescue missions—including the Seal Team Six and Delta Force—but often, because of the vagaries of foreign policy, they aren't deployed. This is where Hurricane Force steps in, à la H. Ross Perot. "We can move rapidly," Liddy argues, "and we don't have bureaucracy to cut through."

But the people at Liddy & Associates have been vague about the actual missions that Hurricane Force performs. Liddy recently said his commandos have pulled off three "extraction missions," but he has declined to mention any dates, countries, or clients. Dr. Olaf Rankis, an "intercultural behavioral expert" who directs the Liddy Academy, concedes that thus far the missions of Hurricane Force have involved nothing more than intelligence gathering.

LESSON II: DEFENSE TACTICS

Over breakfast at the hotel, I chatted with Jim the customs broker about his interest in corporate espionage. "You know, I was just thinking," Jim said. "It would be a cinch to wiretap a telex machine." He sketched out a little diagram on a napkin. "All you'd have to do is . . ."

We waited as long as we could to catch some glimpse of Liddy, but we were already late for our class in self-defense.

Our instructor, Joel A. Kirch from upstate New York, was a badass. Second-degree karate black belt. SWAT-team commando. Nationally recognized master of the twenty-six-inch police baton. He looked like a pit bull: buzz cut, smoldering eyeballs, bulging jugular vein. "The best self-defense," he said, "is one in which you bring your man under control without tissue damage."

Kirch claimed he could teach us to defend ourselves in a matter of eight hours. "Most bodyguards, like those guys who hang around Sylvester Stallone, are old-fashioned goons. They just beat the hell out of people. Today you're going to learn sophisticated techniques— maximum control with minimum effort."

Kirch broke out a couple of large punching bags and lined us up for combat drills: elbow blocks, sucker punches, roundhouse kicks, and a little move that Kirch called "the knee blitz." He barked directions like a line coach. "C'mon, fellas, pop it! Let's see some power!"

Kirch then touched on a few high-tech concepts: the reactionary gap, the body-space theory, the figure-eight nightstick system, Koga and Lamb methods.

"Okay, say you're a cop," Kirch said. "Large Lewis is eating the green off the bar. He's becoming combative. What ya wanna do? You wanna take out your little piece of wood and bonk him over the head, that's what. But you can't do that. You can get your ass sued. You gotta use *humane* methods."

Kirch claimed his revolutionary "pressure point" techniques were guaranteed not to result in a criminal indictment. No lawsuits. "Plenty of pain, but no tissue damage whatsoever."

If you hook your thumb over the little L-curve near the base of your jawbone, and drive it deep into a certain pocket of flesh and nerves just below the earlobe, you'll find that it creates intense pain. This is one of Kirch's pressure points. The idea is to grab your opponent, locate his pressure point, and squeeze like hell, the way Spock does it on *Star Trek*. The pain will leave your man compliant.

The only problem is finding the pressure points. By the time you get your hands on the exact spot, the thug has clobbered you with a crowbar and is on his way. Kirsch didn't talk about this.

Practicing the pressure-point technique was no fun, either. We stood around feeling each other's heads like a bunch of est groupies. When the pressure on the nerve became unbearable, we were supposed to tap our knees—but most of us just screamed.

GORDON LIDDY SPENT MOST of his life waiting for something to happen.

Read *Will* and you get a portrait of a man forever preparing himself for conflicts that never developed, enemies that never materialized, wars that passed him by or were never declared—except, perhaps, in his head.

Born in 1930, George Gordon Battle Liddy grew up Catholic just outside Manhattan in Hoboken, New Jersey. In *Will*, Liddy writes that he was a meek and sickly boy, ashamed of himself and afraid of just about everything: thunderstorms, dirigibles, fire, people, and pain. He stood in awe of his father, Sylvester J. Liddy, a successful Wall Street attorney who ruled the family with his Jesuit's sense of rectitude. Sylvester Liddy was the sort of man who, each spring, would make his boy Gordon sign a formal contract promising that he would try out for the baseball team.

Gordon's uncle Ray was an FBI agent in Manhattan, and some evenings he would drop by the Liddy house and tell swashbuckling tales. Young Gordon was fascinated by this bold world of cops and robbers.

In the late 1930s, the family employed a German maid who sometimes listened to the speeches of Adolf Hitler on the Liddys' radio. Though Gordon didn't understand a word of German, the mesmerizing surges of the Führer's voice had a strange effect on him. Somehow it helped inspire him to embark on the odyssey of self-discipline for which he would become notorious following the publication of *Will*.

He was afraid of lightning, so he strapped himself high up in a tree during an electrical storm. He was afraid of rats, so he cooked one and ate it. He was afraid of pain, so he sizzled his hand over a candle flame. It was supposed to strengthen his will, transforming him into nothing less than an *Übermensch*—a fearless and disciplined soldier.

Liddy graduated from his father's alma mater, Fordham University, an old Jesuit school in the Bronx, where he was a B-plus student and a cross-country runner. More than anything else, the Liddy of that era yearned to prove his manhood on the battlefield. He'd been too young for World War II, but now the Korean War was coming on, so he enlisted in the army with the hope of seeing action.

He remembers vividly the day he overcame his fear of killing—by learning how to slaughter chickens.

"I killed and killed and killed, getting less and less bloody, swifter and swifter, surer with my ax stroke, until finally I could kill efficiently and without emotion or thought. I was satisfied: When it came my turn to go to war, I would be ready. I could kill as I could run—like a machine."

But the killing machine came down with appendicitis just before he was scheduled to go off to Korea. He was assigned to radar detail, with orders to scan the skies of New York City for Russian bombers. By the time he was fully recovered, the war was over. He never killed anything but chickens.

LESSON III: RISK ASSESSMENT/ASSET PROTECTION

Professor John J. Strauchs, an electronic wizard with a background in the CIA and military intelligence, is a big gun in the world of burglar alarm systems. A pale, affable chain-smoker with crafty eyes, he wore a rumpled pinstriped suit and carried an old briefcase crammed with sensors, meters, buzzers, and a jumble of other electronic paraphernalia.

Strauchs's company—the Systech Group of Great Falls, Virginia—designs security systems for Fortune 100 companies, prisons, and military operations.

Strauchs works in a field in which the line between measure and countermeasure, tactic and countertactic, is not always crystal-clear. "Security," Strauchs told the academy class, "is a magnificent cat-and-mouse game with gadgets, toys, and James Bondish stuff. You need to think like a thief. The best way to have a good defense is to imagine what the offense is going to be."

Strauchs quickly moved us into some intricate stuff: Wheatstone bridges, McCullough loops, ultrasound sensors, and a little something he called a piezoelectric crystal.

We learned that if you really want to understand how a building is being used, the first thing you do is examine the trash. "It's like archaeology," he said.

Strauchs said that razor-ribbon fences—the tall, menacing ones with barbed wire curling along the top—are practically useless. "Razor-ribbon is psychologically intimidating, but people can get through it in seven seconds without having to go to the hospital. Sure, there are nicks, but I get nicked shaving in the morning."

At the end of the class, someone asked Professor Strauchs what kind of alarm system he uses for his own home. "None," he said. "I don't even have one of those little stickers on my door that *says* I've got an alarm system."

I searched for Liddy that evening in the hotel lounge, but no luck.

AFTER NARROWLY MISSING ACTION in Korea, Liddy enrolled in Fordham's law school, where he worked on the law review and spent his free time hunting down the perfect mate. He broke up with one longtime girlfriend when he realized her gene pool wasn't too promising.

"I had read Lindbergh and was very impressed by the logic of his emphasis upon genetics in choosing his wife," Liddy wrote in *Will*. "I wanted more mathematical ability in the gene pool from which my children would spring. I also wanted size—height and heavy bone structure—so that my children would be physically as well as intellectually powerful. . . . I had worked long, hard, pain-filled years to transform myself. . . . Now I believed I had earned the right to seek my mate from among the finest genetic material available."

Finally Liddy found the material he was looking for in Frances Purcell, a tall, auburn-haired IBM employee from Poughkeepsie. "I knew she was the woman I wanted to bear my children," Liddy wrote. "A Teuton-Celt of high intelligence, a mathematical mind, physical size, strength, and beauty—she had it all."

They were married in 1957 and moved to Indiana, where Liddy took his first assignment as an FBI agent. He says he temporarily dropped the G in G. Gordon Liddy because he "abhorred the thought that I might be suspected of a fawning emulation of J. Edgar Hoover." During those years in Gary and Indianapolis, he says, he became so proficient with firearms that "I could walk down the mean streets and everyone would instantly know I was the most dangerous person around." Though today Liddy makes much of his handgun prowess, he admits he never actually used a firearm during his years with the FBI.

In 1962 Liddy left the FBI, temporarily joined his father's law practice in Manhattan, and then moved to Poughkeepsie to take a job as assistant district attorney for Dutchess County.

As a local prosecutor, Liddy was flamboyant, confrontational, a headline-grabber. He once fired a gun in court. In another case, he smashed a two-by-four across the rail of the jury box. He conducted a drug raid on a Dutchess County house owned by Dr. Timothy Leary and caught the counterculture figure and his groupies literally with their pants down.

All the while, Liddy was steeling his willpower through his old childhood regimen of inflicting pain on himself. On one occasion, he says, he burned a finger so badly that it needed surgical attention.

In 1969 Liddy moved to Washington to work in the Nixon Treasury Department as a special assistant to the secretary. At Treasury, he earned a reputation as a good soldier who would carry out any mission assigned to him. He was instrumental in waging a sweeping antimarijuana campaign known as Operation Intercept, which amounted to a blockade of the Mexican border.

A few years later, Liddy was assigned to the White House for "special duties." One of his duties was to lead a clandestine investigation of Daniel Ellsberg, the man who had leaked the Pentagon Papers. It was during this investigation that Liddy and a crew of Cuban recruits broke into the Los Angeles office of Ellsberg's psychiatrist, Dr. Lewis Fielding.

In December 1971, Liddy went to work as general counsel for the Committee to Reelect the President. From the beginning, he saw his job in martial terms. "The nation was at war not only externally in Vietnam but internally . . ." Liddy writes. "I had learned long ago the maxims of Cicero that laws are inoperative in war. With an ice-cold, deliberate certainty I knew exactly what I was going to be doing, and it was damn well about time: I was going to throw the Battle Override."

Liddy had a lot of crackpot plans during his days at the Committee to Reelect the President (CREEP). Lucky for him, most of them were never implemented.

He volunteered to assassinate columnist Jack Anderson. He devised an elaborate plot to fire bomb the Brookings Institution. He wanted to wiretap the *New York Times.* He tried to plant agent provocateurs at nearly every liberal rally and demonstration. He wanted to drug Daniel Ellsberg with LSD dusted on the steering wheel of his car. And as the Watergate scandal unfolded, he volunteered to kill E. Howard Hunt—and then be killed himself.

If Liddy was serious about pulling off any of these plots, he would have needed far more cunning than he showed during the break-in at the Democratic National Committee Headquarters on June 17, 1972. The job was, in every imaginable way, a fiasco.

First, there is the matter of the masking tape across the lock of the service-entrance door. Anybody with any sense of caution would have taped the door vertically so it wouldn't show. Liddy's men not only taped it horizontally, they retaped it horizontally after the Watergate night watchman discovered it the first time. Seeing the door taped a second time, the night watchman did what you'd expect him to do: He called the police.

Second, Liddy paid the Cubans in cash minutes before the break-in. So when the cops nabbed the burglars, there they were with wads of sequentially marked $100 bills in their pockets. It was only a matter of time before the bills were traced back to CREEP.

Third, Liddy chose to plot the break-in out of another room in the Watergate complex, room 214. One of the Cubans had the room key in his pocket at the time of the arrest. The cops also found, among other things, an address book owned by one of the Cubans. Penciled in the address book was the name E. Howard Hunt and the words "W. House."

You didn't have to be Bob Woodward to realize something was fishy.

LESSON IV: EXECUTIVE PROTECTION

Professor J. Linton Jordahl, a former security agent with the Department of Justice and a decorated Vietnam vet, hobbled into the seminar room on a cane. He said he had snapped his spine in a high-speed car chase a few years back. The crash had forced him into early retirement after fourteen years in the federal-marshal program. One of his last assignments had been guarding defendant John Hinckley—"that lazy wimp," Jordahl called him.

Professor Jordahl limped around the room and played videotapes of political assassination attempts from modern history. *Click.* In a black-and-white news clip from 1972, a dark Filipino hit man emerges from a crowd and slashes Imelda Marcos with a bolo knife. *Click.* A band of Egyptian terrorists gun down Anwar Sadat and his military brass. *Click.* James Brady sprawls on the pavement as agents shove President Reagan into a limo. Jordahl analyzed each scene for early hints of danger, pausing on a frame to point out the obvious breaches of security. "I like to put the press up front," Jordahl said. "They make a good buffer zone."

Click. The attempted assassination of George Wallace, Jordahl said, was a "textbook case in crisis mismanagement, a real classic." He suggested it might have been "*pro*acted" through elementary measures. Jordahl froze the VCR on a frame showing Wallace's wife kneeling over the Alabama governor's bleeding body and crying hysterically for help. "Look at her," Jordahl said. "She's not serious. She dumped him a little later. She's just doing it for the publicity."

Jordahl then passed out a half dozen pistols and demonstrated the proper technique for wresting a handgun from an assailant. This was not very easy to practice on a live subject, like a classmate. Jordahl told us that in real life, if you're any good at handgun snatching, you're supposed to move so fast that you rip the would-be assassin's trigger finger clear out of its socket.

Jordahl urged us to watch for people who "just don't look right." He had his own terms to describe such a person: "clown, yo-yo, dingdong, raghead, a squirrelly type, a save-the-whatever, a funny one."

Left-wingers or right-wingers, there is an element of science when it comes to spotting potential assailants in a crowd, Jordahl assured us:

"Secret Service agents are aware of the classic assassin profile. Fits every presidential assailant from John Wilkes Booth to Lee Harvey Oswald. A white male, short, slight of build, feels unfairly treated; has no stable masculine figure to identify with; has few meaningful relationships with women; and usually is a paranoid schizophrenic.

"Incidentally," said Professor Jordahl, hobbling back to the overhead projector, "in the last class we had someone who fit the assassin profile to a tee. Boy, was that clown squirming!"

UNREPENTANT AND UNWILLING TO TALK, Liddy was convicted on nine felony charges. Judge John Sirica sentenced him to twenty years, and he served forty-four months in eight jails before his parole in September 1977. He called prison "a mere occupational hazard."

The sphinx of Watergate was flat broke the day he squealed out of the parking lot of a Connecticut prison—free at last, even though he could see reporters chasing him in the rearview mirror. Today Liddy is living prosperously. He winters in the resort community of Scottsdale, Arizona, and summers in Fort Washington, Maryland, overlooking the Potomac in a spacious home he claims was owned by *Advise and Consent* author Allen Drury. The license plate on Liddy's Volvo reads: H20-GATE. Liddy's first book—an intrigue novel entitled *Out of Control*—didn't do so well, but *Will* has gone through multiple printings and is now considered a back-order classic. In some bookstores it even winds up on the "inspirational works" shelf. Liddy also enjoys the profits from the made-for-television movie based on *Will*, starring Robert Conrad as the man with his hand over the candle.

Liddy isn't the only Watergate conspirator who has risen from his own ashes—just the most flamboyant. H. R. Haldeman bought a chain of Sizzler steakhouses. John Ehrlichman wrote best-selling books. Chuck Colson found God and started up his own prison ministry. And E. Howard Hunt reportedly wrote a musical about the Claus von Bülow trial. Liddy says he gets together with some of his old Watergate cronies once a year to talk about "the good old days."

Between his lectures and his films, Liddy doesn't have much time for gun collecting. Besides, as a convicted felon nine times over, he's not supposed to own handguns. "But," he says, "I must tell you that Mrs. Liddy has an absolutely fascinating collection of firearms, some of which she keeps on my side of the bed."

LESSON V: MOTORCADES

Our last day at the academy and still no Liddy. But Jack Sague, the Cuban-American spokesman, told us at breakfast that Liddy would definitely be arriving sometime that day.

Linton Jordahl had us out all morning practicing an elaborate motorcade drill, complete with walkie-talkies, limos, and a follow car. Jordahl wanted us to execute the drill flawlessly because our motorcade would be used later in the day to escort G. Gordon Liddy himself to the lobby of the hotel.

This was to be Liddy's grand entrance. He would play the role of VIP, and we would be Secret Service agents protecting our man from "snipers" and a throng of reporters. Liddy would arrive in style while we showed off our new skills. And, of course, the carefully orchestrated event would make a wonderful photo opportunity for the local papers.

So we put on our finest suits and our aviator glasses. We synchronized our watches. We turned on our walkie-talkies. We waited for the appointed hour of Liddy's arrival. We climbed into our limos and drove to the appointed spot. And then we waited. And waited. And waited.

But Liddy wasn't there.

His associates told us his plane was a little late.

When Liddy finally did show up, two hours after that, it was time for our late-afternoon "commencement exercises" in the seminar room. Liddy ambled in wearing a red blazer and a wide, cream-colored tie. His head was shaved like Mr. T's, and he was looking a little pasty in the face. He stood up and gave a meandering, ten-minute "motivational talk" on the future of corporate security and private investigation that was mostly composed of warmed-over passages from *Will* and his standard college lectures.

"You are going to be the only game in town," Liddy told us. "You're our only hope. You can write your own ticket." He said a couple of outrageous things about guns and killing, but you could see he didn't have his heart in it.

He signed our diplomas, and when my turn came, I went up and shook his hand before the photographers. I looked down and studied my certificate with its gold seal and the fine cursive script, which proclaimed that I had fulfilled the requirements of the board of governors of the G. Gordon Liddy Academy, "with all the rights, privileges, and honors thereto pertaining here and elsewhere."

In the cocktail lounge, the students and reporters were squirming to get at Liddy like pups at a teat. He was cordial and articulate, and he seemed to have a good-natured awareness of the absurdity of the scene. Though his lines were a little stale and his features a little shallow, he was still the consummate showman.

A little later, in a casual conversation with Jack Sague, my worst suspicions were confirmed: G. Gordon Liddy doesn't actually have anything to do with G. Gordon Liddy Academy—other than his little eleventh-hour publicity appearance.

Liddy's name was emblazoned in bright red letters on our navy-blue T-shirts and our diplomas, and the brochure officially listed him as a "course instructor." But Liddy didn't instruct any courses. He didn't plan the curriculum. He didn't hire the teachers. He didn't screen the applicants. And the guy who supposedly *was* responsible for all these details, the behavioral expert they call Dr. Olaf Rankis, never showed up, either.

Sague also informed me that Liddy & Associates was not able to procure that Uzi they had promised us for the firing range the next day. "We're still in the formative stages," Sague kept apologizing. "We're still trying to figure out what people want."

But no one seemed to mind all this confusion. These guys were getting to share war stories with the real G. Gordon Liddy *in a bar*. They kept hovering around this middle-aged celebrity with the shaved head and the red blazer who had made such a fortune off his own mistakes. You could see they were having the time of their lives.

Someone asked Liddy his opinion of the Iran-Contra scandal. "I have the highest regard for Colonel North," he replied. "I would have done exactly the same thing he did—except on a much grander scale."

He answered a few more questions, squeezed in one last photo session with the local paper, and then disappeared into the night. Total time on the scene: two hours.

I wandered over to the bar to order another beer. "You know who that guy was, don't you?" the bartender said, as if he'd seen Bigfoot.

"Yep," I answered. "G. Gordon Liddy. The man who botched the Watergate break-in."

Then the bartender placed a full glass before me and leaned over the rail. "You and me," he said, looking me straight in the eye, "we live in a strange country."

—1987

Chief Without Indians

Chinle, Arizona

FEBRUARY 17, 1997, President's Day. Russell Means is sitting barefoot inside his comfortable prefab house on the Navajo Reservation, sharing his views of some former presidents: "If Washington and Lincoln and Jefferson were sitting here today, I'd take 'em all hostage. I'd have their hands tied behind their backs."

Means peers angrily out the window at the dazzling, bitterly cold day. A gusty wind whistles under the storm door and rattles through the bare cottonwoods all around his house while a feral cat claws at the window screens. A set of old barbells lie rusting in the hard-packed dirt of his yard. Beyond his snow-dusted horse pasture, he can see a jumble of modest ranch-style houses, a Navajo hogan, a few double-wide trailers, and, farther in the distance, a Church's Fried Chicken.

"Washington," Means says, with an edge sharpening his voice, "I doubt I'd even let him go. The man was a despot. He earned his ascension to generalship by slaughtering defenseless men, women, and children in Indian villages. 'Village Destroyer,' that's what the Indians called him on the East Coast. This is the same man who supposedly said 'I cannot tell a lie.' This, the father of your country. An Indian killer."

And Lincoln?

"Lincoln's the worst of them all! In order to prosecute his war against the South, he established the military-industrial complex that has all but destroyed the indigenous peoples of this continent. Two days before delivering the Emancipation Proclamation, Lincoln signed an order to execute thirty-eight Indians in Minnesota for what was called the Great Sioux Uprising. These were innocent Indian men who'd been arrested at random! Sentenced without a hearing! Never even got a trial! So much for your 'Honest Abe.' "

Means is wearing a striped rodeo shirt, a crisp pair of Wrangler jeans, and a substantial amount of turquoise jewelry. Although he is showing signs of his fifty-seven years, he is still an intimidating presence, retaining the aura of unpredictable truculence that Andy Warhol captured so memorably in his iconic silk-screen portrait from the seventies. He's come home to Chinle to be with his wife, Gloria, a Navajo, and their two sons after nearly a month of traveling to promote his autobiography, *Where White Men Fear to Tread,* a five-hundred-page collaboration with writer Marvin Wolf. Means had hoped to spend the week relaxing, riding horses with his twelve-year-old, Tatanka, maybe reading a few scripts. But after only a few days, the pressures of domestic life are starting to mount. This morning the Navajo sanitation department had come by to pick up the trash—President's Day isn't a holiday in the Navajo Nation—and didn't empty one of the large garbage cans outside. "The bastards!" Means says. "Lazy government bastards! God, I hate lazy people! I gotta go find those guys."

Then there were those stray cats yowling outside. "They come over here expecting handouts." He grimaces. "Goddamn cats!"

In late 1991, Means spent a month at a rehab clinic called Cottonwood de Tucson to deal with what he called his "simmering rage." Consumed by hatred of white America, he had made a list of a few dozen people he wanted to assassinate: senators, federal judges, prosecutors, Bureau of Indian Affairs officials, and a few random rednecks. "I planned to die in a gunfight, a martyr to my people," he writes in his autobiography. "I was, of course, quite insane."

He says his anger-management program was a success. But the more he dwells on Washington, Lincoln, and Jefferson, the more he seethes. The stern, resolute voice, which millions of kids would recognize as that of Chief Powhatan in Disney's *Pocahontas,* rises in volume and pitch. His feet begin to fidget, and his huge fingers fuss with the leather strips and silver conchos that ornament his long black braids.

"'Act like real men,' I'd tell 'em!" he yells. "Quit lying! Stop abusing your women! Stop having illegitimate babies all over the place. And maybe, if you're lucky, I might let you go."

FOR MOST OF HIS LIFE, Russell Means has been on the move, confronting history, the FBI, the courts, other Indians, and his own considerable mistakes. His life has been an exhausting series of crises and contretemps. He may be the most famous Native American alive, and yet he is still known, principally, for his actions during the heyday of the American Indian Movement, for which he served as an eloquent and charismatic national spokesman. During those brilliant early years, his identity seemed crystal-clear. Here was an uncompromising man willing to risk his life in the name of Indian sovereignty. In 1973, Means became an integral leader in a seventy-one-day standoff against United States armed forces in the tiny South Dakota town of Wounded Knee. His defiance at Wounded Knee galvanized Indians everywhere and catapulted Means to national leadership. After hearing Means speak in 1973, Vine Deloria Jr., a Lakota scholar, wrote, "In the manner and clarity of Russell Means' speech many Indian people found a strength they did not know they possessed. We should cherish this man as one of our greatest people."

But over the last few decades, Means has become an enigma, a man who has seemed desperate for allies, willing to talk to anyone, go anywhere, entertain any offer, champion any position. Coursing with an all-consuming but thoroughly unfocused wrath, he has forayed with varying degrees of success into politics, acting, freelance diplomacy, CD-ROM publishing, even rap music. Like any great warrior who failed to die young in battle, Means has had trouble carving out a clear persona for himself after the battle was over.

"Ever since Wounded Knee, Russell has seemed more and more like a blind man with a Rubik's Cube," says Laura Wittstock, a Seneca journalist and commentator who covered the standoff at Wounded Knee. "The older he's gotten, the less coherent his career seems. He's been frantically hunting around for a new identity and saying, 'Is this it? Is this it? How about *this*?'"

Means's cowriter, Marvin Wolf, offers another perspective: "Russell was prepared to die at Wounded Knee. On some level I think he might have *wanted* to die. He would have gone down in history as an Indian martyr and everything would have been simple. But, alas, the federal government wouldn't cooperate."

RUSSELL MEANS WAS BORN in November of 1939 on the Pine Ridge Reservation. His mother was Lakota, his father part Oglala and part Irish. Means characterized his mother as a domineering and ruthless perfectionist who didn't spare the rod. His father, a welder by trade, was good-natured but weak-willed and far too fond of the bottle. The family moved to Vallejo, California, a racially mixed, lower-middle-class suburb in the Bay Area. Vallejo offered certain advantages over the Pine Ridge Reservation, with its crushing poverty. But growing up in urban America left Means feeling disconnected from his heritage. He yearned for the summers, when he would visit relatives on the reservation.

In high school Means was a quick study, fiercely bright in a contrarian sort of way. He went on to study accounting at a business school in Los Angeles, but his education was interrupted by frequent drinking binges and restless travel. In 1961, when he was twenty-two, he married a Minniconjou Lakota woman, but that same year, after their son was born, the marriage fizzled. In 1962 Means moved to San Francisco, where he worked as a dance instructor and married a young Hopi woman named Betty Singquah. Soon they had a baby girl, Michele, then a son, Scott.

Throughout his twenties, Means was, by turns, a drug dealer, a con artist, a data processor, an accountant, a night watchman, a pool hustler, a petty thief, a printer, and an itinerant Indian dancer. He lived on the streets of Los Angeles for a time, selling his blood for $4 a pint. As he puts it in his book, "I was adrift, feeling like a failure, hating myself."

Then in 1969, he attended an Indian leadership conference in San

Francisco. There he first encountered Clyde Bellecourt and Dennis Banks, two Ojibway men who had formed the American Indian Movement to combat police brutality against Indians. Means was intrigued by the tactical sophistication of Banks and Bellecourt; they, in turn, were impressed with his gift as a public speaker. Soon Means joined the movement full-time.

"At the time AIM was born, American Indians were ashamed of being Indians," Means says. "AIM looked traditional. We weren't afraid to confront the white man and say, 'I'm your equal.' The Indian people were hungry for that."

For the next two years, AIM members canvassed the country, going to different towns and reservations to demonstrate. At the time, AIM focused on such issues as police brutality toward Indians, biases in the criminal justice system, Indian-themed sports mascots, and America's long and sordid history of abrogating its treaties with various tribes.

In 1970, when AIM leaders seized Mount Rushmore. Russell Means publicly urinated on George Washington's forehead. Federal authorities told them they were illegally trespassing. "We said, 'No, we're not. We have a treaty that says this land is ours—the treaty of 1868,'" recalls Means. (The Fort Laramie Treaty of 1868 had clearly established Sioux boundaries, but the reservation lands had steadily eroded since.) Later in 1970, on Thanksgiving Day, AIM seized a replica of the *Mayflower* that was anchored near Plymouth Rock, Massachusetts. Means gave a speech in which he demanded: "Pilgrims, go home!"

In 1972, AIM embarked on what it called the "Trail of Broken Treaties," a cross-country caravan through Indian reservations destined for the Bureau of Indian Affairs building in Washington, D.C. It began with about a dozen cars; the caravan arrived in Washington with almost a thousand. When negotiations with the Bureau of Indian Affairs stalled, AIM stormed the building, barricaded it for a week, and vandalized the offices almost beyond recognition. Means, already emerging as AIM's most watchable and quotable mouthpiece, told the Washington media in one particularly memorable line, "If we go, we're going to take this building with us. There's going to be a helluva smoke signal!"

It was at Wounded Knee, South Dakota, in 1973, that the face of

Russell Means became virtually synonymous in the public mind with the face of Indian defiance. AIM leaders were looking for a way to protest BIA corruption, the federal government's unlawful seizure of the Black Hills, and two centuries of violated treaties. They were hoping to force a showdown that would draw the United States into a meaningful dialogue. Wounded Knee was grimly symbolic ground, the site of the U.S. cavalry's 1890 massacre of some three hundred defenseless Lakota. Wounded Knee was also said to be the place where the heart of Crazy Horse, the great Lakota warrior, was buried.

On February 27, 1973, AIM seized the town, taking several whites hostage and holing up in a church. The U.S. Sixth Army responded with armored personnel carriers, F-4 Phantom jets, and attack helicopters. A relentless siege carried on for weeks. Two Indians were killed, nine were wounded, and one FBI agent was paralyzed.

As the event unfolded, the international media needed a single figure to focus on, and Means, with his air of intelligent menace and his ear for the nuances of the sound bite, fit the bill. "Dennis Banks was the brains, and Russell Means was the mouth," one law-enforcement official present at Wounded Knee remembers. Stolid, clench-jawed, with a jagged scar across his forehead, Means stood outside the church and told the cameras, "The federal government has to massacre us or meet our demands! . . . This is it! We are making our last stand here!" If central casting had been looking for the archetypal Indian radical, there was Russell Means, with the bone choker, the mirrored shades, and the AIM button that said, CUSTER DIED FOR YOUR SINS.

"We were fearless," Means says, "because we knew we were right."

Thousands of Indians viscerally responded to Means's defiance, and new AIM chapters sprouted all over the country. "People wanted someone to take a bullet for them, and along came this vainglorious warrior who was willing to do it," Laura Wittstock says. "He came along at a time when the stereotype of the American Indian was of a downcast, defeated old man in a cowboy hat, weaving down the street with a bottle of cheap booze in his hand. Means burst that image."

More than a few elders on the Pine Ridge Reservation declared that Means was the reincarnation of Crazy Horse, who defeated Custer in 1876 and died a martyr the following year at the age of thirty-three (he was bayoneted by a cavalryman while trying to escape U.S. custody). It was a powerful analogy, and one that Means did little to discourage. Yet there was at least one important difference: Crazy Horse never allowed himself to be photographed, while Means would spend the better part of his career seeking cameras, using the machinery of the media as his main weapon in his fight against the white man's tyranny. If Crazy Horse was a master of guerrilla warfare, Means was a master of guerrilla theater, adroitly ambushing the signs and symbols of white culture.

"Although it sounds strange to say, Russell had almost a kind of advertising mind—the knack for finding an outrageous symbol that could reduce a complex message down to one visceral image," says Canadian journalist and historian Rex Weyler, who covered the early days of AIM in his book *Blood of the Land*. "He understood that you're not going to beat up the U.S. of A. physically, that the fight was going to be won or lost on the battlefield of images."

After the siege at Wounded Knee ended with the promise of continued negotiations, AIM's treaty concerns were mostly ignored. Wounded Knee became an obsession of the Nixon White House, and AIM was targeted by the FBI's counterintelligence unit known as COINTELPRO, the unit that had infiltrated the Black Panthers in the late 1960s. One government strategy for neutralizing AIM was to tie up its leaders in time-consuming and costly legal battles—"to throw as many charges at you and see what shit sticks," says Means. It was a strategy that largely worked.

Means stood trial for various charges throughout the mid-seventies. Though he beat a murder rap, he was convicted in connection with a 1974 riot at the Sioux Falls Courthouse and went to prison in 1978. Later that year he was stabbed by another inmate in what he termed an assassination attempt. Among other celebrities, Marlon Brando and Harry Belafonte paid him a visit as he recovered from the incident. With Means and many of its other leaders now in jail, the movement was becoming increasingly marginalized.

Nevertheless, Means argues that AIM had a lasting impact. "As an organization, it was a total failure; as a consciousness, it was a total success. We reinstituted Indian self-dignity in America. We got the country to start admitting its deceit concerning the treatment of my people."

AFTER HIS RELEASE FROM PRISON in 1979, Means tried, with limited success, to step onto the political stage. He struck a series of notably odd public alliances with the likes of Larry Flynt, Louis Farrakhan, the Reverend Sun Myung Moon, and Muammar al-Qaddafi—Means's fourth honeymoon was in Libya. "I was looking for allies to the Indian cause wherever I could get them," Means says, by way of explanation, "but all of the legitimate organizations shut their doors in my face." In 1983 he accepted an invitation to be Larry Flynt's running mate in a bid for the Republican party's presidential nomination—a quixotic campaign that got off the ground only long enough to further sully Means's already damaged reputation.

"I took a gamble and I lost," Means says of the escapade. "It was a roll of the dice. I thought Flynt's campaign would give me a platform to raise some serious concerns about Indian issues. I was wrong. Still, I don't have any regrets. I mean, here's a guy who says, 'I'm going to be the best damn pornographer in the world,' and he goes out and does it. You have to appreciate that kind of honesty. He's still a good man."

In 1985 Means became interested in the plight of the Miskito Indians of Nicaragua. After taking a freelance junket to the Nicaraguan jungles, he advanced a hard-line anti-Sandinista position that put him at odds with virtually everyone who had once fought with him in the past. He was publicly denounced by his former AIM brethren—including Clyde and Vernon Bellecourt—and accused of being in bed with the CIA.

Then in 1987, he was off on an entirely different course, seeking the Libertarian party's 1988 presidential nomination—and losing in the primaries. That same year, he called a press conference to announce that he was abandoning AIM forever. As the 1980s came to a close, Means was widely seen as a man without direction and with few supporters, fighting a multitentacled war that raged primarily in his own angry heart.

*   *   *

AND THEN, as Means likes to put it, the Great Mystery intervened. In 1991, film director Michael Mann, recalling the old AIM warrior's classically chiseled features from faded newsclips, cast Means in the title role in *The Last of the Mohicans*. After the film was shot in North Carolina, Means moved to Los Angeles to pursue a film career in earnest. Thus far he's been moderately successful, appearing in a number of documentaries, television shows, and made-for-TV movies. He's also landed roles in a handful of feature films, the most notable being *Natural Born Killers* and *Pocahontas* (as the voice of Chief Powhatan).

He works out of a small, slightly dilapidated Santa Monica office he calls T.R.E.A.T.Y. Productions, where he makes and markets low-budget films, documentaries, and CDs. The office is a sunny, cramped space cluttered with scripts, videos, computers, and weight-lifting equipment. Copies of his two CDs, *Electric Warrior* and *The Radical*, are stacked on the hardwood floor. An old couch is draped with a Pendleton blanket, and eagle feathers are strategically stashed around the room. Perched in the middle of his desk is a single photograph: a picture of the little church at Wounded Knee.

I drop by the offices on a warm winter day. Means has been on the phone all morning conducting radio interviews, and he has a two-o'clock appointment with Oliver Stone. Dressed in gym shorts and a T-shirt, gripping a mug of coffee, he parks himself behind his desk, leans back, and gives a loud yawn. For a while his conversation bounces around in desultory fashion from Indian casinos ("good in the short-term but ultimately suicidal") to his dim view of the film *Dances With Wolves* ("*Lawrence of the Plains,* I call it") to the evils of linear-thinking Eurocentric society ("in six thousand years of history, the white man hasn't made a single move without first considering the dollar sign.").

Finally, he seems to be up and running. "When I was doing *Mohicans,*" he says, "it suddenly dawned on me that the entertainment industry offers one helluva venue. The movies, I realized, could be an extension of my activism, only on a much bigger stage. Instead of just being an activist, I found I could also be an artist. Because, you know, artists are the true revolutionaries. They're always the first ones to recognize the need for change."

What's an ideal role for Russell Means? I ask.

"A *starring* role," he says, with a raucous laugh.

On the wall, Means has taped a picture of Ted Turner to a bull's-eye, as though the CNN mogul were a target glimpsed within an assassin's scope.

So, I say, you're not too fond of Ted?

He runs his fingers through his hair and glowers. "He's an enemy to my people. He's the owner of the Atlanta fucking Braves, and you see him on the television doing that goddamn redneck 'tomahawk chop.' He and Jane both! They might as well be flipping the bird to every Indian in America. I mean, it's bullshit."

A quizzical look then washes over him, and his eyes move slowly around the room. "Bullshit," he says softly. "Why is it that this particular animal's excrement is synonymous with lying? Why not goatshit or llamashit or fishshit or whatever? When you think about it, it's not really fair to bulls, is it?" He busts out laughing.

His assistant, Elizabeth, brings more coffee and gently reminds Means of something he has to do later in the afternoon. His mood darkens. He looks incredulous. "Goddammit!" he yells at her, hunting distractedly for his calendar and grabbing his glasses. "It's Tuesday already?"

"Yes," she says, summoning all the courage she can muster. "It's Tuesday."

He makes a quick phone call, takes a sip of coffee, and then turns philosophical. "You know," he says, "the weird thing is, back in the seventies, I used to get shot, stabbed, beaten, arrested, and imprisoned just for doing my thing, just for trying to get the message out. Now I'm doing the same goddamn thing, but I'm getting paid *well* for it."

Which, in fact, is a bone of contention for many Indians who've followed his career: by accepting Hollywood's lucre, they say, Means has prostituted himself and sold the movement down the river. "When he went out to Hollywood, he signed his own eviction notice from Indian America," says David Melmer, an editor at the South Dakota–based *Indian Country Today,* the largest-circulation Native American newspaper in the nation. "He was so full of himself he forgot his own people."

Means is defensive about all the "selling out" accusations; indeed, he occupies a fair portion of the Russell Means Home Page attempting to defuse the issue. "I haven't abandoned the movement for Hollywood," he writes. "I brought Hollywood to the movement." He says that he only accepts roles that project Indians in a positive light, and insists that he donates most of his Hollywood money to Indian charities. "Anyone and everyone who accuses me of 'selling out' to Hollywood and otherwise, I invite you to spend a week with me."

But in a way, it's Means's insistence that his acting ventures are all in the service of a higher cause that rankles a lot of Indians around the country. "It's not the *fact* that he went to Hollywood," notes journalist Laura Wittstock. "It's the *way* he did it. You know, if you want to pursue a career in acting, that's wonderful. But don't entertain the illusion that you're doing it for your own people."

At times, it is difficult to say exactly who Means's "people" might be. After all, he is an urban-raised Indian with Oglala, Lakota, and Irish roots, who keeps a home on the Navajo reservation and spends much of his time in Santa Monica to maintain a presence among the Hollywood tribe. After a career that's kept him constantly on the road, his personal life is complicated, to say the least. "He was in this pantheon of Indian leaders," says Means's cowriter, Marvin Wolf. "Women literally threw themselves at him. It would have been difficult for Russell to resist them even if he'd been sober." By the early 1980s, after a string of failed marriages, he had a total of nine children, most of whom he had, by his own admission, neglected. It was a failure of responsibility that he viewed with deepening guilt and despair. But when he married Gloria Grant in 1984 and decided to build yet another family, he resolved this time to get it right. "He felt very, very badly that he wasn't able to provide for his first few families," Wolf notes. "He knew that his kids felt tremendous anger toward him for abandoning them. In some ways, his devotion to his two boys in Chinle is in inverse proportion to the way in which he ignored all the others."

As Means traveled across the country to promote *Where White Men Fear to Tread,* signs of his old roistering life kept resurfacing. "When

we wrote the book, Russell thought he had nine children," says Wolf.
"By the time the book tour was over, he had fifteen. We'd be at a book
signing, and there'd be this kid hanging back, waiting. Finally the kid
would come up to Russell and say, 'Mr. Means, you're my father.' Once
his memory was jogged, he'd acknowledge it. All these women would
come forward, too. There were a few cases where he didn't think the
woman was telling the truth, but he went along with it because he could
see how emotionally invested she was in believing that Russell Means
was the father of her child. He didn't want to hurt her feelings."

THERE'S AT LEAST ONE PLACE where Russell Means's version of
events goes uncontested: the World Wide Web. According to Means,
his homepage gets something on the order of a thousand hits a day. It
is plainly a congratulatory representation of himself. It features "the
many firsts of Russell Means," reprints of his "most famous" speeches,
long lists of the innumerable books and documentaries in which he
is quoted or mentioned. One can order the Russell Means Morning
Prayer Poster for $35 (includes shipping and handling), or purchase
political apparel emblazoned with lyrics from Russell Means's various
rap tunes. For only $10 in annual dues, Means invites Web site visitors
to join something called "the AIM Club." Those who send in their
money get "a free T-shirt."

Means's continued use of the AIM banner has angered more than a
few of his old colleagues. Movement leaders in Minneapolis insist that
Means is not authorized to use the organization's name, let alone raise
money under its auspices. "When I saw that homepage of his, man, I just
about threw up," says Clyde Bellecourt. "Russell should be ashamed of
himself—trying to claim credit for starting the movement and using
that to raise money for himself. It's despicable. Back in 1974 a revered
old medicine man told me that one of my brothers would turn against
me, that he'd cause friction and pain and divisiveness among our
people. Now I know that brother was Russell Means."

The internecine battling within the movement dates at least as far
back as the late 1970s. "Like any organization, we've had our growing pains," acknowledges Bill Means, Russell's brother. "In AIM, most

of the real work gets done at the local level. The national organization barely even exists, per se. Because we're so loose and decentralized, it's always confusing trying to figure out who's legitimate and who isn't."

Of his brother's continued use of the AIM banner, Bill says, "You're talking about a man who nearly gave his life for those three letters. He fought too hard and risked too much to give it up."

Those who've closely followed the movement's history say that although the conflict may have started over legitimate differences concerning strategy and ideology, it now largely boils down to a personal feud between the Bellecourts and Means. Certainly the rancor is mutual. "They're tyrants!" Means says of the Bellecourts. "No one listens to those clowns anymore. They're dysfunctional individuals."

AND SO TODAY, bereft of a people, a party, or an organization to lead, and lacking the institutional bullhorn he once had, Means has grown detached and conflicted, constantly forced to defend a career that seems to be strewn with contradictions.

Means likes to say that his public persona changes every decade, almost like a national mood ring of the Zeitgeist. "In the 1970s, I was called a communist sympathizer. In the 1980s I was called a CIA lackey. In the 1990s, I'm called a sellout. And in the next millennium, I'll probably be called grandpa."

Sometimes Means talks about throwing it all away—acting, politics, music, PR companies—all of it. He dreams of returning to South Dakota to set up a self-sufficient village on land once owned by his father. As he explains it, his eyes light up. In this village, people would talk and pray and sing only in Lakota. They would dance the old dances and live in tepees. To hell with phones and faxes, he says. Elders would share their knowledge, and the children would learn the old ways without distraction from the Chicago Bulls or *Beavis and Butt-head*. "We will replant the seed," he says. "We're going to do it without confrontation, without possessing anyone's land. We'll be self-sufficient, like the Amish or the Mennonites. It'll be like starting all over again, rebuilding our clan system, our whole nation."

And you'll turn your back on white America—completely and forever?

"No," he says, "probably not. It's impossible to live in this world today without having to deal with all of the liars and the cheats. Your culture seeps in everywhere. The pressures of the patriarchal society are just too immense."

Then he glances at his watch and grimaces. He's already late for his two o'clock with Oliver Stone.

—1997

The Gay Eminence

MEL WHITE REMEMBERS precisely when his two selves—the two Mel Whites he'd tried for twenty-five years to keep separate—finally met face-to-face.

It was in the spring of 1986; he was ghostwriting the Rev. Jerry Falwell's autobiography, *Strength for the Journey,* and flying around the country with the Moral Majority founder and his entourage. It was White's second book for Falwell, and they'd become pals. On this particular morning he and Falwell were sitting in a limousine on their way to a fundamentalist rally in San Jose when they found themselves nosing through a crowd of gay-rights activists. White could see the rage smoldering in their faces, could hear them attacking Falwell for his fulminations against the "abomination" of homosexual love.

Falwell, who was quick to understand the tactical value of an enemy, only waved to the protesters and proffered his famous Cheshire cat grin. Then, sinking an elbow into the velvety upholstery, he turned to his confidant and said, "Those gay demonstrators—boy, I love 'em. If they weren't here, I'd have to go out and hire 'em."

Mel White tried to feign amusement, but felt only dread. He was the scribe of the religious right, a famous behind-the-scenes figure in

American evangelical circles who had ghostwritten books not just for Falwell but also for Billy Graham, Jim and Tammy Bakker, and Pat Robertson. He had listened patiently to their stories, slapped varnish on the rough spots, turned their stillborn thoughts into living words. White was also a prodigious producer of documentary films and best-selling inspirational books that conservative Christian audiences loved: heart-stirring stories about lepers and burn victims and POWs surviving against all odds with God's help. Mel White moved in a world where right was right and everything else was the work of the devil—or the communists, which was just a synonym. He would later go on to pen the speeches of Ollie North. A former evangelical pastor with a doctorate in divinity, he was a committed Christian and a family man with a wife and two kids in Pasadena, California. Everyone in the Christian right knew him.

But there was a secret that Jerry Falwell and White's other clients didn't know. Falwell's hired voice, the friend to whom he'd entrusted the story of his life, was gay.

"I just sank in my seat," White recalls of the limo ride. "I couldn't look at Jerry. It was the first time that my two worlds had ever collided like that. I knew I couldn't go on living this lie."

White didn't have the nerve to tell Falwell that day. In fact, Falwell learned only in 1992, when White faxed a confessional letter to him in Lynchburg, Virginia, on Christmas Eve. (Falwell now says through a spokesman that "it wouldn't have mattered anyway" and that he still considers White a friend—and the best writer he ever met.)

All the same, it's a safe bet that Falwell won't be hiring White to do any more books. In fact, all of White's contracts with the religious right have been severed. After a long, tortured odyssey strewn with electroshock therapy, several suicide attempts, and a divorce from his wife of twenty-five years, Mel the Ghost is finally, publicly out of the closet.

He's out of the limousine as well, figuratively speaking, standing with the gay-rights activists and shouting back at the biggest names in American televangelism—"homophobic hatemongers," he calls them—whose money he pocketed for years. Since coming out, he has been arrested in several national gay-rights demonstrations, including one in front of the White House.

In 1993, White was appointed "dean" of Dallas's Cathedral of Hope, the largest gay church in the world and the flagship institution of the thirty-thousand-member national gay denomination known as the Metropolitan Community Church. Set in Dallas's Cedar Springs gay district, the cathedral is a stone cavern with lambdas—the Greek letter L, which has come to symbolize liberty in the gay-rights movement— in the stained-glass windows and a bookstore that sells everything from gay hymnals to copies of *Daddy's Roommate*.

At his installation as dean, White announced to a congregation of two thousand that he would be leading a multimedia counteroffensive against Falwell, Robertson, and other televangelists who he contends are whipping up a holy war against homosexuals in America. "Today," he proclaimed, "I give up my place of privilege as a prosperous, upper-middle-class, middle-aged . . . pretend heterosexual male. And I say to my friends on the religious right, I'm gay, I'm proud, and God loves me without reservation!"

"JESUS IS GOING TO DO to Jerry and the others just what he did with the money changers in the temple," White tells me a few days later, as he sits on the living room couch at his ranch outside Dallas. "He's going to pick up the nearest object and chase them out. This was a house of prayer, and they've made it into a den of thieves. Their fundamentalism is just orthodoxy gone cultic. They have to have simplistic answers. They have to have black and white. To me it makes no difference whether you're a fundamentalist Muslim blowing up the Trade Towers or if you're a fundamentalist in Virginia encouraging violence against gays and lesbians."

As he recalls another client, Pat Robertson, his mood becomes positively vitriolic. "Pat is totally homophobic," he says. "He's organizing in every precinct in America to have gay and lesbian influences stopped. He sits there every day on *The 700 Club* for one hour and tells millions of people across America what Bosnia means, what Somalia means. This is what it means! It's another sign that the last days are upon us, that God is working out his final plan—whatever. And people say he knows so much! He must be wonderful. He's brilliant! His program is just an infomercial for hate."

At first glance, Mel White looks like an ordinary guy from the suburbs; you could picture him as the weatherman in Pasadena. He speaks softly in the chipper tones of California. His mustache is trim, his hair thinning, his face genial and splashed with the sun. He's a preppy dresser, but with a certain West Coast casualness: brighter colors, smarter slacks, dress shirt opened an extra button or two to the elements.

I can quickly see why he was such a facile ghostwriter: he speaks in complete sentences ready to hit the page. It's almost as if he's dictating. And in a weird way, he is, at least today. He's got a little microphone from Radio Shack clipped to his shirt, and he's taping his own version of our interview, taking notes for a book he's writing about his experiences in the religious right. It's an odd dynamic—the ghostwriter debriefing himself—and it makes him uncomfortable. "This is giving me a headache!" he grouses. It's hard for someone who's used to inhabiting other people's attics to find himself stuck inside his own.

"It's a creepy process, ghostwriting," White says. "You get inside a person's conflicts. Before long, you're like an actor who's playing a role. You become that person for a while. And when you do it for as many people as I have, you begin to wonder who you are."

He hasn't quite pieced it all together yet—what his new relationship is to the evangelist world, where he goes from here, how he's supposed to complete the bizarre metamorphosis from heterosexual Christian husband and father to closeted gay Christian ghostwriter to openly gay Christian attack dog. As he tells his stories, I sense that there is still plenty of psychological fish line that needs unsnarling. He has an odd habit of referring to himself in the third person—Mel thought this, Mel did that—as if to say, That was a different guy. His headache worsens. His brow furrows. The hulking surrealism of his life story seems to bear down on him. "If you can make any sense of this, I'll be your fan for life," he says.

White also is struggling to acclimate himself to rural Texas, where he has recently moved from Laguna Beach. He knew it was time for a change of venue, and Dallas seemed like the perfect place for him to embark on a new national ministry for gays. "I wanted to be in the Bible Belt," White explains, "and this is, as they say, the Buckle." White sporadically commutes to the cathedral in Dallas, but he does most of his work by computer, fax, and telephone out of his small ranch in the sticks an hour or so south of the city. It's a modest seventeen-acre spread that might suit a minor-league J. R. Ewing, with a nouveau mansion and a backyard pond stocked with catfish. In a nook by his upstairs office he's fashioned a prayer shrine where he watches the sunrise. White sometimes offers the house as a weekend retreat for various church groups or gay celebrities.

The ranch is set inside the circumference of the unfinished and now abandoned Texas supercollider, in hot, flat, Baptist farm country: rustling cornfields, drag strips, your occasional polka festival, and a chain-saw sculptor down the road. White doesn't want to reveal the exact location or even the name of the nearest town for fear of reprisals from antigay vigilantes. He lives here with his longtime companion, Gary Nixon, a friendly, strapping guy with Scandinavian blond hair who sometimes gets mistaken around Dallas for Cowboy quarterback Troy Aikman. Nixon serves as a kind of chairman of the ranch and a gourmet chef. Late in the morning, he marches in with a platter of gorgeous omelets and sautéed asparagus. "Hey, look at this," White says appreciatively. "Faggots can cook."

MEL WHITE GREW up by the big blue scallop of Monterey Bay. His father was the mayor of Santa Cruz. Evangelism ran deep in the family. His grandmother was an itinerant preacher who led tent revivals all over the Midwest, and both of White's parents were stalwarts in the Indiana-based Church of God. They were practical, good-natured, conservative Christians who later became missionaries in Soweto, South Africa. Says White, "We went to church every time the doors opened."

His folks always wanted him to be a minister. "I've always felt that Mel had a special place in God's kingdom, but this isn't what I had in mind," says White's mother, Faythe, a retired speech therapist who lives in the hills above Santa Cruz with her husband, Carl. "Of course, we have known about his homosexual problem for many years. It's really hard for us to understand and it hurts. But Mel will always be our pride and joy. He is a good son. There isn't anything in the world he wouldn't do for us. I just pray that if he's been completely deceived, that God will find some way to show it to him."

When he was a boy, Mel lost a brother in a bicycle accident. Years later, when he told his parents he was gay, they grieved almost as they had after his brother's death. "I went into shock," remembers Faythe White. "I thought I had lost another son."

White felt his first vague predilections toward homosexuality as an adolescent. "As soon as everyone else started thinking about girls, I started thinking about boys. I couldn't help it. I didn't know what was wrong with me. My hormones were raging, and I was feeling as guilty as I could feel. I'd be escorting the homecoming queen at halftime and kissing her in public when I really wanted to be kissing the quarterback. So I became an overachiever: straight As, student council president, and all of that. I kept thinking, if I did enough good things, God would love me in spite of my nasty thoughts. I was trying to be the best little boy in the world. It's pathetic now, looking back on it. I was told that if you're homosexual you're going to hell. And I believed it until I was forty years old."

White met his future bride, Lyla Lee Loehr, when they were in the seventh grade. They went off together to a small religious liberal arts college in Portland, Oregon. After graduation in 1962, they got married and moved to Southern California. His homosexual fantasies continued, however, and one day not long after the wedding, he took Lyla to a Chinese restaurant in Glendale and broke the news. "Honey, I think I'm a homosexual."

Lyla was devastated, of course. She said, "What do you want to do about it?"

"I want to stay married and have a family. I think I can be healed. I don't understand this."

She grasped his hand and said, "I don't understand it either, but, hey, we'll work this thing out."

And for twenty-five years—while White was pursuing separate doctorates in divinity and communications, while he pastored a small Swedish Covenant Church in Pasadena and launched a successful career in the Christian filmmaking and publishing industry—Lyla stood by him as wife, business partner, and closest friend. They wanted a family so badly that they endured five miscarriages before their son, Michael, was born. All the while, White was wrestling with his sexuality, and he dutifully ran the gauntlet of "treatments" designed by various fundamentalist healers and medical practitioners to douse the urges of Sodom.

He went to exorcists who laid their hands upon him and tried to purge the spirit of homosexuality. He racked up tens of thousands of dollars in psychiatric bills. He visited a behaviorist who gave him electric shocks every week as he looked at pictures of handsome men. He underwent "aversive therapy," in which a psychologist would give him a foul-tasting candy bar that made him feel sick whenever he felt sexually attracted to a man.

"None of these things helped, of course," White says. "I held on as long as I could, but I was becoming suicidal. Finally I said to Lyla: 'Good-bye counseling, good-bye to all this fantasy about being ex-gay. If God doesn't love me, I'm sorry, I'm outta here.'" While scuba diving in Hawaii, he swam down to a submarine wreck and pulled out his air hose. But the dive master spotted him just in time to save his life. Later he visited a psychologist who told him, "You're not sick. You're gay. Fall in love with a man."

By 1980, White had given up on changing himself; he moved down the street and lived the life of a gay bachelor, dating occasionally. He continued making films and writing books for the religious right, but never told his clients that he was gay, figuring what they didn't know couldn't hurt them. In some ways, though, his family life remained the same. "I would drive up and fix breakfast every morning," White recalls. "We'd all go out and have dinner together, or go to the movies."

Through it all, White has managed to stay close to his two children, Michael and Erinn. And though White and his wife were divorced five years ago, they are still dear friends. "I don't regret that I was married to Mel for twenty-five years," says Lyla White, a development director of a Pasadena Episcopal church. "He was a good person, a good father, a good husband, and a good friend. There was just one glitch. I knew that if he could choose, Mel would have chosen to be straight and in a family. But it was not a matter of choice."

"Lyla is the sweetest, kindest, most wonderful woman on Earth," White gushes. "God, I love her! And she's single. Boy, she would be the greatest catch! If you know any eligible men, let me know!"

White says he's a lot saner now that everything's out in the open, but he is still sometimes plagued with guilt. "I wrote a lot of books that I wouldn't read—just horrible books," he admits, as he munches another asparagus stalk. "And I feel ashamed by it today. I feel embarrassed that I did anything for the enemy, that I contributed in any way to their ministry. If Mel is on trial for taking money from homophobic people, then he's guilty as charged. I did it to put my kids through college and to keep my bills paid.

"It took me years to find the wisdom and the courage to take a stand. On the other hand, all gays and lesbians have to work for a system that hates us. The military hates us. Industry hates us. The church hates us. So for a gay person to work anywhere in America involves helping the enemy. Look, I believe in Jesus. And I naively thought that I was contributing to people whose ministries were dedicated to the same thing I was: telling the story of Jesus. Gays and lesbians weren't an issue in the books I was writing. I never had to write any ideological stuff about gays."

White insists he had nothing to do with the oft-paraphrased statement—widely attributed to Falwell—about AIDS being God's punishment to gays. "When I heard that he'd said that, I was furious," White recalls. "I dropped everything I was doing. I went to the Hay-Adams Hotel where Falwell was staying, and confronted him. I said: 'Jerry, did you say that? I just want to hear it from your mouth.' And he said: 'No, Mel, I did not say that. That's wrong. I did not say that.' Well, I went back and found it reported in five different places. And he will deny it to your face today."

He downs a couple of aspirin and rubs his temples. The strange thing, he says, is how much he genuinely came to like many of the religious-right figures for whom he worked. "You know, Jerry's been a loyal friend to me. Just very generous. And he is fun to be with. He's such a cutup, always playing practical jokes on people. And he's got all these funny habits. He never lets a day go by that he doesn't call one senator and two congressmen. Wherever he is, whatever he's doing, he'll call. I've been with him when he called them from his airplane. 'Howya doin', Senator? This is Jerry. I'm thinkin' about ya. Prayin' for ya. Knowin' that you got America at your heart.' He told me, 'That's my rule: two congressmen, one senator. Every day.'"

White says that he still considers the Rev. Billy Graham to be one of his "personal heroes." Yet writing for him gave White insights into some of the darker aspects of Graham's role as our de facto national chaplain. "To understand Billy's role in this nation is to understand the role of a person whose smile makes everybody feel that it's okay," White says. "This is why so many presidents have needed him. He is part of that great, smiling leadership. He has enjoyed a lot of power, but I think he is trapped by it. On the road he has to have guarded suites and limos and jets. Everywhere he goes, he's mobbed on the streets. He said to me once that when he walks into a room, he feels like people are taking handfuls of flesh out of him, and that by the time he gets to the end of the room, he feels like a walking skeleton."

Of all the religious-right figures White wrote for, he is perhaps fondest of Jim and Tammy Bakker, whom he describes as "crazy but wonderful—the hardest-working people in the business." As it happened, White was writing their autobiography as the IRS was wandering through their offices. "The whole ship was going down, and I was in the midst of it," he says.

White sat in the Bakkers' home in Palm Springs, California, and watched in disbelief as Tammy dyed her hair three different colors in the space of an afternoon. "She comes out of the bathroom after going through the process of stripping and coloring. She asks, 'You like it, Jim?' He answers, 'Yes, yes!' And she says, 'No, you don't!' Then she runs back in there and does it all over again."

After everything that's happened, after all the disappointments and conflicts of faith, I ask White, Do you still consider yourself a Christian? White looks out toward the catfish pond and sighs. "I'm a follower of Jesus Christ as best I can," he says. "I pray every day. I read the Bible every day. I memorize the Scriptures and the teachings of Jesus. But I don't want to be associated with fundamentalist or even mainline Protestant churches anymore. That's over for me."

His headache has abated, and he looks exhausted. He inspects his tape recorder to see if it's still rolling, to make sure the day's long session of self-analysis has been captured. "It's amazing, when I think about it, how close I am to them," he says, with a prolonged, bewildered stare that eventually gives way to a cackle. "Either God has an incredible sense of humor, or I've just stumbled into something really weird. I know them better than anybody knows them. I know them better than they know themselves. So this war I'm declaring is personal. They're my friends, the enemy."

—1994

The Toughest Guy in Alaska

Iditarod Trail, Alaska

AT EIGHT A.M. on the starting day of the 1990 Iditarod Sled Dog Race, the chute at Fourth and D streets in downtown Anchorage is a blare of klieg lights and hot-colored racing gear. Standing before the cameras of ABC's *Wide World of Sports* is announcer Lynn Swann, former wide receiver for the Pittsburgh Steelers, a black Adonis in a chic down parka. A tape of Jimmy Buffett's "Margaritaville" pours over the crowd of fifteen thousand spectators while bouncers in fox-pelt caps police the barricades.

In back of the chute, several hundred dog handlers are sorting and stacking Ziploc bags of meat and lard. Dander hangs in the air, and everywhere is the reek of excrement.

The mushers inch their way to the chute, a new team blasting off every two minutes. Greasy-haired Norsemen just in from the bush. Arctic jocks waddling in their mukluks and vapor barrier boots. Miners in floppy Yazoo hats, grizzled loggers and wildcatters, Yukon River rats. They hop on their runners, test their footbrakes, fuss with the stanchions on their sleds. Tim Osmar of Clam Gulch. Emmit Peters of Ruby. Rick Mackey of Trapper Creek. Now comes Joe Runyan, the wonder-boy strategist who raises homing pigeons in his spare time. Now comes Col. Norman Vaughan, the oldest man in the race at eighty-four, a 1929 graduate of Harvard who accompanied Admiral Byrd on his first expeditions in Antarctica. Then Martin Buser of Big Lake. Lavon Barve of Wasilla. Bill Hickel, the Anchorage millionaire, son of the governor. Susan Butcher, the famous champion from the Tanana River country.

"ONE MINUTE!"

Now a silver-haired man edges toward the chute. He is seventy-three years old and has a hearing aid in each ear. He flashes the crowd a sly grin, his gray eyes twinkling. He unsnarls his gangline with the patience of an old fisherman. His small wrinkled face is scratched and studded with gray beard stubble.

His five handlers are locked in a tug-of-war with the dogs. He walks over to his sled and calmly parks himself on the runners. In a grandfatherly voice that is barely audible, he calls to his handlers, tells them to let go of the dogs. The huskies spring forward, and the sled lurches to the starting line. "Whoa!" he cries.

"THIRTY SECONDS!"

The announcer's voice crackles over the loudspeakers: "Please give a warm welcome to Joe Redington, Father of the Iditarod."

A deafening cheer wells up from the crowd. Everyone knows Joe Redington—he's a household name from Anchorage to Prudhoe Bay. Redington is called the Father of the Iditarod because he invented it. It was Redington who in the late 1960s came up with the idea of running a sled-dog marathon across the forgotten trails of the Alaskan interior. He saw the race as a way to revive the lost art of mushing, a tradition that had all but died in the tracks of the snowmobile.

Not only did Redington concoct the Iditarod; he has raced in it for the last sixteen years, finishing as high as fifth place. Despite his age, Redington is generally recognized as one of the top twenty mushers in the world.

His seventeen huskies are proud specimens, alert, attuned to his every movement. The urge to pull ripples in their lean muscles, smolders in their yellow lupine eyes. They lunge with all their tensile strength, hairs bristling, the diamond-patterned harnesses pulled taut on their backs, so that Redington's team of handlers must hold back the lines to keep the dogs from skittering away before their time has come.

Redington grips the handlebar with one hand, and waves to the crowds with the other.

"Gentlemen, start your engines!"

"Ten ... nine ... eight ..."

"Well, I gotta go."

"Tear 'em up, Joe!"

"Three ... two ... one ..."

"Smoke 'em!"

"Mush!" Redington calls to his huskies.

His neck slightly whiplashes from the initial jolt. The runners scrape through the crusty snow as his dogs bound forward at twenty miles an hour.

JOE REDINGTON, WHO HAS raised huskies ever since he came to Alaska in 1948, is famous for developing a line of racing dogs with tight feet, tough pads, and an unbridled desire to run. Mushers from all over Alaska speak of "a Redington dog" as if it were a distinct breed. Three-quarters of all the huskies that run in the Iditarod race are "Redington dogs," or their direct descendants. His Knik Kennel is the largest sled-dog operation in Alaska, housing as many as 450 animals at a time. "I've always had more dogs than the average person," he says.

If Redington had never dreamed up the Iditarod, he'd still be a legend in these parts. Of course, every old-timer has a grizzly bear story, or some tall tale about surviving an airplane crash in the Brooks Range. But Joe Redington is the real thing. He's on every Alaskan's short list of certifiable folk heroes. Never mind that he's an old gnome who stands five-foot-six and is deaf as a post. He's the dean of the Alaskan sourdoughs. The *Los Angeles Times* once called him "the Toughest Man in Alaska."

Redington is the sort of man who has a knack for getting into fixes from which he then miraculously extricates himself. He's been missing and presumed dead on more occasions than his wife, Vi, likes to recall. Her motto is, "Try not to worry." On the Iditarod Trail, he's often tumbling off his sled, smashing into trees, colliding with a snow machine, or slipping through the ice and getting a bad case of chilblain.

So far he's always made it home. "I don't scare too easy," he tells me. "Maybe I ain't too smart. Because I think sometimes it might pay to get scared."

Redington has lived the Alaskan life with gusto—as a homesteader, commercial fisherman, bush pilot, guide, and dog-team runner for the army's Search and Rescue Unit, pulling plane wrecks and corpses from the mountains. Once he and his protégée Susan Butcher took a team of dogs to the summit of Mount McKinley (it had never been done before). On one occasion he crashed his plane in the wilderness, straightened out the propeller between two trees, cut a runway out of an alder stand, and flew out six days later. When he was mushing a starving dog team through a blizzard some years ago, he had to slaughter his weakest huskies and feed them to the others. In 1981 the Alaska governor sent Redington to Washington, D.C., to mush a team of dogs down Pennsylvania Avenue in President Ronald Reagan's inaugural parade. Two Maryland youths stole Redington's dog team, but police found the huskies in a suburban Maryland basement hours before the parade. In the end, Redington's team and his sled (equipped with rollers) made the trek down Pennsylvania. "It was good mushing!" he remembers.

When I dropped by Redington's house in the rural town of Knik several weeks before the start of the Iditarod, he was out in his dog yard mixing up a vat of gruel. There were hundreds of dogs chained to separate posts out in the yard, sending up a deafening, anxious howl. Redington's truck, a rusted-out Sierra Classic, wore the evidence of a recent collision with a moose. The front bumper was badly dented, the hood sprung, and dried blood was spattered everywhere. One of his dogs had died over the winter, and I nearly stepped on him as I walked up the icy path to his house. All I could see was a tuft of hair half-sunk in the snow. "Can't really bury him until spring—the ground's frozen solid," Redington said. "He was a good one, though."

Redington's house was a slatternly affair buried in the drifts. Inside, it was an absolute mess. With several hundred dogs holding their attention, he and Vi clearly didn't have time for housekeeping, nor, it seemed, inclination. The place had more of the look and feel of a camp than a house. They were, in every sense, outdoors people, and they seemed vaguely out of sorts beneath a roof. "I hate a damn house," Redington told me. "I was always kind of a gypsy. I slept out all my life. I've lived more in a tent than I have in a house. This is what I was looking for from the time I was born—trapping, outdoor living, mushing."

I had been told that when Redington first came to Alaska from Oklahoma with his brother in 1948, Vi was Redington's sister-in-law. As the story was related to me, Joe was married to another woman, but he and his brother decided to permanently swap wives, with the apparent consent of all spouses concerned. When I asked Joe and Vi about this, they only smiled.

A SPECK OF CIVILIZATION at the confluence of the Takotna and Kuskokwim rivers, McGrath is a mining outpost in the frozen heart of the bush, with a population so small that the entire phone directory is printed on one page. The McGrath checkpoint is 415 miles from Anchorage. To get here, the mushers have to cross the Alaska Range and traverse some of the most treacherous landscape on earth, including a certain stretch called the Farewell Burn, a ninety-mile ghostland of charred stumps and felled trees that was the site of a major forest fire in the late 1970s.

It's twenty below and sunny on the morning I arrive in McGrath, and the town is buried under seventy inches of snow. At the Miners Café, a greasy spoon near the runway, the reporter from the *Anchorage Times* sucks Skoal and hammers out tomorrow morning's story on his Tandy laptop. Lynn Swann saunters into the café with a bevy of adoring women from the ABC Sports crew.

For hours and days, I huddle with the other journalists in the wet warmth of the café nursing cups of bad instant coffee and bowls of chili, trying to imagine the ordeal that Redington must be going through right now somewhere to the east, grateful that it's him and not me, and yet vaguely envious of his experience.

Redington lurches into town at eight one night under a full moon. He parks his team behind the house of an old friend. "Gotta feed my doggies," he mutters to me as he stirs up a kettle of gruel. The dogs eat ravenously, then curl up in straw beds and fall fast asleep, their muscles still twitching in their dreams. Redington waddles into the house and pulls off his mukluks. He sits down at the dining room table and quietly sips a mug of hot Tang. What he really wants, he tells me, is an ice-cold chocolate milk shake, but he's out of luck. "I'm afraid McGrath isn't a milk-shake town," he grouses.

A combination of stormy weather and volcanic ash has left Redington's dogs in sorry shape. Mount Redoubt, a highly active volcano several hundred miles away, has blown its stack for the third time this week, and a dark canopy of ash has descended over much of southern Alaska. More eruptions are expected later in the week, with possible earth tremors to follow. Much of the Iditarod trail is now coated in brown volcanic ash, which irritates the mushers' eyes and burns their lungs, forcing them to cough up blood. The abrasive granules also wear down the slick plastic emulsion on the runners of the sleds. But the ash is hardest on the dogs: it works into their paws and causes their footpads to crack and bleed. When they become thirsty on the trail, the dogs eat the ash-covered snow, and many of them become ill.

This is the case with three of Redington's dogs, and he has decided to "drop" them here at the McGrath checkpoint. An official veterinarian will examine the dogs and then they'll be flown back east to a prison near Anchorage, where the inmates will look after them until the race is over.

Yesterday, Redington tells me, he got into a potentially lethal scrape with a starving moose. When the snow drifts grow too deep, moose often go on mad and desperate rampages for food. A starving moose is an ornery and unpredictable creature that can stomp anything that gets in its path. To defend himself and his team, Redington packs a firearm, like most mushers, but he doesn't like to shoot a moose unless he absolutely must; race rules stipulate that if a musher kills an animal on the trail, he has to gut it on the spot and arrange for the meat to be salvaged. Gutting a thousand-pound moose is a particularly bloody affair, and it can take the better part of a day, especially in thirty-below weather.

In this case, Redington was mushing near the Big Susitna River on a narrow trail when the moose encountered his team. "He come right down the gangline," Redington tells me. "He never touched a single dog, the sled, or me. It was a nice moose. It didn't hurt anything. But when it went over the top of me, my headlamp shined right up in his eyes, and they looked as big as eggs. I think it was scared."

What about *you?* I ask.

"Well, I wasn't really scared. If you'd had something to check my pulse, I don't think it would have ever changed."

Redington had another trying experience near Rainy Pass. "It was real windy, and the hillsides were steep," he tells me. "I couldn't find the trail. It was all blowed over. There was about a dozen teams out there, and we was going in all directions, the dogs just spinning around and around. We was having quite a time out there. At one point my team got wrapped around a tree." He laughs.

I have to ask him: Given the moose and the ice storms and the sleeplessness and the lashing winds, is mushing ever . . . fun?

"There's times when it's miserable," he concedes, "and I might say, why in the hell am I out here, fighting this cold? But if you've ever run a team on a nice moonlit night with the northern lights flashing out there, you'd see why. When you're out there all alone, and the only sound is the runners, and the dogs are going along at a good clip like they're enjoying it, it's a feeling like no other."

THE IDITAROD IS ONLY two decades old, but Alaskans speak of Redington's creation as though it were an ancient ritual sprung from the hyperborean mist, an event without origins. The Iditarod is simply what Alaskans do, a natural outgrowth of the culture. Alaska is a land of migration, where the rhythms of life are marked by the movement of species across great distances. The sockeye salmon make their trek up the Yukon, the caribou herds tramp the steppes with the seasons, the gray whales migrate with the shifting ice floes of the Chukchi Sea. In the context of Alaska, the Iditarod race is simply another peregrination of the species, an exodus sure as clockwork. As a former mayor of Nome puts it, "The Iditarod is what Alaska lives on for the rest of the year."

"Iditarod" is an Athabascan Indian word that means "a far-distant place." Once there was a village called Iditarod, a gold-mining outpost on a tributary of a tributary of the Yukon River, but today it's a ghost town of vacant saloons, a tumbledown rooming house, a brothel of buckled lumber. The race passes through the ruins every other year, but otherwise, the trail has little to do with Iditarod, geographically or historically.

Still, it's a good name for the world's longest mushing marathon, for no one really knows how many miles separate the chute in Anchorage from the burled arch in Nome. Some say it's twelve hundred miles; some say more. The "official" count is 1,049 miles, but that's a symbolic figure: one thousand, because it's at least that many, and forty-nine because Alaska is the forty-ninth state. The race crosses two mountain ranges—the Alaska and the Kuskokwim—and some two dozen rivers.

The Iditarod race commemorates, and was in part inspired by, an earlier race across Alaska—in this case, a race against death. In January of 1925, a diphtheria epidemic broke out in the town of Nome. The contagion crept from one house to the next, with new cases reported hourly. Serum supplies were exhausted. Authorities were unable to summon airplane pilots to rush the desperately needed medicine to Nome, so a group of nineteen dog mushers, led by the famed Norwegian dog driver Leonhard Seppala, formed a relay across the state. A package of 300,000 units of antitoxin was raced by train from Anchorage to the railhead at Nenana; from then on, the serum was in the hands of the dog mushers, who sprinted westward 674 miles in the dead of winter. Seppala's mission of mercy made headlines around the world. The *New York Times* ran the story on page one for a week. The serum arrived in Nome after 170 hours in transit, and the epidemic was averted. Today a statue of Seppala's lead dog, Balto, stands near the arsenal in New York's Central Park. Upon his death in 1967, Seppala's ashes were sprinkled over the Iditarod Trail.

When Redington came to Alaska in the late 1940s, the bush plane and the snowmobile had yet to supplant dog teams as the principal carrier of mail and supplies in the Alaskan backcountry. Redington didn't waste any time getting into the spirit of mushing—traveling overland from Canada, he bought his first sled-dog puppy at a gas station just fifteen minutes inside the Alaska line. "When I first came to Alaska," he says, "there was a dog team behind every house. They was the people's means of transportation, their wood and water. But when the snow machines come along in the early sixties, people started getting rid of the dogs, because you didn't have to feed that snow machine. I decided something had to be done. We had to make a reason for keeping the dogs. So we decided on the race."

It is ironic, and perhaps a hallmark of the national culture, that it took a manufactured event—a high-profile race with a $50,000 first prize—to save a tradition that originally grew out of necessity. In the mid-sixties, Redington, along with a local Alaska historian, sparked a statewide movement to open a trail that loosely followed Seppala's old diphtheria serum route, and soon the Iditarod Trail was established. (It's now designated a National Historic Trail.)

A traditionalist at heart, Redington bristles at the name some of the younger mushers have given themselves. "I'm not a 'dog driver.' I'm a musher. There are all kinds of damn drivers. Pile drivers. Screwdrivers. Truck drivers. I don't want to be no driver. I'm a dog musher. I don't like the word 'driver' because it sounds like you're driving your dogs into the ground. I mush dogs that loves to go. If I tried to drive my dogs with a whip they'd just look back at me like I was crazy."

French Canadians in the Yukon Territory used to shout, *"Marchez!"* (meaning "Go!"), but few racers today actually use the command "mush." This is a matter of some concern to Redington. "I use 'Mush,' not 'Hike' or 'Go.' I learned it from an old mail carrier who came to Alaska in nineteen and four. I say it good and sharp. When I start my dogs out I say, 'Mush!'"

THE FLIGHT BY BUSH PLANE from McGrath to the Eskimo village of Unalakleet takes a little over an hour and costs $500. I decide on Wilbur Air because Wilbur seems like a nice enough fellow and needs the work.

We leave McGrath on a dazzling cold morning, ten below. Wilbur takes me over the Kuskokwim Range, then buzzes the Iditarod checkpoints of Takotna and Ophir. From the air, the stunted spruce trees look like beard stipple. The trail appears as a hairline in the blue-gray snow, occasionally crosshatched with the footprints of a wolf.

From Ophir, Wilbur banks southwest across the Beaver Mountains and passes over the frozen swampland known as the muskeg, a hundred miles of raw country without roads or fences or the subtlest markings of man.

Now Unalakleet slides into view, a snug village huddled against the floes. The town's name is an Eskimo word meaning "where the sea wind blows," and that is a meet description. The wind in question is strong and cold, and comes directly from Siberia. Unalakleet is where the Iditarod Trail joins the Bering Sea coast. The rest of the race will be run here on the ice shelf; the route follows the Norton Sound, then hooks west for a straight shot down the Seward Peninsula.

The village has a population of 850, most of whom are Eskimos. Social life revolves around bingo at the Igloo Arcade. Many of the Eskimo residents still rely on a subsistence lifestyle of trapping, hunting, and fishing with the seasons. Unalakleet is a "damp" town, which means that you can drink alcohol, but you can't buy it. Still, alcoholism is rampant, and the black market is brisk.

At the Lodge restaurant I meet a young Unalakleet resident named Warren. He wears thick black-rimmed glasses. He confesses he is bored with Unalakleet, wants to move to Anchorage and become a travel agent. "Time to move on." He frowns. "Get something going." Warren says the Iditarod is the most exciting time of year. So many people, so much commotion. Warren is collecting the autographs of every musher who passes through town. He can talk about the mushers for hours. He knows them by name and number, knows where they live and how many dogs they've dropped and who their sponsors are. He feasts on the incidental details. He listens to the radio for the updates.

Redington, Warren tells me, is just now on the outskirts of town. Warren is a big Redington fan, and definitely wants to get his autograph. As it happens, Redington used to live in Unalakleet, years ago. In the mid-1970s, he ran a fish-processing plant here in the summer. It was here in 1975 that he met the young Susan Butcher, who was working on a musk-ox farm, just out of town. They discovered that they shared a love for sled dogs and soon became close friends. In the fall, Butcher followed Redington to Knik and lived in a tent on his property for three months, training sled dogs from his kennel. Redington became a mentor for Butcher, and it is widely gossiped that they were briefly lovers. "I adore Joe," Butcher later tells me. "And I give him an immense amount of credit for teaching me what a real Alaskan is supposed to be. He taught me the patience to deal with adversity as it comes. I should have been raised a Redington."

The village elder of Unalakleet is a ninety-one-year-old man named John Auliye, a friendly man whose eyes are clouded with cataracts. His modest cabin is cluttered with caribou hides and ivory carvings. A game of solitaire lies unfinished on the dining room table beside a bottle of seal oil. Auliye, an old friend of Joe Redington, is the sort of traditional musher whose knowledge and skill Redington sought to preserve by creating the Iditarod.

Auliye has witnessed two great episodes of Alaskan history. He served with Colonel Muktuk Marston's Alaskan Scouts when they liberated the Aleutian islands from the Japanese in World War II. And he mushed a leg of the 1925 serum run to Nome, driving a dog team from Shaktoolik to Moses Point, where he passed the diphtheria antitoxin on to Leonhard Seppala. "I didn't know anything about the medicine," he recalls, "but I was willing to take it even if I didn't get paid. If you help people, blessings come back. Years later I meet people from Nome who thank me for saving their life."

Auliye hasn't been on a sled in years ("Too old," he protests, "no good"), but he takes a keen interest in the mushers who skip through town every March. He's glad that Redington's event has helped keep the old arts alive, though he's not sure about some of the newfangled techniques the racers use. "They spoil the dogs now. When we raced to Nome in 'twenty-five, our dogs didn't wear *booties*." He says the word with disgust.

I ask Auliye what he thinks about the prospects for young Eskimos like Warren growing up in Alaska today. He turns somber. "Eskimo boys no longer know how to be an Eskimo. The old life is gone. To hunt and trap. To spear a whale. To call the seal with three scratches on the ice. To kill a bear with one shot only. When I was a young man, I killed with one shot. I hit a brown bear; it dropped."

A look of despair creeps into his face. "But these boys today," he says. "They have nothing. They know nothing about mushing dogs.

They can't make it in the Eskimo way. They can't make it in the white man's way. No education. They go to Anchorage. Turn to drink. Watch TV. They are nothing."

The "white man's way" of dog mushing is perhaps best exemplified by the work of Roy Chapman, a "sports medicine" researcher who has set up camp close to Auliye's house. Chapman is a member of the Arctic Sports Medicine Team, a research project loosely associated with the University of Alaska. Chapman and his scientists are using the Iditarod as a laboratory to study the physiological effects of extreme cold. The researchers concentrate on such arcane matters as "Vo2 max," "core temperature," and "specific gravity." They follow the mushers' "hydration patterns" and "gastric emptying rates." The Arctic Medicine project has its own musher entered in the race, Greg Tibbitts. An Iditarod rookie, Tibbitts is mushing a team of dogs on loan from Redington. The researchers monitor Tibbitts's metabolism at each checkpoint. "The Iditarod is the ideal clinical scenario for studying arctic conditions," Chapman explains. "You couldn't pay people to put themselves through the kinds of things that mushers go through. The cold, the stress to the body, the sleep deprivation. And they like it!"

Chapman says that prolonged sleep deprivation causes some mushers to hallucinate. They may see goblins, a nonexistent cabin, a skyscraper in the middle of the bush. "I've had guys tell me great stories about how they've just had a twenty-minute conversation with their mom. 'How is she?' I'll ask. 'Oh, she's been dead for fifteen years, but she's doing good.'"

I ask Chapman to describe the optimum body type for an Iditarod musher. "It's what we call a 'mesomorph,' which means small and round, not unlike the basic Eskimo physique. The mesomorph can retain his heat better. He doesn't look like an athlete at all. But he turns out to have tremendous upper body strength, tremendous grip strength, and a more efficient metabolism. When I think of the ideal musher, I imagine Joe Redington as a thirty-year-old man. Even in his seventies, Redington is tough as nails. I'm constantly amazed by the man's physical strength, by the way he just slings around those hundred-pound bags of dog food. He has a handshake that will crush a beer can. If Joe Redington was in his thirties, he'd wipe these guys out."

Two days later, Redington straggles into Unalakleet, looking weather-beaten and dazed. He's slept only three hours in the past forty-eight. On two occasions, he's nodded asleep and fallen off his sled. I ask him if he's hallucinated on the trail, like some of the others.

"Nope," he snaps. "I've never seen anything that didn't look right to me."

NOME IS A COMMUNITY OF four thousand hardy souls who take pride in their remoteness from . . . *everything.* It is literally the end of the line—not just for the Iditarod race but for North America. The town is even farther west than Hawaii. From here I could tromp over the ice across the international date line to the coastal village of Provideniya, on the Chukchi Peninsula, the Russian Far East.

On the beach, the town is holding a golf tournament called the Bering Sea Classic, with orange golf balls and six "greens" painted on the snow. The linksmen play in the shadow of a fourteen-story monstrosity of metal affectionately known as the Bima. A floating bucket dredge that looks something like Darth Vader's *Death Star,* the Bima roves the coast during the summer, churning up the sandy shallows in search of gold; but right now it sits dormant, locked in ice.

A fierce blizzard on the Norton Sound has detained the race. For eight hours the mushers were holed up in cabins and roadhouses between Shaktoolik and Elim, waiting for the storm to pass, but now they're sprinting west again. On this blustery Saturday night, it's forty below. The air-raid sirens blare. The word from KNOM radio is that Joe Redington has been spotted at the Fort Davis Roadhouse on the east end of town. Bar patrons pull on their parkas and stumble onto Front Street to greet Redington. Vi is bundled up and patiently waiting at the finish line.

Redington's headlamp bobs down Front Street, the pale white light silhouetting his dogs. He looks fragile on the sled, his short frame slumped against the drive bow, his boots precariously balanced on the narrow slats.

His dogs lope across the finish line, their feet caked in ice up to the fetlocks. The huskies regard the hooting crowds with bemusement.

Their heads are wreathed in white cloud puffs, their own moist breath meeting the cold air. They've run the Iditarod enough times to know that this is the final stop. After eleven hundred miles, the dogs still look impressive, but the stress of their odyssey weighs in their faces. Their muzzles are pulled back in quivery scowls, their eyes glassy and glazed, their whiskers grizzled with frost. They look back at Redington to make sure there are no imminent commands. Then they quietly lie down in the trail and lick the packed snow from their blistered paws.

Redington dismounts without fanfare. He walks up to the platform and signs his name. He looks weary and pale in the glare of the cameras. He can't feel his face and he can't hear a thing: he lost both of his hearing aids on the trail. He drawls into the microphone, "I always like to get here to Nome. I don't even know what I placed, but whatever it was, that's good."

The announcer reports the official time. "Joe Redington arrived in Nome on the seventeenth of March at nine-fifty-eight P.M. with thirteen dogs. Total elapsed time of fourteen days, twelve hours, fifty-nine minutes, and fifty-nine seconds."

Redington steps down from the platform and gives Vi a bear hug. He turns and faces a wall of reporters. Buried inside his furr ruff is a gritty smile.

—1991

AMERICAN EDENS

And the Bureaucrats Said,
Let There Be High Water

The Colorado River, Grand Canyon

WE TETHER OUR BOATS at the mouth of a parched side canyon called Basalt and are just beginning to set up camp when we notice that the water is on the rise. The sun is slipping out of the sky, and the walls of the Grand Canyon are ranged around us, opiates of rock, as stupefying as they always are and always will be. There are fifteen of us on a private river trip, happy and UV-baked, smeared in greasy windbalm and sporting Neanderthal river 'dos after six days of running the cold Colorado. Todd, an exacting brewmaster from Oregon, taps a pony keg of an extraspecial bitter ale and we stand at the water's edge, savoring mugs of the strong, viscous stuff.

Yes, we all agree, it's a fine day for a flood.

With the scent of tonight's dinner—jambalaya—drifting over from the Dutch ovens, we watch as the fifty-degree water licks at our feet, swallowing an inch of shoreline with every wave. It's a businesslike advance, informing every instinct that Jehovah is up to old tricks, better retreat to higher ground—which we eventually do, rescuing our tents and sleeping bags from vulnerable swatches of beach.

Our odd flotilla—three rafts, a dory, three kayaks, and a twenty-two-foot, motorized snout raft that looks something like the *African Queen*—is shifting fast in the swirl of an eddy, forcing us to fasten on more and more lines in an expanding cat's cradle of nylon. Farther out in the river, the current has snapped into a frenzy, and the pellucid blue-green of the Colorado soon turns the hue of turkey gravy. Granules of newly stirred sand peck at the underside of the pontoons, creating a close staccato, like Rice Krispies freshly doused in milk. Dead mesquite and cottonwood trunks shoot out of the eddy and bob helplessly toward Lake Mead. We hear a strange, low grumble that we decide is a boulder rolling somewhere down in the murky channel. A rattlesnake wriggles for higher ground twenty yards from camp, and a couple of red-spotted toads hop along the shore, looking puzzled. Nothing in their short lives has taught them how to read the warning signs of flood—not here in the Grand Canyon, where man has controlled the spigot for thirty-three years.

But this is no garden-variety flood, no mere impetuous gush of runoff. It was rehearsed in elaborate cybermodels and unleashed on schedule by engineering wonks, and right now it's being monitored by battalions of scientists stationed along the three hundred serpentine miles of the Big Ditch. It may be the world's first premeditated flood, and it's certainly the first one whose sole purpose is preservation. The point of this weeklong spasm of water is to blast some 12 million tons of accumulated sediment from the main channel. To rebuild the canyon's beaches. To scour the Colorado's backwaters. To restore habitat for native fish. To re-create some semblance of the old river that was lost when Glen Canyon Dam was built three decades ago. It's designed to be a grand simulation of nature's corrective riot—the gargantuan effort predicated on the paradoxical truth that in order to get back to where we once were, we must further manipulate an already overmanipulated landscape.

The Bureau of Reclamation, which oversaw the building of the dam and is now staging this week's festivities, prefers not to call it a flood at all. No, this is an experimental beach/habitat-building test flow. Not that anyone can tell the difference between whatever the hell that is and a real flood, certainly not from our vantage point here at Basalt, some eighty miles downriver from Glen Canyon Dam.

At six o'clock this morning, March 26, 1996, Secretary of the Interior Bruce Babbitt donned a hard hat and strolled across a catwalk outside the humming ramparts of concrete that Edward Abbey once dreamed of blowing up. Then, with the twirl of a wheel, he let the foam fly. From the blue fathoms of Lake Powell, the water came roaring through the penstocks in four jets that shot hundreds of feet over the river. Over the course of the day, the flow rate has escalated from 8,000 cubic feet per second to 45,000. More than 117 billion gallons of water will spew through the floodgates by week's end.

Reporters will later grope for analogies. It is, they'll say, enough to fill Chicago's Sears Tower in seventeen minutes. Enough to fill Arizona's Sun Devil Stadium in less than ten minutes. Tourists will ask the park service when and where they can expect to see the tidal wave that will come churning through the canyon, mowing down wildlife, vegetation, and hapless rafters like us. A television producer from an extreme sports show will call to inquire whether a crew could be helicoptered in to shoot footage of a daredevil surfer shredding the big tsunami. (Request denied.)

Alas, the tsunami never arrives, but the hydraulics are huge enough to make me grateful for the party I'm with. Nearly all of my companions are or have been professional rafting guides. They are some of the best river runners in the world, out on their own private trip, happy not to have to baby tourists or enforce brainless rafting-company rules. All told, they've racked up more than one thousand trips through the canyon, a collective wisdom that I find reassuring under the circumstances. Some of them even boated in the high water of 1983, when a record snowmelt caught bureau officials off guard and forced them to spill huge amounts of water—in excess of ninety thousand cfs at certain points—in a frantic effort to prevent Lake Powell from running over.

For my hosts, rafting in this massive test flood wasn't part of the original plan, just a happy coincidence. The application for their permit had languished, as they all do, for six years on a park service waiting list. When the number came up, they realized, with very large smiles, that the put-in date fell only a few days before the high water. And now here it is. By nightfall the river is deafening, and some of the canyon rats are sitting by the fire, talking about the storied rapids we'll be bouncing through tomorrow. Hance. Sockdolager. Horn Creek. They know every coming kink and eddy and can draw in the sand the exact layout of each rapid. They speak of the nuances in an intimate, fraternal shorthand, sounding like a bunch of old Scots discussing a certain enigmatic hole at Muirfield or St. Andrews. They're understated elitists, sure of their craft, sure of the proud if not especially remunerative life they've chosen, sure in their belief that the staggering place they've spent so much of their adult lives mastering is the closest thing we have to Xanadu.

The sky ripens from pink to indigo, and soon the Comet Hyakutake floats into view, inching like a ghostly flagellate across the cosmos. We've been admiring it all week, treating it as our night-light. But now I'm thinking this isn't natural, this is a sci-fi flick. Surely this scene has been enhanced for our benefit by an obscure special-effects division of the Department of the Interior. We've got a flood at our front and a comet at our back and a couple of impossibly ancient walls defining our aperture. We've got everything but the word "epic" written on a billboard in the sky.

All of which could be skewing my sense of scale. But from where I'm sitting, never having run the Colorado before, the water out there appears to have turned homicidal.

"Yeah, it'll be big tomorrow," says Dennis, a coolheaded, ponytailed river guide of fifteen years, looking over the river.

Big? I ask.

"Yeah. Big and squirrelly."

Squirrelly?

"Look, if we flip, we flip," Dennis says. And then, borrowing a line from a deceased canyon legend named Whale, who before becoming a river runner had seen action in Vietnam, he adds, "I mean, it's not like there's going to be snipers."

THREE DAYS BEFORE the flood, the river had indeed taken on a martial cast, looking like a staging area for some imminent assault. As we floated down from the put-in at Lees Ferry, past Badger Creek, past Indian Dick Rapid, and on through the Roaring Twenties, we kept spotting impressive evidence of our government at work. Surveillance planes droned overhead. Choppers dropped in. Motorboats shuttled fish guys, bug guys, dirt guys to their stations. Scientists were submerging cables, tagging plants, inserting radio transmitters into the soft bellies of fish. They were wiring up the whole channel, converting it into a three-hundred-mile-long laboratory primed to receive the mother lode of data.

At one point we met a young technical assistant whose job for nearly two weeks was to take hourly water samples and then pick out all the organic matter—"orgs." He then was to separate the damp stuff into neat little stacks and label them: piles of midges, piles of flies, piles of gnats. It sounded like a sentence on Alcatraz. "I'm going crazy!" she confessed. "Can I hop on board with you guys?"

Most of the time I was riding with veteran guide and *National Geographic* photographer Dugald Bremner in his dory, the *Skagit*. The canyon dorymen are a traditionalist subset within the river-running tribe, and he is one of the best. "Graceful in repose, high and dry in the heavy going," he likes to say of his boat, quoting an old river-running brochure. He is a soft-spoken purist of the river, with a desert-baked face and a punctilious taste for single-malt scotch. His attitude with regard to watersheds is summed up in a bumper sticker affixed to his camera case: DAMS SUCK. "They do," he says. "Literally."

At mile thirty-two, we rounded a bend to confront two long mares' tails of springwater hissing out of the canyon wall, some two hundred feet up. It's a famous little spot called Vasey's Paradise. The constant spray from this pair of natural faucets has created a lush microclimate, like a green wadi in the Sahara, with hanging gardens of fern and watercress and monkey flower covering the limestone down to the river's edge.

Vasey's was crawling with scientists on this blustery day. "Come on up!" a young biology student called, waving us into the cove. He looked glad to see some fresh faces.

"What's going on here?"

"Snail duty!" he replied. "We're using nine-irons to chip these guys up the bank."

Over by the twin falls, a few biologists were crouched in the wet weeds, hunting for specimens of the Kanab ambersnail, an endangered species. It is believed that this tiny terrestrial snail is a last vestige of an age when there was a great deal more moisture in the canyon. The objective was to tag the snails with a teensy-weensy number for future studies and then gently place them, one by one, a short distance up the bank, so that the population here wouldn't be hammered by the high water. This was a mission of mercy, in other words, to minimize mollusk carnage. At this point, they were up to number 638 and were still hunkered in the muck, continuing their search for the biological equivalent of lost contact lenses.

It was a surreal scene, all the more so when one considered the fact that these painstaking biologists were ultimately being paid and marshaled by the Bureau of Reclamation, erstwhile destroyer of riparian ecosystems. The notion that the bureau's apparatchiks were now overseeing this elaborate environmental project came with loud ironies— shades, one might say, of the fox guarding the henhouse. Then again, times change, and even government agencies may be capable of an about-face. As one contract scientist I'd met earlier, a lifelong adversary of the bureau, had told me, "This is an enormous redemptive act. Not that they're doing this out of guilt—there is no guilt in government—but the bureau boys are wearing the green hats here." Bruce Babbitt, in his quavery Jimmy Stewart drawl, would put it another way: "After so many years of concentrating on water capture and power generation, this test is a symbol of our new commitment to making environmental restoration an equal part in the water equation of the West."

But what environment were we seeking to restore? What sort of conditions were we, to borrow bureau parlance, "managing for"? Floods, often bigger than this one, were once a regular spring fling on the Colorado, a swell of Rocky Mountain snowmelt and sediment glurping down through the canyon. The spectacle was not only impressive to watch; it was a crucial part of the natural order of things, a seasonal flux to which all life was intricately tied. But after the dam went up in 1963, the spring floods no longer cleaned out the river. The environment of the Colorado below the dam changed dramatically. The muddy, warm water turned clear and cold, drawn as it was from

245 feet below the surface of Lake Powell. Life on the river became tied less to the seasons than to the whims of the Western Area Power Administration and the diurnal power pangs of cities as far away as Los Angeles and Denver. One of the results of these wildly fluctuating daily flows was that many of the canyon's beaches, prime camping grounds for the 22,000 rafters who annually float the canyon, began to erode at an alarming clip. An estimated 40 percent had disappeared between 1963 and the start of the test flow.

It took more than a decade for scientists to figure out just what kind of havoc all these changes were wreaking on the river—and what could be done about it. Thirteen years and $60 million were spent studying the various options in a vast, tedious process that took into consideration more than 37,000 public comments and the findings of the country's finest ecologists. What emerged from this morass of paperwork was a new bureaucratic buzzword, *adaptive management*, and a recommendation that would have been heretical in 1963: Why not use some of the water in the Colorado for purposes other than generating electricity or irrigating the Cadillac Desert or sprinkling the putting greens of Scottsdale and Las Vegas? Why not use the water to *mimic* the pre-dam floods? The dam taketh away, but the dam might also provideth.

No one was sure the test flow would do what it was supposed to do, but if it worked, the bureau hoped to stage these faux floods every few years, viewing them as a Roto-Rooter maintenance plan on a big, big scale. The scheme was extremely ambitious, and this initial test alone would cost upward of $3 million, when you tallied up all of the scientific work and the estimated lost power-generating revenues.

And yet this wasn't any river; this was the Ganges of the environmental movement, hallowed waterway of John Wesley Powell, David Brower, and Edward Abbey. It was already perhaps the most regulated, most studied, and most politicized swath of water in the world. If the history of grandiose public-works projects has taught us anything, it's that playing God can be a little like telling lies: One act eventually begets another.

★   ★   ★

"HELLO, VARIOUS HUMANS!" a skinny, auburn-haired biologist called down to us from the camp at Vasey's. He was wearing squishy irrigation boots, short pants, and an Australian outback hat, and he had a distracted air about him, like a director on opening night.

A contract scientist for the bureau, Larry Stevens has been intimately involved in the flood's planning for the past four years, a vital voice in the byzantine process. River runner, author of one of the canyon's definitive river guides, restless polymath, and biologist with a Ph.D. in zoology, Stevens has devoted a quarter century of his life to figuring out this monumental puzzle of water and sediment and rock. Call him Professor Grand Canyon. For all practical purposes, this stretch of the Colorado is his office, and throughout the week he'd been hopscotching around, giving interviews, overseeing teams of scientists, checking to make sure everything was in order for the high water's arrival.

I shook hands with Stevens and asked him if he had a minute to talk.

"Nope," he said, glancing at his watch. "Got a helicopter to catch."

Just then a chopper popped over the rim and perched on a flat spot just below the talus. "Maybe I'll see you somewhere downstream!" he yelled as he grabbed a briefcase and ran down the footpath to hitch his ride.

Yeah, right, I thought. *There's only 245 miles of Grand Canyon left to go. We'll see you down there.* Then up he floated, whisked to the rim like some raja of the river.

Yet sure enough, two days later we ran into him. It was at mile fifty-five, at a placed called Kwagunt Marsh, where he was conducting a survey. "There's going to be a lot of loss of life here tomorrow," he said, looking out over an expanse of rustling cattails that would be fully inundated within twenty-four hours. "It's one of the things about this flood that I'm not too crazy about." Before 1963, he said, there were very few marshes in the Grand Canyon; their creation was one of the unforeseen results of the dam, and depending on your point of view may have been a positive thing, drawing a rich trove of new wildlife.

At nightfall Stevens sauntered over to our camp, his survey complete. We were having margaritas on the big snout raft, the whir of the blender resonating obscenely down the canyon. After a few drinks, Stevens was howling old sailor ditties, a guitar on his knee, the scientist metamorphosing into his old river-rat self.

It was turning cold and windy, but it didn't matter, for tonight was sauna night, a time-honored river-running tradition. We baked a dozen stones in the fire and draped a tarp over a pair of kitchen prep tables, insulating the structure with sleeping bags. When the stones were ready, we shoveled them into a pit dug in the sand. Then we stripped down and crawled toward the amber glow.

After we got a handle on the furnace heat, the conversation turned to the dam, and the irony that the very thing that had made a mess of the canyon environment was now being used to move back the clock. "Yes," Stevens said, "but we'll never really get back to that other river. That river is long gone. What we have now is something else entirely, something that's not altogether natural."

There was a long silence, and then Stevens started crowing an unfamiliar song: "Bring back the river! Set that muddy water free!" It was a piece of doggerel he once wrote about the humpback chub, a prehistoric-looking Quasimodo of a fish that's native to the canyon. The chub is the closest thing the canyon has to a mascot, but because it does better in warm water, its population was clobbered by the advent of the dam. "We survived the droughts when the water was low / the trouble started when the bureau built the dam, thirty-three years ago. . . ."

After the song was over, we sat for a few long moments, thinking chub thoughts, paying silent homage to its sorry humpbacked fate, but the verdict was unanimous. We couldn't take the heat anymore. Our brains were turning to consommé. We scrambled out and plunged ourselves into the Colorado. Someone had to devise a way for people to actually *want* to take a dip into this river of Freon on a cold night like this, and here it was: Poach yourself alive.

I stayed under as long as I could bear it—three seconds, maybe. It was an otherworldly cold, all out of character for a river that runs through desert lands. It felt wrong.

We could make it warmer if we really wanted to spend the cash. The scientists have proposed a special intake mechanism that could be rigged up at the dam, drawing water from different thermal levels of the lake. Which would be good for the chub but bad for the trout that have flourished in the canyon and thus bad for the bald eagles that have come to feed on the trout. There were infinite unforeseen quandaries up and down the food chain. Every move had unintended consequences; every doctoring of the potion left a funny taste on the back of the tongue. Once we've taken up the business of "managing for" entire ecosystems, juggling the incomprehensible calculus of nature, it's hard to know when to quit.

ALL THE RIVER-RUNNING ADVICE in the world cannot adequately prepare me for my first encounter with truly gigantic white water: the basso profundo rumble, the fugues of froth, the million watery rhythms bombarding the senses. I'm standing on a promontory above a monster rapid called Hance, feeling the mist rising off the water, smelling the turbid river smells. Some of the canyon rats are peering through binoculars, trying to figure out which of Hance's several slots will make the best run today, the run least likely to end in hypothermia and the dispatch of a rescue helicopter. "Couple years back, someone lost it here," Dugald tells me, shouting over the boom. "His boat wrapped around that rock over there. Went down and didn't come back up."

Well, that's some comforting news there, Dugald. Kind of you to share.

As we've already experienced this morning, the high water has made everything more dynamic, less predictable, harder to read. There are strange "boils" that keep bursting to the surface, causing us to lift and spin out of the current like water bugs. The tranquil pools between the rapids are no longer tranquil at all, more like pneumatic tubes suctioning us downstream to the next big attraction. On the other hand, the flood has actually washed out many of the rapids in the canyon, turning once dicey patches into extraswift but easily navigable runs.

Not so with Hance. Hance has only gotten mightier, louder, *squirrellier.*

"They ever find the guy's body?" I ask.

"Well," Dugald shouts back, "they helicoptered me and this other guy in with kayaks, and we spent a couple days searching downstream. Never did find'm. Probably got trapped under some rock. Had to swell up with methane before it would pop back up. Couple months later, a science team spotted the body floating past Phantom Ranch, and they retrieved it."

To further blacken the morning, there's a park service "observer" stationed on the banks here, a clipboard in hand. He inquires as to how the high water's been treating us thus far, asks a series of pointed questions about flips and near flips, and then waves us off to our doom.

Sufficiently steeled, our running strategies figured out, we jump on our boats and slip back into the mainstem. I'm riding with Dennis and his wife, Chris, on the snout raft, which will afford me enough height and stability to watch the fate of our armada unfold. Dennis runs right, and soon we're drifting toward a hundred-yard gauntlet of holes and eddies, boulders and haystacks, that right now is looking as grotesque as any Hieronymus Bosch painting. But hey—no snipers.

I won't give you some ridiculous yahoo account of the proceedings, because you can well imagine: it's huge, it's wild, we take on many gallons of water—but somehow we make it through without flipping.

As we're flung out of the swirlies and back into the main channel, we can plainly see the enormous redistribution of sand that's taking place all around us, can sense the floor plan of the canyon rearranging itself. Indeed, a week after the flood recedes, officials will estimate that beaches and sandbars have been restored by as much as 30 percent. In some places, twelve feet of new beachline will be created. At mile 122, a USGS team will underestimate the rate of sediment accumulation, and $60,000 worth of scientific instruments will be buried under a fresh sandbar. Later, Babbitt will say the entire flow experiment "worked brilliantly" and will announce that what has been learned here might be applied to other ecosystems mauled by man—the Platte, the Columbia, the Everglades. Dave Wegner, the Bureau of Reclamation official who was more or less the czar of the flood, will say that he is "elated—the event seems to have followed the script very well."

Yet as we point our boats into the Inner Gorge, feeling the black walls closing in, the script is perfectly unreadable. We're wet, shivering, and inexplicably euphoric, lurching toward the soul of the Grand Canyon, toward Granite and Crystal and Lava. At this point it makes no difference who or what unleashed this great brown roil we're riding, or for what reason. It's an authentic life force now, moving to its own powerful caprice.

—1996

In Darkest Bohemia

Monte Rio, California

ON A BEAUTIFUL JULY MORNING, I drive north from the Golden Gate Bridge on Highway 101 for an hour or so, and then make my way west toward the town of Freestone, where I pick up a little two-lane road known as "the Bohemian Highway."

The Bohemian Highway is one of the loveliest stretches of road in California. It cuts through twelve miles of vineyards and olive groves. It climbs over arcadian hills of pastel pink and burrows into ancient stands of redwood filled with fog and mist and motes of primal forest dust dancing in pale shafts of light. When I come to the little resort of Monte Rio, on the silty banks of the Russian River, the scenery suddenly shifts from somewhere in the south of France to Cold War Berlin. The road narrows and hooks to the right, and concertina barbed wire is strung up along a fence. The traffic signs grow in severity: NO THRU TRAFFIC. SPEED LIMIT 15 MILES. NO TRESPASSING. NO PARKING. PRIVATE ROAD. SLOW. CLOSED GATE AHEAD. MEMBERS AND GUESTS ONLY. NO TURNAROUND. The road stops at a gatehouse installation that looks like Checkpoint Charlie. A series of guard stations reaches far into the compound. Back in the redwoods, I sense a beehive of activity: buzz saws, hammers, forklifts, generators. Utility trucks are hauling cords of firewood up a paved canyon road. Valets scurry around in red jackets, toting luggage and parking cars. The place has the air of rusticity achieved at stupefying cost.

Eventually a burly man in a forest ranger's suit emerges from the gatehouse and asks me whether I can read English. "You're on private property, pal," he says. "You gotta turn around." He has a stern look on his face as he shows me the way out. And if for some reason I still don't get the picture, he says he'll call the police.

I'm not the first person who's been turned away from this curious compound in the Pacific forest—nor am I the first to contemplate schemes for an illicit break-in. The Bohemian Grove is the most exclusive summer retreat in America, if not the world. For over a century, members of the prestigious all-male Bohemian Club, an artistic and literary society in San Francisco, have made a pilgrimage to this three-thousand-acre redwood stand in Sonoma County. The men come here to escape their wives and the vexations of statecraft and corporate stewardship. The Bohemians call it the Midsummer Encampment; Herbert Hoover called it "the Greatest Men's Party on Earth."

For three weeks in late July, the Grove turns into a self-sustaining city. More than two thousand members and guests sleep in Crusoesque tree houses with names like Derelicts, Cave Man, and Whiskey Flat. The Bohemians do a lot of drinking and pissing on redwoods. They shoot skeet, play dominoes, and go on nature hikes. Stanford botanists lead safari excursions on the perimeter of the Grove—"Rim Rides," they're called—in open-air Land Rovers. Some members slip across the river for illicit evenings with hookers from the Vegas–Reno–Kentucky Derby circuit.

Art and live music are omnipresent. Oil portraits by Bohemian painters sit on easels beneath the redwoods, gathering dust. Over fifty pianos are stored in a dehumidified warehouse and wheeled out to cabins on demand. The Grove's pipe organ is housed in a special air-conditioned building. At the center of the compound is a 2,500-seat amphitheater where, on the peak night of the encampment, the club stages the annual "Grove Play," an extravagant epic drama written and performed exclusively by Bohemian talent and usually starring an odd cast of sprites and wood nymphs played by men in drag. Though a Grove Play typically carries a price tag upward of $30,000, it is performed only once.

But the Midsummer Encampment is much more than booze and thespian antics in the redwoods. It is the conspiracy theorist's greatest nightmare, a daunting roster of leading conservative politicians, corporate CEOs, and military brass who gather privately every year in a Tolkien forest to reaffirm their faith in big business, small government, and the good life. Forget about the Trilateral Commission. Forget the thousand closed-door cabals of Wall Street. If the American plutocracy has a secret clubhouse, it is the Bohemian Grove.

Left-wing political groups in California first caught wind of this decades ago. By the early eighties, a few hundred environmentalists, peaceniks, feminists, and lesbian separatists had banded together to form a militant protest group called the Bohemian Grove Action Network (BGAN). The demonstrators held vigils at the entrance of the compound every summer to denounce what they called "ruling class bonding." The BGAN logo pictured a tuxedoed patrician in a top hat, swilling a martini as he straddled an MX missile.

BGAN has called the Grove, with good reason, the birthplace of the atomic age. In the 1930s Berkeley physicist (and Bohemian) Ernest O. Lawrence forged crucial ties to government and business leaders at the Grove, paving the way for construction of the first cyclotron, which led, in turn, to the discovery of plutonium. In the autumn of 1942, Manhattan Project physicists, wary of Hitler's spies, secretly met inside the Bohemian Grove clubhouse to discuss isotope separation and to map out the initial development plans for the atomic bomb.

Despite Lawrence's precedent, it is considered supremely bad form to strike deals of any kind inside the Grove. The club's motto is "Weaving Spiders, Come Not Here"—a line from *A Midsummer Night's Dream* meaning no networking or shoptalk allowed. But contacts made beneath the gas-fed lanterns on Saturday evening can, without effort or prolonged introductions, be followed up by phone calls on Monday morning. "The Grove isn't designed for business, or even statecraft," observed one fairly prominent member of the military-industrial establishment, Bohemian Caspar Weinberger. "But it's a very pleasant place, and, inevitably, talk sometimes turns to substantive matters."

The Midsummer Encampment has long been a favored retreat for mandarins in the Republican party. Teddy Roosevelt was the first in a long line of Republican presidents who've hobnobbed at the Grove, including Taft, Eisenhower, Nixon, Ford, Reagan, and Bush Senior. And striding in after them, all the presidents' men: George Shultz, James Baker, Henry Kissinger, Nicholas Brady, Harold Brown, William Clark, Donald Rumsfeld, William French Smith, and Alexander Haig are all Bohemian Club members, no doubt the most *un*bohemian lot ever assembled in one place.

Herbert Hoover is still affectionately known among Bohemians as "the Chief." Hoover joined the club back in 1913 and became a member of Cave Man camp, where he took great pride in being the earliest riser each morning. It was largely at the Grove that Hoover, disgraced after the Great Depression, transformed himself into the party's elder statesman. From 1935 to 1964, Hoover was given the honor of delivering the final Lakeside Talk, and Republican hopefuls made pilgrimages to Cave Man camp to pay him homage.

Republican honchos represent, to be fair, only a small fraction of the Bohemian membership. The club ranks are primarily composed of San Francisco businessmen and professionals, with a healthy smattering of professors from Stanford and Berkeley, research scientists from private R&D labs, policy Brahmins from the Hoover Institute, and a few wine barons from Napa and Sonoma valleys. There have also been an astounding number of nationally known authors and media stars (Herman Wouk, Walter Cronkite); Hollywood celebrities (Bob Hope, Charlton Heston); multinational corporate heads (Ray Kroc, Henry Ford II); press lords (William Randolph Hearst); old-money scions (Laurance and David Rockefeller); and a few astronauts thrown in for good measure (Neil Armstrong).

The wealthier Bohemians fly in from all over the world, parking their Learjets and company turboprops on the crowded tarmac at tiny Sonoma County Airport, fifteen miles from the Grove, near Santa Rosa. Some have been known to sail their yachts up the Pacific coast and drop anchor in Bodega Bay. The less fortunate members drive their Saabs and BMWs up from San Francisco.

The encampment officially lasts for seventeen days, but most members just drop in for one of the two big weekends, when the bacchanalian revelry cranks up to its highest level. By midweek the Grove population dwindles to as low as three hundred, mostly retirees and club diehards who plan extended vacations in Bohemia. The others jet back to their boardrooms and trusteeships on Monday morning. "Some of us have to *earn* a living," working Bohemians are fond of saying.

MY FIRST PLAN OF ATTACK is to go in by canoe.

The Grove keeps a boathouse on the Russian River where the Bohos sunbathe and swim laps in the milky green water. The club couldn't purchase rights to the whole river channel, try as it might, so visitors are free to drift by the boathouse and get a long—and legal— glimpse of Bohemians at play. It's the closest outsiders can get without risking a trespassing rap.

My plan is simple: I'll paddle by the boathouse under the cover of night and hide my canoe in the brambles. Then I'll slip by the guardhouse and turn down Bohemia's main drag, River Road, toward the heart of the Grove.

On the first day of the encampment I rent a banged-up metal canoe for five bucks. I want to scout the riverbank by day to see if my scheme will work. I paddle upriver against a gentle current, gliding past some ramshackle river cabins and the Northwood Lodge and Golf Course, where AWOL Bohos are out hitting a few rounds. An osprey hovers over the river, hunting for fish. Suddenly the channel grows shallow, and I find myself paddling through rapids. Finally I have to drag the canoe across the rocks and silt for twenty yards, struggling against the current. It almost looks as if, long ago, the Bohemians had hired the Army Corps of Engineers to dam the river to discourage upstream traffic.

Privacy—some might say secrecy—is clearly the Bohemian way of doing things. The club mascot is itself a symbol of secrecy: the owl.

Everywhere in Bohemia one sees owls. Owls on stationery, cuff links, and bolo ties. Stuffed owls, papier-mâché owls, bronze owls. The forty-foot Owl Shrine, a dark and brooding concrete beast overgrown with moss and lichens, looms over the pond where the Bohos hear their Lakeside Talks. Originally the owl was chosen to reflect the nocturnal habits of the journalists who founded the club, but in the last half century it has come to symbolize, quite succinctly, the shadowy perch to which the Bohemians have removed themselves.

Beyond the rapids there is an abrupt kink in the river, forming a naturally protected enclave for the Bohemian swimming hole. Here the river looks almost artificial, like the green-dyed lagoons of Disneyland. Instead of flamingos, turkey vultures brood on a sandbar. The boathouse is a sprightly affair with green-and-white canvas awnings and Adirondack chairs where a few Bohemians sit shirtless, playing backgammon. A big American flag flaps in the breeze. From the dock, a bowlegged, ruddy-cheeked man in his sixties performs a perfect swan dive and surfaces with a howl. Farther out in the water, a liver-spotted old-timer is floating on his back and squirting geysers of water through his teeth. On the left bank, three bronze Bohos are lounging in the sun, flicking their toes in the sand. As I drift by, snippets of their conversation ("... get out the spreadsheets," "... interest-free loans," "bad judgment call ...") float over the water. One of the men, wearing a star-spangled meatsuit à la Mark Spitz, turns from the conversation, removes his sunglasses, and flashes me a proprietary look—an odd mixture of suspicion and obvious regret that this is a *public* river. "Nice day?" I falter, letting my paddle trail in the water. He coolly replaces his shades and resumes the discussion of spreadsheets.

I can see my chances of getting in by the boathouse are slim. The bank is nearly vertical and overgrown with briars and thistles. The boathouse is swarming with activity. And there is a permanently manned guardhouse perched high above everything, linked to the river by a single wooden staircase that zigzags down the hillside.

It's obvious the Bohos took precautions against a river invasion a long time ago.

*   *   *

DESPITE ITS PERSNICKETY adherence to secrecy, the Bohemian Club seems intensely interested in maintaining the Grove's place in history as a kind of American Olympus. Over the decades, Club archivists have seen to it that the major libraries in California, not to mention the Library of Congress, are supplied with the reams of official literature that the club publishes under its own imprint. At Berkeley's Bancroft Library, you can read the yellowed scripts of every Grove play ever produced, dating back to 1902. You can read all five hardback volumes of the club's tediously documented history, *The Annals of Bohemia*. You can spend weeks sifting through maps, wine lists, cartoons, lyrics, scores, transcriptions of Lakeside Talks, and tinted daguerreotypes of bewhiskered old men dressed in togas. The club seems to welcome the public's curiosity, as long as it takes the form of historical scholarship pursued through acceptable channels of research. It's the same sort of obsessive history-consciousness that led the Nixon White House to work its mischief behind closed doors, but all the while, *to tape-record everything!* Every word that is spoken in Bohemia is supposed to be off the record, and yet, absurdly, everything is recorded, photographed, and neatly cataloged for . . . for whom? Not for the general public, but for the faithful scribes of some far-distant posterity. "What's the point of being brilliant," Henry Kissinger lamented at the opening of a 1982 Lakeside Talk, "if you have to do it in obscurity?"

The Club itself is in many ways the West Coast equivalent of New York's Century Club, or Washington's Cosmos Club. The six-story ivied brownstone at the corner of Post and Taylor streets in downtown San Francisco has the same sort of fusty Victorian charm: the creaky floors, the crystal chandeliers, the redolence of pipe tobacco and malt, the dapper old men sitting in overstuffed chairs reading moldering hardbacks from the library. Women, if they're invited in at all, must enter by a side door and confine themselves to the banquet halls downstairs. A steady succession of sex-discrimination suits over the years has exerted considerable pressure on the Bohemians, but the club has held fast. (In 1989, however, the club was forced to hire women as Grove employees for the first time, the result of an employment discrimination suit brought by the State of California.)

Membership comes dear: $8,500 to join as a voting Boho, with monthly dues of $110. Men's clubs are said to be a dying phenomenon around the country, but the Bohemian Club has never been more popular. It typically takes fifteen years for prospective members to inch their way to the top of the three-thousand-name waiting list.

The club was started in 1872 as an informal drinking society for freethinking men in the San Francisco area who were interested in matters of art, literature, and music. At the time, the European notion of the "bohemian" lifestyle—the wandering, carefree *artiste*—had come into vogue in America, inspired in part by Puccini's opera *La Bohème*. Jack London, Bret Harte, Ambrose Bierce, and Mark Twain were among the club's early members, as was Sierra Club founder John Muir. The club rented a few rooms at the Astor House on Sacramento Street and blackballed all wealthy men as a matter of course.

But the Bohemians—being bohemians—couldn't pay their bills. So before long they reluctantly invited businessmen with professed avant-garde yearnings into the ranks, and within a few years "men of affairs" dominated the club roster. Oscar Wilde, visiting the club as part of a transcontinental tour of America, was moved to remark: "I have never seen so many well-dressed, well-fed, businesslike-looking bohemians in all my life."

Yet the name stuck, and membership in the Bohemian Club steadily grew, building on a curious alliance between businessmen and artists that could have thrived only in a city as wide-open and socially pliable as San Francisco in its youth. The Bohemians' musicals, reviews, and art shows grew more elaborate each year, and over time the club developed a latter-day version of Europe's court patronage system. Artistically gifted men were invited to join at greatly reduced rates, but were obligated to share their talents for full-paying members drawn from the wealthy class. The Bohemian Club thus gave the starving garret musician or actor of Victorian San Francisco an appreciative audience and the financial freedom to perform, while the railroad tycoon could soften his philistine edges in the fashionable presence of similarly well-dressed, well-fed "bohemians." It was a social arrangement reminiscent of the Medici, and it continues to this day. "You have joined not only a club, but a way of life," the Bohemian Club admonishes initiates. "Talented types," as gifted members are called, are expected to put out.

The first summer encampment, held in Marin County in 1878, was little more than a colorful picnic in the country. But the pilgrimage continued, year after year, the elaborate rituals becoming overlaid with a bizarre combination of Greek drama, Druidic legend, Shakespeare, the Book of Common Prayer, and the American Wild West. Somewhere along the way, the Midsummer Encampment began to take on a vaguely spiritual aura. Today, Bohemians at the San Francisco clubhouse speak of "going up." The Bohemian literature is strewn with descriptions of the Grove as a "cathedral," "sanctuary," "temple." It is said that some Bohemians, upon their deaths, have had their ashes sprinkled over the forest floor. Other Bohos concentrate their affections on specific trees. At the base of a three-hundred-foot redwood not far from the dining circle, you will find a little plaque that reads: I LOVE THIS TREE AS THE MOST SOUND, UPRIGHT, AND STATELY REDWOOD IN THE GROVE. LET MY FRIENDS REMEMBER ME BY IT WHEN I AM GONE.

THE TOWN OF MONTE RIO is an improbable site for an Establishment retreat. The town's population is an odd fellowship of gays, hippies, loggers, bikers, and eco-bandits. It's the kind of place where Earth First! warriors strap themselves to condemned redwood trees and "Appropriate Technology" is the ruling creed. A Bible camp and a Buddhist temple cling to the hills near the Grove. The Korbel Champagne Company, founded by two Czech brothers who moved to Sonoma County from the *original* province of Bohemia, owns a few thousand acres of vineyards nearby.

The Village Inn, where I'm staying, is a gracefully sagging Victorian hotel on the banks of the Russian River, named for the Russian fur trappers who, in the early 1800s, seasonally migrated here from the czar's colony in Alaska. The hotel is less than a hundred yards from the Grove fence line. Standing on the steps, I can hear the report of shotguns booming down the hollow from the Bohemian trap and skeet range. Next door to the inn is a modest residence faithfully guarded by two Doberman pinschers. Each blast of the shotguns sets the dogs off on a fit of barking, and they pace the length of a chain-link fence beneath a sign that warns, TRESPASSERS WILL BE EATEN.

The downstairs bar at the Village Inn is a popular hangout for Bohemian Club employees who've punched out for the night. The bar surface is strewn with an odd collection of toys and puzzles—Rubik's Cubes, Hot Wheels, trick ropes, battery-operated gizmos. On a busy night, you can meet Secret Service men, call girls, personal valets, and other servants of Bohemia gathered around the bar, fidgeting with the toys. A facetious cloak-and-dagger atmosphere pervades the place, *Casablanca* meets *Pee Wee's Playhouse*. Everyone is eyeballing one another. A heavily perfumed woman in a leopard-skin cocktail dress sits cross-legged on a bar stool, drinking daquiris in a gauze of cigarette smoke. Two men in dark suits stand in the shadows, playing with one of those metal-ball pendulum clackers from the early seventies: *Rackata-rackata-rackata-rackata*.

In the dining room, there are four actual Bohemians wearing owl bolo ties and cardigan sweaters, but no one is paying them much attention. "Who cares about them?" a local woman tells me. "They're all a bunch of yawners!"

Most of the Grove workers are hired from the rolls of the San Francisco waiters union, and are sworn not to assist journalists or other snoops in their research. But some are willing to cut a deal. Throughout the night, a Grove waiter in a pleated, food-stained tux shirt has been trying to sell me a "permanent pass" to the encampment for $500. "I could do it in a second," he assures me.

A garrulous fireplug of a fellow named Emmett says he's been in charge of the Bohemian bar and grill for seventeen years. Emmett's discourse on Grove life is all good-natured bluster, his anecdotes reeled off in a tone of mock condescension that seems to say, *You don't have a clue about how this country really works.*

"Say, Emmett," one of the locals says. "You must have seen some pretty heavy stuff up there in seventeen years. You know, political deals, CEOs divvying up the continent . . ."

"Man, they don't talk about shit up there," Emmett answers. "They talk about stuff like who stole the last bottle of Kahlua. They go someplace else to talk about their business." He stares at me for a moment.

"Who *you?*" he asks, breathing whiskey in my face.

A writer, I tell him.

"Don't be bullshittin' Emmett now. I've been keeping my eye on you. Seen you up there shootin' skeet. All you Secret Service cowboys think you're pretty hot shit with a shotgun, don't you?"

Emmett's got me pegged for some redneck hoss from the Secret Service and there's no convincing him otherwise.

"Listen up, James Bond. I'm the best shot in the state of California. I could break your neck before you even *get* to your gun. Who you workin' for? Reagan? Kissinger? Don't be messin' with Emmett. I'm the mayor of the Russian River."

Later, I meet a chain-smoking waiter with lugubrious, bloodshot eyes who informs me that he's the shop steward of the San Francisco restaurant workers union that serves the encampment. "The Grove's a magical place," he says. "I've personally had eye contact with Ronald Reagan three times! *Three times.* Eye contact! Another time I heard Burt Bacharach singing with Merv Griffin on the piano. Or was it the other way around? But I mean, *together!*"

The locals are eager to share their tips on the Grove, but getting in, they assure me, is out of the question. Some local hippies supposedly know a secret overland route from the backside of Bohemia. But I'd have to hack through miles of thickets, and I'd likely meet some pretty tough characters back in the hill country that surrounds the Grove, river rats straight out of *Deliverance* who wouldn't think twice about shooting me for trespassing on their property.

Even if I did succeed in penetrating the boundary somewhere, the odds are I'd get hopelessly lost. I could wander around in there for days and never see a soul. It's all switchbacks and ravines and cul-de-sacs, a tangle of pathways in the green gloom of redwoods, whose massive fluted stalks all begin to look alike after a while.

The trail system, someone tells me, is designed so that each path eventually doubles back to a guard station. Some trails in remote areas have infrared sensors that can detect an intruder's movements. Roving TV cameras stationed along the perimeter feed into a central monitoring station where Bohemian sentinels keep constant vigil. At strategic places, the Grove police have built tree houses high in the redwood canopy, where guards scan the pathways with binoculars.

"You might as well try to break into Fort Knox," the Village Inn bartender tells me, pouring another Bass Ale. "Trust me, you're going to wind up in the Santa Rosa jail with the worst cast of poison ivy you've ever seen."

MONTE RIO AVENUE tumbles from the high hills above the Bohemian entrance. The only marker is a sign that announces, NOT A THRU ROAD. The "avenue" turns out to be a single-lane residential road that winds through a warren of cabins, then cuts along a steep ridge. In places it is little more than a wobbly platform on stilts, cantilevered over a canyon. Finally the road doglegs to the right and dead-ends at a blocked entrance.

A sign over a gate says, BEWARE OF DOG, and judging by the general appearance of the place, it looks like a sign that means business. The wooden gate is half a foot thick, wrapped in chains and padlocked shut. The fence is draped in barbed wire. Another sign announces PRIVATE PROPERTY: NO TRESPASSING.

I hurl a stone over the gate to stir up the dogs. It tumbles down the hillside, and I can hear it smashing into tree trunks before landing in a clump of maidenhair ferns. I think I hear barking, but at 4:45 A.M., I could be imagining things.

Down in a valley, through the tree limbs, I can see a parking lot filled with Jags and Mercedes-Benzes gleaming in the moonlight. The road continues beyond the gate for a hundred yards or so, then drops behind a hill. It appears to be an old service road of some kind, an access route for trucks and heavy machinery, though it clearly hasn't been used in a long time.

I'm calling their bluff on the dogs. I'm going in.

I'm wearing my best approximation of a Bohemian uniform: a blue blazer, a cotton dress shirt, and crisply pressed Levi's jeans. I'll be posing as a Bohemian early riser heading for his morning dip in the river, so I fling a towel around my neck and carry a pair of swimming trunks for good measure. In my coat pockets I've stashed a penlight, a Sony tape recorder, and a faded map of the Bohemian Grove that I'd copied out of the Bancroft Library. The map is dated September 1935.

I spread the beach towel on the ground to shield my blazer from the dirt and conifer needles. I lie on my back and squeeze into the narrow passage under the gate.

Snoops like me, burning with a peculiar lust and feeling of entitlement, have been breaking into the Bohemian Grove ever since the start of the Woodward-Bernstein era. *Mother Jones,* National Public Radio, *Time,* the *Los Angeles Times,* CBS News, and *Spy* magazine have all sneaked reporters in over the years. Two nonfiction books and several novels have been written about the place. A Vanderbilt anthropologist has compared the Bohemians' elaborate rituals to those of a misogynist tribe of Indians in Central Brazil, the Mehinaku, and more than a few observers have compared the "Cremation of Care" ceremony, in which Bohos don hooded robes and chant before a burning effigy, to a Ku Klux Klan rally.

But the most indefatigable researcher of Bohemia is a shy freelance photojournalist named Kerry Richardson. Working alone out of his parents' house in nearby Santa Rosa, Richardson has spent the past several years compiling a computerized dossier on every Bohemian club member. When I caught up with him he had just completed the Ls. Richardson is a tall, fair-complexioned man in his late thirties with thick spectacles and long dun-colored hair pulled back in a ponytail.

The fruits of his research can be found in a small underground newsletter that he publishes from time to time entitled *Kerry Richardson's Journal.*

If universities had a formal department for the kind of research Richardson does, it might be called Establishment Studies. His bookshelves sag with titles like *Missile Envy, The Man Who Kept Secrets, Friends in High Places.* He scours the Fortune 500, *Who's Who in America,* Standard & Poor's Index, and Dun & Bradstreet, hunting for clues to questions like which Bohemians sit on the boards of which of their friends' companies, or which Bohemians have made financial contributions in excess of $1,000 to the political campaigns of fellow Bohemians. He can tell you the names of the executive vice presidents of Lockheed, Rockwell International, and Pratt & Whitney. He can tell you who Stephen Bechtel invited last year as a guest to the Grove. "There's a lot of evil concentrated up there," Richardson says. "Or rather, there are a lot of people concentrated there who are responsible for . . . evil processes."

Richardson's real love is photography. Each summer he drives out to the Sonoma County airport and takes snapshots of Bohemian bigwigs as they step off their Learjets. Most of the men aren't easily recognizable, so Richardson spends a lot of his time trying to verify the identities of those he's photographed. Sometimes he looks up the annual reports of major corporations and studies the official photographs of board members until he finds a likeness. Other times he copies down the tail numbers on the planes and writes the FAA to learn the owners' names. "I think that's John Kluge, but I'm not sure," he says, holding up a negative to the light.

One year Richardson put on diving flippers and swam by the Bohemian boathouse, taking photos with an underwater camera. "Why don't you just leave us alone?" one of the Bohos told him. Richardson snapped off a few more shots and then disappeared in the green water.

Interlopers like Richardson have justified their trespasses on the Grove by appealing to lofty principles: to expose the pernicious ways that power cross-pollinates, to hold the nation's oligarchs accountable. But for others, myself included, one suspects a baser motive. It is the ancient boyhood impulse to Get In—to break the spell of secrecy. It's not a noble enterprise, and certainly not a legal one. But it can't be helped.

NOW THAT I'M INSIDE, I expect air-raid sirens to go off, halogen floodlights, the squawk of a hidden PA system: *Turn back, intruder! This is a final warning!* Instead . . . nothing. Only the frogs and owls and miscellaneous thicket sounds of the forest. As I creep down the spongy path, the only animal I see is a doe quivering in the shadows, her frightened eyes shining back at me through the silver moonlight.

There is a feathery artificiality about the trees, all those giant asparagus stalks stretching skyward in perfect uniformity. A deciduous forest is an imperfect world of crooks and elbows and broken limbs of different species rotting together in democratic heaps, and the leafy ground is always crawling with bugs. But not in a redwood grove. Where are the bugs? Occasionally I see a perfect spider spinning a perfect web between two perfectly straight trees, but no bugs.

The air is cool and damp and still as a cellar. The clump of my footsteps is swallowed by a corrugated wall of timber. At times when the wind stirs in the upper reaches of the trees, the branches rub together to create a frightful keening sound, high-pitched and insistent, like the cry of a trapped animal.

The Grove is the last remaining old-growth stand of any size in Sonoma County—all 2,800 acres purchased in 1925 for the paltry sum of $99,000—and it's a priceless piece of real estate. Some of these trees are two thousand years old. To walk in here is to walk among superlatives—oldest, biggest, tallest, darkest, thickest—not to mention the superlatives commonly associated with Bohemians themselves: richest, smartest, mightiest, best connected. Any living thing that was around during the reign of Charlemagne has a way of mocking you. The Kayasha Pomo Indians who once lived and hunted in Sonoma County believed the groves were haunted places, filled with evil spirits. Just crawling over these ancient roots, I feel like an intruder twice over. On some cosmic level that transcends the mere illegality of trespassing, I sense I do not belong here.

According to my map, I'm on Mt. Heller Trail, but I keep blundering onto subsidiary paths that evidently didn't exist in 1935. I'm getting farther and farther from the encampment circle. Little cairns are laid out by forks in the path, but these tell me nothing. It's no use: I'm hopelessly lost in the Bohemian Outback. Occasionally I stumble upon a concrete trail marker bearing the chiseled image of an impish owl on the wing. But it's not until dawn that I see any convincing sign of Bohemian civilization. Taking Middle Ridge Road, I come to a desolate clearing that turns out to be the trap and skeet-shooting range. The grass is drenched in dew and littered with the green casings of shotgun shells.

I walk for twenty minutes on an access road that winds out of the woods and climbs over several miles of weedy hill country. I've wandered clear off the map now, to some no-man's-land on the outskirts of Bohemia. In the distance I can hear the rumble of a heavy truck, and it's growing louder. The Grove police, I suspect, making their surveillance rounds. Now that darkness has lifted, the guards will spot me a mile away; there are no redwoods to duck behind out here. And they'll assume I'm a spy right off: I'm miles from camp, and farther still from the Russian River, where, ostensibly, I'm heading for a swim. No real Bohemians would be hiking this treeless periphery, certainly not at this godforsaken hour.

Now I can hear the police truck chuffing up the hill behind me, just a hundred yards back and gaining. I'm frantically hunting for a place to hide. I hear the sound of gears grinding, tires shaking the earth. They're coming after me.

I crawl into a culvert just before the vehicle crests the hill: a large truck from the Bohemian utility fleet, fire-engine red, clanking and rattling with chains, winches, heavy tools.

I think they missed me, but I stay low for a few minutes until the road is clear.

JUST WHEN I THOUGHT I'd managed to elude all of the Grove's fabled security traps, I round a corner and see that I'll have to pass by a guard station after all. I pick up the pace and try to look natural, swinging my towel over my shoulder and whistling a tune. To my surprise, the uniformed man in the little kiosk just smiles and waves me on through.

It's about nine A.M. when I finally work my way down to River Road. The Grove is waking up now. I can smell bacon and percolating coffee. Smoke is curling from the camps, and everywhere I can hear the clinking of porcelain and flatware. Tyndall beams of light angle through the canopy. Inside the camps, old guys are sitting in their boxer shorts, yawning, stretching, belching, hacking. On a hillside, two stout souls in lederhosen burst out of the woods, their whittled walking sticks smacking the ground as they return from a brisk morning constitutional.

In many respects, the Grove is a rustic place. No TVs, stereos, or radios are allowed. Most of the buildings are rough-hewn cabins, their rickety steps carpeted in moss and forest needles. The public clearings are strewn with wood chips. A salt lick stands in the middle of the Grove, to attract deer. Tacked to a redwood tree near the dining area is an admonition to campers: GENTLEMEN! PLEASE NO PEEPEE HERE!

Each of the Grove's 135 camps has its own personality. Some are bungalows spread on the forest floor; others are jumbled boxes that seem to bounce down the hills. The public spaces are furnished with faded sofas and morris chairs, and all manner of bric-a-brac is lying about: stuffed animals, road signs, naked mannequins, fur pelts. The camps have boyish-sounding names that conjure up half-forgotten tales from *Treasure Island* and the works of Kipling: River Lair, Shoestring, Woof, Moonshiners, Toyland.

Aviary is the camp for singers. Tunerville is where the orchestra members stay. Medicine Lodge, a cluster of tepees, is inhabited exclusively by doctors. ThreeThrees is a camp for navy admirals. At Poison Oak Camp, they serve Bull's Ball Lunch, a hearty entrée of testicles from the castrated herds of a central California cattle baron.

There's a boastful competitiveness about these little lairs. The fancy hinged signs that swing outside the camp entrances seem like a form of advertising, as if to say, *Come try life in our condo village*. These ruddy campmates hunkered over their fires are instinctive company men, the kind of people who draw a large part of their identity from institutions. Their sweatshirts say EXETER, SEMPER FIDELIS, YALE CREW. Their baseball caps say AIR FORCE, UNIVERSITY CLUB, STANFORD LAW. The borders of each camp are clearly marked with gates and tidy fences, bright flags and escutcheons. In one of the camps, someone has propped up a stolen sign from suburbia—WARNING: NEIGHBORHOOD CRIME WATCH—as if burglary were a problem in the Grove.

I'm a little young-looking to be a Bohemian (the average age in the club is fifty-five), though I could pass for a son or a nephew, or perhaps some junior executive that the boss brought along. But no one gives me a second look. It is the height of bad taste for a Bohemian to openly question the legitimacy of another guest's presence. Still, I've decided to forestall any suspicions by going out of my way to be friendly, making myself look at home here. As I stroll toward the dining circle, I'm constantly waving, smiling, making direct eye contact with everybody I meet. Outside Monkey Block Camp, I have an encounter that gives me a start: it's the surly guy who wore the little Mark Spitz number on the Russian River the other day. But he clearly doesn't recognize me; this time he's all smiles. "How ya doing?" I gingerly ask him. He gives me a chipper salute and says, "Boy, what a day! Goooooooooooood morning, Bohemia!"

I wander over to the campfire circle and take a seat on one of the enormous benches hewn from redwood logs. The cinders from last night's bonfire are still smoldering. Placed about the circle are full-length portraits of the men responsible for producing the various entertainments during the week. "Sires," they're called. A Sireship is a title of special honor and responsibility in Bohemia, and these portraits reflect it. All the Sires are depicted as discerning men of unerring taste. They stare off into the middle distance, their spectacles pushed back over their furrowed brows.

Over at the telephone bank, an unidentified Bohemian wearing only a towel and flip-flop thongs is deep in conversation with his broker. "*Whaddayamean he said no? Hey, I've got a controlling share.*" Another gentleman in bermudas and a UCLA T-shirt is sipping a Bloody Mary and talking, in a somewhat defensive manner, with his wife. "*Honey, honey . . . l-l-look, I promise I won't get too smashed. I'm flying United down tonight, okay?*" At a little amphitheater near the museum, a Berkeley professor is delivering a lecture on "chaos."

A young guitar player—a "Talented Type"—comes over to say hello. "What camp you in?" he asks politely.

"Bromley," I answer. (Bromley Camp is the large residential limbo at the Grove where most new members stay until they're assigned a permanent camp.)

"Oh, that's funny," he says. "I'm in Bromley, too. Where you sleeping, exactly?"

"Uhhhhhh," I stammer, "I-I-I . . ."

He gives me a long bewildered look. But then, lucky for me, one of his buddies comes over to congratulate him on a guitar performance he had given last night. I take my cue and disappear through the bushes and down the nearest trail.

AN ORDINARY PERSON cannot stay very long inside a grove of *Sequoia sempervirens.* As beautiful as it is in there, all that cloistered monochrome green becomes suffocating. There is a spooky quality about the timelessness, the noiselessness, the *bug*lessness of this utopia. I'm beginning to understand why the Pomos believed the redwoods were haunted.

I don't linger long at the Bohemian Grove. I'd spent the past week snooping around like a jackal for a way in. Now that I've succeeded, I'm itching to leave. I can easily stay all week, crashing camp parties, attending free concerts, hearing Lakeside Talks until I'm Groved out of my mind. But I have no interest in it. I don't feel like hunting down celebrities or eavesdropping on policy eggheads as they carve up the planet. I have no interest in going on a Rim Ride or taking in the Grove Play, which this year will be based on the theme of Pompeii.

At its worst, maybe the Grove really is all those evil things that Kerry Richardson and the BGAN protesters say it is: the playpen of the plutocrats, the spawning ground of God only knows how many nuclear weapons. Like all men's clubs, the BC is by its nature elitist, and, in sometimes frightening ways, it perpetuates a closed system by which political leaders are often selected in this country.

But at its best, Bohemia is more than a men's club. It is founded on an intriguing idea, an illusion that is uniquely American and essentially Californian: the illusion that a man can shuck his identity for a time and bend reality to suit himself. The Grove is a fantasyland where masters of the American Dream can "cremate" the world they've conquered; where powerful men can feel talented, and talented men can feel powerful; where undistinguished men can feel famous, and famous men can melt into the crowd; where gentlemen of leisure can enjoy the amenities of cultured society while "roughing it" in the forest.

The Bohemians couldn't be a friendlier tribe. This is part of the problem. Maybe, on some level, I wanted a confrontation. I had believed the local lore. I had blanched with fear each time I heard about some new layer in the Grove's onion skin of security. I had imagined the Grove to be an impenetrable preserve, like some inner sanctum of the Vatican. But I just crawled under a fence and walked in.

That afternoon, with a feeling of great relief and maybe a little disenchantment, I slip through the barbed wire and drive back to the Village Inn. Next door, the two Doberman pinschers are curled up in their little lot. This time, when I walk by, they're wagging their tails.

—1990

Mystery! Science! Theater!

Oracle, Arizona

"THIS IS ONE of the magic moments of history," proclaims Jane Goodall, the eminent primatologist, in her quavery, genteel voice, "and we are all here to share it together."

Dawn has broken purplish and cool on Arizona's high desert. An apricot sun peeks over the Santa Catalina Mountains and softly backlights the glass domes and ziggurats of what may be America's most misunderstood edifice. Goodall is on hand to serve as the keynote speaker at the "Re-entry" ceremony for Biosphere 2, an odd piece of ecological drama that will be televised worldwide. It's the morning of September 26, 1993, and in a few short minutes the eight Biospherians will walk through the air lock after two years spent inside their terrarium. As Goodall runs overtime with dotty reminiscences about Louis Leakey and her African chimps, the Biospherians remain sealed behind the metal door, zipping up their *Star Trek* costumes, practicing their lines, checking their makeup.

BEFORE DAYLIGHT, spectators anxious to witness this "magic moment" had lined up in a two-mile-long bumper-to-bumper jam on the highway leading to the Biosphere site, which occupies 3,200 acres of dusty desert about an hour north of Tucson. Headlights bored through the darkness, revealing hillsides of prickly pear and slumbering saguaro. The bright-eyed parking aides wore Re-entry sport shirts printed especially for the occasion. They carried walkie-talkies and clipboards and cheerfully reminded people to keep moving. "Better hurry," one said, "or you'll miss the Vivaldi."

On hand for the event were some five thousand souls, each willing to fork over $12.95 to gain entrance to the grounds. "Witness the Biosphere 2 crew's historic RE-ENTRY to Earth," said the ads that had been running in the regional papers. "Bring the whole family for a day of discovery at this major ecological event. Meet the Biospherians in person! Hear special Eco-Talks from top scientists!"

Driving toward the heart of the vast compound, it was impossible not to be impressed by the huge glass pavilion winking on the ridge ahead. Two years of controversy and bad press couldn't diminish the spectacular visual effect of the structure's unique architecture—the crystal arches, the white minarets, the gleaming geodesic lungs. In concept and construction Biosphere 2 was an act of hubris on the grandest scale, and yet somehow it looked appropriate out here. This was Arizona, after all, the state that gave us the mirage civilizations of Charles Keating. Technicians trundled along the canyon roads in souped-up golf carts. Generators hummed. A helicopter wheeled in the sky. Adding to the high-tech tableau was the snarl of cables, booms, and cameras of television news outlets from around the world, competing for air superiority.

From the parking lot, the crowd made its way on foot along a trail carpeted in webs of Astroturf. Cresting the hill, I could hear strains of Vivaldi's *Four Seasons*. A symphony orchestra played down by the air lock, the musicians dressed in tuxedos and evening gowns. At the edge of the path stood a souvenir booth with a sign that read, LIMITED EDITION RE-ENTRY COLLECTIBLES. On sale were Biosphere 2 shot glasses, commemorative coins and stamps, thimbles, paperweights, and copies of the Biospherian cookbook, *Eating In*. There was a cuddly teddy-bear mascot, Bearospherian. The vendor informed browsers that though the Biosphere project is supposed to continue for more than a hundred years, only souvenirs from "Mission One" will retain any value as collector's items. "Better get 'em now," he said, "because there's only gonna be one first time."

Scattered about the grounds were scores of sculptures by a New Mexico artist named Tony Price, who has given expression to one of Biosphere 2's dark subtexts: that Planet Earth (known in the parlance as Biosphere 1) may reach a calamitous state, through either nuclear war or environmental collapse, possibly making Biosphere 2–type structures a future necessity. Price's sculptures were fabricated out of torn and melted scrap metal salvaged from the nuclear junkyards around Los Alamos. Bearing such grim titles as *Nuclear Kachina* and *Prince Yama God of Death,* these installations reinforced the notion that the Biosphere project was driven, in part, by a peculiar brand of survivalist millennialism.

Spectators couldn't enter the structure itself, but they were free to press their faces against it. Peeking through the honeycomb of glass, I could see a tangle of fronds pushing against the foggy panes. Crawling in manic, erratic patterns were vast armies of tiny brown ants, scurrying along the space frames, carrying nuggets of concrete and dead plant debris. The population of these "crazy ants," as the South American species is called, had exploded out of control, and because pesticides were off-limits the Biospherians were stumped about how to remedy the problem. On closer inspection, I could also see thousands of identical-looking ants outside the glass. Were there separate populations on each side of the biospheric divide? Or had the ants, oblivious to Biosphere 2's man-made boundaries, found an access route?

ON THE LARGE CONCERT STAGE, the planners and architects of Biosphere 2 sit cross-legged and beam with pride at the futuristic landscape they have wrought. Here are the masterminds of a project that has been accused of bad science, hucksterism, legal badgering, and the doctoring of data—not to mention cultic practices and a secret doomsday agenda—but none of this is registering on their faces. They survey the scene with frozen smiles, like old-time Kremlin leaders on a reviewing stand. Video images of Biospherian life flicker on a huge screen overhead—Abigail Alling swimming in the "ocean," Sally Silverstone milking the goats, Mark Nelson cutting grass in the "savanna."

On one side of the stage sits Texas oilman Ed Bass, the sugar daddy of Biosphere 2, wearing a natty blue blazer, his long blond hair smoothed back and lacquered to his patrician head. On the other is John Allen, a metallurgist and sci-fi poet who's said to be Bass's guru and the prime mover behind the Biosphere project. Back in the seventies, Allen ran a theater troupe that lived on a commune near Santa Fe. Known as Synergia Ranch, this social experiment was harrowingly documented in *The Communal Experience*, a book by historian Laurence Veysey, who spent five weeks at the commune in 1971. Allen's vision of approaching doom was tinged with the hope that an elite corps of space explorers, versed in the brave new discipline of "eco-technics," might preserve human life by venturing to other planets and establishing self-sustaining communities beneath giant glass domes. Up on the stage, Allen wears a bolo tie and a maroon fedora and keeps exchanging smiles with emcee Margaret Augustine, the willowy CEO of Biosphere 2's parent company, Space Biospheres Ventures.

In front of the reviewing stand, row upon row of spectators sit in plastic folding chairs on an incongruously verdant lawn, the product of assiduous water sprinkling. In the audience are families of the Biospherians, scientific dignitaries, and various eco-chic types with raisiny hides and earlobes sagging from the weight of turquoise earrings.

In the back-row seats, tourists from Nevada discuss the burning question of the day: "Two years in there and you don't think they *did it?* Get real!" Next to them, an elderly woman holds a sign that says, WELCOME BACK TO EARTH!

When the action finally kicks off, Bass is the first to speak. He seems nervous and a little befuddled by the whole spectacle, but nothing in his expression indicates that he has any regrets about the millions he's sunk into the project. In fact, he keeps looking over his shoulder at the bubble like a child doting on his coolest toy. "Less than half an hour from now," he says, "the human population of our Earth's biosphere will be swelled by eight in number—eight brave pioneers who stepped apart from us two years ago today and have been living a glass pane's breadth away in a whole other world." Bass turns toward the portal window. "Welcome home," he says with a laugh, "and save me a good hug."

HALF AN HOUR LATER, the brass section swells with Aaron Copland's *Fanfare for the Common Man.* On the screen, the audience can see a live picture of the Biospherians waving from inside the air lock. Suddenly the door is thrown open and the four men and four women emerge. The look on their faces is a mingling of confusion, elation, and relief. Few of them are smiling. Several gasp for breath as they fill their lungs with the clean desert air. Two years without ultraviolet rays has turned them fish-belly gray, and their palms are orange from the beta-carotene in their staple diet of carrots and yams. They are extremely gaunt, having dropped an average of twenty-one pounds each. During their two years inside the bubble their metabolism slowed to what one specialist, quoted in a newspaper story, describes as a "state of hibernation."

The Biospherians wear matching blue jumpsuits styled by a Hollywood fashion designer who once made costumes for Marilyn Monroe. As the crowds cheer, the crew marches with ramrod posture down a red carpet toward the stage. Each comes to the podium to make a few remarks for the cameras.

"It's a different atmosphere," declares ocean biome specialist Abigail Alling, "a very different atmosphere." She clasps her hands together and peers up into the heavens.

Some of the greetings are a tad cryptic. Roy Walford, a bald gerontologist who has devised a high-fiber diet that he claims will enable people to live to 120 years of age, has this to say: "It's nice to be back among the magnolias." Magnolias? Walford offers a grandfatherly smile and explains, "Lest you think I've lapsed into arboreal madness," that the line is from an old movie starring Red Skeleton, "my favorite comedian."

Perhaps the most discerning comment of the day comes from crew cocaptain Mark Van Thillo, a string bean of a man who in his thick Flemish accent utters precisely what is on the minds of millions of TV viewers around the globe. "Two years ago," he says, "I stood here wondering what would happen. Today I stand here wondering ... *what happened?*"

AFTER THE RE-ENTRY CEREMONY, some two hundred journalists are shepherded into a big white tent that bulges with cool air piped in from portable air conditioners. Several dozen phones are set up in the back, against flapping canvas walls. People stand around sipping coffee and eating granola bars amid the clacking of laptops and the shrill song of modems.

The Biospherians saunter in to face the lions. "After two years," Mark Nelson says, "we begin to crave outside human contact. And as journalists, you are humans, too."

The press conference is brief and for the most part lighthearted. Some of the journalists may be feeling a bit chastened for beating up on the Biospherians so much over the past two years. It's difficult to cross-examine eight people who have just returned from seven hundred and thirty days of self-imposed exile and who look in desperate need of a T-bone steak and a fifth of Jack Daniel's.

Much of the bad press was deserved, of course. As an experiment in self-containment, Biosphere 2 had proved to be, in many ways, a failure, and the Biosphere administrators used aggressive spin control. The planners went into the project with a vow of total self-sufficiency. The bubble, they said, would be hermetically sealed. In fact, by the end of the mission the air lock had been opened a total of twenty-nine times. Among other things, the Biospherians had ordered in makeup, seeds, Sominex, mousetraps, and computer equipment. Jane Poynter actually had to leave the building for five hours to undergo surgery after severing the tip of her finger in a rice thresher.

The Biosphere's atmosphere needed frequent rejiggering, too. Carbon dioxide rose to dangerous levels, despite a scrubber that was installed a few days before closure. For reasons that are not entirely clear, the oxygen level plunged to 14 percent, about two-thirds the level in Earth's atmosphere. The Biospherians gasped for breath and suffered from insomnia. On two occasions, oxygen had to be pumped in.

"Was the Biosphere trying to kill you?" one journalist asks.

"No," Mark Nelson answers, "but it was trying to tell us something."

The portrait of daily life that emerges during the press conference sounds Spartan at best. The smell of mildew, algae, and animal excrement hung in the air. Instead of toilet paper, bathrooms were equipped with a "bidet system." Women had to menstruate into special reusable cups. And despite its vaunted wilderness areas, Biosphere 2 afforded little pastoral tranquility: the ceaseless drone of fans, generators, compressors, and pumps made the interior sound like the boiler room of a battleship.

Because the crew couldn't produce enough food, hunger was a constant companion. Hoarding and stealing were inevitable results. "The hunger became so bad," Mark Nelson says, "that it was sometimes difficult for some of us to follow the movie plots on our VCRs. Whenever food appeared we just stared at the screen."

But there were also good times inside the ark. "I glimpsed paradise in there," Biospherian Linda Leigh says. *Life Under Glass*, an intriguing account on sale at Biosphere gift shops, recounts tales of feral-pig feasts, elaborately themed birthday parties, and "al fresco dining" on the veranda overlooking the Intensive Agriculture Biome. Some afternoons the Biospherians would knock off early and go snorkeling in the "ocean" or pop the bonfire video in the VCR and have a clambake on the "beach." They would then pass their evenings on a man-made strand lapped by the artificial waves of their synthetic ocean, basking in the orange glow of a virtual flame.

After a while someone asks what is apparently taken as an impertinent question: "Who took the Sominex?"

"It's a common sleep-inducing agent!" Roy Walford insists. Sally Silverstone, the moderator, evidently senses that the conference is turning hostile. "As you can imagine, we're very tired and we have much to do," she says, declaring that the press conference is now adjourned.

The Biospherians abruptly rise to leave, but the photographers protest. "One last picture!" they bellow. The crew reluctantly draws together to strike an arm-in-arm pose, as if the last thing they want is more togetherness. "Say 'goat cheese'!"

⋆　　⋆　　⋆

LATER IN THE DAY, a small group of journalists who had been invited as part of a special "press pool" to tour the Biosphere's insides return to share what they've seen. A reporter named Arthur Rotstein from the Associated Press leads the briefing. "We spotted several cockroaches in the stairwell," he says.

"Were they alive or dead?"

"They were . . . *squished*. We then went to the holding pens for the animals. It stank pretty bad in there, like a barnyard. There were a few goats and these chickens that they call African jungle fowl."

"How about pigs? Were there any pigs?"

"We saw no pigs, but there used to be some in there. They were going to have Vietnamese potbellied pigs, but the animal-rights people raised a fuss. So they got these wild ones called Ossabaw feral pigs."

"How do you spell that?"

"O-s-s-a-b-a-w," says Rotstein. "It's an island off of Georgia. I'm told there were two pigs, a male and a female. They had one litter of six. All became food."

"Wait! About that smell. What was it like again?"

"It was, you know, urine, feces. Animal smells."

"Did it smell bad only in the animal area?"

"No," concludes Rotstein. "It smelled pretty much everywhere."

—1993

Panther Falls

The Blue Ridge Mountains, Virginia

AS WITH BARS and women, it would be foolish of me to try to convince you that my swimming hole is better than yours. Mine *is* better, though. Mine is the platonic form of swimming holes. You might as well take all the old pastoral images and chuck 'em—Huck and Tom in Missouri, the rising-sap innocence of Walt Whitman's buck-naked boys. Spare me your lame tales of swinging ropes and tractor-tire tubes, your blue-jean cutoffs, your cypress-lined sinkholes and hidden hot springs. My ears are closed. Whatever you've got to offer, I have but one response: Mine's better.

When I first came upon it from the top, I sensed its presence before I saw it. A sibilant hiss, a sheeny mist rising from the mountain-laurel thickets, a plume of negative ions. Suddenly, the air temperature dropped. My skin tingled, my breath quickened, an atavistic grin crept across my face. I climbed one last rise in the trail, and there it was below me. A waterfall spilling between two mighty sandstone boulders. Froth tumbling down a staircase of limestone ledges to a deep pool of blue-black water that emptied, in turn, into a narrow rock channel carpeted with shaggy green moss. The channel dropped into one pool, then another, then, impossibly, a third. Ranged all about this labyrinth of water were aprons of lichen-covered rock. I feasted my eyes on the whole improbable arrangement, watching the water spill from pool to pool to pool, wondering how this place came to be and why Nature went to so much trouble.

Without even knowing it, I spent the summers of my youth just down the mountain from this magical place, in the Shenandoah Valley of Virginia, working on my grandfather's farm. In the hot afternoons, we'd head for any one of our favorite swimming spots: Swink's Bottom, Jennings Creek, Buffalo Bend, High Rock, Goshen Pass. These were Pappaw's places, places he'd known about since he was a kid growing up in the "aught years" of the last century. In their own way, they were all perfect. Later in life I traveled about the country and compiled my own short list of idyllic American swimming holes—including a certain spring in Idaho, a cenote in Florida, and a waterfall pool near Ithaca, New York, where the old Tarzan movies were filmed.

But then I learned of the greatest pool in God's wet world, and it was in my family's own backyard: Panther Falls, a ferny spot on a freestone trout stream high in the Blue Ridge, not far from the Appalachian Trail. (As for its precise coordinates, I can only say that if you go to the trouble of finding it, then you deserve to be there.) Some college kids told me about it, and, skeptically, I made the pilgrimage with these seasoned Panther druids on a sweltering day in late June. At first sight, I knew that my whole worldview would have to be revised. I threw off my clothes and dove into the main pool, into water that was a bone-wincing cold—water that had come posthaste from a deep mountain spring. I spied a few crayfish brushing along the margins, a brook trout churning in the shadows. But even these denizens seemed to understand that Nature had tailor-made this place for humans.

We spent the day there, leaping from the high boulders that over the years had spelled death for several young divers who miscalculated the tricky plunge to the black hole below. We sunned on the ledges and slithered down natural water slides slick with algae.

My friends were right—damn them—Panther was incomparable.

It was a painful concession to make: our old, familiar places, our ancestral haunts and hideaways, are always superlative until we discover something that's quite obviously better. It hurts for a while, but eventually we find the humility to make the new places our own.

—2001

Smells Like Zippy Spirit

THE HULKING WHITE TRUCK veers quietly off the main road and slips through the backwoods in the spitting rain. The metal side panels rattle, the big GMC engine grinds away, and yet the truck is hard to detect in the night: its headlights are off.

Just ahead on the road, Fraser Clark is smoking a hand-rolled cigarette and trying to distract a group of U.S. Forest Service law officers. They're clustered around their four-wheel drives at the entrance to a gathering of some six thousand hippies, spiritual seekers, and seemingly misplaced cyberpunks who have pitched camp on a golden meadow deep inside a northern Arizona forest. Standing at the checkpoint, Clark is engaging them in a friendly debate over what the U.S. Constitution may or may not have to say about the people's right to erect mammoth concert speakers in a national forest.

Gotta have a permit, the officers demand.

Bollocks, Clark amiably replies.

Clark is a fifty-one-year-old Dionysus with a Scottish brogue, a stringy goatee, and a wispy mane of caramel hair. The look on his face says that something sneaky is afoot and that he's at the center of it. He has come to Arizona from London to test a pet theory he has about mankind and the millennium, and now he's got a gaggle of reporters following him, trying to get to the bottom of it. He wears a yellow cardigan over a Mickey Mouse shirt and moves with a studied languor, as though he's providing clues to the zeitgeist with every facial tic and gesture.

Somewhere beyond the checkpoint, way back in the shadows of the ponderosa pines, beyond the Krishna Tent and the Peace Hole, a soggy field of fescue lies dormant in the late-August night. An elk herd grazes. Crickets fiddle in the weeds. A pale moon seeps through gauzy rips in the storm clouds.

If they knew any better, the elk and the crickets—indeed, every creature within a ten-mile radius—would run for cover while there's still a chance. Packed inside the big truck, which just now is bouncing through the forest to sneak around the ranger checkpoint, is a sound system capable of strafing the entire area with forty thousand watts of viscera-thumping racket. Twenty-four monster cabinets. An air force of tweeters. Mule-tough Honda generators. And to drone underneath it all, four dozen fifteen-inch bass speakers with enough seismic rumble to make every worm in the vicinity spit out its dirt and hunker down for the apocalypse.

Yes, Fraser Clark likes to have a good stereo when he goes camping. And so, one way or another, those speakers are getting through.

Sorry, pal. Strict orders. No amplified music.

Clark flashes a spritely smile, knowing that the diversionary tactic has worked, that the contraband has probably reached the field, and that his big outdoor bash can soon begin. He bids the rangers adieu and vanishes into the fog.

Thanks to the Forest Service, the festivities are getting off to a late start—two days late, in fact—but Clark seems unfazed. "If you want things to start on time," he says, "then go to Woodstock. With an event like this, you don't ever know when it's going to start—you don't even know *if* it's going to start. But see, people don't *want* a guarantee. They want a bit of adventure. They want the excitement of bringing this semilegal stuff out here beyond the System."

Before long, as cars start pouring into the encampment, their headlights swirling in the woods, Clark, the happy impresario, surveys what he has created. "These people," he says with a sly wink, "have all come to experiment with the future."

FOR THE PAST YEAR CLARK, a native of Glasgow, Scotland, has run a trendy London nightclub called Megatripolis. It's a rambling affair where people can dance to ambient music, quaff "smart drinks," network on computers, and listen to New Age lectures in a continuous seminar known as the Parallel University.

Last June, hoping to spread his club's gospel, Clark came to America with an entourage of fourteen young Megatripolis denizens to embark on a national ramble whose avowed goal was to ignite a new social craze, something Clark calls "the zippy movement." A zippy, as he tells it, is a "hippie with zip," an electronic seeker who can harness computers, modems, and other techie geegaws for the betterment of an ever-expanding tribe of enlightened beings. Zippies, who like to boast that their "brain hemispheres are in perfect balance," like to surf the Internet and dance till dawn at impromptu outdoor "raves," fueled by vitamins and mood-enhancers such as Ecstasy and LSD. Underlying the whole scene is a hazy millennial premise—that the planet needs help, fast—and a diffuse environmental consciousness. "How do you get city people to care anything about the countryside if they never bloody get out there?" says Clark, groping to explain. "You put on a big rave, see, and they get the sunrise, they get nature. They see what it's all about."

Above all, Clark says, zippy-ism is about a feel-good spirit that he calls pronoia, "the sneaking suspicion that people are conspiring behind your back to help you."

Clark launched his so-called Pronoia Tour of America because he decided that the movement would never succeed unless it succeeded here. "If we can make the zippy message fashionable in America," he said, "America will broadcast it to the planet. And Americans are ready. Americans, see, are bored shitless."

Armed with loads of self-confidence ("I'm just a guy," he told one British reporter, adding, "Jesus was just a guy, too, of course"), Clark also wanted to perform a cultural marriage, to bring together two heretofore separate tribes—the technoheads of U.S. rave culture with the good old-fashioned hippies who still dot the landscape—in an unstoppable new supertribe. What it would do wasn't exactly clear, but such particulars were farther down the road. The first step was to oversee the nuptials. "The hippies have the wisdom to live beautifully on the land," Clark liked to say. "The ravers have the energy and the connections. Put them together and it would send a message to the world's leaders: New scene in town! No more bullshit!"

Clark's confections were so lusciously quotable that they instantly struck a chord in the American media. *The New York Times,* the *Los Angeles Times,* National Public Radio, and other major outlets covered the zippy "phenomenon," complete with slang and fashion primers. The longest article, a spring cover story in the computer-culture magazine *Wired,* called the Pronoia Tour "the most radical musical invasion of America since the Beatles and the Stones first kicked up the shit 30 years ago."

Wired also broke the news that, in late August, Clark and the zippies would culminate their tour by throwing the mother of all raves, one that, as Clark put it, would "touch the mythical clitoris of the culture." Details were sketchy. All anyone knew was that it would be somewhere along the South Rim of the Grand Canyon. Rumors about what was called the Paradigm Jumping Off the Grand Canyon Omega Rave were soon broadcast on a thousand alternative music stations and computer bulletin boards.

The zippies spent the summer more or less as planned, staging $12-a-head raves from New York to California. In Wyoming, they hit the annual gathering of the Rainbow People, latter-day hippies who camp out every Fourth of July in a selected national forest. At a rave in Boulder, Colorado, they hooked up with the grand icon of mobile celebration himself, Ken Kesey. "Our turn is over," Clark claims Kesey said at the end of their evening together. "Now it's your turn." By which Clark took him to mean that the old Merry Prankster chieftain was passing the mantle to the zippies.

* * *

"EXCUSE ME," inquires the young reporter from the London magazine *i.D.* as she coasts into the zippy camp, clattering to a stop. "Do you happen to know where I might find Fraser Clark?"

"You and everybody else," answers Michael John, an owl-eyed confederate of Clark's who is famous for giving long, cryptic lectures at Megatripolis under the name Professor Paradox. "Let's just say you're getting warm."

It's Saturday afternoon at the Omega rave site, the day after the great sneak-in. The zippies are making much of the fact that, according to some revisionists, today is the first day of the New Millennium, since the Christian calendar is allegedly off by five years and four months. If that's so, then the year 2000 is getting off to a rotten start. Everyone in this sprawling tent city—including God, it seems—is in a surly mood. Rain has turned the footpaths into a red-clay paste. Storm clouds are sulking overhead; the thunder is scattering flocks of vultures. Two mangy hounds are scavenging in the wet field, their angry growls periodically erupting into full combat. "Whenever the spirit gets high," Professor Paradox notes, "the dogs are the first to react."

The zippies have set up their camp, such as it is, in a secluded cove off the main meadow. A big tarp is strung between some ponderosas, along with an odd clutter of iridescent streamers, disco mirror balls, and psychedelic billboards. The sound system has been erected nearby, an ominous, black, multideck V jutting out in the grass like some medieval siege device.

The Omega rave starts tonight—that is, if the lawmen don't swoop in to kibosh it—but no one here seems up for it. A few zippies are hunkered around a Coleman stove, slurping Ramen noodles and shivering under their blankets. Orka and Judy, a Colorado fashion duo who have fallen in with Clark's posse, are drearily rummaging through their collection of platform shoes. There's also K.J., the Pakistani mix master and thrift-shop aesthete, who's in a swivet because someone has driven off with his "trance music" records—all 150 of them. Nearby sits Earth Girl, who is serving up mugs of her trademarked Psuper Psonic Psyber Tonic, a vitamin-packed smart drink sold at Megatripolis. "This drink proves that intelligence levels can be completely played with and amped up," she says, spooning lemony crystals from a big plastic jar. "Oh, and it's *excellent* for stoners!"

We reporters are very much in evidence—in fact, we outnumber the zippies. *Newsweek* is here, as are *Life, Rolling Stone, Spin, Paris Match,* the BBC, and several German magazines. A couple of know-it-all photojournalists work the periphery, manically narrating the scene like Dennis Hopper in *Apocalypse Now.* "We're witnessing history here," one of them says, dead earnest. "Years from now we can tell our kids, 'Yeah, I was there—I was with the zippies.'"

Clark, meanwhile, is shut up in his tent with his girlfriend, Sionaidh, a porcelain-skinned Scot about half his age. They've been in there an hour, unveiling the zippy master plan to a filmmaker who's shooting the official tour documentary. Clark sits in the lotus position, gesturing wildly, peering out a mosquito-mesh window. It's hard to hear his spiel, but he's definitely on a roll. "So you see," he exclaims at one point, "instead of *excreting* the whole system onto the planet, we can *inhale* it into cyberspace!"

Suddenly a wicked argument starts, with Sionaidh yelling that he's a "typical male, like all the others!" The tent unzips and out hops Fraser, red as a beet, lobbing Gaelic obscenities. He turns and smiles awkwardly at the journalists. "Hello," he says, feigning courtliness. "Merry Christmas and a very happy New Millennium to you all." Then he marches alone into the woods.

"Ugh," a zippy sneers. "Could you guys get lost for a while?"

Zzzzzzeeerack! An angry lightning bolt saws across the tree line. The zippies frantically cover the speakers in plastic and then dive for their tents, just as the rain starts coming down in sheets.

WHEN *WIRED* FIRST TRUMPETED the planned Grand Canyon rave, a few pesky details were swept under the mouse pad—details that now haunt the zippies in the Omega meadow. The biggest one being that the National Park Service would never have allowed the ravers anywhere *near* the Grand Canyon. Still, the idea of a "rim rave" sounded so perfectly epochal that it took on a life of its own.

As the big date approached, however, the tiny troop of fifteen zippies decided to shift locales and join forces with another large alternative gathering that, as it happened, was also scheduled for late August on national forest land in northern Arizona. The World Unity Festival and Conference, organized by a twenty-eight-year-old percussionist from Flagstaff, was billed as the more authentic alternative to the grossly overcommercialized Woodstock II. With an estimated sixty thousand New Age healers, environmentalists, American Indians, Deadheads, and back-to-nature hippies expected to show up, the festival would be, according to its advance hype, a benchmark happening on par with the 1992 Earth Summit in Rio de Janeiro. The Dalai Lama and Nelson Mandela were "sort of confirmed" as guest speakers.

The zippies, Clark decided, would hold their Omega rave side by side with the World Unity bunch. The gathering wouldn't quite be on the "rim" of the Grand Canyon, but some forty-five crow-miles away in the Kaibab National Forest. Not ideal, yet the zippies hoped it was close enough to retain the epic patina of the original plan.

But as the zippies trekked westward, details about the Omega rave remained so exasperatingly vague that a growing number of American cybersurfers started to smell a rat. "This gathering has either no mind or no conscience," one cynic from Berkeley wrote on alt.culture. zippies, a newsgroup forum on the Internet. "Only the children of P. T. Barnum are going to trek to the Kaibab Desert to see this event. The people (ir)responsible for turning the rave scene in the U.S. into a farce should be sacked immediately and shipped back to where they came from."

Late in the summer, when the zippies ran out of both money and psychic steam, things really began to fall apart for the Pronoia Tour. A mysterious schism after a big early-August rave in Santa Cruz, California, resulted in ten of the original fourteen Pronoids breaking ranks and heading south for parts unknown. It was like something out of the Old Testament, the restless upstarts dissing their patriarch, the tribe cleaving in two.

Clark, just days before the Omega rave, was left holding the bag with a skeleton crew of three loyalists and a few recruits. Somehow they scraped together the bucks to rent the sound system, borrowed a truck, and humped in from California, only to have the Forest Service deny them access—thus forcing the zippies to lose another couple of days smuggling in their stuff.

Now, at the meadow, the zippies were admirably trying to put the best face on things, but so far it's been an unmitigated disaster. Across the way, the World Unity Festival has likewise bonked. Only a tenth of the predicted sixty thousand revelers have come. A week earlier, the festival's planning committee collapsed, leaving clueless wraiths wandering the streets of Flagstaff, trying to nail down directions and sort out rumors. Wisely, the Dalai Lama and Nelson Mandela chose to stay home.

Before ending up here, some of the World Unity planners had led a thousand or so people to an alternative site on the Hopi Indian Reservation, a parched piece of northeastern Arizona badland called Big Mountain. Inexplicably, they neglected to secure approval from the Hopi elders. The next day a team of Bureau of Indian Affairs officials swaggered in and set up roadblocks. Choppers throbbed in the sky. The whole tattered throng was ordered to leave.

At the last minute, aid for the zippies and the World Unity crowd came from yet another group, the Rainbow People, who are the grand masters of throwing spontaneous bacchanals in the wild. The Rainbows, who had been informally recruited to help plan the World Unity gathering from the very beginning, suddenly took control, salvaged the wreckage, and brought it all to the Kaibab. They dug latrines, organized kitchens, established order. Thanks to them, the gathering has a pulse again. But something is off. The Rainbow camp feels a world away from the zippy enclave, and there's been little interaction. Truth be told, the Rainbows don't seem to like the zippies, despite Clark's connubial overtures. The rave just isn't their scene.

As for the journalists, we're drawn to the peculiar energy of the zippies like helpless, thumping moths. Still, none of us can get a fix on the story. Or whether we even have a story. What we've got are schisms, bad weather, and chaos on a Cecil B. DeMille scale. The Hopis don't like the hippies. The hippies don't like the zippies. The zippies are at odds with themselves. The dogs are at one another's throats.

And where's that Fraser guy anyway?

*   *   *

THE TEMPEST HAS RAGED for an hour, two hours, going on three, the driving rain flecked with white shards of hail. Finally, late in the afternoon, an orange Nerf ball of a sun pokes through, and a perfect rainbow appears. The Rainbows yowl with joy, pounding out hosannas on their congas.

"Maybe it's a sign!" Professor Paradox offers, staring at the rainbow.
"What of?"

"I dunno. Hippie-zippy unity. The New Millennium. *Something.*"

The rain has cleared the bile from the air and replaced it with an invisible pronoia cloud. The smart drinks are flowing again; brain hemispheres are getting balanced.

Clark returns from his walk in the woods, wet but smiling. He gives Sionaidh a hug, and by all appearances everything is rosy again in the girlfriend department. Soon he's posing for a *Newsweek* photographer, sitting sidesaddle on a borrowed mule with a borrowed laptop across his thighs, as if he's perusing his e-mail up there: Fraser Clark, the Electronic Horseman.

"Press conference!" a zippy minion announces. "Fraser will be addressing the members of the media in five minutes!"

As the reporters head back to camp, Clark strokes his beard and gazes proudly over at the speakers. Ambient music has begun to warble and moan like a pod of humpback whales.

Clark starts off slowly, mysteriously, as the reporters scribble. "I ask you, the media tribe, to consider that there is a higher moral ethic than simply reporting history—and that's helping to *create* history. I invite you to join in a conspiracy with us to send out positive viruses to the universe."

He's just getting going, and already we're feeling perplexed. One of the German reporters, a wiry hipster, asks under his breath, "Viruses? Vot do he mean, *viruses?*"

"Imagine," Clark resumes, lighting up a cigarette. "Imagine a planet covered in rain forests. A naked couple, slightly hairier than we are, walks through the woods. They stop. The man leans over and picks up a flower. Suddenly an electrical connection is made. Menus drop down in their eyes. They plug in, travel to New York, have a little virtual-reality meeting. That's the zippy dream, see. We can all be naked psychedelic apes out in the forest and yet still be all connected up together."

Clark pauses to let the imagery sink in, as the whale moans give way to a swirling panorama of celestial mood music.

The Pronoia Tour is now officially over, Clark declares. It's time to take the next step in the zippy revolution. In the fall he and his comrades will open a series of rave clubs on the West Coast, starting with Megatripolis San Francisco. "We'll do smart drinks, of course," he says. "We'll also have an aboriginal snack shop where we'll serve, you know, bark and berries and Indian foods all mashed into a paste—some kind of dip thing. Strong, but *very* nutritious."

The floor is open for questions. Nearby we hear the whine of tires spinning in mud, which prompts me to ask Clark how the zippies can call themselves environmentalists. Because, looking at this mashed and rutted and pissed-on field, it seems obvious that assembling thousands of ravers in a secluded forest isn't the best way to tread lightly.

"No," he admits, his cigarette's amber light dancing in the dark. "It's not the best thing for this particular two square miles of America. With all the public shitting and the hygiene problems, I'm obviously not recommending it as an ultimate lifestyle. Bringing large numbers of people together is just the first thing we have to do to win the battle against the System."

There's a loud visitor in our midst. We turn to behold a hirsute, middle-aged prophet in religious robes, looming like Bugs Bunny's nemesis, the Tasmanian Devil.

"Who're you?" Clark demands.

"My name is Jesus Christ," the man says emphatically. "Today I'm two thousand years old. It's a New Millennium, in case you didn't know. What I wanted to say was, this rave thing of yours is okay, man. It's *holy.* So I say, let's *do it!* I want to *die dancing!* Remember, Jesus *raves!*"

Clark tries to shoo Christ away before he steals the show. "Happy birthday, Jesus," he says. "And thanks for the endorsement."

*　　*　　*

THE PRESS CONFERENCE breaks up, and Jesus disappears into the growing rave crowd. The gale-force music is full of bleeps and belches stitched together with a jackhammer beat, 140 pulses per minute. K.J., the Pakistani mix master, says 140 bpm is more or less the rate of a fetal heart. Which is fitting, because it's designed to send you straight back to the womb, wrapped in an electronic sac. "What you are hearing," he yells, "is the voice of electricity."

Overhead, a screen flickers with fractal images: monarch butterflies floating in the cosmos, paramecia grooving across the Mojave Desert. A few trillion stars wink through the fog. In the fringes of the meadow, the Rainbows stumble from their tents, barefoot and baffled, to investigate the racket and light. Most of them are Hacky Sack–playing Luddites who ordinarily wouldn't be caught dead around all this raging technology. Soon a hippie woman stalks over and yanks the generator plug.

"Babylon music!" she hisses in the sudden silence.

But the juice is quickly restored, and the offensive wages on. Orka and Judy take the spotlight, he in a Captain America getup, she in an aluminum-foil space suit with Madonna-like cone breasts spewing out red strobe beams. A few big American rental cars roll into the field, disgorging crews of young ravers from Denver, San Francisco, and New York. Some, lit with Ecstasy, have a deer-in-the-headlights look on their faces as they dive into the soundscape.

After a while the Rainbows accept the fact that this aural blitzkrieg will last until dawn, and so, tepidly at first, they join in. Soon the field swarms with trance-dancers, five hundred strong, spinning in the reefer fog, stamping the wet grass into a hard plate of dirt.

AT HIGH NOON ON SUNDAY, a small party of celebrants gathers by the FOOD NOT BOMBS sign. Today Earth Girl, the smart-drink peddler, will be "married" to Max, an eligible young Rainbow brother. It's Clark's merging of the tribes in action, a ceremony he calls "a techno-pagan wedding."

A Rainbow shaman opens the service: "Hear ye, hear ye. This symbolic wedding will unite the Earth People from the South with the Techno People from the northern Zippy Kingdom."

Just behind the wedding party a couple of scruffy Rainbow hounds are doing the wild thing, hunched awkwardly in the dirt with mortified scowls on their faces, but no one pays them any mind.

Clark takes a theatrical bow. "Today," he says, clearing his throat, "we offer up Earth Girl, a nubile, media-friendly, techno-literate maiden." Applause. "And she comes fully reproductive, as guaranteed by the whole tribe." Drums. Laughter.

Now Clark grows solemn. "We hold this great techno-organic wedding, that we may unite as the entire alternative nation. The two should never have been apart."

The crowd shouts, "Ho!"

Clark: "You may now kiss the bride."

Earth Girl and Max embrace and then hold hands as they leap over a broom into their "future."

With the marriage sealed and the GMC truck all loaded up, the zippies shove off for California, like a bunch of high-tech Joads. But this time, instead of creeping along the back roads, they decide to take the main way out.

Big mistake. There's a khaki phalanx waiting for them at the entrance—Forest Service cops, all licking their chops. "We warned you, buddy," officer Mark Zumwalt tells the driver, one of the sound system techies. (Clark himself has managed to slip through unscathed in another vehicle.) Grumbling that "You can't bring that stuff in without a permit," Zumwalt writes up two separate tickets totaling $800. "You know," he says, grimacing at the trashed meadows, "this *used* to be a national forest."

—1994

AMERICAN RIDES

The Silver City

South Bend, Indiana

"WE ALWAYS LIKE A GOOD PARADE!" Esther says. She salutes the grand marshal as he sails by in a Cadillac convertible, his blue beret pulled down at a rakish angle. "We like to get gussied up and look at ourselves."

"Oh, there's no beating a parade," agrees Esther's friend Pauline, holding a parasol to block the sun. "Especially on the Fourth of July!"

The golden dome of Notre Dame hulks over the Indiana flatlands. Outside the football stadium where Knute Rockne coached his last season, the marching band is playing John Philip Sousa—cymbals smashing, trombones punching the sky. Along the parade route, five thousand spectators are squeezed into lawn chairs or sprawled on picnic quilts, Velma and Clarence and Gertrude and Dale, zinc oxide slathered on their noses, hearing aids squeaking in their ears. A drum-and-bugle corps trots by, then a kazoo band, then a Dixieland jazz ensemble doing a Bourbon Street dirge.

"My goodness, what a wingding!" Pauline chuckles. "Have you ever seen such a thing?"

They're all hooting and horselaughing, Orval and Mildred and Chester and Blanche, watching the stream of humanity drift by: Pil-

grims and Indians, kings and queens, Yanks and Rebs . . . a troika of
Boy Scouts bearing flags, flapper girls dancing the Charleston, dignitaries doffing tasseled hats . . . cowpokes, hoboes, baton twirlers . . .
Studebakers, Model Ts . . . papier-mâché rockets, prairie schooners, a
vintage fire engine with sirens screeching . . an outhouse on wheels
with a sign tacked to the door that says BACK OFF OR I'LL FLUSH!

And finally, at the end of the procession, comes one of the familiar
silver bubbles—the silver bubble that brought them all here in the first
place, Horace and Twila and Ray and Pearl. Teardrop from the age of
Sputnik, spaceship from the pages of H. G. Wells. The bubble noses
down Juniper Road and coasts toward the famed "Touchdown Jesus,"
the fourteen-story mosaic on the facade of the Hesburgh Library that is
directly aligned with the stadium goalposts and seems to depict Christ
raising His arms to signal yet another score for the Fighting Irish. On
the side of the bubble, spanning the full length of its fuselage, a sign
proclaims: AIRSTREAMING IS A WAY OF LIFE.

Beyond the procession, on the athletic fields, 3,350 Airstream travel
trailers are parked in meticulous rows, a vast grid of metallic silver
lozenges baking in the sun. The owners of these nearly identical capsules have come to Indiana from nearly every state and Canadian
province to celebrate the vision of their club patriarch, the late Wally
Byam, dean of the American RV industry. Tinkerer, author, businessman, and relentless impresario, Byam was the inventor of the Airstream,
widely considered the world's preeminent travel trailer. Every July for
three decades the Wally Byam Caravan Club International (WBCCI),
the social club of Airstream owners, has picked a different site in
which to hold its International Rally, which is both a family reunion
and a birthday celebration: Wally Byam was born on the Fourth
of July.

Byam conceived the name "Airstream" in 1936, when he introduced
a line of travel trailers with riveted aluminum shells. Drawing from
advances in the aviation industry, Byam's monocoque bubble was
designed to ride "like a stream of air." Byam was an apostle for the high
romance of group touring. He caravanned around the globe in a gold-
plated Airstream (bearing the number 1) with an observation hole

punched through the roof, where he perched himself and shouted instructions to his fellow campers through a bullhorn.

"We shall go where angels fear to tread," he used to exhort his followers before embarking on his far-flung trips. "We shall lead our caravan down roads that are still but a gleam in a cartographer's eye."

Byam's caravans were massive logistical feats, celebrated in the pages of *National Geographic*. In 1959 he and his wife, Stella, led a team of Airstreams through Africa—from Cape Town to Cairo. In Addis Ababa, he gave an Airstream to Ethiopian emperor Haile Selassie as a personal gift. Another caravan took him and a large group of friends to Central America along the Pan-American Highway.

Byam had a notion of traveling in what he called "the vehicular village," a moving town with constitutional bylaws and democratic institutions. "I wanted to show how much fun trailering could be en masse if we ran the whole shebang like a New England town meeting and let democracy have its head," he wrote in his book *Trailer Travel Here and Abroad*. In the vehicular village, everybody had a job, each person contributing according to his ability, taking according to his need. There was a postmaster, a doctor, an official greeter, a keeper of the kitty, and a rearguard officer called the "caboose." Byam wore several hats: he was, in the words of one fellow caravanner, "mayor, secretary of state, protocol officer, and toastmaster on ceremonial occasions."

The Wally Byam Caravan Club was chartered by a group of Byam's friends who were taken with his idea of self-sufficient travel. The first International Rally was held in 1958 in Bull Shoals, Arkansas, deep in the Ozarks. The Airstreamers parked in a giant wagon-wheel formation, concentric circles of space capsules radiating from a central bonfire. Pat Boone's grandfather sang, and a fireworks display on the Fourth lit up the stormy sky with the words, HAPPY BIRTHDAY WALLY.

HERE IN SOUTH BEND, the Airstreamers have built a self-contained city on the Notre Dame campus. They've set up their own post office, with a designated zip code—46556. They have a news program known as "Wally Byam Control." They've laid five miles of water hose and four miles of electrical wire. Everybody draws from the same water supply: a universal five-eighths-of-an-inch hose that courses through the Silver City and enters each trailer through a Y-junction. A fleet of red Honda mopeds serves as the Wally Byam Scooter Patrol, delivering messages in the Silver City. The club has a committee to oversee every facet of life: lost and found, macramé, even pancakes. But the most prestigious is the sanitation committee, charged with pumping the "black water" from every Airstream trailer. A quirky esprit de corps has developed among the sanitation workers, who wear overalls and red roses and call themselves "the Effluent Society."

In the Silver City, everything is done in a punctilious fashion, as if disorder were a disease. Every rally has a theme. Every trailer has a number. Every meeting follows parliamentary procedure, and no decision is made unless the ayes have it. The Airstreamers are masters at what they call "precision parking." A team of traffic experts in orange vests and safari helmets docks the incoming rigs according to blueprints drawn up months in advance. The rows have identifying codes, and every section is marked off by color: Red-6, Gold-8, Blue-7. The location of each trailer is posted on a "Locator Board," so no one at the rally can remain incognito.

It's a neighborhood built on conformity and a shared commitment to well-choreographed leisure. Members pledge to obey the WBCCI Code of Ethics, which essentially demands that they be nice people at all times. "[Members agree] to say or print nothing that may reflect unfavorably on others," states the code. "Membership in this organization is an assurance of our courtesy on the road and goodwill to all peoples and countries."

Though the median age of the club is sixty-six, it's difficult for me to think of the Wally Byam Caravan Club as a society of old folks. Everywhere I look, I see vigorous, ruddy-skinned people marching around the college campus, fighting age. Constant motion is the antidote to infirmity. There are square dances, horseshoe and shuffleboard tournaments, Jazzercise classes, metal-detecting excursions, talent shows. "The club extends the life of our members," says WBCCI president Ed Minty, who theoretically lives in Phoenix but has been "full-timing" three years now with his wife, Pat. "We have a lot of people who are in their eighties pulling trailers around. It keeps them interested in getting out and doing things. I know that's true in our case. This club's the best thing that ever happened to us."

Airstreamers know exactly where they are—longitude, latitude, county, precinct, and mile marker. The interiors of their Suburbans and GMC trucks are rigged with compasses, altimeters, barometers, temp gauges, TripTik charts. Crisp efficiency is the operative ideal—road science. Their seat cushions are orthopedically correct, and their soft drinks are securely anchored. They keep a close eye on weather patterns two time zones away, and their hands are firmly wrapped around the wheel. "Truck drivers always toot their horns at us," one club member tells me. "It's a salute. They say Airstreamers are the best drivers on the road."

Walking down the long rows of docked trailers with model names like Excella and Land Yacht, I can see the blue flicker of television sets inside. Occasionally the sweet smell of cakes or brownies wafts from the kitchen ovens. Filmy gray water from the drains of bathtubs and sinks trickles out of hoses and seeps into the soft ground. An old guy in a floppy fishing hat and lime-green golf slacks whirs through the alleyways on his Rascal electronic cart. The air crackles with CB radios, as the announcer from Wally Byam Control breaks in: "All parties who wish to participate in the cribbage tournament should meet in room two-fifty-eight at nine o'clock for further instructions."

In Blue-19, an Oregon woman sits under her Zip Dee ratchet awning doing needlepoint and listening to Paul Harvey on an AM transistor radio, while her husband rummages through his rock collection piled in the back of their Silverado.

In Gold-6, a couple from Delaware practices dance steps to a Glenn Miller tape, the music periodically interrupted by a sizzling sound coming from their electric bug zapper. The sticker on the back of their trailer says

NO PHONE

NO CLOCK

NO WORRIES

NO MONEY

Bumper stickers like this one are a rarity among Airstreamers, who as a rule practice discretion. They like the handsome look of all that unsmirched aluminum, and have trouble understanding why an RV owner would want to junk up his rig with detritus from his travels—tacky souvenirs in the I DID YELLOWSTONE vein. It's understood within the club that you're not allowed to tinker with the exterior of your Airstream. You can gut the insides if you like and customize everything yourself, but the argentine shell must remain intact.

The WBCCI is a society built upon an iconic shape with an ideal sheen, and no one presumes to improve upon perfection. "You see, it's the *styling* that we like," club president Ed Minty told me. "The Winnebagos and all these others, they're good trailers. But they don't have that classic look about them. There's a reason why ours costs more. It just looks different. It's round. It's that aluminum—it gives. It's flexible. Boy, that thing's alive!"

Club member Eelco Tinga explained the obsession with a uniform aesthetic this way: "If you go by a pasture where there's Holstein cows, they're all black and white, and it looks good. If you go by another pasture where they're mixed in with Jerseys and Guernseys and beef cattle, they look—*pfffff*. Right? See, this is what we like about what we've got here. Everything looks the same."

Over the years the WBCCI's cliquish obsession with appearances has led more than a few owners of less distinguished rigs to resent Airstreamers as the self-appointed Brahmin class of the RV world. The charge of elitism is only reinforced by the slang used by Airstreamers, who sometimes refer to other RV makes as "cheeseboxes," "Squarestreams," or "SOBs" (some other brand).

"Oh, sure, there are a lot of people who think Airstreamers are just plain stuck-up," Carl Bateman, a retired Caterpillar equipment dealer from Nashville, told me one afternoon. "It's just that you're naturally friendlier with someone who's got something in common with you. It's human nature."

Bateman shifted in his Zip Dee lawn chair and squinted at the space-pods glinting in the afternoon sun. "The other thing that makes people think we're snobs is that when we caravan around the country; we don't need contact with the outside. Anything we need, we got it right here.

You want music? We've got our own orchestra. Feeling sick? We've got retired doctors in the club. You see, we're a city unto ourselves."

"IT'S A LIFESTYLE THAT GETS INTO YOUR BLOOD," says Gene "Stubby" Stubbs of Vienna, Virginia. "We're the kind of people who, when we get into something, we give it a hundred and ten."

Gene and his wife, Shirley, have been members of the Wally Byam Club for fourteen years. Stubby is president of Region 2 of the WBCCI, a large dominion that extends from Ontario to Maryland. The Stubbses' trailer, a thirty-four-foot Limited, is parked near the stadium, its wheels leveled and chocked. Their rig has all the options: Corian galley tops, oak cabinets, cedar-lined closet, overhead tambour storage bins, wooden venetian blinds, convection microwave, solar panels, shag carpeting, ceiling fans. It's a cheerfully decorated space appointed in soft burgundys, with an Astroturf welcome mat and a needlework greeting by the door that says, HOME SWEET HOME. Everything inside the cabin folds out, slides in, tucks under, and snaps down. "A marvel of space utilization." Stubbs beams, leaning back in the swiveling captain's chair and sipping a Coke fresh from the fridge. "Now you take a trip in one of these, and you won't ever want to stay in a motel again."

Stubbs is an avuncular man of six-foot-five who wears a gemstone bolo tie and hefty turquoise rings. A semiretired accountant for a division of the Department of Defense that researches what he calls "way-out Buck Rogers stuff," Stubbs was born in northern Alabama and grew up on the Navajo reservation in New Mexico. "From the beginning, we liked the *idea* of an Airstream," Stubbs says. "It was aerodynamic. There was nothing to break or bend. It was the ultimate."

Stubby's wife, Shirley, is an elegant woman in her early sixties with limpid eyes and a warm smile. "To tell you the truth," she confesses in a whisper, "when we joined the club, Stubby and I thought it was too much togetherness. We weren't used to being structured all the time." She chuckles. "Now look at us! With Airstream, you have instant friendships. It's a big silver magnet that draws people together." She says that if she or Stubby spot another Airstream driving down the road, they can look up the number in a membership directory and immediately find out who's driving and where they're from. If they were to pass Airstream number 21383, a glance in the directory would tell them that Howard and Mildred Dixon of Chattanooga, Tennessee, were behind the wheel. The Stubbses could pick up their CB radio and talk to the Dixons on 14, the channel all WBCCI members use, and perhaps they would agree to meet for lunch down the road.

Another amenity found in the club directory is courtesy parking. Nearly one thousand members across the country offer free parking space for any Airstreamer who happens to be passing through their town. These generous hosts have the designation "CP" at the end of their listing in the directory. If an Airstreamer finds himself in Kenai, Alaska, he can park on the property of Jack and Willie Mae Bowen (#5708) (CP). Courtesy parking amounts to a national motel chain for Byamites, enabling them to hopscotch around and never pay a cent in camping fees.

More than half of all Airstream owners decline to join the Wally Byam Club. Such killjoys are called "baldies." Their rigs have no ID numbers and thus are "bald." Byamites view baldies with pity and disappointment, laced with hope that they'll be tomorrow's convert. Stubbs concedes that he might be less likely to stop for a broken-down baldie than for a properly numbered Byamite trailer. "Oh, I might stop because I'm a Good Samaritan. But once I've stopped, I'll be working on him. I want him to know what he's missing."

SELF-CONTAINMENT. That was the lifelong ideal of Wallace Merle Byam. He spoke the phrase like a mantra. From his earliest days in the business, Byam wanted to construct a trailer that could keep its septic fluids and foul odors to itself. With the careful arrangement of battery packs, propane tanks, and storage cells, he sought to build a traveling vessel that could go for weeks without having to drop umbilical cords to the outside world. For Byam, self-containment amounted to a declaration of independence from the messy uncertainties of the road. One of the names of his early models neatly captured the spirit of self-containment. He called it "the Sovereign."

Byam was a distinguished-looking man with piercing eyes and downy silver hair. He had a chiseled face and an aquiline nose popping with capillaries. When he was deep in thought, he had a habit of nibbling at the ends of his black-rimmed reading glasses. In the company photographs, he was pictured leaning against a globe in a black flannel suit, looking like an august patron of the Explorers Club.

He was born in Baker, Oregon, on July 4, 1896. His parents died when he was young, so Wally, an only child, went to live with his grandparents in the dry foothills of eastern Oregon's Blue Mountains, where he spent his summers working as a shepherd. His interest in self-contained vehicles is said to have dated back to these summers, when he would live for weeks at a time out of a donkey-drawn cart that was equipped with a sleeping mat and a kerosene stove.

He went to sea as a cabin boy before attending Stanford, where he graduated in 1921. In the early twenties he worked as an advertising copywriter for the *Los Angeles Times* and then published how-to carpentry magazines. One of his magazines ran an item showing how to build a trailer on the chassis of a Model T. The item brought complaints from readers, who said the instructions were faulty. Byam tested the plans himself and agreed, so he set out to design his own. In the next issue of his magazine he wrote an article about his new trailer, claiming it could be built for less than one hundred dollars, including materials. He sold instruction booklets by mail and began building weird-looking contraptions straight out of Jules Verne, with bat wings and portholes and webbed fins of chrome. With each new model he made subtle improvements: He dropped the floor between the axles so people could stand upright; he put in water pumps and chemical toilets; he installed gas stoves, iceboxes, heaters. The first trailers were built out of plywood, Masonite, and furring strips, much of the raw material pulled from the junkyard.

By then other moonlighters were building travel trailers, too. In the late twenties, trailer construction had become a thriving cottage industry in the United States, and in Europe the trailer business was even better established. Most of the new trailers were improbable-looking vessels with names like "the Auto-Kamp" and "the Prairie Schooner." It became fashionable among wealthy adventure seekers to tour Europe in customized rigs, dubbed "house cars." Harvey Firestone, Thomas Edison, Henry Ford, and John Burroughs traveled around together in one such house car, with Edison's bulbs lighting up their camps at night.

In 1933 Byam built his first teardrop-shaped trailer, the "Torpedo Car Cruiser," and sold the design plans by mail for five dollars. Three years later, working under the new company name of "Airstream," Byam unveiled "the Clipper," an aluminum-shelled trailer with a cedar closet and an experimental air-conditioning system that worked on dry ice. Cost: $1,200.

Impetuous, flamboyant, prone to manic spurts of inspiration, Byam built his trailers in much the same way that Preston Tucker built his futurist cars. He was a maverick, brilliant with his hands, expert in the theatrics of promotion—but the sort of man who sometimes forgot to dot his Is. From a practical standpoint, he was a terrible businessman. But he was smart enough to surround himself with competent people, and charming enough to retain their loyalty. "He was good with an idea," recalls Helen Schwamborn, Byam's cousin and a longtime employee of the Airstream company, "but he ran around so much, he couldn't keep his mind on what he was doing. Someone else had to do the work." He would come home from one of his long field trips and want to turn the factory upside down, rip the place up from the roots and rethink everything. His engineers hated to see him coming.

During the second World War, Byam was forced to close down the Airstream factory and take a job at United Aircraft, where he worked nights as a production supervisor, a job that would strongly influence his design of future Airstream models. He resumed building Airstreams in 1947, and the business took off. In the postwar housing shortage, trailers were serving as temporary living quarters for newlyweds and college students matriculating under the GI bill.

The Wally Byam Caravan Club was chartered in 1956—a propitious time for the birth of a society of recreational vagabonds. The Korean War was over. Gas was plentiful and cheap. And with the passage of the Interstate Highway Act the following year, the largest road system in world history was rapidly being blasted from the bedrock.

The club led tours through Canada, Central America, Europe, and Cuba, where President Batista greeted the caravanners outside his palace in Havana. In 1958 Byam came up with the most quixotic dream of his career: a trailer caravan through Africa from Cape Town to Cairo. It didn't take long for the pied piper to find one hundred takers. "He could really paint a picture," says Helen Schwamborn, recalling how Byam charmed his African caravanners. "He made traveling around so exotic and glamorous. He made Africa sound like a dreamland. No one ever stopped to think about all the hardships the trip would involve. Sometimes he'd really stretch things and I'd have to say, 'Now, Wally—you know that's not true!' And he'd say, 'Oh, what difference does it make? You can see they're enjoying it!'"

The trek would require a year of planning, including meetings with State Department officials in Washington and Vice President Richard Nixon. Finally in 1959, forty-one Airstreams were shipped by sea to South Africa. Heading north from Cape Town, the caravanners traveled for eight months and covered nearly fifteen thousand miles, often on roads that were so bad, as Byam later put it, "not even the elephants would walk on them." The media dubbed the Airstreamers "the Lost Caravan," because they had a habit of disappearing for weeks at a time. On some legs of the journey, they averaged no more than three miles a day, and on several occasions they even had to build their own roads and pontoon bridges. In the Belgian Congo, the natives mistook the Airstreamers for an army that had come to liberate them from the colonial authorities. A pygmy tribe in Uganda thought they were gods. Byam looked like Livingstone in his pith helmet and safari khakis, a French interpreter standing by his side. Tribal chiefs often assumed he was a king, so he had to act like one, making up protocol as he went. But in the final months of the African caravan, his eyesight started to fail him. Back in the United States, he went to see an ophthalmologist, who, in turn, sent him to a neurologist. The diagnosis was grim: Byam had a brain tumor. In 1962, Mr. Trailer, the man who once said, "Life beings at sixty," died at the age of sixty-five.

The club kept growing after his death, and the caravans continued unabated, including an incredibly ambitious 403-day odyssey across Europe and Asia. By 1975, the Wally Byam Caravan Cub had swelled to 24,000 members, and the international rallies were drawing 10,000 pilgrims each July.

Over the years, the Airstream has consistently drawn committed caravanners less likely to drop out with the vagaries of the economy or increases in gasoline prices. Veteran Airstreamer Frank Sargent of Fort Myers, Florida, told me that the Wally Byam Club appeals to something that will never go out of fashion. A retired engineer whose numerous patented inventions include the Porta Potti, Sargent worked with Byam on the early principles of self-containment and now wears Byam's mantle as the club high priest. It was Sargent who organized a monthlong Airstream caravan through China in 1985. "Why do people go caravanning?" Sargent asks. "It's elemental. The nomadic instinct is something deep in us. It's as old and powerful as our need to stare into an open fire. People for thousands of generations have moved in caravans. Gadding around in groups is a part of what we are. It fulfills the tribal instinct."

THE WEEK BEGAN INAUSPICIOUSLY in South Bend. High temperatures sent more than sixty Airstreamers to the hospital with heat exhaustion. There were ten emergency ambulance calls, and at least one participant died—evidently of a heart attack. It got so hot one day that hundreds of Byamites left the rally and spent the entire afternoon in an air-conditioned mall. Later in the week, an elderly woman was hit by a car and broke her hip. Another Airstreamer was struck by lightning. Rainstorms turned the parking fields into mud (someone put up a sign in a water puddle that said WARNING: ALLIGATOR CROSSING), and there were two tornado watches in the area. Worst of all, hailstorms have been in the forecast. Airstreamers are particularly leery of hailstones, which can leave tiny pockmarks on the soft aluminum skins of their trailers—an unsightly and difficult-to-treat condition known as "Airstream Acne."

Luckily, much of the action has been indoors at the Notre Dame auditorium. On Sunday evening, Rhonda Knight ("Miss Ontario") was crowned Teen Queen before a howling crowd of seven thousand. On Tuesday night, next year's officers, attired in white tuxedos and blue berets, were installed in a formal pageant that featured the national anthems of Canada, Mexico, and the United States. Vegas crooner Roger Miller gave a concert one night, singing his old classic "King of the Road" for an encore—*Two hours of pushing brooms buys an eight-by-twelve four-bit room; I'm a man of means by no means . . . King of the Road.*

Now it's Thursday morning and the Silver City is rapidly being dismantled. The Byamites are folding up their lawn chairs, ratcheting down their awnings, and pulling up their gray water hoses. Wally Byam Control has fizzled off the air. Caravans are heading up and moving out in all directions. Teams from the garbage committee are scouring the abandoned parking lots, picking up litter.

In Blue-7, Jaimie and Susan King of New Bern, North Carolina (#7018), are preparing to shove off for Missouri and parts west. As self-described "youngies" (they are both in their fifties), the Kings represent the future of the Wally Byam Club. A semiretired human physiology professor who wears a zip-up astronaut suit, Jaimie climbs into the driving center of his twenty-eight-foot Airstream turbo diesel motor home and fires up the big rock-cruncher engine. He then runs down a safety checklist that would probably satisfy the FAA, while Susan scurries around in back securing everything. "How's the refrigerator?" he inquires.

"The refrigerator is locked."

"I got the porch platform, but how about the bomb-bay doors?"

"They are closed and locked."

"Countertop?"

"Secured."

"Tables?"

"Secured."

"Bathroom sink all right?"

"Secured."

"And the bathroom mirror?"

"It is . . . locked."

"Water pump?"

"It is . . . off."

"How about the water heater?"

"Off."

"Well, okeydokey," Jaimie proclaims, Notre Dame receding in his side-view mirrors. "That's it. WE ARE ROLLING!"

—1991

Woodstock in Leathers

THE HARLEY BOYS stood silent at the base of Mount Rushmore, looking up at the granite faces, thinking big.

In a single day, eleven thousand bikers had ridden their hogs down from campsites in Sturgis to marvel at it, shattering the all-time attendance record at the monument. Huge, bedraggled men with deep-baked Conan faces and bloodshot eyes and sour-smelling T-shirts and tattered hanks of oily hair blown back from the road winds. Scarred and blistered men, men with stubs and busted legs, hobbling on canes. Iron-butted men in steel-tipped boots, their faces splattered with the gooey carcasses of bugs. A few biker babes in reptile-skin miniskirts and Sleezy Teez halter tops. All-American outlaws, patriotic in a hard and unsentimental way, revving their unmuffled engines.

The one called Mule stood off by himself, licking a cone of "Teddy Roosevelt Maple-Nut" ice cream. Mule wore spurs on his boots and leather gauntlet gloves on his hands. A tattoo of a buffalo skull ran down the length of his arm. Mule had never seen Rushmore before, and he was searching for words. "What can I say?" he said. "It's awesome. It's class. It's so . . . *big*!"

Craggy old Uncle Abe off to the right, his downturned face full of noble doubts. Teddy Roosevelt set back in a shadowy recess, no doubts whatsoever, grinning the bluff grin of Empire. Jefferson aiming high over the plains, a dreamer restless in his rock. And at far left, Washington, telling no lies, his chiseled forehead shining bone-white against the big cerulean skies.

"Those are the dudes who made this country what it is," Mule proclaimed, ice cream tinting his beard. "I don't know about the others, but I betcha Theodore Roosevelt, being a Rough Rider and all, woulda gone for a Harley." With that, Mule hopped on his shovelhead with the Grim Reaper airbrushed on the peanut gas tank along with the words, IS THERE LIFE AFTER DEATH? FUCK WITH THIS BIKE AND YOU'LL FIND OUT, and shoved off for points north.

ELEVEN MONTHS OF THE YEAR, Sturgis is a somnolent town of six thousand in the Dakota gold country. But in the second week of August, the town holds a motorcycle rally known as the Black Hills Motor Classic, and almost overnight it becomes a Gomorrah of steel and hobnail boots. The population swells to over two hundred thousand, making it the largest city in the state. For a week, Main Street is lined with tens of thousands of Harley-Davidson motorcycles, parked at cocked angles from the curbs. Heritage Softails. Cafe Racers. Low Riders. Fat Boys. Day and night, the bikers growl their engines down the strip, their mamas holding on behind. The street signs are plastered with fliers advertising THUNDER KLUNDER'S WALL OF DEATH! and BIG DADDY RAT'S CHOPPER SHOW! Side streets buzz with the reedy sibilance of electric tattoo needles. Bikers gather in open-air beer gardens with makeshift walls of chicken wire and sawdust strewn on the concrete floors. As the parties intensify across the Black Hills, evangelist groups like the Good News Riders and the Tribe of Judah hold tent revivals to save their wicked brethren from certain damnation.

Milwaukee is the home of the Harley-Davidson Company, but Sturgis is the capital of the Harley Nation. For biker purists, the Classic has an aura of religious grandeur, like Cannes for filmmakers or Westminster for dog breeders. Hundreds of bikers get married at the rally (twenty-five dollars and no blood tests required). Sturgis and its environs appeal to the bikers' sense of themselves as heirs to the hard-riding, hard-drinking traditions of the Wild West. The town was named after J. G. Sturgis, a cavalry lieutenant who fell with Custer at Little Big Horn. The Black Hills region, sacred ground for the Lakota Sioux Indians, is widely considered America's finest riding country for street bikes. Highway 385, a state road that runs along the spine of the Black Hills, passes through meadows matted in daisies and high sierra blown dry by the Chinook winds. From Sturgis, the bikers can make day runs in any direction. To the east are the Badlands, spectral realm of buttes and gulches. To the west, in Wyoming, is Devils Tower, the monolithic shaft of granite that served as an alien landing pad in Steven Spielberg's *Close Encounters of the Third Kind*. To the north is the barren spot that marks the geographical center of the United States. And to the south, a few miles beyond Rushmore, is Crazy Horse Mountain, where a local family has spent forty years blasting the hillside into the likeness of the Sioux warrior.

This year—1990—is the rally's fiftieth anniversary, and the bikers have turned out in record numbers: 400,000, according to one estimate, though no one can say for sure. It is, quite simply, the largest biker rally ever held. The Sturgis newspaper, the *Meade County Times-Tribune*, has called it "Woodstock in Leathers."

It's eight o'clock in the morning, and the Sturgis Strip is already a solid bank of Harleys—six blocks long, four rows deep. Through the morning haze, I can faintly see the town's name spelled in white boulders on a distant hill, except the first two letters are missing—URGIS.

Tens of thousands of bikers are out posing and profiling. Guys with names like Iceman, Lizard, Bandit, and Lurch. So much reverence on the faces of so many bad seeds, or at least people trying to look like bad seeds, roistering in their riveted concho vests and latigo belts. Some are fiddling with their engines, packing for day runs to the Badlands. Others are riding down the center lane of Main Street, flashing the crowds hungry looks that say, *If you don't check me out, I'll kill you.*

The crowd is a wall of T-shirt slogans—

INJECTION IS NICE BUT I'D RATHER BE BLOWN

WHO DIED AND LEFT YOU IN CHARGE?

KILL 'EM ALL AND LET GOD SORT 'EM OUT

FLATHEAD, PANHEAD, KNUCKLEHEAD, GIMME HEAD
JUST BEND OVER AND TAKE IT LIKE A MAN, LADY!
BURN THIS FLAG AND YOUR ASS IS MINE
IRAQ SUCKS
THE SUPREME COURT SUCKS
DAYTONA SUCKS
YOU SUCK

It doesn't take long to realize that biker men are truly mammary obsessed. "Show your tits!" they cry day and night, and whenever a woman obliges—which is surprisingly often—all the men in the vicinity are duty-bound to rush to the scene and pay homage.

Local establishments in Sturgis have undergone a curious metamorphosis. Lynn's Country Market has opened a studio where bikers can get their pictures taken with a live black panther. The ladies at St. Francis Church welcome the hordes every morning for huge breakfast "feeds." The Rapid City Hospital, in anticipation of extra orthopedic work, has been running an ad in the newspaper that shows an X-ray of a fractured arm: WE'LL DEVELOP YOUR UNPLANNED VACATION PHOTOS.

Practically everyone in the Harley world has trekked to Sturgis for the fiftieth. Peter Fonda has come to sign autographs for fans of *Easy Rider,* and to take grief from Vietnam vets still lathered up about Jane's infelicitous trip to Hanoi. ("I love my sister," Fonda tells them. "She was right in perception, just wrong in delivery.") Neil Diamond has put in an appearance, and unconfirmed sightings of other celebrities have been reported—Clint Eastwood, Sylvester Stallone, Jay Leno. The late Malcolm Forbes, who attended the 1989 rally with his famed riding posse, the Capitalist Tools, is here in spirit. His two-hundred-foot hot-air balloon in the shape of a Harley looms over the Black Hills.

And then there are the colors: the Bandidos, the Sons of Silence, the Gypsy Jokers, the Hell's Angels. Outlaws have been coming to the Classic for decades, but gang violence is surprisingly low. The Classic is said to be the one time during the year when the gangs agree to a cease-fire.

All the same, there was a gang fight here last night in front of Gunners Lounge on Main Street that ended with one man shot in the neck and two others stabbed. Yellow police tape marks the scene, and the sidewalk is stained with blood. A dozen Hell's Angels are standing outside Gunners, garnering stares. Rumors of a major showdown between the Angels and the Outlaws have been circulating. (A story in the Rapid City newspaper has warned that gang members have bought all the baseball bats on sale at an area Kmart.)

Eleven people have died during this year's rally, nine of them in highway accidents. One woman was instantly killed when her bike, traveling seventy miles per hour, struck an antelope. Another woman died of carbon monoxide poisoning in her tent, and police killed an Australian biker after he went on a rampage with a bowie knife.

But the topic of death is seldom heard on the sidewalks of Sturgis. This is a celebration, a time of rejoicing. On the streets, the huge men are bear-hugging, weeping like babes. Everyone wears the smile of Harley brotherhood.

And everyone wears the same clothes. For people who pride themselves on individualism, Harley boys look remarkably alike, as if they'd all bought their threads from the same mail-order catalog. Bikerdom is a fossilized culture. The uniform hasn't changed in thirty years. As always, only three clothing materials are acceptable: denim, leather, and metal.

Instead, they pour their originality into their bikes. Each machine has a slightly different look and feel. Every detail on the bike speaks worlds about its owner's personality. Enormous attention is lavished on the gas-tank pinstriping, the air-brushed cameo on the fender, the custom chrome work. The length of the front fork or the shape of the cylinder head reflects one's chosen caste; it is through these details that bikers pledge their fealty to the smaller clans (such as the "panheads" or the "knuckleheads") that delineate the Harley cosmos.

Bikers also express themselves through their proximity to various kinds of animal flesh. They like being around dead stuff. Everywhere I look there's carrion—rooster claws, bear heads, elk antlers, horse skulls—anything that was once alive or was once part of something that was alive. People sit on street curbs gnawing turkey drumsticks. Vendors sell bobcat tails, bull scrotums, and fox pelts. The air is filled with the gamy smell of alligator, wild boar, and venison sizzling on open grills.

Live animals are popular, too. People like to bring menacing-looking beasts for shock effect. Like the biker from Nevada who has two pit bulls riding in his sidecar. Or the muscleman outside the Fireside Lounge with the python wrapped around his body. Farther down the strip there is a tarantula in a Mason jar, an iguana on a chain, and a timber wolf curled up in a motorcycle trailer, his yellow eyes full of doom.

After I walk the strip for a while, the animals, live and dead, begin to blur together—the hides and fangs, the hairy arms, the smell of meat, the throaty grumble of engines, the tattooed dragons, the serpents and spiders and hellbounds. The whole dark menagerie begins to coalesce in my mind, and what emerges is the Harley Beast, a human-animal thing, pure and stripped down, a creature of basic urges, predatory and mean but also natural and therefore good.

Bikers often refer to the Harley itself as a beast—"a hog," "a steed," "a steer." Or, as Willie G. Davidson calls it, "an iron horse." Willie G. is the grandson of one of the company founders and perhaps the biggest celebrity at the Classic. People wait in line for hours to shake the hand of the scraggly bearded man in the black beret. A formally trained designer who once worked as a stylist for Ford, Willie G. is given much of the credit for recapturing the company's sense of itself when it went astray during the dark days of the early 1980s, when Harley-Davidson came within hours of declaring bankruptcy. Today he is known as the "keeper of the company soul."

Willie G. talks a lot about things like "the Harley essence" and "the Harley mystique." He understands that the mystique comes wrapped in the flag, for although the first Harley was manufactured in 1903, it did not become the quintessential American motorcycle until World War II, when the company won a government contract to build ninety thousand bikes for the Allies. He understands that a Harley isn't meant to be an agile or particularly fast machine. It's supposed to be a hefty bike for the open road, a living thing with a big braying engine, a long, low, sagging chunk of metal with lots of exposed parts. It is tail fire, chrome and rivets, Western saddlebags, and endless folds of lustrous black leather. While the Japanese companies race toward a sleek modernity, rigging their machines with aerodynamic shells and liquid-crystal instruments, Harley reaches back in time, to a wide-open era.

"The Japanese try to tame the Beast," Willie G. told me when I met with him in Sturgis. "Harley aims to keep the Beast alive."

ALTHOUGH THE CULT OF HARLEY now rules the Black Hills Motor Classic, the gathering actually began as a rally for one of Harley's principal competitors, the Indian. The late Clarence "Pappy" Hoel, a motorcycling enthusiast who ran an Indian dealership in town, started the Classic in 1938. For fifteen years Indian was king, but when the company folded in 1953, the Harleys took over. Today you can still find plenty of vintage Indian Scouts and Chiefs parked on the strip, their Art Deco chromework glinting in the sun. The Harley boys treat the Indians deferentially, like village elders.

Other motorcycle makes are welcome in Sturgis, though not with open arms. Britbikes like Triumphs or BSAs are taken in as distant cousins from across the pond. BMWs get respect but little love. Motor trike owners, known as Brothers of the Third Wheel, are regarded as colorful sideshow freaks; their weird-looking rides, imaginatively fashioned out of hearses or welded to look like the space shuttle, fetch a lot of stares.

Japanese-made bikes, on the other hand, are *non grata*, dismissed as "Jap Crap," "rice grinders," and worse. Occasionally a Honda owner will have the temerity to park his Goldwing on Main Street, but he is inviting trouble. In the early eighties, when the Harley company was getting clobbered by Tokyo, vandals in Sturgis made a sport of burning Japanese bikes in the public park at the edge of town.

Until the sixties, the Classic remained a regional affair, dwarfed by older rallies in better-established biker meccas like Daytona and Laconia, New Hampshire. The Jackpine Gypsies, Pappy Hoel's riding group, ran the rally on a shoestring budget. Visiting motorcyclists pitched tents in Hoel's backyard. There was a race, a buffalo feast, and a beauty pageant in the park. On the final day, Hoel would lead a tour to Mount Rushmore, where his wife, Pearle, would fix a picnic for the men.

Pearle Hoel is a sweet lady in her mid-eighties with watery eyes and a high, quavery voice—not the irascible old hellion you'd expect as the grandmother of the Harley Nation. She still keeps Pappy's tarnished racing trophies in the basement. "I was never into motorcycles," she told me when I dropped by her Sturgis house. She pronounced the word motor*sickles*. "I just rode behind Clarence. It's hard to believe how this thing has just grown and grown and grown. There's really no accounting for it. A lot has changed over the years, that's for sure. For one thing, the ladies don't wear clothes anymore.

"I look forward to all of this, you know," she says, the Harleys thundering outside. "But I guess I'm like everybody else—I'm kind of glad when the week is over."

AMONG THE THOUSANDS of Harley owners who waited until the fiftieth to make their pilgrimage to Sturgis were Peter Morrochelio and Paul Ganno, two Italian-American friends who grew up together in the Boston area. Both in their mid-thirties and still single, Peter and Paul live on separate floors of the same house in Stoneham, Massachusetts. Peter is a stout, clean-cut fellow with a salty Boston accent. He looks as though he could hold his own in a barroom brawl, but there is a gentleness in his face that suggests he isn't the fighting type. He's in charge of the trucking fleet for the New England division of Grossman's Lumber Company.

Paul is shaggier, shorter, more withdrawn. A self-taught mechanic, he owns a motorcycle repair shop, Ganno's Machined Assemblies, in the heart of Stoneham. Paul looks a bit like Robert De Niro with a smear of oil on his face and black grime under his nails. He is the intuitive sort of grease monkey who can spot a rebuilt shovelhead at twenty paces and quickly sniff out the archeology of every magneto and carburetor spring.

For Peter and Paul, riding a motorcycle isn't a social statement. It is pure freedom—an escape hatch. "Motorcycling is the cheapest form of therapy I know," Paul says. "It clears the mind."

"When you're in a car," says Peter, "you're numb to what's going on around you—the wind, the temperature, the heat of the asphalt, the bird on the wire. On the bike you're not just observing this pretty little picture. You are *in* the picture. You're enveloped."

Which is why Peter, like most Harley riders, is so adamantly opposed to state helmet laws. "Why ride a bike if you're going to lock your head in a steel tank? A helmet takes out all the rawness. The sounds get muffled and the peripherals get blurred."

As they grew up, Peter and Paul kept postponing the trip to Sturgis. Money concerns, girlfriends, family troubles—something always got in the way. They made treks to other rallies, like the big spring blowout in Daytona, but for them, Sturgis was the ultimate gathering. And with the fiftieth looming on the calendar, they decided 1990 was the year.

So Peter and Paul rounded up a group of four other local riders, among them a former butcher who goes by the name "Captain Coldcut," a lanky character who wears an air-cleaner cover for a belt buckle.

The trip to Sturgis took four days. The group hopped the Massachusetts Turnpike heading west out of Boston, crossed the Berkshires into New York, then took Interstate 90 through the wrinkled steel country and the mill towns of Pennsylvania. For the next five hundred miles it was perfect flatness—the lulling farms of Ohio and Indiana giving way to the pastureland of Wisconsin and southern Minnesota. Two hours into South Dakota, they were jolted by the drop to the Missouri River. Suddenly they had slipped into an entirely new landscape: buttes and dusty ranchland, the first faint suggestions of the West.

As they crossed the Cheyenne, they could see a dark mass hanging in the distance, a wave of dark pine and granite rising from an ocean of gold: the Black Hills. "It's such an awesome experience to look over at your friend on his Harley, and to be living out this dream that you'd been talking about ever since you were kids," Peter says. "Here we were, two old friends, Peter and Paul on the road to Damascus. Suddenly we're in the *Wild* West. It's then that you realize that you aren't just going to a motorcycle rally. Names you remember as a kid come rushing back to you. It's like, So *this* is where all that history happened."

LIKE DANTE'S HELL, living quarters at the Classic are arranged in descending circles of depravity. Bikers seek out their preferred level of sin and settle down for the week. Gentlemen bikers stay in the fancier hotels around Rapid City. Serious gamblers prefer lodgings near Deadwood, where they can be close to the blackjack tables. Gangs like the Hell's Angels stay far outside of town in semifortified encampments. But the great unwashed masses sleep on the outskirts of town in communal campgrounds with names like Wild West, Hog Heaven, and Covered Wagon. By far the most notorious of these camps is Buffalo Chip. It's the ninth circle at Sturgis—vats of beer, lakes of puke, clouds of reefer—and it's where I've decided to park my rent-a-relic for the week.

On my first morning at Buffalo Chip, I'm awakened around dawn by two loud voices. "So I took the motherfucker's arm like this, and I broke it over my knee."

"I did a guy in prison like that once, 'cept it was over a locker-room bench. Wham—broke it clean in half! Asshole had stolen my smokes."

I look up from my sleeping bag to see two Visigoths leaning against my rental car, oblivious to my presence inside. Their chopped hogs are parked a few yards away. The two bikers have bugged-out Benzedrine eyes, and they're sharing a fifth of Jack Daniel's. One of them turns to relieve himself on my front tire. I keep my eyes closed and try to play possum. Occasionally the conversation stops, and I can hear the sound of chemicals shooting up nostrils.

"... so I took out my blade and cut him up bad. Turned out the fucker died, man! I *killed* the son of a bitch!"

"Hey look!" the other voice interrupts. "There's someone inside this thing!" I hear a tap on my window. "Jeeeezus—you think he's a narc?"

There is a long silence as the bikers inspect me.

"Should we fuck with him?"

"Hmmmm."

"Naw. Look at him. He's crashed. He didn't hear nothin'. Let's get outta here."

I hear them kick-start their engines, but I don't budge. I'm shaking in my sleeping bag. I hear them blasting off across the field.

A bright orange sun has risen over the encampment. On the tattered hillsides, thousands of tents and plastic tarps are fluttering in the breeze. In the distance I can trace the outline of Bear Butte, an odd-looking swell in the golden prairie that Custer once used as a landmark for moving his cavalry. Utility trucks are sprinkling the land with water to keep the dust down, and now the camp is a mud bog. I slither over to the money exchange booth and get a stack of "buffalo chips," the camp currency. Then I stop at one of the open-air bars for a morning glass of "Purple Passion," a stout concoction of pure grain alcohol and grape syrup. Down in the immense crater that serves as the camp's natural amphitheater, a band is playing an obscure biker tune called "Boozin, Cruisin, and Losin."

Among the hundreds milling in the bar is Pam, a hard-core biker chick from Albuquerque, New Mexico. Pam is a wildcat of the desert, wiry and watchful and tough. She has a nearly permanent sneer and a nest of dishwater-blond hair. Pam says she roams the Southwest with a posse of outlaw bikers. She is especially proud of the fact that she rides a "hardtail," a bike without shock absorbers. Riding a hardtail means that her body "wears" every groove and pebble and varmint she's ever hit on the road, the knocks and shakes transferred directly from asphalt to flesh like the vibrations of a jackhammer. "Hardtail is the only way to go," Pam boasts. She's been coming to Sturgis for eight years. "It's the granddaddy of them all," she says, her sneer melting for a moment into a look of earnest sincerity.

As night falls, the Buffalo Chip starts to fill up. Twenty thousand people have come to hear Steppenwolf, perhaps the greatest biker band of all time. The crater is brimful of cycles. Beer and vomit smells mingle with blue motorcycle fumes. The stage is a mountain of Marshall amps and liquor billboards. Spotlights comb the skies. The Miss Buffalo Chip pageant is in progress, and the biker beauties are parading the stage in string bikinis and high heels. Someone in the audience tosses a cucumber onto the stage and yells, "Make it disappear!"

At the far end of the dust bowl, a dozen bikers are playing Chickenshit Bingo, a game of chance that involves a rooster defecating on a large bingo card. Nearby, a group of friends from Canada are doing the "wienie bite"—a traditional agility test in which a biker rides beneath a foot-long hot dog dangling on a string while his woman kneels on the back of the seat and attempts to bite off a chunk of meat.

Now Steppenwolf has taken the stage—haggard dinosaurs with tubercular-blue skin, their scaly forms mailed in black leather. The band belts out oldies like "The Monster," "The Pusher," "Magic Carpet Ride." The crater is now a pulsing mass of bodies. Women are perched on shoulders, hurling their halter tops into the air.

I'm standing with a catatonic biker who calls himself Nemo. "Biggest party on the planet!" he raves, tossing back another cup of Purple Passion. "Gonna remember this one the rest of my life."

An hour passes, and Steppenwolf leaves the stage. The crowd revs for an encore, creating a din that carries twenty miles across the prairie. A galaxy of butane lighters speckles the floor of the crater.

"'Born to Be Wild!'" Nemo screams. "They gotta play 'Born to Be Wild!'"

Finally, Steppenwolf slinks back onstage.

Now the whole crowd is chanting: "'Born to Be Wild!' 'Born to Be Wild!'"

"Ladies and gentlemen!" announces the low, rheumy voice of Steppenwolf's lead singer, John Kay. "Please remain standing for our national anthem!" Suddenly a typhoon of guitars, and then Kay is screeching—*Get your motor runnin'. Head out on the highway.* Nemo lets out a caveman scream and shakes a fist in the air. When the chorus comes, he bellows the beloved lines—*Like a true nature's child, we were born, born to be wild*—and the Black Hills tremble with the contented roar of the Harley Nation.

—1990

Waterlogged

"I SUPPOSE," the judge says, sizing me up, "we *could* give you a bucket and find a place for you as a substitute bail boy."

On this Friday evening in late June, retired circuit court judge John C. North II is standing under the broad elms of his Miles River estate in St. Michaels. The judge is a short, regal man in plaid bermudas, black socks, and espadrilles who could pass tolerably well for Thurston Howell on *Gilligan's Island*. Peering over half-glasses, he fusses with a pile of old rigging laid out on rickety trestles. He's doing his best to feign graciousness. But when log canoeing runs thick in the blood—and today is the eve of the first race of the season—an inquisitor like me is nothing but a nuisance.

"Or perhaps," he says ominously, glancing up from his electric drill, "we could put you out on the boards."

I was afraid he would say that. I've already heard about the boards. And I'm not too sure they're for me. "Yes, one has to watch out for those boards," Judge North adds, chuckling. "If one isn't watching, they can knock you out cold."

Brittle in the bones and in perpetual need of mending, log canoes are vintage sailboats indigenous to Maryland's tidewater rivers. What junks are to the Yangtze River and feluccas are to the Nile, log canoes are to the watery fingers of the Eastern Shore. No one knows or cares much about these arthritic boats except for a few intensely antiquarian mariners in a few hidebound communities along the close and crabby Chesapeake.

With proud, faded names like *Persistence, Tenaceous,* and *Flying Cloud,* the log canoes have acutely raked masts, stiletto sterns and prows, and entirely too much canvas for their own good. And because they have no weighted keel, they're extremely tippy and prone to capsize. This is where the boards figure in. To counterbalance their exaggerated heel, log canoes make use of long "hiking" planks that are cantilevered as much as twenty feet over the windward side of the boat. In response to shifting winds, the crew members (specifically, "boardmen") shinny up and down these varnished sticks of lumber in manic spurts of group activity, practicing the strenuous art of human ballast.

After a day of this Sisyphean scrambling, a boardman can expect to take home a lovely collection of splinters, mashed fingernails, charley horses, and bruises—not to mention dozens of sea-nettle stings. But such are the incidental hazards of keeping a moribund tradition alive.

The spiritual capital of the log canoe is the relentlessly quaint town of St. Michaels, home of the Miles River Yacht Club. Ever since the late 1920s, log-canoe racing has been the marquee attraction at the club, which nowadays is an unpretentious cinderblock affair with sixty or so slips. It's here that some of the most hotly contested regattas of the twenty-seven-race summer season are held, and where, in the late afternoons, log-canoe aficionados gather by the bar to debate the "six-second handicap" and other stunningly trivial fine points in the rules.

Judge North's estate, Broadview, is located no more than a hundred yards from the yacht club, a proximity that affords him a sort of custodial vista on the sport from one season to the next. That seems appropriate, since the judge, a naval architecture buff, is the sport's de facto conservator-in-chief. "There is so much history to log canoeing," North says, "that to enjoy this sport you have to be both a sailor and a classicist."

Log canoes trace their lineage back to the Indians of the Chesapeake, who were known to hack stout vessels from whole tree trunks. (It's not clear where they stood on the question of the six-second handicap.) When Capt. John Smith explored the Chesapeake in 1608, he was surprised to find fifty-foot canoes that would bear as many as forty men. "These they make of one tree." he noted, "by burning and scratching away the coles with stones and shells till they have made it in the forme of a Trough."

Soon the colonists had adapted the Indian technique, fashioning craft from several logs instead of one, and adding sails. Over time, the log canoe became a kind of riverine pickup truck, used by oyster tongers and commercial fishermen to navigate the shoals and narrows of the bay. When the British blockaded the Chesapeake during the War of 1812, the swift, shallow-draft canoe proved crucial in eluding the enemy.

In 1880, the U.S. Census reported 6,300 log canoes on the Chesapeake. But with the arrival of steam (and then gasoline) engines, the sailing vessels were left to rot in weedy coves and marshes. Today, of only twenty-one log canoes still sailing the Chesapeake, most are older than their owners—and only three have been built since World War II. "We're the last in the line," the judge tells me gravely, "the keepers of the flame."

As the sun melts into the Chesapeake, the judge lays down his drill and strolls across his kelly-green lawn to the riverside patio for a bottle of Heineken and some maritime conversation. Thick steaks sizzle on the grill. Grandchildren splash in the pool. A catamaran skids across the open Miles as the judge's fleet of vintage cars gleams in the big garage at the edge of the property.

The judge's family has lived and sailed around Talbot County for the better part of three centuries. His great-grandfather built canoes, as did his great-uncle. It's always been that way with these boats, a few deep-rooted families keeping the old art alive. Today the North clan owns three canoes: *Island Bird* (built in 1882), *Island Blossom* (1892), and *Jay Dee* (1931). The judge is a fiercely competitive sailor, and wastes no time showing me his silver Governor's Cup, the most prestigious trophy in log canoeing.

It's a complicated task keeping these old boats on the water, the judge says, let alone racing them. To make allowances for the odd shapes and lengths of the various canoes, the racing rules employ an elaborate handicap system. It's the sort of arcane formula that the judge's minutiae-loving mind feasts on, and he explains it with the but-of-course tone of a calculus professor: "The length of the deck is added to the maximum beam plus the afterquarter beam, which is the width of the boat halfway between the aftermast and sternpost. You add those three dimensions, then multiply it times six seconds, then times the number of miles in the course. That gives you your rating differential, you see."

Then he adds, "It's quite simple, really."

The judge, I quickly discover, is a martinet about canoe rules, and deeply skeptical of change. "You must understand," he says, "that we've been around these boats a very, very long time. We've got a lot of years invested in them. Nothing is done hastily."

Naturally, he is also a member in good standing of the Chesapeake Bay Log Canoe Association, the local organization that has fostered the sport since 1933. A former president, no doubt?

"That's commodore," he answers, with a pained scowl. *"Please."*

IT SEEMS I'M DESTINED for the planks after all. It's Saturday, the first day of the season, and I've been signed on as a boardman for *Jay Dee* (which the judge pronounces something like "Juh-aaa-yuh Duh-eee-uh"). Thirty-five feet from stem to stern (but closer to seventy feet counting her full rigging), *Jay Dee* is a magnificent boat, the largest log canoe in existence. She was built by the judge's aforementioned great-uncle, John B. Harrison, on Tilghman Island, during the latter years of the Hoover Administration. With her fifty-six-foot foremast, *Jay Dee* races with a suit of what seems like twenty acres of Dacron sail: jib, foresail, mainsail, staysail, and kite.

Today *Jay Dee* has a crew of twelve, skippered by a resolute, ruddy-faced man with the suitably Conradian name of Corbin Penwell. A building contractor and transplanted Washingtonian, Penwell has suffered the humiliation of capsizing in a race earlier in the day and is determined not to let it happen again this afternoon—even though much of his crew is, like me, hopelessly green.

We maneuver for position with six other log canoes near the starting line, listening for the report of the five-minute gun. Abruptly, and with great volume, Penwell curses as another canoe slyly angles in front of us, momentarily stealing our wind and coming within inches of ramming us. The ensuing exchange between the two crews—friends onshore but operatically bitter enemies on the river—is best not quoted here.

At the first puff of wind, we immediately sense the boat heeling, like some prehistoric beast turning in its sleep. It's unsettling to be in a vessel this large that's also this precarious. Now Penwell is yelling, "Out, out, out!" The boardmen, six of us, slam the sixteen-foot-long hiking boards into place under the inside lip of the leeward gunwale and scramble halfway up the boards on the windward side. "I mean *all the way out!*" Penwell cries, grimacing at the water pouring in. Now we lean farther out over the water, feeling the cool spray on our dangling legs. For a moment the boat has righted herself, and Penwell is tolerably happy. But suddenly the wind shifts again, forcing *Jay Dee* to tack. We scramble madly down the planks, but not quickly enough to avoid getting soaked by the waterline that has suddenly risen to meet us. We must reverse ourselves—removing the heavy boards, lodging them in the other side, and scooting back out. And so it goes, all afternoon, this frantic seesaw game with wind and water. I imagine myself as a bubble in a mason's level.

From a distance, the spectacle is comical to watch; it has the Chaplinesque quality of sandpipers scurrying in the surf. But in the boat, it isn't amusing in the least. To be in a log canoe is to be ill at ease. Something is always in need of desperate correction. Every moment is lived with the awareness that catastrophe is imminent. Stay on a log canoe long enough and you'll get ulcers.

Right now, though, mostly what we're getting is blisters, bad ones, and they're smarting all the worse from the constant gush of salt water. Still, we've begun to develop a galley-slave camaraderie, and the suffering feels good, or at least less bad, for the sharing.

Jay Dee tacks from marker to marker along a seven-mile course that follows the oxbows of the Miles. Off to one side, I catch a quick glance at Judge North, who's looking perfectly magisterial as he skippers his little canoe, *Island Bird*. Along much of the course, we're also trailed by the judge's mammoth Onassis-sized motor yacht, *Midnight Lace*.

On board, I can see some midday revelers tossing back chardonnay while others follow the action with binoculars.

I'm thinking how much more fun they must be having than we are, as we ride, cramped and sore-assed, sixteen feet out over the water, blood streaming down our shins. Yet on this crystalline Chesapeake day, I can think of no place I'd rather be than straddling my hard plank of misery.

An hour and a half later, sunburned, splintered, and generally walking funny, we head for the yacht club. At the bar, under the grainy photographic gaze of bygone commodores, we compare blisters, strawberries, and other honorable flesh wounds.

"Ooooooh."

"Nice!"

"*Very* tasty."

An elderly St. Michaels woman, wife of one of the more avid sailors, has been sitting at the bar watching the boats return, and she interrupts our little dermatology seminar. "Look at them—they're just like swans!" she says. I can see that she's been drinking, but the tears in her eyes are real.

After the last canoes straggle into their slips, the race officials begin the laborious process of calculating the handicaps. For a moment, it looks as though our *Jay Dee* is the victor, and our black-mooded Captain Penwell is momentarily jovial. But then the judge comes forward, and with a pedant's mordant delight, points out a minor discrepancy in the way we've assessed our boat's handicap. Alas, when all is tallied, Judge North and the crew of his *Island Bird* are declared the winner.

The judge does his best not to rub it in. "Everybody makes mistakes," he says, clutching his trophy. "You know, when I was a judge, I hanged a few innocent men in my time."

—1994

Blazing Saddles

Washington, D.C.

TUESDAY THROUGH FRIDAY NIGHTS, the bike messengers congregate at Asylum for a little-known event, the "Courier Happy Hour." At six P.M. they come skidding in from the streets, Lycra spider-men with names like Beaver, Beetlejuice, and Bam Bam. Concrete cowboys with shaved legs and holstered Motorola radios, scabby knees and earrings, guys who look like some weird cross between Greg LeMond and Sid Vicious. Soon the place is reminiscent of the alien bar in *Star Wars*, all sorts of interesting-looking beasts and hard-shelled insects hobnobbing in the dim lounge, speaking a strange argot. "Made a *major* southwest slice, man. Cut a big hole in the traffic in front of this Murphy at Faragut and then I shredded 'em, man, had him eating my dust. . . ."

The conversation often centers on perennial peeves—jaywalkers, elevators, security guards, cops, potholes, tourists, Capitol Hill metal detectors, suddenly opened car doors, or, most common of all, cab-drivers. "This cabbie's cutting me off, so I kick in his fender. Then the prick flips me the bird. So at the light I take out my radio, ride up to his window, and bash him good across the face, like *this*."

The war stories told at Asylum are tinged with the peculiar pride of a tough profession whose numbers have dwindled down to the hardest of the hard core. "Send it by courier" was the catchphrase of the Reagan-era workplace. Not only was a bike messenger fast and dependable, he was your slave for the hour. The courier epitomized the inflated urgency of the times. Sending it by regular mail wouldn't do. You needed hot colors, physical toil, the fanfare of having some coolie handing over a document in person. As a result, courier companies became a multimillion-dollar cottage industry in the eighties. Meanwhile messenger work appealed to a new class of urban malcontents who saw a way to find personal expression on a bike, while earning $800 a week or more, depending on how fast they could pedal. The mystique of the courier was romanticized in the 1986 movie *Quicksilver*, starring Kevin Bacon. "On the street, I feel exhilarated," Bacon's character rhapsodizes. "I go fast as I like, faster than anyone. If the street sign says one way east, I go one way west. They can't touch me."

But by the turn of the decade, telecommunications technology caught up with the bicycle, and the new watchwords of the officescape were "Fax it," or "Send it e-mail," or "Modem it in ASCII text." Today the bike messenger finds himself sprinting against fiber-optic lines like John Henry racing against the steam-engine drill.

ASYLUM IS A SMOKY, fermented space above an Ethiopian restaurant in a derelict section of northwest Washington that was torched during the 1968 riots. The house drinks are Blackened Voodoo Lager and Jägermeister shots. It's the kind of club that attracts extremely pallid people in extremely black clothes who go for obscure bands like Clutch or the Meat Puppets. Asylum is the only bar in town that welcomes bikes inside. The messengers like to haul their battered Bridgestones and Cannondales up the stairs and arrange them in a dense, circular formation known as a "clusterfuck." It's a symbol of group solidarity that dates back to the days when the couriers used to hang out at d.c. space, a now defunct downtown club where they had to park their bikes outside. The messengers would lock their rides together—as many as a hundred at a time—to keep them from getting ripped off.

Once they've stashed their bikes, the couriers begin to peel away their chain mail—the knee and elbow pads, the helmets with side-view mirrors, the Velcro arm pouches and slick sheathings, the gauntlet gloves with the fingers ripped out. They sidle up to the bar for the night's first Jägermeister shot, yelling their order over whatever skull-cruncher music happens to be emanating from the Asylum tape deck.

At Courier Happy Hour you meet people like Scrooge, a quiet, imposing figure in Olympian good shape with ocher skin, matted dreadlocks, and missing front teeth. At forty-one, Scrooge is the dean of the Washington bike messengers. He works with Action Couriers (Dispatcher #135) and makes about $500 a week. "We do real work," Scrooge boasts. "And we're good at it. We're like the Pony Express, man—heroes, thirty times a day."

Scrooge's friend Suicide is a rangy, gregarious, hyperactive man with a sponge of frizzy hair and various black leather strips and thongs dangling from his appendages. A veteran messenger of nearly a decade, Suicide won his nickname years ago when he used to wear a Japanese kamikaze headband on the streets. It was Su, as he is known to friends, who first organized the Courier Happy Hour at Asylum, where he sometimes tends bar.

Suicide also aspires to be the Eugene Debs of courierdom. He wants to organize Washington's messengers and strike for better wages. Courier companies take advantage of them, he insists. Since messengers are considered "independent contractors," companies refuse to pay benefits or workers' comp. "If we could have a work stoppage," he says in brittle tones, "you'd hear it around the world! This city would grind to a halt, man, just completely shut down! They would never fuck with us again."

Su misses the glory days of the late eighties. Then, he and Scrooge used to play in a rock band called Scooter Trash. Among their more popular songs was "Happy Trails," a raucous sledgehammer of a tune that became something of an anthem for D.C.'s messengers. "Well, my brakes aren't working quite like they should," Su would sing:

> *So I left him lying in a pool of blood*
> *One less pedestrian but who cares?*
> *Shouldn't have been there in the first damn place*
> *The "Don't Walk" sign means don't walk, of course*

Laid him out, man, no remorse,
I don't care, I make my own right of way
I got a rush red alert so get the
Fuck out of the way!!!

The few messengers who are still around tend to be die-hard romantics, a leaner breed scrapping for a dwindling number of pickups. They know that, beleaguered as it is, the courier business is not likely to vanish altogether. There will always be vital documents that must be notarized, blueprints to be hauled crosstown, depositions and payroll sheets in need of signatures. The laws of human procrastination being more or less constant, one can assume there will always be people with packages that absolutely, positively must get there in fifteen minutes. And there will always be a handful of American business districts—New York, Boston, Chicago, San Francisco, and Washington—where crowds and thick traffic make bicycle travel the only practical form of express delivery.

The couriers are detached from the establishment that depends on them—and they like it that way. As much as they may hate the drudgery of their jobs, they share a kind of mordant chauvinism in working at the bottom of the city's food chain. Once Scrooge was called upon to deliver a fish to a taxidermist; another time it was a six-pack of "sample bricks" from the National Brick Institute. Once he delivered $6.5 million to a Washington bank. Messengers sometimes get calls from government fat cats who've left an umbrella at a restaurant or a shirt at a hotel room tryst. They even get paid to wait in lines. Say a lobbyist wants to be guaranteed a seat at an important committee hearing on the Hill. Instead of waiting in line himself, he'll pay a messenger to save a place for him. "That's our job, man," Suicide says with a raspy laugh. "To do dumb shit for people."

Even so, Scrooge says that many of the "squares" he passes on the street would gladly trade places with him. It's hard for deskbound wonks not to envy the couriers. They're in terrific shape. They get to be buccaneers every day. They don't have to wear monkey suits, and they never get hung up in traffic. What's more, they don't have to answer to a real boss, only a disembodied voice crackling over a radio.

*　　*　　*

THE BIKE MESSENGERS who don't go to Asylum usually hang out at Dupont Circle after hours. At dusk they ride up to the white marble fountain with six-packs of Heineken in their fanny packs, unclip their Shimano shoes from the pedals, toss their "brain buckets" on the grass, and fall into the easy, familiar body language of boon companions. Scrooge coasts over on his Trek aluminum. He nods at Suicide, who is splayed out in the grass sipping a bottle of Hydra Fuel. Heavy metal pours from a blaster, and a couple of West African drummers are on the far side of the Circle. "Murphy! Murphy!" someone squawks over Scrooge's Motorola, code language for "Cops ahoy!" Scrooge passes the word on to the other bike messengers—"Murphy! Murphy!" Thirty seconds later an officer from the U.S. Park Police jumps the curb at Dupont Circle and noses his patrol car beside the fountain.

Couriers love to hate the police. The antagonism animates them. They scramble to clean up the scene, stash their beer cans in the shrubs, snuff out their joints. Murphy jumps out of his car and slips on a pair of rubber gloves. He forges into the crowd with an eye toward busting somebody or impounding an unregistered bicycle. The messengers whisk their bikes off the pavement and stand defiantly in the officer's path.

"You gotta problem, Murphy?" demands one of the messengers. Murphy sniffs the air suspiciously, then scowls at the wall of fluorescent spandex. "Go home, Murphy!" Murphy gives them the evil eye, but finally relents. He slips back into the patrol car.

The West Africans resume their polyrhythmic pounding. Scrooge and Su sit on the fountain wall, eating bean burritos. Scrooge says he's been spending most of his free time lately noodling on his laptop computer. He's thinking of publishing a courier newsletter. And he's got bigger plans afoot—a hacker's dark conspiracy. "I'm going to create a virus that will ruin all the fax machines. You know, kind of like a Michelangelo for faxes," he says. "I'm gonna send it out over the phone lines like an epidemic. Then *watch out*. All the bike couriers of the world will unite! And we're going to take this country by storm!"

—1993

AMERICAN BY BIRTH, SOUTHERN BY THE GRACE OF . . .

Jerusalem on the Mississippi

Memphis, Tennessee

"SATAN IS A LIAR!" shrieks the girl from Detroit, the tears welling in her unblinking eyes. "Satan is a liar and we have a victory NOW!!"

Onstage, the swaying choir has reached a crescendo, singing "Yes, Lord, yes, Lord, completely yes!" and now the Saints are strumming washboards and pounding tambourines to the mounting frenzy of the gospel anthem. "From the bottom of my heart, to the depths of my soul, Yes, Lord!"

"Satan is a liar!" the girl keeps saying. She turns and hugs her sisters crowded in the aisle, taking care to step over the elderly lady in the white sequined dress who has dropped to the floor for a conversation with the Ghost.

"Baabaabaawambidawambiooooobaabaabaawangwongbaa!"

"Get it!" the sisters scream, gathering around the woman and locking arms in a tarrying circle. "The tongue is here!"

"Baawoooooodoingdoingwooooobaabaahangeeeeeeeeeeeee!"

At the height of the fever, the presiding bishop gathers the flowing skirts of his robe and rises to survey his flock of believers crowded inside the Memphis Cook Convention Center. "Sweet Jesus!" he declares, extending his hand over the crowd. "This thing getting hotter by the minute! We are positively having us a Holy Ghost explosion!"

In some other setting, twenty thousand people losing control like this would be called a riot. But here there are subtle economies of emotion that keep the scene from flying into chaos. Some people are jogging in place, an old man is seizuring in the aisle, and the lady two rows back is shouting something about how the good Lord—praise His holy name!—has just shrunk the goiter off her neck. "Was big as a cantaloupe, but now it's gone!"

"He's a good God! Sweet Jesus! He's got the power over sickness! He's got the power over the sickle cell! God is here to help you deal with all your isms and your schisms!"

Standing next to me is Teressa, a coltish girl with smooth ocher skin. She wears white gloves, a white linen dress, white high-heeled shoes, and a white hat. She cannot be more than fourteen years old. She throws her arms around me and hugs me tightly. Then she steps back and looks deep into my eyes. "You *know* he is a liar," she proclaims. "But we have a victory now!"

The bishop's speech is traditionally a joyous occasion, a final drenching in the Holy Spirit before the Saints' long journey home. Yet there is a sense of foreboding in the air, a new uncertainty about the future. By now everyone here has heard the grim reports that have made front-page news in the Memphis paper this week: the bishop is dying of cancer of the pancreas—inoperable, they say—and may have only a few months to live.

A hush descends over the hall.

"Not long ago," the bishop begins, his voice ominous and quavering, "I went to the doctor. And he said, 'Cancer . . .'"

Why, Lord, why.

"And he said the treatment is chemotherapy."

Lord save ya', sweet Bishop.

"But I didn't want no chemotherapy, because I'd heard it makes your hair fall out . . . and I didn't want to be buried bald! No, I want to look *pretty* when I die!"

Praise the Lord!

The Saints begin to stir again as the bishop's voice opens up, the pace quickening, the fire gathering inside him. "So . . . instead of going to the hospital . . ."

Preach it!

". . . I checked into the *Saints'* hospital!!"

Say it, Bishop!

"Because I *know* the treatment of prayer . . ."

Uh-huh, uh-huh.

". . . is better than the treatment of chemotherapy!!!"

Sweet Jesus-God-ah-Mercy!

"And I want you all to know today . . ."

Preach it!

". . . that I'M NOT MAKING NO FUNERAL ARRANGE-MENTS!!!!!"

Pandemonium.

Teressa, tears streaming down her cheeks, raises her hands to heaven and starts to quiver, a power rumbling inside her. "We have a victory!" she cries out. Then she, too, feels the tongue coming on and drops to the floor for a bout with the Ghost.

"Issshawambiflogishyishyidwangolowaogowambologi!"

WHEN I WAS A BOY growing up in Memphis, I'd sometimes take out my transistor radio and scan the stations for baseball games on Sunday afternoons only to discover that the airwaves were still being hogged by religious broadcasts. Every pulpit in town was competing for airtime: Southern Baptists, Primitive Baptists, Freewill Baptists, Reformed Baptists, Two-Seeds-in-the-Spirit Baptists, United Methodists, Seventh-Day Adventists, and a great yodeling slew of freelance revivalists. The farther up the dial I got, the freer and livelier the worshiping became. The radio needle would sweep over the polyester prophets of the white suburbs, past the local Jerry Falwells and the latter-day Elmer Gantrys, and then it would enter the more expressive realm of the black faiths.

Finally I'd get over to the very end, to a scratchy low-watt station that played the liveliest broadcast of them all—three or four uninterrupted hours of keening, whooping, and Delta stomp music. These were the black Pentecostalists, the ones who spoke in tongues and laid their trembling hands upon the sick. The largest Pentecostal denomination in the world was based in Memphis, its headquarters just a few blocks from the Mississippi River. It was called the Church of God in Christ (normally written COGIC, but pronounced "*Ko*-jik"). Here was a church where people stood up whenever they pleased and where hardly anything was written down. It was another culture on the other side of the city—the other end of the dial. One thing was unmistakable: *This* was worshiping.

My hometown is known the world over as a pilgrimage city, fabled in song and film for the legions of Elvis Presley fans who come each August to gaze on the King's tomb at Graceland and purchase relics. But every November, the Church of God in Christ hosts a substantially larger gathering of pilgrims that makes the scene on Elvis Presley Boulevard seem quite tame. For more than eighty years the church's believers have returned to the "Mother City." The Memphis riverfront becomes a tent revival, and the autumn air stirs with some of the most beautiful, gasket-blowing gospel music in Christendom.

They come here from Bedford-Stuyvesant, Watts, the East Side of Cleveland, the South Side of Chicago. They come from Kosciusko, Mississippi; Tuscumbia, Alabama; and a thousand one-mule towns across the South. They come from COGIC missions deep in the shantytowns of Soweto, South Africa; Monrovia, Liberia; and Port-au-Prince, Haiti. Memphis is the church's international headquarters and burial place of founder Charles Harrison Mason, the beloved prophet who reigned over the COGIC kingdom for sixty-five years. It was Mason who, in 1907, conceived the idea of holding an annual revival following the cotton harvest each November. Mason predicted that the Holy Convocation would grow so large one day that Memphis wouldn't have a place large enough to hold all the pilgrims, and his prediction more or less came true. Today, COGIC has to stretch the fire codes each year to pack in all of the returning Saints.

Bishop Mason lived long enough to see much of the tremendous growth he'd predicted for COGIC. He died in 1961 at the age of ninety-five, and is buried in a marble crypt in the foyer of Mason Temple, a cavernous, Quonset-roofed auditorium in the projects of downtown Memphis where Martin Luther King delivered his "Mountaintop Speech" the night before his assassination.

Today the church that Mason built claims a membership of 3.7 million souls worldwide, yet little is known about this mysterious denomination born nearly a century ago in a cotton gin. COGIC kept such a low profile throughout its history that the federal government didn't officially recognize it as a religious body until 1975.

Yet quietly, almost clandestinely, COGIC has grown from a ragtag religious sect of Delta sharecroppers to a major international denomination, with missions in forty-seven countries on four continents. The Church of God in Christ is a Pentecostal body, which puts it in the same spiritual tradition as televangelists like Jimmy Swaggart, Oral Roberts, and Jim and Tammy Bakker. Like all Pentecostals, the Saints believe in the inerrancy of Scripture and the imminent Second Coming of Christ. They view the Ghost as an active force in their lives, responsible for such paranormal phenomena as faith healing, the gift of prophecy, slayings in the spirit, and glossolalia (speaking in tongues).

Pentecostalism is a uniquely American tradition, born of a series of evangelical revivals that swept the United States in the late nineteenth century and culminated in the historic Azusa Street Resurgence of 1906, a spiritual jamboree that energized a Los Angeles ghetto for more than three years. All Pentecostal groups trace their origins to the Azusa Revival, where it was reported that thousands spoke in tongues and were washed in the healing powers of the Spirit. Among the thousands of pilgrims who traveled to Los Angeles that fateful year was COGIC founder Bishop Mason, whose experience at the revival was so intense he was struck dumb for a month. "Getting back to Azusa" is a common refrain in Pentecostal churches, carrying with it the notion of returning to an era free of the cynicism of the scientific age, a time when the supernatural powers of the Ghost spread like a contagion among the believers.

Theological beliefs aside, COGIC is vastly different from its white Pentecostal brethren. COGIC was founded by a black man, the son of slaves, for black believers. COGIC customs grew directly out of the cotton fields and shacks of the Mississippi Delta. As machines steadily forced the sharecroppers off the land and the black families migrated to the smokestack cities of the North, the Church of God in Christ became a source of solace, a means of preserving the spirit of the old

in the face of urban life. Something powerful was pre-
raw idiom faithfully passed down.

Reverend Al Sharpton got his start preaching in a Brooklyn
COGIC church at the age of nine. Sharpton is no longer associated
with the church, but his scrappy style still bears many qualities of
the COGIC pulpit tradition—mistrust of the written word, reliance
on theatrics and sheer volume to advance an argument, the street
preacher's dogged championing of the underclass. The live-wire spiri-
tuality that runs through the COGIC experience has long appealed to
the poorest and most desperate segment of the American black population, the same people whom Sharpton has sought, in his own way, to
represent. "The Church of God in Christ traditionally viewed itself as
the church of the unlettered black masses," Lawrence Jones, dean of
the Howard University Divinity School, told me. "It offers a highly
emotional faith unadulterated by Western intellectualism."

THE SUPREME LEADER of the Church of God in Christ for the
past twenty-one years has been Bishop J. O. Patterson. Church literature describes the seventy-seven-year-old clergyman as "the man who
fathers three million sons and daughters around the globe." Patterson
is the son-in-law of founder Mason, and only the second presiding
bishop in the eighty-three-year history of the church. His full title, if
you're a stickler, is "the Most Reverend James Oglethorpe Patterson,
Sr., Presiding Bishop, President of the Corporation, Chairman of the
General Board, Chairman of the Board of Directors, General Over-
seer and Chief Apostle of the Church of God in Christ." Others just
call him "Big Daddy."

Patterson is an affluent funeral parlor executive and pastor of the
city's largest COGIC congregation. He presides over the all-powerful
executive board of the national church, a body of twelve bishops that
meets behind closed doors inside the COGIC world headquarters,
based in a dilapidated former luxury hotel. Patterson's tenure as presiding bishop has been marred by intense controversy, but his ultimate
authority is unquestioned. "God selects the leaders in this church," he

once said at the Holy Convocation. "This church is not a democracy. It's a *theo*cracy."

Pancreatic cancer is a particularly deadly disease; few of its sufferers have been known to live more than a year after diagnosis. Yet most of Patterson's congregation seems to believe him when he says he's cured: faith healing is one of the hallmarks of the COGIC experience. And Patterson has made testimonials of dramatic recoveries before, such as the time he claimed the Spirit saved him from a dangerous allergy that had caused him to swell up "twice my normal size."

The bishop's illness has left him gaunt and sallow, but he is still a commanding presence in the pulpit. He is a tall, mustachioed man with a baritone voice and steely eyes that methodically scan the room. He wears a white robe with a purple stole. Swinging from his neck is a hefty crucifix of gold and rubies. When he preaches, he clenches his teeth and hunches slightly forward, dropping his head down like a bull moose. One senses that Patterson, a mortician by trade, is a man distrustful of motion.

Patterson is a master of the well-timed stage entrance, and knows how to build suspense by keeping himself scarce. His photographed image, however, is everywhere. For months prior to the Holy Convocation, his likeness has been plastered over the slums near Beale Street. He stares out from the diesel-blackened ads on the rear panels of city buses and glowers from billboards pitched high above the red-light districts, his dour image competing with the Kool cigarette and malt-liquor ads. THE SAINTS ARE COMING! the signs announce. In these billboards, as in all his official photographs, Patterson never smiles. There is only a scowl and an inscrutable fish-eye stare that seems to register disapproval over downtown Memphis.

The church treats Patterson like royalty: He rides in a black Fleetwood limousine with a license plate that reads COGIC-1, and is escorted by minions who wear black suits with white gloves and constantly shield his movements. During Sunday services at his church in Memphis, Patterson sits quietly on a large throne known as the Apostolic Chair and sips coffee from a silver chalice, occasionally picking up the phone to confer with the sound engineers. He lives in a plantation-style mansion near Graceland with a wrought-iron gate and a permanently manned guardhouse. On his travels abroad, his schedulers book first-class flights and accommodations, carefully choreographing red-carpet receptions at foreign airports. Bishop Patterson rarely meets with members of the press. Arranging a personal interview with him, I'm repeatedly told by his office, is "out of the question."

For all the trappings that surround Bishop Patterson, his followers insist that he is still a man of the people whose tastes and views haven't strayed far from his simple origins in rural Mississippi. Patterson wears blue jeans and flannel shirts around the house, they say, and his culinary tastes run in the direction of beans and molasses-soaked corn bread. For his vacations, he still likes to fish for crappie in the muddy oxbow lakes of the Delta. One of his common refrains in sermons is "Thank God for the ignorant folk!"

Patterson once summed up the full sweep of his theological views in one sentence: "I am not frigidly formal or foolishly fanatical, but I am fervently fundamental, earnestly evangelical, and purely Pente-costal." His positions on specific matters of national church protocol or vice can be found in one of the many informal pronouncements that he has delivered at Holy Convocations over the years:

On cigarette smoking: "Smoking is wrong. I've never seen any-body get the Holy Ghost while they were smoking!"

On premarital cohabitation: "The Holy Ghost don't believe in shacking. We've got to stop dragging holiness in the dust."

On clerical attire: "I don't believe that preachers ought to be wear-ing skintight suits and high-heeled jitterbug shoes."

On homosexuality: "God put us here to replenish the earth. God made Adam and Eve, not Adam and Steve."

On tithing: "Are you giving God a tip or a tithe? I have never in my life seen a U-Haul trailer hitched to the back of a hearse."

All week long, as I mill about the Convocation, I hear a lot more about the church founder, Bishop Charles Mason, who's been dead for more than thirty years, than I do about the ailing Bishop Patterson. The Saints speak of founder Bishop Mason as if he were still watching over them with a sweet, grandfatherly vigilance. One bishop referred to him as "that great prophet of God, greater than a Moses, greater than an Isaac, greater than a Jacob!" Bishop Mason was a short, spry man with close-cropped grizzled hair, leathery brown skin, and a pencil mustache. "The Diminutive Holy Man," the Memphis papers dubbed him. Every day he wore the same uniform: a black serge suit, a white broadcloth shirt with removable collars, and a black bow tie. He had a disarming habit of closing his eyes for minutes at a time. His only vice was chewing gum.

Despite his humble demeanor, church accounts describe Mason as a "militant." He prayed two hours on his knees every morning before breakfast. He advised his church members to keep a Bible in every room of their house, even the bathroom ("Don't waste your time in there!"). Some Saints will tell you that Mason raised people from the dead and turned away tornadoes by the muscular force of his faith. In 1918, federal authorities arrested Mason for his opposition to World War I. The FBI suspected Mason of collusion with the Germans, and maintained a secret file for decades, hoping to build a case against him for treason.

During his sixty-five-year reign, it was unheard of for church members to disagree with Mason. He was a pious man. Unlike Patterson, he never had personal servants or bodyguards. The church structure grew out of a few simple principles set down in his *Book of Discipline*.

The son of slaves, Mason was an untutored mystic who instinctively turned to nature for signs of the Holy Ghost. His was a kind of Christian animism. The Ghost was everywhere—in that cypress stump over there, in the pecan groves, in an ornery old mule. It was said Mason could divine God's will by studying the freakish shapes of certain twisted roots and petrified vegetables that he had pulled out of the black soil. He liked to haul his gnarled specimens into the church and use them as visual aids. "Mystical wonders of God," he called them. There was a root that resembled a crippled human hand, a branch that vaguely resembled a serpent, a gourd that had the "exact likeness of an animal's head." Mason could slice open a watermelon and augur a drought or a war based on the configuration of the seeds.

Mason was born a year after Appomattox on a Tennessee cotton plantation not far from Memphis. Even as a young boy he showed a spiritual predilection. Often he would walk into the woods alone and pray for hours at a time. He liked to sing the old slave hymns with his parents and their friends in the Missionary Baptist Church. As an old man he always used to say that his life's work had been to recapture the simple vitality of the "slave religion" he'd learned at the knee of his parents. In 1878, a yellow fever epidemic hit Memphis, decimating the city's population. The Masons fled west to Arkansas to escape the mosquito-borne plague, but not soon enough: within a year, yellow fever had claimed his father's life, and young Charles fell ill a few months later. His chills and delirious fevers persisted for several weeks, and his mother feared for his life. But one morning, the fourteen-year-old boy suddenly recovered, a dramatic healing that would clinch his decision to pursue the ministry.

In 1895 Mason set out on his own as an itinerant preacher. He worked the gins and sharecropper shacks of the Cotton Belt, following the railroad tracks from town to town. He preached in brush arbors and carnival tents. He conducted all-night revivals from the beds of hay-wagons. At the outset, he attempted to work within the Baptist and Methodist traditions. But everywhere he went, Mason found that the established churches rejected his teachings. Some local ministers were uncomfortable with all those weird roots and rotten potatoes he doted on, and were alarmed by the way his freelance evangelizing stirred the people's emotions. Others were troubled by his theology. Mason had begun to preach a radical definition of "holiness" that was derived from the teachings of John Wesley. He held that the true believer can achieve a state of perfect holiness, or "sanctification," that is very nearly Christ-like; the "sanctified" Christian is not of this world, and should therefore take pains to "separate" himself from society. Mason's otherworldly message threatened the authority of established black ministers, who served not only as spiritual leaders, but also as the de facto political heads of black communities throughout the Jim Crow South.

In 1897, Mason landed in Lexington, Mississippi, where he established his own denomination and called it the Church of God in Christ. Today Lexington is a drowsy county seat shaded by magnolias and a dozen grain silos that rise over the rusty hills and gulches to the east. To get there, I took Highway 61 out of Memphis and headed south through the Mississippi Delta, the Mesopotamia of the blues. It is a stark landscape with languorous bayous and thick piney woods swallowed by kudzu. Little has changed in the nearly one hundred years since Mason first arrived. Cotton is king, though the soybean has made a considerable dent in the order of things. Mason's church, the St. Paul Church of God in Christ, is still here, newly renovated and drawing large crowds on Sundays. The road out of Lexington was lined with trailer bins piled high with cotton to be ginned. For miles the white wisps fluttered in the air and blanketed the roadside ditches like a deep winter's snow.

"BACK TO PENTECOST AT ANY COST" is one of Bishop Patterson's trademark expressions, and it seems an appropriate slogan for the Holy Convocation. Getting souls back to Pentecost is big business. The Chamber of Commerce estimates that the Saints sink more than $16 million into the Memphis economy each November. The pilgrims are known for buying fancy suits, jewelry, perfume, and luxury cars. Business is brisk at the Madison Cadillac dealership downtown. A salesman there remembers one COGIC bishop who used to trade in his used Fleetwood for a new showroom model each November. It has long been a tradition for COGIC women to buy fur coats and hats during Convocation Week.

At the convention center, sour pickles, peanut brittle, yams, and new-crop pecans are the big items. A nearby congregation is offering plate dinners at the church cafeteria for $8.99; the entrées include chitterlings, neckbones, oxtails, hamhocks, pig's feet, and buffalo fish. Preaching on a corner near an outdoor concession stand, a thin, dour-faced holy man—clearly put off by all the talk of eating—brandishes a Bible and hollers at the swarming crowd: "This here's the only food you be needing! Now stop being tourists, y'all, and let's have church!"

J. O. Patterson Ministries, Inc., has set up a flashy multimedia display by the main escalator. Here there are $25 videocassettes of the bishop's sermons, which are continuously flickering on four large color television sets. Throughout the day, wide-eyed young preachers cluster around the monitors, soaking up Patterson's pulpit style, mastering the subtle cadences the way hungry young boxers might study old footage of an Ali bout. "See the way he do?" one of them whispers to a mesmerized colleague. "Listen how he's always sneaking up that volume." This is the closest many of these Pentecostal understudies will get to formal seminary. COGIC does have a small seminary on the campus of Morehouse University in Atlanta, but most of the church's ministers still rise through the ranks in the traditional way—establishing a grassroots following at the local storefront church, learning the Pentecostal idiom in the desultory way that jazz musicians pick up their licks.

Other rooms at the convention center are lined with secular goods. Fannie's Sales is offering panty hose and five-hundred-dollar silk suits. The racks at Bea's Custom Millinery are overflowing with ladies' designer hats, netted and ribboned and outfitted with purple ostrich plumes. A persistent saleslady on the first floor is pushing something she calls the AcuVibe Foot Massage, a "revolutionary" new podiatric remedy. "C'mon, brothers and sisters," she coaxes. "You been standing on those feets all day long. Let me put the AcuVibe on you!"

Also on the first floor is Mary Kay Cosmetics, its display done in trademark pink and peach. Carrie Datson, the Mary Kay saleslady, lives in Cleveland, where she has been a member of the Church of God in Christ for thirty years. Standing proudly over her toners and skin creams, she can scarcely contain her enthusiasm for the Dallas-based direct sales company. "I don't put anything before God," she hastens to note, "but I'd say that after my church, Mary Kay is the best thing that ever happened to my life."

Actually, there are several Mary Kay sales counters at the COGIC convention, but Datson's booth is the only one "authorized" by the official church hierarchy. This is because Datson, in keeping with strict rules governing the modesty of women in the church, has agreed not to sell what are called "glamour or vanity items." Blushes and mascara, for example, are definitely contraband, considered nothing more than vulgar face paint to seduce men. But toners, astringents, cleansers, and perfumes are deemed "nonglamour," and thus enjoy the church's sanction.

The church comes down hard on women members who persist in wearing vanity items. One of the common punishments, Datson points out, is a practice known as "silencing"—the offending Jezebel is simply not allowed to speak in church. She is shunned by her friends, ignored by her preacher, and forbidden from giving public testimonials or offering even so much as a prayer. "Not supposed to be any parading around in our church," Datson explains. "The preacher has got to put those kind of women in order."

Keeping women "in order" seems to be one of the ongoing concerns of the COGIC leadership, in fact. Though women form the backbone of the church, constituting well over 70 percent of the national membership, they are not allowed to train for the ministry and are forbidden from holding any office that does not fall under a broad category that the church literature unabashedly calls "women's work." Women's work includes service on the Hospitality Committee, the Ushers Unit, the Food Division, the Nurses Unit, the Ministers' Wives Circle, and the Sewing Circle. ("Sewing is important for the concentration and relaxation of women," a church pamphlet explains.) At the Holy Convocation, the church holds a sexually segregated Women's Day that is reigned over by a stern matriarch from the San Francisco Bay area named Mother Mattie McGlothen, general supervisor of the Department of Women. Mother Mattie's position on femininity is concisely presented in an official manual, written under her direction, that is circulated among all new women members. "The holy woman," the manual advises, "should be temperate, disciplined, self-controlled, chaste, a homemaker, good-natured, adapting, and subjecting herself to her husband."

Carrie Datson sees no problem with any of this. "The Bible says that men should lead," she reasons. "A woman has no business being a pastor because then she'd be in a position of authority over men. She'd be totally out of order. That's not the way God planned it."

Aside from her saleswork for Mary Kay, Carrie works full-time as a registered nurse at a Cleveland hospital. She spends many of her free hours caring for her husband, Ollie, a retired truck driver who is a diabetic requiring kidney dialysis three times a week. Since Ollie became disabled in 1981, Carrie has been the breadwinner in the household, but in no way does she consider herself in charge. "As long as there's breath in my husband," she declares, "he's the authority in our house."

A few months after the Holy Convocation, I visited Carrie at her home in Cleveland. The Datsons live on the city's East Side, a crumbling precinct that bears the telltale scars of the crack wars. When I arrived, a winter storm had just blown off Lake Erie, dumping a half foot of wet snow on the ground.

The Datsons are members of the East 105th Street Church of God in Christ, the second-largest COGIC in Cleveland. Carrie and Ollie have six grown children spread over the Midwest.

Carrie is a strong woman with a broad, motherly smile full of pearl-white teeth. She is fifty years old but looks forty. There is the simple strength of pragmatism in her eyes, an inner placidity that seems at odds with the stoked fires of her church doctrine. Yet Carrie speaks convincingly of her experience with the supernatural, of the glorious white-hot emotion that surges through the believer when the Holy Ghost comes. "Can you remember when you were a child," she says, "getting something that you really, really, really, really wanted real bad? And one day you finally got it, and you were surprised? There's nothing that can be compared to it, but that's sort of the feeling. You just want it so bad, and then you finally get it, get the Ghost. You feel like you can conquer the world. You feel totally free. It's something you have to know for yourself. It's joy unspeakable. You're just totally happy. Something takes hold. You feel like you're really going to fly away. You can try to govern it down, but you can't. You go to uttering. It just comes out of your mouth. You don't black out or anything. You are still in control of your faculties. The Holy Ghost is a perfect gentleman—he doesn't make anybody go crazy."

TERESSA, FROM DETROIT, has just finished her talk with the Ghost, and the energy inside the Cook Convention Center has begun to dissipate. Suddenly an aide to Bishop Patterson rises to the podium and shouts at the Convocation crowd:

"He's the most unselfish leader in the WORLD! Every time you see him you're seeing a walking miracle! I don't want you to even THINK about giving your leader anything less than ten dollars!"

Everyone knows the cue. It is time for the annual cash gift to the presiding bishop, a ceremony known as "the Love Offering." The ushers pass around bright orange plastic pails that say "COGIC Finance Department" (in previous years, the church simply used large Kentucky Fried Chicken buckets), and the Saints dutifully drop their bills into the growing piles of cash. Some $200,000 will be collected in under fifteen minutes. The recipient of all this largesse, Bishop Patterson, quietly rocks in a Naugahyde office chair behind the podium.

"Don't be shirking an offering now!" the speaker shouts in a vaguely menacing voice. "You just don't come before God empty-handed! Look around you—EVERYBODY's giving! We'll take traveler's checks, personal checks! C'mon now, let's see that ten-dollar bill. Hold it up high so EVERYBODY can see who's giving and who's shirking his responsibility! Ten dollars is the LEAST you can give. God's kept your body well all through the year. Give your ten dollars to the KINDEST, HUMBLEST, most UNSELFISH leader in the WHOLE world!"

Finally Bishop Patterson rises to acknowledge his followers' generosity. "There's no church in the world like the Church of God in Christ," he says. "Because our church is rooted and grounded in the spirit of Jesus!"

Then his voice becomes grave. "Now at one time we may have been a little fanatical. Everything was wrong in the early days of our church. Dental work was wrong. Neckties were wrong. Everything was wrong! But now . . . *something's* got to be wrong. Something's got to be wrong today when little fourteen-year-old girls are becoming mothers! Something's got to be wrong when we see the ladies of our church going around looking like Zsa Zsa Gabor, worshiping hats and wigs! Something's got to be wrong when some of our preachers are riding around in cars that look like pimpmobiles! That's too vain. Preachers got no business looking like members of the Mafia."

The bishop is already short of breath. He is clearly a frail man, not the marathon preacher he was in the days of twenty-four-hour roadshow revivals. "Who knows why God gave me the strength to stand here and talk to you today? Who knows? If my illness can do anything this week, I would hope that it could clean up this church's political ambitions, and bring us hastily to judgment. There are people clamoring for this job! Well, to them I say, 'I ain't gonna die, and I ain't gonna resign!' "

Hallelujah, good bishop!

"Whoever clamors for the job don't get it. See, promotions don't work that way."

That's right!

"To hold this job you've got to love people, not dollars!"

No, sir!

"I hope that in some way, my illness can lead our church back to old-time holiness. . . ."

Preach the word.

"Back to the kind of holiness that makes people call us fanatics!"

Yes, yes, good Lord!

"All the way back to Azusa, where God was real! Back to Pentecost at any cost!"

Postscript: Bishop J. O. Patterson died of pancreatic cancer two months later in a Memphis hospital. The funeral at Mason Temple on January 4, 1990, was attended by some ten thousand people— including Benjamin Hooks, Oral Roberts, and U.S. Senator Jim Sasser of Tennessee. President George Bush sent a message of condolence that was read aloud at the memorial service. A horse-drawn carriage, bearing the casket, led a cortege through the rainy streets of downtown Memphis.

—1991

Let Us Now Praise Famous Fish

Richmond, Virginia

AT THE OSBORNE LANDING a few miles downstream from the Virginia capitol, forty-one fishermen are sitting in identical nineteen-foot fiberglass boats, fiddling with their quivers of graphite rods, rummaging through their giant plastic tackleboxes filled with plastic buzzbaits and crankbaits and worms, plastic frogs and crawdads and minnows, and endless miles of nylon monofilament line. Dawn is breaking. A tangerine sun is just beginning to burn through the fog that has blanketed the James River. Gray tidewater laps at the undersides of the boats and gives off a faint miasmal stench. Tournament officials scurry over the docks with clipboards in their hands, checking the last-minute details. The men will soon be roaring out to the river channel in staggered heats, but now they sit idling in the shallows, talking fish jive.

"You ready?"

"Yeah, I'm ready!"

"You don't look ready to me!"

"Where you headin' today?"

"Appomattox Creek."

"Appomattox, huh? You going down there to rewrite that ol' treaty, ain't ya, bubba?"

"Nope, just doin' a little fishin'. You?"

"Going *way* down. Down to my secret place."

"They say you got yourself a real honey hole down there, huh?"

"Sho-nuf."

"Ya lettin' anyone in on it?"

"Tell ya this: It's somewhere between here and the Chesapeake Bay."

"Why, *thanks* for the big tip there, slim!"

Through all their macho banter, the fishermen can't conceal the nervous anticipation that burns in their faces. This is opening day of the Bassmasters Classic, the country's premier fishing tournament. The winner of the three-day competition will take home a cool $50,000 and the world championship title. The windfall of corporate sponsorships that will rain down upon the victor will ultimately amount to more than a million dollars. Gathered this early August morning on the historic James River are the best bass fishermen in America. Each angler earned his berth in the classic by dint of ten months of qualifying competitions on the Bassmasters Trail, fishing in tournaments that ranged from the boulder-strewn St. Lawrence River in upstate New York to the lime-green desert lakes of Utah and Nevada to the murky old TVA impoundments in the very heart of the Bass Belt. A year of hard casting has come down to these three days. Now here they are, thirsting for glory, sizing each other up, wondering who among them will be standing in the Richmond Coliseum three days from now with his day's catch flopping on the scales as twelve thousand fans howl in awe at the new King of Bassdom.

The Bassmasters. They are stolid men with thick, brown hides and crow's-feet around their eyes from constant squinting in the sun. They wear denim shirts crowded with the patches of their corporate sponsors: Zebco reels, Skeeter boats, Strem fishing line. They come from places like Arkadelphia, Arkansas; Broaddus, Texas; and Gravois Mills, Missouri. There is a musky smell about them, the brackish smell of the river. Their hook-scarred hands are redolent of outboard gasoline, Skoal tobacco, and gill slime.

The forty-one boats crouch in the water—broad and square in the sterns, sharp-nosed in the prows. Forty-one American flags fly over the transoms. The big Evinrudes splutter and cough and blue fumes seethe from the frothy swirls of the propellers. The raspberry polyflake finish on the boats catches glints of the morning light. On board, the liquid-crystal instrument panels cast a dim green glow as the gauges register the pH of the water, the temperature of the water, the light intensity of the water, the depth of the water, the structure of the bottom, and the presence or absence of fish. The swiveling captain's chairs rise from the carpeted casting decks, upholstered thrones surrounded by arrays of electronic footpedals and kill switches. The aerated livewells bubble with fresh oxygen. Boat by boat, the tournament officials peek into the livewells to ensure that none of the men has sneaked any previously caught fish on board.

On the dock, a few extra-loyal wives, still half-asleep, wave their husbands off to battle. Also in the crowd is an eleven-year-old boy named Woody who rose at five this morning and rode his bicycle down to the boat landing to catch a glimpse of his favorite fishermen, the ones he'd seen on *The Bassmasters* cable television show countless times before. In a sweep of the eye, Woody can see the full pantheon, bassin' giants like Hank Parker, Tommy Martin, Larry Nixon, Guido Hibdon. Roland Martin, towheaded author and television star who has built a world-famous bassing resort on Florida's Lake Okeechobee. Gary Klein, the fair-haired Californian who claims he's never had a *real* job in his thirty-two years. Woo Daves, the local favorite, a little fireplug of a fellow out of Chester, Virginia. And in the far corner of the cove, keeping off to himself, perhaps the greatest bassman of all time: Rick Clunn, the veteran from Montgomery, Texas.

There may be more consistent bassmen than Rick Clunn; there may be fishing personalities who are better known and better loved; there may even be a few in the bassing world who have earned more money over the years. But when it comes to high-stakes fishing tournaments like the Bassmasters Classic, Rick Clunn is the undisputed king. No one can outfish him in the clutch. He has won an unprecedented three BASS world fishing championships and the coveted Angler of the Year Award; he has also won major titles on rival bass-fishing circuits, including two U.S. Opens and the Red Man All-American. All told, Clunn has earned more than a million dollars in tournament prize money, and twice that in endorsements and corporate sponsorships.

When Clunn is having a good day—which is often—he is very nearly unstoppable. He fishes with a chilling, cyborg efficiency, which accounts for his nickname among sportswriters: the Ice Man.

I have been selected to be the Ice Man's "observer" for the day. As part of tournament protocol, each of the pros is randomly paired each morning with a different writer who serves as an official witness to discourage cheating. Many sportswriters have found these all-day outings to be ideal for conducting interviews with the pros, but this won't be the case for me. Rick Clunn is notorious for tuning out the world—his boatmate included. He can go a whole day without saying a word. He likes to shut out the extraneous dock-talk and contemplate the day's work in perfect silence. Even when the fishing is over and he's returned to the hotel, Clunn observes a strict regimen of mind purification. No TV. No newspapers. No heavy meals or unnecessary conversation. People often mistake his quirky introspection for rudeness. "I'm warning you," Clunn says as I climb into the boat. "I don't want you to think I'm being impolite. I'm filtering out my externals. You're going to be bored out of your mind. All you're going to do is sit there for eight hours and stare at my butt!"

The details of Clunn's life story are well known to viewers of *The Bassmasters:* How he gave up his comfortable job as a computer programmer for Exxon. How his wife, Gerri, supported him and their two daughters through the lean years. How at the 1984 Bassmasters Classic in Arkansas, he caught a record seventy-five pounds of bass to win the tournament, and then stood alongside Governor Bill Clinton and Vice President George Bush to tell the adoring crowds: "Only in America can a boy grow up to make a living chasing little green fish!"

Rick Clunn is something of a mystic. A lot of the other fishermen think he's daft, with all his strange talk of Zen Buddhism and *Jonathan Livingston Seagull.* He says he experiences "visions." He has a black belt in hapkido, a Korean martial art that stresses mind control. He's been known to wear disguises out on the water so that the other fishermen can't recognize him. For reasons that no one can understand, he buys only hooks that are manufactured in Europe. Sometimes he camps by the lakeside the night before a tournament to get every cell of his body "in tune" with the energy fields of the water. "You have to achieve a spiritual connection to the environment," he explains. "You have to *be* the bass."

Whatever the other fishermen may think of Clunn's unorthodox methods, they can't argue with the results. Clunn is an intuitive genius at solving the great puzzle that is modern bass fishing. He can instantly break down the environment into its constituent parts—the current, the time of day, the season of the year, the wind, the clarity of the water, the approaching cold front or thunderstorm, the foliage, the submerged human garbage, and the hundred other variables that factor into the vast and ever-changing calculus—and then superimpose that calculus over what he knows about the capricious behavior of bass. "It's an enormous puzzle that you're constantly trying to put together," Clunn says. "If you want to catch a bass, you're going to have to understand his world down there. It's a tremendous challenge to your mental being."

Still, the Ice Man hasn't won a Bassmasters Classic in six years. This is the third year in a row that the tournament has been held on the dingy tidewaters of the James River, and so far Clunn has been jinxed. The first year, 1988, Clunn ended up in eighteenth place with a paltry sixteen pounds. The second year he did a little better: tenth place, with a total weight of twenty-two pounds, eleven ounces. But this year, Clunn is confident that the trophy is his. How does he know? He had a vision. In fact, he looks like he's having a vision right now. He sits mute in his boat and stares vacantly over the iron-colored river, like a man in a voodoo trance.

An official tournament vessel slips through the throng of bass boats and circles in front of the dock. Inside the boat is a strapping man in a white cowboy hat who holds an electronic megaphone. "Uhhhh, gentlemuhn . . ." the man announces in a heavy Alabama drawl, with a note of solemnity in his voice. He clears his throat, removes his hat. The Bassmasters know the cue. They all bow their heads as Ray Scott, the man who more or less invented the sport of big-league bass fishing, says the morning prayer.

"Heavuhnly Father . . ." Scott begins, his megaphone slightly squeaking with feedback, ". . . bless each and evuhry one of these fishahmuhn here today. Lord, watch over'm as they make their way to their favuhrite holes this mornin'. Let them enjoy an All-American experience on the waddah, and return them safely to us. In Jesus' name, Aaaaaaaaaa*men*."

One by one, the fishermen blast off for distant points on the James. The fiberglass noses rise magnificently over the surface. Soon the sleek boats are hydroplaning at forty . . . fifty . . . sixty miles per hour. A few of the fishermen speed upstream toward the slumbering skyline of Richmond, but most turn downriver, gliding past the antebellum plantations and duck marshes of the Lower James and on toward the salt line near Williamsburg.

Finally, Clunn's name is called, and we slip out of the cove for the river channel. The wives all turn from the dock and sleepwalk back to their cars. But Woody, the eleven-year-old boy from down the road, doesn't budge. He wants Ray Scott's autograph. "Why, sure, little fella," Scott says, bending down to sign the proffered sheet of paper.

Beaming, Woody hops on his bike and races home for breakfast, with the engines of the Bassmasters still roaring through the land.

"YOU CAN ARGUE THAT BASS fishing is a huge waste of time and money," Scott admits. "But what a wholesome way to blow your paycheck! What a wholesome disease it is! The ancient Assyrians used to say that the gods do not subtract from a man's allotted life span the hours he spends fishing. The urge to fish is deeply embedded in the human soul. Theoretically, we came from the water. And the water still attracts us, pulls us like a magnet. Some of us want to swim in it. Some of us want to look at it. But there are others of us out there who have to *fish* it. It's a primeval motivation."

Ray Scott is the founder and president of the Bass Anglers Sportsman Society (BASS), a national federation of two thousand amateur fishing clubs that is headquartered in Montgomery, Alabama. Since its inception in 1967, BASS has been the organization chiefly responsible for turning the lazy pastime of the Deep South into a commercial juggernaut. The BASS tournament circuit has created a new class of sports celebrities and helped fuel the technological transformation of angling in America. Today, Scott is recognized as a folk hero, the father of a new sporting universe for the rural man. To fishermen across the country, the jowly ex-insurance salesman in the trademark Stetson hat and lizard-skin boots is known as "Mister Bass."

Drive down any interstate in America for five minutes and chances are good you'll see one of Mister Bass's crested logos, with its leaping, gape-mouthed fish, pasted to the window of some mud-splattered Bronco or Suburban. There are an estimated twenty million bass anglers in the United States. More than 80 percent of all fishing tackle purchased in the United States is devoted to the capture of a single species of fish—*Micropterus centrarchidae,* the black bass. Once the butt of jokes on *Saturday Night Live* (Dan Aykroyd got a lot of mileage out of a skit about the "Bass-O-Matic," a special blender that grinds up fish into tasty shakes), the bass has become the All-American sport fish. "The most sought-after critter in America," Scott calls it.

Scott's various angling ventures include a popular cable television show and *Bassmaster* magazine, a slick monthly journal with a readership of 2.5 million and an advertising rate of $20,000 per page. Scott's bass empire generates $30 million in revenues each year. "I know this sounds like something Jim Bakker would say," Scott told me, with an odd mixture of pride and embarrassment, "but it all rolled out for me, just like it was providential. I didn't ponder it for a second. I knew bass fishing was ready to emerge from the lily pads to the front page. I knew there was this subculture out there. I could feel the enthusiasm. All I had to do was roll away the rock and let that guy out. Now everybody's got the bug. These people are critically ill!"

For the bassophiles, the Bassmasters Classic is the Super Bowl, the Masters, the World Series. First held in 1970 on Nevada's Lake Mead, the classic is the crowning event of the tournament season. Since bass fishing isn't much of a spectator sport, the main attraction is the weigh-in ceremony, a kind of fishing pageant cum boat show held each afternoon before crowds of ten thousand or more. While Scott works the audience in his rodeo announcer's brogue, the fishermen make their grand entrance. Seated in their boats towed by glistening Chevy trucks, they make a triumphal half lap around the arena, like charioteers in the

Circus Maximus. One by one, they hold up their fish for all to see. The bass are then placed in perforated plastic bags and weighed on an enormous set of digital scales.

Typically, the fishermen haul in more than seven hundred pounds of bass during a classic, but it's not the massacre it seems. Few of the fish perish and none ends up in a frying pan. BASS practices a policy of mercy called "catch-and-release." All fish under twelve inches are immediately thrown back, and keepers are handled with extraordinary care. The contestants are penalized one ounce for every "deceased" fish they bring in. After the bass are weighed, BASS technicians place them in a metal holding tank filled with cold water and a bright green liquid called Jungle Tournament Formula, a "scientifically designed" electrolyte potion that helps keep fish calm and infection-free until local wildlife authorities can return them to the river.

Though a special cash prize of $1,000 is awarded for the biggest fish caught each day, the tournament is ultimately decided on cumulative poundage: the Bassmaster with the largest weight tally at the end of three days wins the $50,000 check. Often the decision comes down to a matter of ounces.

More than a fishing derby, the Bassmasters Classic is a carnival, a trade show, and a kind of family reunion. It is the annual mecca for the nation's bassheads, a theme-park pavilion erected to the greater glory of a piscene god. Tens of thousands of fisherfolk come from all over the country to inspect the newest rods and reels, to finger the latest electronic paraphernalia, and to collect autographs from the pros. They plan their vacations around the classic, dragging their poor wives and kids from booth to booth. They study the endless charts and diagrams purporting to explain the fish's breeding and feeding habits. They stare lustfully at the live bass swimming in bubbly green aquariums. Everyone in the fishing industry puts in an appearance: boat manufacturers, lure designers, outdoor writers, resort owners, fishing guides. For three days, they mill about the huge convention center, spinning fish stories, collecting freebie lures, and taking comfort in just being around so many others who are suffering from the same sickness.

"There's a certain amount of peer pressure involved in bass

fishing—no question about it," Ray Scott says. "People are parrots. They like to copy each other. They want to feel like they are part of some larger world. You can build a world around anything if you take the vertical approach. You've got to find that sleeping demand and amplify it, magnify it, exaggerate the need! In other words, don't try to do every species of fish. *Specialize!* Just pick one and do it better than anyone else. One of the great things about this crazy country of ours is that you can specialize in anything. Hell, you can specialize in salt and pepper shakers if you like. Or better yet, *just* the salt shakers. In my case I specialized in a fish, and built a whole world on it."

Lately, though, Scott has diversified. He's set up something he calls the White Tail Institute, a kind of hunters' think tank that conducts scientific studies on the foraging and breeding habits of the white-tailed deer, which he calls "the second most sought-after critter in America." Among its various projects, the institute is building a deer sperm bank for future eugenics studies. To that end, Scott has been collecting the testicles of trophy bucks. He's also marketing a high-protein variety of clover that he claims "the deer just can't resist." He advertises that all a landowner has to do is plant a plot of the new miracle seeds in the spring, and when deer season rolls around, it'll be a cinch to bag a big one. Scott admits it all sounds a little strange, but says, "I think way-out sometimes."

BY MOST YARDSTICKS, the bass doesn't measure up as a sport fish. The muskie is a more aggressive fighter. The walleye tastes better. The trout is more elegant and makes a nicer trophy on the wall. The catfish yields a finer filet. A fisherman can fill up his stringer faster with perch or bream or crappie. And the bass is not especially large, usually weighing no more than five pounds.

Even fanatics will acknowledge that the bass is not much to look at. Red Smith, the Pulitzer Prize–winning sportswriter, once described *Micropterus* this way: "He is thick lipped and pot-bellied. Loop a watch chain across his bay window and he would look like a Thomas Nast caricature of vested interests." The bass is an extremely scaly fish with splotchy green flanks and a pale underbelly peppered with tiny black flecks that look like skin cancer. Its spiky dorsal fin gives it a vaguely prehistoric look. As if its exterior weren't ugly enough, the bass will graciously exhibit its insides, too: You can look down its yawning, cartilaginous mouth and plainly see its guts. Its gills open wide, exposing pulsing ringlets of blood-rich flesh.

But the bass has something going for it: a confounding personality. It is a moody, inscrutable phantom of a fish. "The reason we're all after the bass so much is that we can't figure him out," Ray Scott explains. "He's as unpredictable as Wall Street. The bass is a little like a cat. He's a solo operator. He doesn't pal around a lot. There's a certain mystique about him. You want to know what makes him tick. He'll drive you crazy!"

For all its feline fickleness, when the right bait floats by in the right way at the right time, and all the other environmental conditions are right, the bass can strike ravenously and without mercy. The bass undergoes a dramatic personality change, entering what is called "the Feeding Mode." It becomes, according to Red Smith, "the swaggering bully of lake and stream—truculent, greedy, overbearing." Says Rick Clunn: "He's a brute and a redneck and a predator. He'll hit just about any kind of bait, depending on his mood. He'll also strike for reasons unrelated to food. He'll snap at a lure just because he doesn't like the noise it's making. He would be scary if he could grow to fifty pounds. He'd literally eat children who were wading in the water—would just jump up there and take them off the bank."

Bassers compare their style of fishing to hunting, and often talk about their quarry as if it were not a fish at all, but some kind of menacing wild beast (a common term for a big bass is a "hawg"). It's hardly the "contemplative man's recreation" that Sir Isaak Walton rhapsodized about in his 1653 paean to the English outdoorsman, *The Compleat Angler.* When old man Walton went "afishing," as he called his serene sport, his maxim was "Study to be quiet." But there is nothing quiet about modern bass fishing. It is a brawling, labor-intensive process, with bleeping electronic encumbrances and big engines grumbling at full throttle. "Bass fishing is like a chase," says Clunn. "You are *pursuing* something, not waiting for it to come to you. A lot of people like to go fishing as an escape from the demands of their life. They want a peaceful and uncomplicated situation. Well, bass fishing is not for them."

Because bass tend to live in murky waters, in dark, weedy lairs deep in the shadows of stumps and rotting tree limbs, they rarely get a good look at their bait. But they don't need to. The bass is such an aggressive fish that it may strike at the slightest provocation: a strange movement in the water. A silver flash of light. An unfamiliar smell or color. It may strike out of curiosity, surprise, or pique. Thus the bass fisherman may try to taunt and rile his prey in the way that the matador agitates his bull. Many of his lures are designed purely to grab the bass's attention. They shimmer and pop in the water. They are rigged with fluttery tassles and bright green skirts and spinner blades that swivel and whir through the weeds. They have names like the Bomber, the Hula Popper, the Devil's Toothpick, the Big, Bad LeRoy Brown. They are agile little annoyances that can invade all the bass's favorite hideouts. There are surface lures, deep-diving lures, and lures that bounce along the bottom. There are lures that are designed to travel through Sargasso Seas of hydrilla and milfoil weed without getting hung up. Some are amazingly lifelike replicas of real creatures—minnows, worms, crayfish—and some are bug-eyed mutations of warped Day-Glo plastic, melted monsters straight out of a Dali painting. Some are coated with the scent of pig fat to arouse the bass's sense of smell. Others have hollow cavities that are filled with tiny ball bearings that rattle loudly in the water. A trout wouldn't think of biting one of these garish torpedoes, but to the bass they hold a strange appeal, triggering some atavistic reflex to avenge violated turf.

"The black bass is eminently an American fish," argued naturalist James Henshall, an early advocate of bass fishing. "He is wholly unknown in the Old World except where recently introduced, and exists naturally, only in America." In Henshall's estimation, delivered in his 1881 treatise *Book of the Black Bass*, the scrappy, irascible bass behaved as an American sport fish ought to behave. It was the Everyman's fish. It was a survivor. It stood up for its rights. It was a creature of appetites. What it lacked in refinement and grace it made up for in sheer lust for living. While the effete trout might insist on the delicacy of a newly hatched fly, the bass would eat anything that was set before it. While the trout required a certain fragile balance of temperature and oxygen and current conditions, the bass could live practically anywhere, and could be caught any season of the year, any time of day, in any kind of weather. "He has the faculty of asserting himself," Henshall observed, "and of making himself completely at home wherever placed."

BBBRRRRRRRRRRrrrrrrrrrrRRRRRRRRRRRRRRrrrrrrrr!!!!

The James River valley slides by at sixty miles an hour. Foam spews over the bow. I am sitting deep in my bucket seat, cinched in tight, my life vest buckled. Rick Clunn is at the wheel, his head tucked behind the windshield. Watching him negotiate the river channel, I realize that in addition to being an expert fisherman, a Bassmaster must also be something of a speed demon, a NASCAR racer of river and lake.

Twenty miles downstream, Clunn kills the engine and glides to his first hole. He opens the bright red locker and selects one of his five rods. And then, without saying a word, he climbs to the casting deck and goes to work.

Rick Clunn is a lean, tautly built man with ginger-brown hair. He speaks softly in a Texas Gulf twang that is as sharp as turpentine. He is forty-four years old, but has a face that could belong to a boy of fifteen or a man of sixty. He has frosty, slate-colored eyes that seem simultaneously spacey and intense. There is a jittery restlessness to his movements in the boat, but his face is calmly absorbed in concentration, his mental energies neatly husbanded. He works his mouth into strange contortions. His tongue curls and slides around with his casts, as if *it* is doing the casting. He has the surefootedness you'd expect from someone who spends 130 days a year in a bass boat. His tiny feet look like suction pods on the casting deck. Sometimes he stands on one leg and drapes the other over the bow, keeping it cocked at the knee, so that from a distance he looks like a stork. He works the foot-powered trolling motor like a wah-wah pedal, inching the boat toward his chosen targets in quiet spurts of humming energy.

Today he is wearing polarized sunglasses, fuschia shorts, and a denim shirt discreetly sprinkled with a few company logos—companies, he says, that he actually believes in: Daiwa. Tracker boats. Poe's plugs. A sticker on Clunn's tacklebox says, DON'T MESS WITH TEXAS.

Watching Rick Clunn fish is an exhausting experience. He is what is known as a "Run 'n' Gun" fisherman, which means that he moves around a lot, bouncing from hole to hole in a frenetic effort to "eliminate unproductive water." It is not uncommon for him to cover 150 miles in a day. Sometimes he will stop at a hole, make a single cast, and then head downriver ten miles before stopping again. Once he finds a "productive" stretch of water, he works at breakneck speed. It is said that Clunn is the fastest caster in the sport, averaging around five thousand tosses per tournament. He can't keep still. Now he's kneeling, now he's sitting down, now he's standing up again. He is constantly changing rods, tying on new lures, checking the depth sounder. His movements are carried out with an urgency bordering on desperation. He skips lunch. His eyes methodically scan the water, searching for promising holes. He always seems to be thinking three or four casts ahead, like a rock climber strategically plotting his course. The barrages of casts come so fast that the component sounds begin to blur together: the wheeze of the line overhead, the splash of the fat lure in the water, the rapid grinding of the reel's gears.

Clunn catches his first bass on a bogus worm in a pile of submerged riprap. The initial strike is fierce, but the battle is over in five seconds. Clunn lands the bass without fanfare, removes the purple worm from its grisly maw, and tosses the fish into the livewell. "Two pounds," Clunn says, his tone expressionless. He hurls his lure back into the James as if nothing has happened. The captured fish thumps against the side of its tank. At regular intervals, the timers in the livewells pop on, and fresh oxygen pumps into the swishing chambers.

Five minutes later Clunn is working a surface lure along the edge of a rotten dock, threading it in and out of the creosote pilings. Suddenly he spots a suspicious-looking ripple thirty yards off. He glances over at the Hummingbird depth sounder and sure enough, scads of fish (to me, little red blurbs) dart across the high-definition screen. *Wheeeeeeeeeeze-Splooosh.* He hits the spot on a dime, taking care to avoid the mossy ledge to the left, the clump of cattails to the right, and the live wire overhead. But nothing bites. *Wheeeeeeeeze Splooosh.* Another perfect cast. This time—*Bam!* A strike. The rod buckles under the weight. Clunn hauls in his second fish of the day, but he is unimpressed. "Pound," he mutters, placing it in the livewell. "Maybe pound'n a quarter."

Clunn may catch as many as twenty bass during a day's fishing, but he is allowed to bring only five to the weigh-in ceremony. Thus he must constantly cull his livewell, replacing the smaller specimens with ever larger ones to ensure that the final collection represents, in effect, the day's "greatest hits."

Sportswriters often compare bass fishing to golf. They note how the bassman moves from hole to hole, sizing up his terrain, selecting his rod and lure with the same discrimination that a linksman uses in choosing his iron. But as I watch Clunn fishing, the comparison that keeps coming to my mind is not golf but *dentistry:* he methodically works the river, flossing the banks, brushing the weeds, scraping the stumps clean, constantly changing his tools for greater precision, taking little X-ray pictures of the unseen cracks and cavities—laboring, all the while, in a confined world of swiveling chairs, pneumatic booms, bubbling chemicals—until suddenly, the fish answers the command and bites down hard, so that Rick Clunn, River Dentist, may finally pull the offending specimen up by the roots.

Clunn began delving into what he calls "the mental stuff" early in his professional career—in the mid-1970s. He found that by visualizing the next day's fishing, he could predict the outcome of his tournaments in sometimes uncanny ways. He could predict how many fish he'd catch. He could even predict where the bass would be, and how large. Sometimes he would experience magical days on the water, days in which everything played out exactly the way he'd visualized it. Sometimes the fishing would be so precisely executed, so beautifully choreographed—so nearly perfect—that he felt he had broken through a mental barrier and entered a higher realm of pure intuition. In those moments, he felt a clarity of perception that was almost frightening to him. He called it being "in the flow."

"It was kind of like skipping through a door into a new dimension," Clunn explains. "It usually would come at a point of pure exhaustion in which I was ready to give up. My intellect would shut down and suddenly something else would take over."

The problem, for Clunn, was that these moments of inspiration did not occur with any consistency, and they did not last long, sometimes only a few precious minutes. They could backfire, too: a moment of pure "intuition" could prove to be nothing more than a dumb hunch that led him on a wild-goose chase. "It was a mystery to me. How could I access this thing? How could I control it? What part of my being was it coming from? I knew there was something else going on here that I had to understand."

So Clunn hit the books. He read Whitman and Thoreau. He read the Koran. He studied Hindu and Buddhist philosophy. He read a smattering of Plato and New Age literature. He devoured biographies of great historical figures, men like Mozart, Einstein, and Pasteur, to find out how they experienced their breakthroughs. Over time, Clunn began to develop an angling "philosophy." He felt that the only way he was going to improve his fishing was to step *outside* of it. His regimen was simple: Pare down your life. Follow your instincts. And integrate yourself with the total fishing environment.

You might be fishing in a cove one afternoon when a bird flies over your head. That bird is not inconsequential. It may provide clues to the whereabouts of bass. It may be that the bird is pursuing shad or crayfish. It may be that it is eyeing a particular insect in the water. "Everything is made of one hidden stuff," Clunn says, quoting Emerson. "It is a giant play out there, and we are all actors in it—the birds, the fish, the water, the wind. And humans, too. We sometimes think we are superior to the natural world, apart from it. We keep forgetting that we are nothing but little molecules and electrons, an energy field."

For Clunn, tapping into the hidden stuff is a matter of consciously turning on the unconscious. This is a tricky task that Clunn compares to "exercising an atrophied muscle." It is a matter of meshing yourself so completely with the environment that you "become" the water, become the fish, become the lure threading through the weeds—like the Zen warriors who imagined they were arrows. Clunn says, "Fishing, to me, is just a small scenario in all the scenarios of life. It's a pure vehicle for learning about the inner mind. As soon as I stop learning, I reckon I'll quit and do something else."

Late in the afternoon, when the day's fishing is almost through, Clunn works beside a collapsed duck blind at the mouth of a small creek. A fine drizzle pecks at the water surface. He climbs into his neo-prene rain-suit "system" and remains dry. Across the creek, obscured behind a stand of cypress trees, is an antebellum mansion with a greensward sweeping down to a boathouse. Clunn spots the cypress trees and starts working along their roots, bombarding the folds and pockets. *Wheeeeeeeze Splooosh*.

He glances at his watch. He grimaces. A half hour until check-in. The impending deadline reanimates him, and he executes his casts even faster.

Suddenly I notice that another boat has pulled beside us. In it are three men with binoculars. They are not fishermen; they are *spectators*. Evidently they've spent the day tailing the Bassmasters in the hope of gleaning hot bassin' tips. "Oh, my God!" one of them gasps. "It's Rick Clunn! Right there! LOOK! Right *there!* Rick Clunn!! Shhhhh! What's he usin'?"

But the Ice Man is oblivious to their presence. He has stopped fishing for a moment, and seems to be daydreaming. He turns his face up into the rain and stares at a flock of birds.

"A-A-A-A-A-ND NOW, LADIES AND GENTLEMEN . . . it's . . . MISTER BASS!"

Ray Scott stands beside the digital scales and grins mischievously at the roaring crowds packed into the Richmond Coliseum. *Also Sprach Zarathustra*, the theme from *2001: A Space Odyssey*, booms over the loudspeakers, and spotlights swirl through the arena. Scott wears an electric-blue coat, a neckerchief, and his usual Stetson hat. He holds a wireless microphone in his hand. A giant laser image of a bass is danc-ing in the air over his head, its flickering outlines etched in lime green.

"Richmuhn, Viginiah!" Scott shouts to the crowd. "Let's make lotsa racket today! Let's blow the soft stuff off the roof!"

Today is the final weigh-in of the 1990 Classic. The pit of the coli-seum is carpeted in Astroturf and landscaped with plastic green shrubs. Hanging from the rafters are bunting advertisements from the classic sponsors: MotorGuide trolling motors, Delco Voyager batteries, Wran-gler jeans. Behind a blue curtain, BASS statisticians diligently plug numbers into their computers. Cameramen from *The Bassmasters* roam the arena taking footage.

One by one, the forty-one fishermen emerge from the main portal and display their fish. As it happens, Rick Clunn is the last man to come out of the chute. The crowd gives him a warm and boisterous welcome, but no one expects much from the Ice Man this year. He's had a mediocre tournament, and is far back in the standings: tenth place. To win today, he'll have to bring in eleven pounds, nine ounces of bass, which would be an astounding feat. "He's gotta have a lot of weight," Scott informs the crowd. "It's going to be very difficult. But Rick Clunn is no ordinary fishermuhn. It always pays to lay a little of yo' money on Rick Clunn."

Clunn digs into his livewell and pulls out a plump bass.

"Lip him!" Scott shouts. "Hold him up nice 'n' high! He's proud to be here!"

Clunn raises the fish above his head, its gills flaring, its tail flopping wildly in the air. The ten thousand humans let out a bloodcurdling scream, a scream that sounds a million years old. A dot-matrix sign on the scoreboard displays a running commentary:

N*I*C*E   C*A*T*C*H,   R*I*C*K!!!!

While Clunn reaches for another fish, Ray Scott keeps the patter going—"Whoa! Look at him! He's about to give himself a hernia on that one!"

Clunn drops a second big fish into the plastic bag. Another primal scream erupts from the crowd.

"Look out!" Scott's voice booms. "Two bass! Look at that! Another James River beauty!"

W*H*A*T   A   L*U*N*K*E*R!

Clunn pulls out another one, even bigger than the first two.

"He gonna win this thing!" Scott says, his voice now tinged with genuine surprise. "I believe he's gonna win it! He got any more?"

Clunn digs out still another one.

"Bingo! We *definitely* got us a winner!"

N∗I∗C∗E   G∗O∗I∗N∗G,   R∗I∗C∗K!

Clunn places a fifth fish in the plastic bag and saunters up to the grandstand, where Scott and the BASS technicians are waiting. The digital screen shows that Clunn's catch weighs eighteen pounds, seven ounces—the largest single stringer caught in the three James River Classics. Scott drapes his arm around Clunn's shoulder and for the first time today is speechless.

R∗I∗C∗K   C∗L∗U∗N∗N,   C∗H∗A∗M∗P∗I∗O∗N   B∗A∗S∗S   M∗A∗S∗T∗E∗R

Clunn is smiling from ear to ear. In the glare of the cameras, he holds up $50,000 worth of black bass.

—1990

Crawl Space

FOR THIRTEEN HOURS, David Gant bobbed in the blackness, his head pressed against a lucky wrinkle in the limestone ceiling. His scuba tank was out of air, his headlamp out of juice. He grew dizzy as the oxygen in his tiny crevice thinned dangerously, leaving him on the brink of unconsciousness.

Gant was a young logger from Alabama who'd dabbled with scuba diving but had no experience in caves. Late on the night of August 15, 1992, he'd gone spearfishing with a diving buddy in the mouth of a flooded cave on Nickajack Lake, not far from Chattanooga. The two men weren't supposed to be there: The fenced site warned trespassers of $25,000 fines. But local legends of two-hundred-pound catfish—reputedly fattened on a food chain enriched by the guano steadily dropping from resident gray bats—had been too tantalizing for the two friends. Sometime that night, the entrance clouded to "zero-viz" when one of the spearfishermen stirred up silt. Gant's friend panicked but managed to swim out of the murk and safely surfaced in open water. Gant unwittingly swam *into* the cave, bumping his tank along the ceiling until he found a cavity several thousand feet in. Exhausted and scared, he grabbed onto a stalagtite and treaded water in the darkness.

By the time cave rescue specialist Buddy Lane arrived on the scene the following day, the local incident commander had long since declared the operation a "recovery." In his judgment, it was inconceivable that Gant was still alive. Open-water divers had probed the initial cave passages, and now authorities were dragging the depths for the victim's body. Nearly one hundred people, including distraught members of Gant's family and a welter of TV reporters, were gathered around the site. It was a deathwatch.

Buddy Lane strongly advised the incident commander that it was premature to regard this fellow Gant as a corpse. Lane, the captain of Tennessee's Hamilton County Cave Rescue Unit and perhaps the nation's preeminent subterranean rescuer, had seen too many situations like this. Lane's team was the first and for years the only true cave rescue unit in the country. Over the past eighteen years, Lane had spearheaded or participated in some 150 underground extractions. Above all, his font of experience had taught him a few things about the tragedy of rushing to conclusions. Lane recalled, "I thought of myself in there all alone while everyone outside was declaring me dead."

IT'S NO COINCIDENCE that the nation's foremost cave rescue team is based in Chattanooga. The Civil War city, set in the hard limestone crotch where Tennessee, Alabama, and Georgia wedge together, is one of the leading karst regions of the world. Some eight thousand caverns are known to exist within an hour-and-a-half's drive of Chattanooga—and it's anyone's guess how many have yet to be discovered.

I met Buddy Lane on a dazzling autumn morning in Chattanooga. He was teaching a course in cave rescue techniques as part of a national wilderness medicine conference. A group of us followed him deep into a cave on Lookout Mountain and then proceeded to undertake a mock extraction, with one of the conference participants serving as the "victim" cinched to a stretcher.

Lane is a large, gangling man with thinning dark hair and a wry grin that lingers on his face as if there's a punch line coming. Despite his enormous size, he slips effortlessly through the cave's labyrinthine tunnels, a man utterly at home in the cold, wet dark. He runs a steel fabrication company, a position which has afforded him the wherewithal to range widely over the planet, "sport pitting" wherever the caving's good—Alaska, Switzerland, Belize, Honduras, New Mexico. At first, I found it inexplicably difficult to carry on a conversation with him until I learned that he has a prosthetic left eye, the result of a brutal facial injury he sustained in a cave in 1975. His numerous scrapes and close calls have convinced him that, in the end, "cavers have to look after our own—no one else is going to come after us when we get in a jam." Cavers are "specialist sportsmen" who themselves need specialist rescuers. "As our techniques and equipment have improved, we're increasingly getting ourselves into places where, if we get hurt or stranded, only other technically proficient cavers can get us out."

There is something of the good ol' boy in Lane's personality, yet he has a fiercely analytical intelligence and an amusing disdain for any sort of caving incompetence. His rescue anecdotes are peppered with descriptions of "dumbshits" and "doofuses." He has no tolerance for the sort of jackassed behavior that often necessitates an emergency call, yet once the mission is over, he clearly savors the stories.

Buddy Lane, a native Chattanoogan, ventured on his first caving trip when he was fifteen years old. "I knew immediately it was my calling," he said. He participated in his first cave rescue in 1973, and he was instantly hooked on the gritty intensity of the challenge. Cave rescues, he learned, are laborious affairs requiring, among other things, extensive rock-climbing techniques, intricate belays, and specialized litters. Belowground communications are difficult at best, since ordinary radio and cell phone signals can't travel far through rock. Rescuers often face the tricky task of squeezing the injured person through constrictions no wider than a man's shoulders, or hauling the victim up through gelid waterfalls. Every single piece of equipment that might be needed must be hauled underground. "A cave rescue is about the hardest thing there is; it's just a ton of work," he told me. "That's what's so great about it."

Although he works strictly on a volunteer basis, Lane has responded to rescue calls from all over the United States. In his most ambitious effort, he led the evacuation of an injured explorer from deep inside New Mexico's Lechuguilla Cave in 1991. Taking five days to reach the surface, the Lechuguilla rescue ended up being the longest, deepest, and technically most difficult cave extraction ever undertaken.

During big, complicated rescues, Lane typically spends much of his time aboveground, choreographing the efforts of law enforcement and emergency response crews. He is a quiet, cerebral field commander, expert at managing the constant flow of information and equipment while coordinating interagency communications so that the right people know what they're supposed to know, when they're supposed to know it. His mobile command post is a cobalt blue Suburban turbo diesel crammed with electronic equipment—two cell phones, two global positioning devices, a CB radio, a police scanner, several pairs of walkie-talkie radios, a console-mounted platform for his laptop, and a voice-activated tape recorder to capture distress calls. "I like to stay connected," Lane told me, as he trolled the dispatcher frequencies. He was the sort of man who was perpetually on call, always at least half-attentive to the airwaves. There was an unseen world beneath us, many thousands of miles of cavities and limestone tubes, and soon enough someone down there would need him.

BUDDY LANE APPROACHED THE rescue at Nickajack Lake with the coolheaded precision for which he is well known in rescue circles. Within hours of hearing that David Gant was missing, Lane's team succeeded in laying hold of an old map of the cave surveyed by the Tennessee Valley Authority before Nickajack Lake was created in 1969. A quick study of the map's vertical profiles convinced Lane there was a chance the cave had air pockets where Gant could still be breathing.

Lane's team then contacted a state emergency official who, in turn, persuaded TVA to do something extraordinary: open the floodgates of Nickajack Dam to bring down the level of the thirty-mile lake. The utility authority had never done anything like this before; it was a quarter-million-dollar squandering of reservoir water earmarked for hydroelectric power. Yet opening up the dam, Lane felt, was the only option that could turn a "recovery" back into a rescue.

Once the waters began to recede, Lane was itching to search the cave. But the turf-proud and woefully inexperienced rural emergency crew at Nickajack had insisted that Lane's services weren't needed. The situation, they assured him, was under control. This was no longer an active rescue, they reiterated. Gant was certainly dead.

Employing a little diplomatic finesse, however, Lane eventually persuaded the incident commander to let his unit explore a few of the cave's newly dry side passages. Lane and the team lieutenant, an impressively mustachioed park service cop named Dennis Curry, put on floatvests and slipped into the lake. The water level had receded fourteen inches since the TVA had opened the dam, enough of a drop that a steady breeze of potentially lifesaving air was now blowing through the cave: the first good sign.

For the next half hour the two rescuers finned their way two thousand yards in, to the point where they had but a few inches of airspace. With waning optimism, Lane swirled his fluorescent searchlight over the far reaches of Nickajack Cave and inched ahead.

NOT ALL CAVE EXTRACTIONS ARE rescues, of course—far too often they're corpse recoveries. While the stakes aren't as high, recoveries are no less demanding in logistics and technical prowess. In July of 2002, Lane and Curry were called in to retrieve the body of a Tennessee man named Jeffrey Wayne Young who had apparently committed suicide in a pit beneath a place called Gum Springs Mountain. A known methamphetamine user, Young was missing for three weeks when his Rottweiler, Spike, was discovered (alive, but sixty pounds lighter) inside the Gum Springs cave entrance. Lane and Curry followed a cookie-crumb trail of the victim's personal belongings—his marriage license, his house deed, then his own clothing—which he had evidently burned to create a light source while venturing deeper into the cave. Finally Lane and Curry reached the sixty-foot pit where Young had plunged to his death. Heaving the corpse out of the hole was a grim business involving miles of rope and multiple bolt settings in dangerously crumbly limestone. "The rock was rotten, and so was he," Curry says. "Even with two body bags, I couldn't get enough Vicks VapoRub in my mustache."

All types of people end up stranded in caves, some of them legitimate speleologists, Lane says, some of them "asswipes and shit-for-brains who have no business underground." A few years ago Lane and Curry cave-rescued a young, reefer-befogged man wearing cowboy boots who, in a series of remarkable maneuvers, managed to get himself in a crouched position with his head pinned between two five-hundred-pound boulders. How do cave rescuers feel about risking their necks to save people who, in a strictly Darwinian view of things, may not *deserve* the effort? "I let God sort that out," Curry says. "My thing is, I don't want them littering up the pristine caves."

Lane puts it another way. "Even doofuses," he says, "are entitled to a second chance."

DAVID GANT BRIEFLY LOST consciousness after thirteen hours floating in Nickajack Cave. Yet in what seemed a near-miraculous stroke of good timing, he was soon revived by a breeze of fresh air that came whistling through the passage. Gant then noticed with some curiosity that the water level had dropped, and that his tiny air pocket had grown by more than a foot. He couldn't see anything, but at least he could breathe again.

It was some eighteen hours into his ordeal that Gant experienced a spiritual vision. He was dying—he was quite sure of it. The cave had become a white tunnel. A pair of intensely bright lights approached. Everything was clear to Gant as he peered into the blinding luminance. "You're angels, aren't you," he said, "coming to take me away."

One of the angels had a funny mustache. "Dude," he said, "we've been called a lot of things, but never angels."

Eventually, Lane and Curry convinced Gant that this was not a hallucination, that they were of-this-world rescuers who'd come for him. Slowly the three men breaststroked out of the cave. When they emerged into the late-afternoon glow, the deathwatch was still in progress. Hundreds of people along the banks turned in stunned amazement. Waterlogged and weak, Gant stumbled ashore and embraced his family.

From start to finish, Lane and Curry had been on the scene just over an hour. Hurriedly, they packed up the rescue truck while the incident commander, visibly irritated that his show had been upstaged by outsiders, proudly took credit for what the papers would call the "Miracle at Nickajack."

Captain Lane's official report was considerably more understated. "Found victim alive," he wrote. "Everybody happy."

—2002

A Murder in Falkner

THE HILL COUNTRY around Falkner, Mississippi, is swallowed in kudzu vine, the climbing green thickets occasionally cut back to reveal brick ranch houses or trailers set back in the hollows. Driving along State Highway 15, I spot an old engine crankcase shimmering in the weeds, a pull-start lawn mower, a rusted tricycle turned on its side. Patchwork quilts flutter on a clothesline strung between loblolly pines. Geraniums sprout from the hub of a used tire that's coated with white spray paint. The tin roof of a collapsed barn tells me to SEE 7 STATES FROM ROCK CITY.

Along the highway, an elderly woman in a sundress creeps across the road to the row of mailboxes for her copy of the *Southern Sentinel*, the weekly newspaper printed in nearby Ripley. Kids in cutoff jeans slither in the mud by a hand-painted sign that says, BAIT.

The town of Falkner derives its name from the same Scotch-Irish family that produced the great novelist. (Back in the twenties, William Faulkner added the U as a literary extravagance.) Faulkner's great-grandfather, William Clark Falkner, settled in the area around 1842. A Confederate colonel and a flamboyant trial lawyer, Falkner was passionate, violent, impulsive. He made a name for himself at the age of eighteen, when he interviewed a convicted murderer in the local jailhouse the night before the man was to be executed. Falkner rushed his lurid account of the crime to a printer the same night, and made a bundle the next day selling copies of the murder story at five cents apiece to the hundreds who had gathered for the public hanging in the courthouse yard. Later in life, he gained notoriety for his turgid romance novels, such as *The White Rose of Memphis*.

Colonel Falkner was called, by turns, a great statesman, an incorrigible braggart, a Southern gentleman, and a cold-blooded murderer. He was also a fast-talking promoter who single-handedly arranged for a new railroad to be routed through the area in 1872. For a short while, the town that bore his name enjoyed a boom as a small-time cotton and transportation center.

But that has all changed. The local population has dwindled over the past century, a consequence of agricultural mechanization, depleted soils, and the declining importance of the railroad. Though the land is not rich enough for much farming anymore, the residents still plant milo and cotton and soybeans. Most people scratch a living from the ground however they can. Some raise gamecocks or pit dogs; others cut timber. Narcotics officials say some of the outlying fields are covered with marijuana, or "wacky-backy," as some of the locals call it.

The modern town of Falkner is scattered across a few dozen gulches and ravines, where the north and south forks of Muddy Creek merge. It is in the middle of Tippah County, one of the poorest and least populous in the state. Driving along Highway 15, one can see a redbrick high school, a Gulf station, a feed mill, and a water tower with the town's name painted in square letters. Falkner is a series of hills, a pocket of houses, a crossroads, a swath of fragmented images seen from a truck or a school bus. The people of Falkner are spread across a ten-mile landscape, living along the dusty gravel roads that course through the county. Because of this, affairs in Falkner often seem tentative, unresolved. Public grievances are seldom confronted out in the open. Grudges fester, suspicions flourish, and the stories people tell take on a life of their own—much more so than in a snug little town with a barbershop or a beauty parlor, where every day's rumors get tested and refined.

People in Falkner live close to their impulses, just as they did nearly

y ago, when an unknown local author penned what he called
erning code" of Tippah County. "A man ought to fear God
and mind his own business," the writer declared. "He should be
respectful and courteous to all women; he should love his friends and
hate his enemies; he should eat when he is hungry, drink when he is
thirsty, dance when he is merry, vote for the candidate he likes best, and
knock down any man who questions his right to these privileges."

IN MARCH OF 1981, Steven Vance Brown was something of a golden
boy at Falkner High. He was a tall and athletic sophomore, with a swirl
of blond hair brushed back in waves and plaintive blue eyes that made
the girls pass notes in class. There was only one flaw: he wore ortho-
dontic braces to correct a pronounced underbite.

Steve worked Saturdays at the Tropical Seasons nursery off Highway 15, and played three sports. He performed in the "gifted" singing
group at the school, and sang in the church choir. His music teacher at
school that year, Sammy Broder, arranged for him to appear on a wake-
up television show in Tupelo one morning, where he sang a little number called "A Sad Song." ("I know that life goes on perfectly/and
everything is just the way it should be/still . . . sometimes I feel like a
sad song/like I'm all alone without you.")

Steve wanted to enroll at Mississippi State in Starkville after high
school. One day he hoped to be a large-animal surgeon. It was only
natural that he was an active member in Future Farmers of America,
the largest organization at Falkner High School. Steve's father, Dwight
Brown, was the agriculture instructor. In fact, the Brown family lived
beside the school in a modest brick house, from which Mr. Brown—a
taciturn man with a sun-baked face—could watch over the vocational
ag shop.

Steve grew up in the heart of Falkner. He was the community's
favorite son from one of its most visible families, surrounded and
shaped by the school all his life. Grown-ups may have thought of him
as a saint, but to his Falkner peers, Steve was an ordinary country boy
who romped and partied with everyone else. Although Tippah County
was dry and Baptist teetotalers seemed to keep an eye on everything,

Steve and his friends bought beer from an old bootlegger in neighboring Benton County. Then they would cruise the streets of Ripley or meet at the Pizza Hut. Sometimes they'd have parties on Saturday nights at the edge of some secluded milo field, where they'd park their cars close together and turn up Rock 103 on the car stereos. These were the times when Steve and his football buddies in their letter jackets would wrestle and sing. The couples would neck in the shadows, and the raspy voice of a deejay named Red Beard would dance the airwaves out of Memphis, vanishing with the songs of the katydids into the Mississippi hills.

STEVE HUNG AROUND with a Falkner High junior named Mike Miskelley. They played football together. Though close friends, theirs was an attraction of opposites. Mike was the high school clown, a kind of buffoon tramping around the halls. He was small and agile and witty, with a suspicious grin creeping across a face that glowed with freckles and adolescent mischief. He was number seven on the football team, a cornerback. He had straight red bangs that edged across his forehead in a perfectly even line. Except for one late night when a cop caught him skinny-dipping with two others at a swimming hole in Booneville, Mike seemed to scurry like a leprechaun from one stunt to the next without getting caught. This was why Mike's folks nicknamed him "Slick"; though he was an incurable prankster, he could always fast-talk his way out of trouble.

Steve and Mike were hunting buddies. They hung out on lazy afternoons, listening to Mike's one Lynyrd Skynyrd tape, and shooting at anything that moved. "Hunting in Falkner just means a bunch of kids driving around the place with shotguns," explains a classmate. "There isn't anything else to do. You might hunt possum, coon, beaver, turtles. But usually you was just out hunting for something to pass the time."

On the afternoon of March 23, 1981, Mike and Steve planned to go out hunting for the first time in a long while. There had been something of a grudge between the two boys, and they had only recently decided to reconcile their differences.

The rift, not surprisingly, had to do with a girl. Impetuous and dreamy-eyed, Maggie Biggers was known at FHS as a romantic who wrote love poems. She was short and pert, with sandy-blond curls. She had the sturdy legs of a practiced cheerleader, and could turn flips and cartwheels without a thought. She played basketball for the Falkner Eaglettes. In the summer she would tan to a dark brown, and her hair would bleach out. There was a charm about her that attracted most of the boys. She had a reputation for being friendly and not a little forward, with a mercurial temperament. "She could turn on the tears at the snap of your finger," says Reggie Jones, a classmate. "And they was real live tears, too. The next second she could be all smiles again, like nothing ever happened."

Maggie and Steve Brown had been dating periodically for two years. Many of their friends believed that they had actually become engaged that winter. Maggie herself called it "preengaged," a status of amorous affairs that one Falkner classmate described as "not buying a ring, but just sorta looking at them."

Whatever the case, Steve's folks hadn't exactly approved. After all, he was only fifteen. He had plans to go on to veterinary school. The Browns thought Maggie was distracting Steve from his studies. They didn't want to see their son's grades suffer over a frivolous high school romance. So they told Steve to stop seeing so much of Maggie.

To make matters worse for Steve, Maggie had been seeing some of Mike Miskelley. Mike visited over at the Biggers home quite often between Christmas and March. Yet Maggie's friends claimed she wasn't genuinely interested in Mike, just fooling around with him to make Steve jealous. "She didn't have anything to do with Mike unless Steve was around," recalls one of Maggie's best friends, Tammy Garrett. Still, Steve had no way of gauging Maggie's motives. He was hurt by her disloyalty, especially since the other boy happened to be one of his closest friends.

Perhaps this accounted for Steve's moodiness that March. Steve's friends say he acted "spacey." They say he seemed distracted, troubled, forgetful. Others noticed he often fell asleep during classes. His grades plummeted. He ignored his buddies. Sometimes he didn't show up for work. Reggie Jones, a classmate who worked with Steve at the Tropical Seasons wholesale nursery, said Steve couldn't keep his mind on what he was doing. Their boss, Jim Wohlfarth, even called the Browns to express his concern about Steve's behavior on the job.

So on Monday afternoon, March 23, when Mike Miskelley planned to go out hunting with him, Steve was not exactly his old self. Yet it seemed the friendship had been repaired. The two boys were speaking again. As a token of the reconciliation, Mike decided to give Steve one of his family's new bullpups. The Miskelleys raised purebred bulldogs, and Mike knew Steve was fond of them.

The same day, Maggie and Steve had announced that they were back together again, though this time they had decided "just to date."

MIKE ARRIVED at Falkner High School around 4:15, after Steve's Monday-afternoon baseball practice. Mike was driving his light blue 1972 Gran Torino. He had to brake and accelerate with his left foot, because he'd injured his right leg during a football practice the previous fall and was still wearing a clumsy plaster cast.

Steve was waiting by the steps at the south end of the school, chatting with a teammate named Dwayne Hopkins. He was wearing lace-up work boots, a rodeo cap, denim jeans, a maroon sweatshirt, and a red coat with a patch advertising Wayne's Feed Company. Slung over his shoulder was his rifle, a bolt-action .22 Mossberg.

Steve hopped in. He laid his rifle next to Mike's 20-gauge double-barrel shotgun on the backseat. They said good-bye to Dwayne Hopkins and headed out Highway 370, toward the woods that lay between Falkner and Ashland.

TWENTY MINUTES LATER, Dwight Brown walked behind his house, saw Dwayne Hopkins sitting on the steps of the school, and waved him over. "Hey, Dwayne," he said, "you mind helping me with these here berry plants?"

"Sure, Mr. Brown, be glad to."

They worked together in the garden, planting the strawberries until just before five P.M. Then Dwight Brown walked back inside his house to watch the news on one of the Memphis television stations. Soon Dwayne's ride arrived, and he headed home for supper.

THE SAME AFTERNOON, some of the FHS girls had organized a slumber party to plan the decorations for the upcoming junior-senior banquet. Maggie Biggers and Sharon Hurt were staying over at Tammy Garrett's place for what promised to be a late night of laughter and gossip.

Maggie didn't arrive until around five that afternoon. The other girls were waiting for her. They noticed that Maggie seemed upset. "I've got to call Steve!" Maggie said. "I've got to reach him. He's got something to say to me."

Maggie was so worried that she couldn't concentrate. She was crying and pacing the floor. Tammy and Sharon tried to calm her, reminding her that Steve had only gone out hunting with Mike Miskelley for an hour or two. They couldn't imagine why Maggie would be so hysterical. "You don't understand," Maggie cried. "Steve has a rifle and he is going to kill himself! He loves me so much he is going to kill himself! We've done broke up for good, and he's so upset, he's going to shoot himself!"

AT 5:20, Dwayne Hopkins and his classmate Robbie Albertson were traveling west on Highway 370 when they spotted Mike's blue Torino coming toward them in the distance. When they passed each other, Dwayne rolled down the window and waved his hand at Mike. Dwayne was a little surprised when he noticed that Steve Brown wasn't riding in the car.

AT 6:15, three Falkner boys arrived early at the ag shop behind the school for a meeting of the Future Farmers of America. Mr. Brown had scheduled a meeting to make plans for a special agricultural contest, and all the boys, including Steve, were told to show up by 6:30. Jerry

Barkley and Randy Moore started working on a corn picker, giving it a fresh coat of blue paint. Timmy Hopper began shooting a basketball at a milk crate tacked to the wall. It was turning dark outside, and the lights from the shop were streaming out the windows. The boys had rolled a pickup truck halfway through the big sliding garage door and flipped on the radio.

Timmy missed a shot, and the ball rolled over toward a woodpile. He walked over and stooped to pick it up. He rose with the ball tucked under his arm, and recalls seeing Steve Brown, wearing a maroon shirt, standing in the doorway of the shop, no more than twenty feet away. "Going to look good, ain't it, Jerry?" Steve shouted over the music, pointing at the corn picker. Then he wandered through the shop and slipped out the back door silently.

AT 6:30 Dwight Brown walked into the shop. "Anybody seen Steve around here?" he asked.

"Yes, sir," Timmy Hopper told him. "We just saw him in here a few minutes ago."

MIKE WAS SHAVING in his bathroom around seven o'clock when Dwight Brown knocked on the front door of the Miskelley house on Clemmer Road, four miles west of Falkner. Steve hadn't returned home yet, and Mr. Brown was growing a little concerned. He thought Mike might know something. So Mike, with a dollop of shaving cream accenting his chin, sat down in the living room and recounted his version of the afternoon's hunt.

Steve was in a crummy mood in the car. He seemed withdrawn, melancholy. He stared vacantly out the window.

Together, the two boys drove out Highway 370 toward a woodland lake behind the Little Hope Primitive Baptist Church, about four miles from the school. They planned to hunt for beaver from the edge of the water.

Mike parked the Torino behind the Little Hope church, and the two ambled across an old cemetery—Mike with his shotgun, Steve with his rifle. Mike had to work twice as hard to keep up with Steve. The steel walking stob on his cast kept sinking into the soft red earth of the graveyard.

They hiked through some woods, kicking up the wet leaves with their boots. They found two old jars from a trash dump for target practice. Steve stood them up against a tree, and the boys took turns firing at them with Steve's .22 rifle.

Steve and Mike then wandered down to the edge of the lake, but found nothing to shoot. "C'mon, Red," Steve called to Mike, "there ain't no beavers down here." They decided to return to Falkner early.

But Steve said he wasn't quite ready to go directly home, where his parents wouldn't be expecting him for at least another hour. He asked Mike to drop him off at the Bank of Falkner, just around the corner from the school. Mike didn't ask questions. Clutching his .22, Steve climbed out and slammed the door. As Mike drove away he glanced into the rearview mirror and watched Steve receding into the twilit distance of Falkner. Steve was ambling down the railroad tracks by the bank, his rifle over his shoulder, hands thrust into pockets, head drooped forward in apparent contemplation.

Mike stopped by the Griffin's Grocery to get his weekly paycheck for his part-time job as a stockboy. His boss had designated Monday as payday, so the boys wouldn't blow all their money on the weekend. Then he bought some gas at the Falkner Gulf and drove back home. He arrived at around 5:35, returning his 20-gauge to the gun rack in his bedroom.

AROUND NINE O'CLOCK, Pam Biggers, Maggie's mother, called over at the Garretts' house to relate the news to the three girls that Steve was missing. Mrs. Biggers said her husband would be coming over soon to drive the girls to the school, where they would join the gathering crowd in the search. While waiting for Mr. Biggers to arrive, Tammy Garrett and Sharon Hurt tried to reassure Maggie, who seemed certain that something awful had happened to Steve. "I know it, I just know it," she said, "Steve's going to shoot himself. He's got himself a gun and he's going to do it."

*   ★   ★

"WHEN IT COMES down to it," Dale Biggers said while driving his Chevrolet to the school that night, "Miskelley will be the one. I told you not to fool with him."

Sharon Hurt and Tammy Garrett, riding with Maggie in her father's car, thought it strange that Mr. Biggers was already pointing fingers. Most people simply assumed Steve had run off for a while without calling home, as he had done several times before. The girls were convinced that Steve would turn up later in the evening. They suspected that Mr. Biggers had been drinking (he told them that he had been out hunting all afternoon).

A carpenter by trade, Maggie's father was known around the county as a man with a short fuse. Maggie's friends described him as a possessive father prone to issuing ultimatums; she seemed to be Mr. Biggers's favorite daughter, "his pick," as one friend described her. He seemed to watch over her with an eagle eye.

Because Mr. Biggers had recently suffered a serious back injury, he was no longer able to take on much carpentry work. One of his major sources of income was raising gamecocks, an activity on the fringe of legality. While the fights themselves are strictly outlawed, Mississippi has no statutes forbidding the raising of the birds. And in poor hill country like this, gamecock farming is a viable way to generate income from otherwise useless land.

Driving by the Biggers place, four miles east of Falkner, one can still see scattered across the front property scores of rusted metal drums staked lengthwise to the ground, each housing a separate rooster. Gamecocks must be chained apart to prevent them from killing each other, for they will instinctively fight to the death if free to do so. Once or twice a year, buyers from Mexico would come in and pay as much as $300 per gamecock. Biggers took special pride in his rooster-raising operation. "I got some pretty birds out here," he said on one occasion. "I like raising birds. I like it better than anything I've ever done."

Not all of the residents of Falkner had a high opinion of Dale Biggers. "He's taboo in the county," says one lifelong resident of Falkner. "You just don't want to rock the boat with him. He's a mean, hot-tempered man. Most people won't open their mouths for fear of meeting up with him or some of his cronies on a dark road late at night."

The circumstances surrounding the death of Dale Biggers's brother, Marshall Biggers, in March of 1978 led many Falkner residents to have special reservations about Maggie's father. Marshall was severely injured at Dale Biggers's home on the evening of March 1, taken by ambulance to Ripley, then rushed to Memphis's Baptist Hospital, where he died several days later. The death certificate on file at Shelby County Health Department lists the cause of death as "a severe blow to the head." No charges were ever filed; according to sources in the county court system, it was dismissed as "a family matter." As then–Tippah County sheriff Roy Yancy explained to me, no one was present in the Biggers home at the time of the incident except for the two brothers.

While many Falkner residents seemed to fear him, it's also true that Biggers maintained a close circle of friends and relatives. He lived in an area of Tippah County known as the Hatchie Bottom. The "Hatchie People"—as they are called locally—have developed a special notoriety through past generations. "Hatchie Bottom is a little place all its own," one resident told me. "Hatchie People won't have folks poking around in their business. They'll do anything to help a friend or destroy an enemy. It's all black or white, and they hadn't got no in-between."

ABOUT THREE DOZEN townspeople convened on the Falkner High School grounds that evening. People stood idly by the ag shop, trading opinions on Steve's whereabouts. Some of the boys wandered out with flashlights into the surrounding countryside, crying Steve's name.

It would be a long night for Falkner. Everyone helped out in some way. The Tippah County Sheriff's Department and the Mississippi Highway Patrol were notified. Friends stayed up until dawn consoling the family, drinking coffee in the Browns' kitchen. Dwight and Mary Ruth Brown were terribly upset. They feared that Steve might have run away for good, or worse, that he'd had an accident in some secluded place where no one could hear his cries for help.

* * *

MIKE WAS STANDING outside the ag shop when Maggie approached him. "What did you do with Stevie?" she asked. "Where'd you put him?"

"I didn't do anything with him, girl," Mike answered.

Mr. Biggers walked over and nudged his daughter aside. "Don't talk to him, Maggie," he said. "Just leave him alone. He ain't going to tell you anything."

THE MEN FORMED larger search parties to scour the back roads of Tippah County in trucks with spotlights. Some of the boys went on foot. After five hours of fruitless search, they finally decided to head home for a few hours of sleep. Mike Miskelley searched with a group of kids who covered the fields all around the school. By the end of the evening, Mike had walked his cast to shreds.

The searches continued through the week. Steve's disappearance so disrupted the community that half the students missed school. "There wasn't a whole lot of learning going on that week," Billy Bolden, the principal, told me.

Overnight, the town of Falkner had produced what seemed to be an endless supply of amateur sleuths. Everyone had his own theory regarding Steve's whereabouts. Had he been kidnapped, injured, or murdered? Did he elope with a girl? Had he slipped into a lake and drowned? Most people, however, had already ruled out the possibility that Steve had run away; his savings account had been left intact, and even his wallet was found at home.

As the days passed, more elaborate hypotheses evolved, stories that concerned drug trafficking, illicit deals, and vice of all kinds. It was speculated that Steve might have stumbled into some dirty business. All the latent fears and deep-seated suspicions of hill-country life suddenly ignited. In private circles, accusations flew, grudges resurfaced. People kept a cautious eye on each other. Others climbed into their trucks and drove around the county looking for their own answers.

Those who had heard about drug dealings in the area could easily imagine a scenario in which Steve walked into the wrong place at the wrong time. And no one could deny the prevalence of drug cultivation and trafficking in the remote hill country. "Marijuana could very well be the largest cash crop in Tippah County and, likely, in any poor area of the state where agricultural cultivation is not very successful," says Charlie Spillers, captain of the Mississippi Bureau of Narcotics for the north region of the state.

Of course, the people of Falkner were most curious about Mike Miskelley. Everyone wanted to investigate his story of the hunting excursion. And here the precise sequence of events and the corresponding times were absolutely crucial. Already there were "concerned citizens" out figuring up mileage and estimating elapsed time.

Then, too, people wanted to learn the sordid details about Maggie Biggers's romances with the two boys. It was only a matter of time before unflattering tales were told in the general community. There was an intriguing simplicity to the idea of a love triangle—a jealous sixteen-year-old moved by passion to dispose of his best buddy, all under the seemingly innocuous circumstances of a friendly hunt deep in the woods.

Mike could not exactly be called a suspect. Most people were still confident that Steve would turn up, so any kind of public accusation was premature. Second, several people had seen the two boys together and knew they had planned a hunting trip. It would seem to be the height of stupidity for Mike, if he indeed entertained the idea of committing murder, to plan it on an afternoon when a number of his Falkner classmates knew the two boys were supposed to be together in the woods with their guns. Third, the Miskelleys were a respected family in the county, with a reputation for decency and hard work. Wayne Miskelley was a contract electrician who was working on a TVA project, the Yellow Creek nuclear plant; Ann Miskelley worked at Kenwin's dress shop in Ripley, the county seat ten miles down the road. "The Miskelleys are fine folk," said Dwight Brown, Steve's father. "You're not going to find better people in Tippah County. And when I taught Mike, I gotta say I never had any trouble out of him."

Last, and perhaps most important, no one could discount the fact that three friends claimed they had seen Steve in the ag shop hours *after* the outing with Mike. (This had become the accepted version of

Steve's last sighting. It was reported in the local newspapers for many months, and the police authorities had begun their investigation on the assumption that the three boys were the last to see Steve Brown alive.)

It appeared that Mike was covered on every front, for even his description of the hunting trip seemed to fit with the evidence. There, in the graveyard of the Little Hope Primitive Baptist Church on the day after Steve's disappearance, a group of Falkner parents discovered Steve's bootprints running alongside the depressions left by the steel stob on the bottom of Mike's walking cast.

THE DAYS STRETCHED to a week, then two weeks, and Steve still did not turn up. Tippah County sheriff Chester "Pete" Crum, a soft-spoken man in his fifties, undertook a countywide manhunt. The search was meticulous—with four-wheel drives, horses, a forestry plane, several helicopters, and over a hundred residents organized by the volunteer fire department. The Game and Fish Commission dragged several lakes.

Some of Falkner's leading citizens, including Mike's father, formed the Steve Brown Search Committee and posted a handsome reward for "information that leads to an arrest and conviction." They staged a telephone campaign, securing pledges of money from industries and businesses to add to the reward fund. The committee printed and circulated two thousand bumper stickers bearing Steve's photograph and advertising the reward. A psychic from Memphis was consulted for tips on Steve's whereabouts. Child-search groups across the country were contacted, and thousands of flyers were distributed that read:

"This misfortune could have happened to our child or yours. He was reared in a Christian home in a small town of 255 residents. This is evidence that such things don't just happen in large cities where crime is high. . . . Steve collected baseball caps, not enemies, and took music, not drugs. His world was defined by the redbrick buildings of Falkner High School, and even the family home is on the campus . . . He spent Saturdays working in a nursery and Sundays in church. He visited his grandparents and the orthodontist, not the poolroom. He might take in a movie in Ripley, but only after asking for his parents' permission."

Several reported sightings didn't pan out. A woman named Beth Reed, a truck driver for a van lines company, said she had picked up a tall blond boy from Mississippi who seemed to fit Steve's description; she said she let him off at a 76 truck stop in Long View, Texas. In addition to this account, the Browns took several collect calls from people who claimed they'd seen Steve. But the reports never checked out.

As time slipped by, pressure began to build on the law enforcement officials to unravel the mystery of the disappearance. The ordeal had agitated the whole community. There were stories of prank phone calls, threats, and strange black limousines driving through the area. One Falkner mother discovered that her son, fearing that he was the next in line to disappear, had been sleeping for weeks with all the lights turned on and a loaded shotgun under his bed.

An energetic young Highway Patrol investigator out of Holly Springs named Kenneth Dickerson was assigned to the case. Dickerson said he had "checked into several leads," but nothing was turning up. All the officials could do was cross their fingers and hope that something would develop.

THEN IT EMERGED, the piece of evidence the investigators so desperately needed to proceed with the case. Maggie Biggers came forward with new information that suggested some level of involvement by Sammy Broder, the music teacher at Falkner High School.

Broder taught the "gifted" class in which both Steve and Maggie had been enrolled. As a singing coach and roving talent agent, he had cultivated many young performing artists in the area. A nervous man with a prim black mustache, Broder and his South American wife, Maria, had lately been inviting groups of students out to their place in Corinth for parties. The kids would tell their parents they were going to Broder's house for an evening of rehearsals for an upcoming singing engagement, and sometimes they would even spend the night. They would indeed rehearse, but often they would party and play music and watch films on Broder's VCR.

Broder was regarded by Falkner parents as a friendly but rather strange man. After all, this was a small town that, by nature, did not take kindly to outsiders. Not only was Broder from Corinth, but he had also traveled around a good bit and had a wife who was a foreigner. To locals, he seemed unsettled.

Sammy Broder was a teacher who seemed to dote on his most talented pupils. He collected photographs of them and even taped home videos of the kids for entertainment. His prize student was a boy named Kenny Graves. Kenny was considered the most talented one of the bunch. Broder liked him so much he once offered to adopt him. After Kenny, Steve was Broder's favorite. Broder even promised to take Kenny and Steve on a musical tour of Europe someday. "Steve wasn't a great singer," Broder later said. "But he was good, and I liked his values. I mean, he was somebody that everybody looked up to."

Sheriff Crum and Inspector Dickerson had already considered Broder to be a suspect. But they had no evidence to go on, other than a few wild rumors. What was more, Broder had an alibi that was seemingly airtight: he had been performing in Oxford for the Shriners Club with twenty people the night of Steve's disappearance. This led investigators to conclude that Broder could not have been involved in the kidnapping or murder of Steve Brown unless he had hired an accomplice. But until Maggie offered her account, the investigators could only speculate.

Maggie signed an affidavit on April 8, 1981, two weeks after the disappearance. Though she volunteered her statement to Sheriff Crum, her role in implicating Broder was never openly acknowledged or reported in the local papers. The affidavit told of the Thursday night following Steve's disappearance, when Broder took Maggie out to his house in Corinth before a scheduled singing engagement. She said the walls of his house were covered with photographs of Steve. She recalled that Broder answered a phone call and that during the course of the conversation Broder referred to Steve repeatedly. "I got his girlfriend here with me now," he said.

After he hung up, Broder showed a home videotape of Steve that made Maggie "cry and cry." Then he began to tell her a story about a recent evening when he showed Steve an adult movie on the VCR. At this, Maggie started crying again, but Broder told her not to worry because "Steve fell asleep during the bad parts." He showed her a room with a "big bed" where Steve supposedly had slept before. Then Maggie said she wanted to walk upstairs and visit a room where the kids would often hang out during Broder's parties, but he wouldn't let her. He told her he couldn't let her see it, because "it's a mess up there."

After Maggie's statement was released, the authorities began to question the parents of the students who studied under Broder. Some of them suggested that Broder could easily have had a motive for making Steve disappear. Perhaps something had happened one night at Broder's house, something that Broder feared Steve would tell his parents about; perhaps he feared this would jeopardize his teaching position at the high school. Thus, there was speculation that he had hired a hit man to clean up the situation on an afternoon when he had a surefire alibi.

Maggie's affidavit raised more questions than it answered, but it was enough to prompt further investigation by the authorities. Several days later, Sheriff Crum procured a search warrant, and the local police broke into Broder's home while he and his wife were away. They overturned furniture, flipped through personal letters, peered under mattresses and carpets. "I think they more or less ransacked the place," Investigator Dickerson later acknowledged. Though they didn't find what they were looking for, their interest was undiminished.

WHEN BRODER RETURNED HOME and found the place in shambles, he was naturally furious. He called the police, he called the highway patrol, he called an attorney; in a rage, he even called the Browns, thinking they must have had something to do with the search. (He came by the Browns' house the next day and apologized.) Broder threatened to sue the police for what he contended was an unwarranted search.

Meanwhile, Sheriff Crum began a more thorough investigation into Broder. The police interrogated him on several occasions. After doing some checking on his own, Crum made some interesting discoveries. Among other things, he found that Broder had a rather erratic employment history, moving across Mississippi from one teaching position to the next, year after year. Without explanation, Broder had been dismissed from the Alcorn County school system before coming to Falkner. "I've already found out enough about that man that we don't need the son of a bitch in our school system anymore." Sheriff Crum told one concerned mother whose son had studied under Broder.

Soon a group of outraged parents started petitions calling for the immediate removal of Broder from the North Tippah County schools; formal complaints were lodged with the county school board. Broder successfully defended himself, however, dismissing the movement to fire him as "a witch hunt." He managed to stay on the rest of the year, but some of his students, including Kenny Graves, dropped out of his classes.

SOON THEREAFTER, to almost everyone's surprise, the investigation ground to an abrupt halt. Locals say this was largely the result of Broder's decision to hire one of the most prominent trial lawyers in the state of Mississippi.

John B. Farese, Sr., had established an immensely successful criminal law practice in Ashland, the county seat of neighboring Benton County. A native of Boston who grew up in that city's Italian section, Farese married a Mississippi belle and studied law at Ole Miss during the fifties. As a young attorney, he established a reputation for representing blacks at a time when such a thing simply wasn't done.

A criminal trial for John Farese was a form of public entertainment, a match of wits in the shirtsleeve tradition of the old populist orators. Farese was perhaps the closest thing northern Mississippi had to a William Jennings Bryan. He was a brilliant performer who presented his arguments slowly, patiently, methodically, homing in on his central point, taking great care to avoid legal jargon that country juries might not understand. He was the sort of attorney who often hauled in props to the courtroom to make even the simplest of points—visual aids, hand-drawn diagrams, posters. In the end, he almost always won over the jury. (*Esquire* magazine listed Farese in a register of the nation's most successful trial lawyers.)

Farese's skills were so legendary, in fact, that they inspired this local witticism: If you commit a murder on Saturday, go to church on Sunday and call up Big John first thing Monday—and all your sins will be forgiven. "They say Big John will pat a man on the back just to find a place to stick in the knife," one Ashland resident says. "He'll read from the Good Book; he'll cry his eyes out; why, he'll do just about anything to get that jury on his side."

Political influence, reputation, rapport with the local folk—these were the crucial components to a successful defense. And these were precisely the qualities that Farese brought to his new client, Sammy Broder. A criminal investigation into Broder might well prove to be more trouble than it was worth.

With Broder retaining Farese, the police began backing off. They apologized profusely for having been so overzealous, and decided that Broder's relationship with Steve was not so mysterious after all. "We just really couldn't relate anything very strong to Broder," explains investigator Kenneth Dickerson. "He employed Mr. Farese as counsel, and after the search of his house was made, we couldn't even talk to him anymore without his attorney being present." Dickerson and Crum eventually dismissed Broder and his wife as a middle-aged couple who simply loved young people; Sammy Broder was no kidnapper or murderer, just a peculiar sort of man who probably had no business teaching in Tippah County.

So Sammy Broder faded from the picture, quietly resuming his teaching job with the tacit understanding, it seems, that he would leave Falkner once the year was over. Whenever investigators came around his house in Corinth, Broder simply told them to go see Farese, and that was the end of that.

IT WAS NOW May of 1981. Weeks had passed without anything significant turning up for Crum or Dickerson: no leads, no body, indeed, no provable crime. And yet the letters were pouring into their offices day after day, the pressure to solve the case forever building. The public cry for a solution even prompted the local authorities to request an FBI agent to look into the case.

Not only was it the biggest case Crum and Dickerson had ever dealt with, it was also becoming a matter of politics. If they could crack the Brown case, their reputation as law enforcement officials would be immeasurably enhanced. For Crum, it would help ensure reelection as Tippah County sheriff. For a young investigator like Dickerson, it could mean a coveted letter of commendation, or a promotion within the investigative division of the Mississippi Highway Patrol. High-profile cases like these don't come along very often, particularly in rural areas. When they do, it can be a real feather in an investigator's cap if he turns up enough evidence for a conviction.

THOUGH STEVE'S DEPARTURE had upset the kids at FHS, school soon resumed its normal operations. The parties and the baseball practices and the meetings of the Future Farmers of America (and its female counterpart, Future Homemakers of America) carried on as usual. Later in the spring, Maggie Biggers and Mike Miskelley began seeing each other again. They were always on the phone; they sat together in the back of their classes, passing notes and cutting up.

The rekindling of their romance no doubt disappointed Dale Biggers. Not only was Maggie's father protective of his favorite daughter, there was also some history between the Biggerses and the Miskelleys. One fall several years earlier, the community had been embroiled in a fierce debate over the matter of deer hunting with dogs. Wayne Miskelley was one of a number of Falkner residents who regarded deer hunting with tracking hounds as a low and distasteful sport. They claimed it was a dangerous practice that essentially allowed hunters to wait with their rifles in their four-wheel-drive trucks until their dogs illegally ran the deer out of posted lands. (The rationale: dogs can't read "posted" signs, so they can run wherever they like.)

On this occasion, a group of citizens led by Miskelley was determined to have the sport outlawed in Tippah County. Dale Biggers, on the other hand, was a vocal proponent of the practice. One night, when the Mississippi Game and Fish Commission staged a public hearing over in Holly Springs to permit debate, both Biggers and Miskelley showed up. There was a bit of an altercation between the men, and the meeting degenerated into a shouting match. Biggers and Miskelley had avoided each other since.

MIKE MISKELLEY WAS HOME with his mother, Nita Ann, and his brother, Todd, early on the evening of May 18 when Sheriff Crum and Investigator Dickerson knocked on the door. The kids were getting dressed to go roller-skating in Ripley.

"Mrs. Miskelley," Sheriff Crum said, "we've got a little statement here that we took earlier today from Miss Maggie Biggers over at her parents' house. Now, we're going to have to read it to you and Michael."

They all sat down in the living room and Sheriff Crum began to read:

> Me and Mike Miskelley were at Falkner School several days ago. Mike said, "I've got something to tell you. . . . I'm going to hell." I said, "If you ask forgiveness, you might not." I told Mike to tell me what it is. Mike said, "It is about Steve." His eyes got red. The next day he talked to me on the phone. Mike said, "It would have been me or him. I done it for a four-letter word call L-O-V-E, because of you. Because I loved you. I knew he was coming between us." I got off the phone. The next morning, I wanted to know the whole story. I told him I'd hate him if he didn't tell me. Mike said, "OK."
>
> The next morning at school Mike said, "You remember the Sunday before Steve was gone. He got jealous and mad at me. That Sunday, I dug a hole. I invited Steve to go hunting with me on Monday. I picked Steve up and we headed down Highway 370. Steve was upset, you know, he wasn't talking about much. We got to the woods and Steve had his gun. I didn't have a gun. There was a bucket and a Coke bottle we set up to shoot at."
>
> Mike said, "I saw where I had dug the hole but Steve didn't see it. This was the time I had to do what I had come to do . . . but I couldn't do it. Steve said, 'I don't believe we're going to find any beavers around here.' I saw the hole. I knew I had to do it. I turned my head and pulled the trigger. I turned back

around and I saw Steve take a couple of steps and he went to his knees. I looked at him and he sort of mumbled and gradually fell down."

Mike told me not to cry. I had started crying. I asked him, "Did it look bad?" and Mike said, "Not at all." I had to know everything, I said, "A twenty-two rifle, if you didn't aim it just right, it wouldn't hurt anyone." Mike said, "No, it took only one. It didn't look bad. Steve only had some blood coming from his nose. He must have been turning around to tell me something. It hit him behind the left ear." Mike showed me on my head where the location was where the bullet hit Steve. I asked Mike if he had blood on him and he said he had some on his blond hair. Mike said he leaned against a tree and cried. "I loved him," Mike said, "but I also loved you. . . ." He put Steve in the hole he had dug and threw dirt on top of him and the gun. Later Mike told me that Mr. Brown and some others had walked over the grave when they were at this location. Mike said he covered up the grave with the limbs and leaves to make it hard to see.

"Did you tell this to Maggie?" Kenny Dickerson asked Mike.

"No, sir," Mike said.

"Mrs. Miskelley," Sheriff Crum said, pausing, "we're going to have to take Mike down to the station for a while. We have to ask him a few questions."

She hesitated at the threshold of the front door, wiping her hands with a dish towel. "Couldn't you wait until my husband gets home from work? Wayne just had to stop off at the Union Hall in Corinth on his way home. He'll be back any minute."

"No, ma'am," Sheriff Crum said. "It's really quite urgent that we get down to the station right now, if you don't mind. They're all pretty stirred up about this back in town. We reckon he'd be safer in our custody."

"Will he have to spend the night in jail?" she asked.

"Yes, because we don't know but someone might try and harm Mike. We need to take him into protective custody."

Ann Miskelley broke into tears, pleading with them to wait until her husband arrived.

"I'll tell you what," Sheriff Crum said. "We'll take Mike on over to the sheriff's office, and then when Wayne gets back, y'all can drive over and we can talk then."

Mike assured his mother he'd be fine. He said he had nothing to fear from their questions. He climbed into the patrol car and they drove off down the gravel road toward Ripley.

ANN MISKELLEY LEANED against the doorjamb of her ranch-style house of gray cypress siding and collected her thoughts. She waited for her husband for about thirty minutes, but apparently he was running late. Finally she decided to drive down to the sheriff's office alone.

Yet when she arrived, about fifteen minutes later, she discovered that Mike and the policemen had not yet returned to the station. Worried— and a little puzzled by the sheriff's earlier suggestion of urgency—she questioned the clerk, who claimed that Sheriff Crum had just radioed to say they were on their way back. They didn't arrive for another twenty minutes.

When Sheriff Crum arrived, he proposed to Mike's mother that if he would submit to a polygraph test in Jackson the next day, and the test came out favorably, the authorities could clear him of all suspicion. While lie-detector tests are inadmissible as evidence in most court-rooms, investigators customarily use them to determine whether to pursue or abandon leads in cases that have reached a stalemate. For Crum and Dickerson, this was just such a case. Mike agreed to take the test. Then Crum told Ann Miskelley that Mike didn't have to spend the night in the jail after all, but he recommended that he stay away from home to avoid the threats of vigilantes. (In fact, he spent the night at his grandparents' house.)

On the way back to Falkner, Ann Miskelley asked Mike where Sheriff Crum had taken him. Mike told this story:

> Crum and the patrolman drove me out to Little Hope Church. We walked across that old cemetery and down toward

the lake, just like me and Steve had walked together the day we went hunting. Then we came to a little mound of dirt way back up in them woods. Crum radioed to Deputy Quincy Cook to come bring a shovel over to the site. They was going to dig up the mound. They said it was Steve's grave site. When Officer Cook returned, he got down and started digging. Sheriff Crum told him to stop, and said to me, "You put the damn thing there; now you dig it up, you redheaded bastard." So Officer Cook handed over the shovel to me. I never been so frightened in my life. But I begin to dig and dig, and my hands was shaking so on the shovel handle. But it turned out to be nothing but a little old animal burrow, like where a possum or beaver had dug in the dirt. There was nothing in it. Sheriff Crum, he looked kinda mad and then he said to me, "Where in the goddamn hell did you put him?" I told him I done nothing with Steve. We all walked back to the squad car and drove to the station.

THAT NIGHT Wayne Miskelley sat down with Mike on the couch in their den and said, "Son, if there's anything you haven't told us, you'd better tell us now. We don't want no surprises tomorrow." Mike said there was nothing. He wanted to take the test.

So on May 19, the Miskelleys rode in the squad car with Kenneth Dickerson and Deputy Donald Butler to the Mississippi Highway Patrol Headquarters in Jackson. Mike was scheduled to take a lie-detector test that would be administered by one Donald G. Bray, whom Inspector Dickerson lauded as the "finest polygraph examiner in the state."

Bray administered one three-part test that asked straight yes-or-no questions such as "Did you kill Steve Brown?" and "Do you know who killed Steve Brown?" During the first run-through the needle was erratic because Mike was so nervous. After Bray studied the readings in the lab, however, the Miskelleys claim that he walked out into the ante-room where Mike was sitting, slipped his hand around his shoulder, and told them: "Congratulations! It looks like Mike is telling the truth. He's clean. I'm completely satisfied with the results." They said Bray told them that polygraph tests were ordinarily 90 percent reliable, and that he felt quite sure about this one.

Mike returned to Falkner with a feeling that the ordeal was finally over. He hoped the test would allay the community's suspicions; he felt he'd been officially absolved. "After he took the lie-detector test, he got kind of cocky," recalls Tate Rutherford, a friend of the Miskelleys. "It was kind of a joke to him. It was just like, 'See there, I haven't done anything.' He really didn't understand the seriousness of it."

SHERIFF CRUM invited Wayne Miskelley to his office the next day and apologized for all the trouble the police had caused the family. He said he genuinely appreciated their cooperation throughout the investigation. Wayne Miskelley says he remembers the conversation vividly. "Crum told me, 'People've been hollering at me, but, you know, I got a job to do. But you don't let nobody throw this at Mike anymore. If they do, you just tell them where to get off at.' Those were his exact words: 'You tell them where to get off at. Or send them to me, and by God, I'll tell them where to get off at.'"

After the lie-detector episode, Mike Miskelley went several weeks without speaking to Maggie Biggers. Then one day during a football practice, he saw her on the field with the cheerleading squad. During a water break, he approached her. "Why in the hell did you do that to me?" he says he asked her. "How come you told them all that stuff?" He says Maggie apologized and exclaimed, "They *made* me. If I hadn't, I would have been in trouble."

In Mike's yearbook, Maggie jotted a note in the back. *I hope you don't hold a grudge against me for nothing,* she wrote. *Love ya, Maggie.*

SUMMER PASSED. It was now six months since Steve Brown's disappearance. The law enforcement officials had turned up nothing. The district attorney, Kenneth Coleman, was deluged with mail urging him to do something. There were accusations that Investigator Dickerson had all but abandoned the case. "I caught hell from the victim's family at first," Dickerson told me, "and then from a number of individuals who didn't like the way I was handling it. But you know, it's easy to be a Monday-morning quarterback. They were all criticizing me because I couldn't bring the boy home alive to them for Christmas. Then the family called the governor's office. There was a lot of pressure coming from the top down. Headquarters was calling every week, and not only that, I was trying to work five more murder cases at the same time."

When the 1981–82 school year began that fall, Principal James W. Bolden announced that Maggie Biggers and Mike Miskelley were to be separated at all times in a special kind of quarantine arrangement. Everybody in the school was asked to help monitor the couple. Bolden laid down the guidelines in a memo dated September 23:

> Due to problems that have arisen between Mike Miskelley and Maggie Biggers, the administration, faculty, and board members feel that some action should be taken.
> A. These students will be separated in classrooms in different sections where possible.
> B. They are not to associate with one another at all on school property (day or night). This means *all* contact.
> C. Any obscene language, gesture, or physical contact will be grounds for dismissal.
> D. Any messages carried by other students, notes, staring, etc. will be considered contact and will be punished.

Though these seemed to be rather sweeping measures for a high school setting, Bolden's "quarantine" could only go so far. Mike says he sneaked out with Maggie quite often. Evidently a reconciliation had taken place that fall. The quarantined classmates used to rendezvous at a secluded place known as Braddock Lake. Later in the year, they would meet at the garage apartment of a mutual friend named Lawrence Jay Roberts in Ripley. Roberts was a manager at the Sonic Drive-In, where Mike had worked during the summer.

During the 1981–82 school year, Maggie wrote scores of love notes to Mike: lyrics to songs, original verses, lines copied out of old poetry books. He kept a few of them, like the one entitled "The Way I Want It":

> *Our love will be a special one*
> *A kind that everybody will want to see*
> *Holding, sharing, loving, caring*
> *Is the way I want it to be*
> *I'll never leave you and hope*
> *You'll never leave me*
> *Both of us together . . . forever*
> *Yeah . . . That's the way I want it to be.*
>
> *Love ya, Maggie*

IN MAY OF 1982 a rather peculiar incident caught the eye of local newspaper reporters. Law enforcement officers claimed they had reason to suspect that Steve's body had been dumped in Braddock Lake, a flood-control reservoir in Tippah County, but they refused to reveal to reporters what prompted the suspicion. The only evidence suggested obliquely in the newspaper reports was the fact that Mike Miskelley had been seen "fishing" alone at the lake. "All we know is, he's the last person that saw Steve," explained Sheriff Crum, "and that's all we've got to go on." The newspapers now reported Crum's contention that the three boys who claimed they had seen Steve later at the ag shop were "mistaken."

So on May 15, under the supervision of the Soil Conservation Service of the Department of Agriculture and the Mississippi Department of Wildlife Conservation, the police officers had the fifty-seven-acre Braddock Lake drained.

"I can't do anything without them thinking it has something to do with Steve," Miskelley told Tupelo's *Northeast Mississippi Daily Journal* at the time. "I went fishing at that lake and now they're draining it. I don't really care if they drain it or not. . . . In one way, I'd be glad [if they found Steve's body] because then it would all be over for the Browns. But I'd be scared, too, because I'd be afraid they would try to stick me with it."

Later, Mike would concede that he'd been disingenuous in explaining his presence out on Braddock Lake that day. He said the *real* reason he was at the lake was to meet secretly with Maggie. According to Mike, Dale Biggers was also down at the lake that day. He spotted Mike just before Maggie was supposed to arrive. Suspicious of some kind of rendezvous, Biggers drove Mike off the premises. Mike claims Biggers was the one who alerted the law enforcement officers and recommended draining the lake.

It took several weeks to drain Braddock Lake. Once the water was shallow enough, Crum and Dickerson began a search for Steve's body. "Concerned citizens" volunteered by the dozen. Milton Lester of Byhalia brought out his metal detector, and David Smith of White's Crossing tried his hand with a homemade contraption similar to a divining rod. (Smith claimed the rod would detect anything from metal to dollar bills.) But the search was a failure. After dragging and wading through all fifty-seven acres of the lake, they turned up nothing but beer cans, garbage, and dead fish.

SHORTLY THEREAFTER, Falkner High School's class of 1982 finally graduated, marching through the school's wrought-iron gates with their senior-week slogan, "We're lots of fun, just a crazy crew/ 'Cause we're the class of '82!"

In a student poll, the senior class chose, as their favorite movie, *Endless Love*, the steamy tale of teen romance starring Brooke Shields. Maggie Biggers, who had enjoyed a popular senior year as captain of the cheerleading squad, had a lengthy listing in the Class of 1982 yearbook. She was voted Best All-Around. Mike Miskelley had spent a much more low-key senior year—not surprising in view of all the controversy—but he had played a major role in the senior class play, *Toga! Toga! Toga!*

THE MONTHS PASSED. Mike and Maggie continued to see each other until that August, when Mike enrolled at Northeast Mississippi Junior College in Booneville. In November, Maggie married a man from Ripley named Jack Nathan "Boom Boom" Jones.

On December 27, 1982, Danny Ross, a fifteen-year-old from Corinth, was deer hunting with his father in the National Forest lands of eastern Benton County. They were hunting in a secluded place, about a quarter-mile walk down a steep ravine from the Old Blackwell Baptist Church, seven miles west of Falkner off Mississippi Highway 370. That day, while hiking by a small stream, Danny came across something strange: a rusty rifle, stuck barrel-down into the mud of the shallow creekbed. He pulled it out of the sand and studied it for a while. Walking on by the stream he stumbled upon something that scared him, lying partially exposed in the old damp leaves. He hurried through the woods to where his father, Herman Ross, was hunting, and said, "Daddy, what does a human skull look like?"

The skull was marked with several hairline fractures and two round holes, like bullet wounds. Nearby, Danny and his father found some scattered bones.

Soon the locals were streaming down to investigate. They trampled over the brush and marked a clear path with red ribbons. When the police authorities arrived, they organized a thorough search of the site. Some kids found a nylon sock that had several small foot bones inside it. Others found the inside pocket of a pair of denim jeans, and a human mandible. A man with a metal detector turned up some bullet fragments, and several human teeth held together with dental braces.

Some of the circumstances surrounding the discovery were rather peculiar. Though it was an out-of-the-way place, this woodland area was a favorite spot for numerous local deer hunters. What was more intriguing, four-wheel-drive tracks were discovered within fifteen feet of the bones, and some of the trees around the site were skinned up, suggesting that someone recently had driven a truck through the area. And while the .22 rifle was found in a conspicuous position—driven into the creekbed with the stock straight up in the air—the stock of the rifle was muddy and riddled with insect holes, which seemed to indicate that it had been lying on its side at one time.

Whether or not the remains were planted, however, the police authorities were confident that they had found Steve Brown. When the officers presented the old rifle to Dwight Brown, he immediately recognized it as his son's Mossberg .22 bolt action. "That's when I knew it was all over," Mr. Brown later said.

The remains were sent to Dr. Michael West, a forensic odontologist in Jackson. After analyzing the teeth against Steve's dental records, Dr. West was able to positively identify the remains as belonging to Steve Brown.

Thus, the twenty-one-month search finally ended. Now the law enforcement officers could proceed with the case. "I don't want to use the word 'relief,'" said Walter Tucker, chief investigator for the Mississippi Highway Patrol, at the time. "But at least we know we don.'t have to look anywhere else for him. The not-knowing is what's been so bad."

An autopsy was conducted at the Mississippi Crime Laboratory in Jackson. The report, signed by a state pathologist named Dr. Rodrigo Galvez, indicated that a small-caliber bullet entered the back of Steve Brown's head and exited through the front of the skull. Walter Tucker said the authorities were now definitely treating the matter as a homicide case.

The North Tippah County schools were closed all day for Steve's funeral on January 6, 1983. At the Ripley Funeral Home over fifteen hundred mourners—six times the population of Falkner—gathered for a thirty-minute memorial service. A color photograph of Steve was placed atop the casket. The wreaths lined the walls and spilled out into the hallway. "In our minds, an unbelievable nightmare has come to an end," eulogized Reverend Billy Foley. "An awful crime has been committed, and an awful injustice has been done. I know his family thinks the whole world has caved in, but they know today how many friends they have." In the audience, sitting near the back with his family, was Mike Miskelley.

ON DECEMBER 28, the day after the remains were found in the Benton County woods, Sheriff Pete Crum and Investigator Kenneth Dickerson picked Mike Miskelley up at his grandmother's house, and brought him to the Tippah County sheriff's office for questioning. Two days later, they obtained a warrant and searched the Miskelley house.

On January 13, 1983, the authorities scheduled a meeting of a regular grand jury to present the results of their investigation. "We got to narrow this thing down," explained Kenneth Coleman, the burly, good-natured district attorney for the Third Circuit Court District. "We got to figure out who did it and then prosecute them."

The grand jury met in the Benton County seat of Ashland, some fifteen miles from Falkner. The case was now under the jurisdiction of Benton County, not Tippah, because Steve Brown's body had been discovered several hundred yards on the Benton side of the boundary between the two counties.

After a thirty-minute proceeding in the Benton County Courthouse on January 13, a grand jury indicted Mike Miskelley for the murder of Steve Brown. The evidence law enforcement officials presented centered on the statement Maggie Biggers had offered back in May of 1981. "The only motive that we know," Benton County sheriff Pat Gresham told the *Northeast Mississippi Daily Journal*, "is that the two boys dated the same girl at one time." Though the alleged crime presumably took place when he was a minor, Miskelley, now eighteen, would be tried as an adult, on a charge of first-degree murder. Miskelley spent eight days in the Benton County jail until bail could be arranged.

On January 26 he entered a plea of not guilty, and was released on a $75,000 property bond put up by his grandfather, John Elmer Miskelley. Before this, few people in Falkner were aware that the Miskelley family had that kind of money, so the announcement of the bail created a bit of a stir. It was at this point that a number of lawyers in the surrounding counties suddenly took interest in the Miskelleys.

THE MISKELLEYS HIRED an eloquent young patrician attorney from the Delta named William O. Luckett, Jr.

This was no random choice. Bill Luckett was the son-in-law of none other than "Big John" Farese, the influential Ashland attorney. The Miskelleys had first sought the services of John Farese, but Farese had told the Miskelleys that he could not take on the case, for there was a conflict-of-interest involving another lawyer in the Farese firm, an attorney named John Riemenschneider, who was also the Benton County prosecuting attorney. In this capacity, he would be called upon to assist the DA's office in preparing the prosecution against Miskelley. Another reason Farese wouldn't represent the Miskelleys was that in the course of defending Mike he might be required to indulge in the unethical practice of implicating a former client, Sammy Broder, the former Falkner High music teacher.

But if the Miskelleys couldn't have Farese, they could have his son-in-law. So Farese referred the Miskelleys to the Luckett Law Office, an attractive colonial brick building with holly shrubs and monkey grass fronting Yazoo Street in Clarksdale.

Bill Luckett was a formidable attorney in his own right. He cut a dashing figure in a courtroom, with his James Davis suits and his imposing stature. He had a Delta dialect that came off as smooth as custard pie. He was a real workhorse, always on the go, full of steam. He was well educated, with a B.A. from the University of Virginia and a law degree from Ole Miss. The Luckett firm had an old and well-established practice with tastefully furnished offices in Clarksdale and Memphis. With its legal expertise and its big-city connections, the Luckett firm could surely put together a strong defense.

Still, there were other aspects to the choice of Luckett. Living as he did in faraway Clarksdale—over a hundred miles distant—Luckett could not know a tremendous amount about the politics of law enforcement in Benton and Tippah counties. Nor did he have very much experience with big murder trials like these; the Luckett firm had established its reputation for handling insurance and real-estate claims, not criminal cases. Then, too, Luckett's style was in some ways contrary to the sensibilities of the Mississippi hill people. He flew his own airplane, drove a Mercedes, wore a gold wristwatch. He projected an image of legal sophistication and confidence that might easily backfire on a suspicious country jury. There has traditionally been a kind of regional hostility between Mississippians of the Delta and those who hail from the hill country farther east. It came as no surprise when Luckett received an angry letter from an anonymous elderly resident of Booneville. *Hello, William,* the note opened. *You come out of the rich land trying to pull the wool over the hill people's eyes.*

*   *   *

PRESIDING OVER THE frowzy square of Ashland, the Benton County Courthouse with its gray cupola and its country Victorian styling seems like a temple sprung from the mud. Originally constructed in 1873, the courthouse is a two-story building of white brick with white columns and gray trim, surrounded by an attractive yard with magnolias and boxwoods and a white lattice gazebo. The old-timers sit in rocking chairs by the steps of the building, whittling and spitting tobacco juice.

Across the street from the courthouse lawn, tucked away in a one-story building on the south end of the Ashland square, is the Farese law firm. There is also Roger's Dollar Store, PJ's Treasure Chest, the Mississippi Farm Bureau, a post office, a Piggly Wiggly grocery, and the offices of the weekly *Southern Advocate* ("We Favor Continuous Progress").

The State of Mississippi v. Michael Wayne Miskelley (Benton Case No. 2904) opened on March 22, 1983—one day before the second anniversary of Steve's disappearance. The trial would become the biggest and most publicized event in the history of Ashland. Over forty witnesses would testify in the five-day trial.

Each morning at 8:30 the spectators would crowd into the second-floor courtroom—a bright room filled with musty portraits of judges and statesmen out of northern Mississippi's past. The trial attracted some three hundred spectators each day. Stragglers would bring along folding chairs to set up in the empty spaces. For most of the trial, there was standing room only.

Presiding over the court was Judge W. W. Brown (no relation to Steve Brown), a small, ruddy-faced gentleman with a corncob pipe and scrolls of graying blond hair. The center aisle quickly became the line of demarcation for the crowd's loyalties. Those supporting the Browns congregated on one side, those supporting the Miskelleys sat on the other, while the undecided spectators shuffled back and forth to honor both families. The two families themselves sat in reserved seats in the front.

Each day at noon, a group of Falkner women served box lunches out of one of the offices downstairs. Spectators who had good seats often refused to leave during the lunch break for fear of losing them.

School was unofficially called off for the Falkner students, and most of them showed up every day, either as spectators or witnesses. Maurine Bain, the county court clerk, said it was the largest and most emotional crowd she'd ever seen in a courtroom. "I was scared the upper floor would cave in from the weight of all those folks," she said.

THE FIRST THREE days were uneventful. The prosecution had to prove through the use of forensic experts that the body found in the Benton County woods was, indeed, Steve Brown. It was also necessary to establish the corpus delicti, literally, "the body of the crime." The State had to prove beyond a reasonable doubt that there had been a crime, that Steve had been killed by a gunshot wound to the head.

Luckett questioned why Dr. Galvez, in his report, had failed to mention the several fractures that appeared on Steve's skull. Luckett argued that the fractures presented the possibility that Steve had been beaten as well as shot. Here, Luckett implied that it was highly unlikely that someone as small as Miskelley—he was five-foot-five and 130 pounds—would be powerful enough to assault a larger and stronger boy like Steve Brown in this way, particularly since Mike was wearing a leg cast at the time.

Second, Luckett questioned why the prosecution had built its case around the unqualified assumption that Steve died from a head wound caused by a .22-caliber bullet, when Galvez had only specified *a projectile, small caliber (.22?)* in his report. What was more, Luckett said, the prosecution was attempting to create the impression that the bullet that killed Steve Brown was one of the same projectiles the authorities found in the woods, and, further, that it was fired from Steve's Mossberg rifle. Yet John M. Allen, the state firearms examiner in Jackson, had concluded in his report: "It is the finding of this examiner that the projectiles and cartridge cases in [these] exhibits were not fired in the [Mossberg] gun." It was determined, in fact, that the projectiles were fired from a Marlin rifle. So the exhibits were only props, Luckett maintained, with no relevance to Steve Brown's death.

Third, Luckett claimed that the firearms experts whom he consulted had never encountered a situation in which a .22-caliber bullet was powerful enough both to enter and exit a human skull containing a living brain. Was it possible that the bullet holes were caused subsequent to Steve's death, after his brain had decomposed?

The defense attorneys were willing to acknowledge that the remains belonged to Steve Brown, but they claimed the State had not proven the other crucial element of corpus delicti, criminal agency. "Well, I will say to you they have probably proven that Steve Brown is dead," conceded Luckett's assistant, Robert Norman. "But that's all they've proven. They have not developed the proof you need to send this man to jail."

The focus of inquiry then shifted to the details surrounding the discovery of Brown's body. The prosecution maintained that Mike shot Steve in the woods behind Blackwell Church and immediately buried him in a shallow grave nearby. Kenneth Dickerson said he found a slight depression "of somewhat precise design" in the ground about thirty steps north of Steve's skeletal remains. He claimed the hole was three feet deep, three feet wide, and six feet long. He originally concluded that it was the grave alluded to in Maggie's statement, theorizing that the buried remains had somehow washed out during heavy rains. But when the defense pressed Dickerson to describe this "grave" more specifically, he admitted that he wasn't sure what it was:

Q: Let's get right to the point if we can, Mr. Dickerson. Are you saying that's a grave?

A: I'm saying it's a depression or hole. I'm not just . . .

Q: You're not saying it's a grave?

A: I'm not saying it's a grave.

Q: Could have been any number of reasons for that hole. Is that not true, sir?

A: Well, yes, sir.

DEFENSE WITNESS TIMMY HOPPER testified that he saw Steve Brown at the Falkner High ag shop around 6:30 on the night he disappeared. Luckett emphasized that if Hopper was telling the truth, it would have been impossible for Miskelley to have committed the murder. The other two boys in the building that evening, Jerry Barkley and Randy Moore, testified that they saw someone who looked like Steve, but conceded that they could have been mistaken. Fearing that the prosecution had coerced Barkley and Moore into changing their stories to convey uncertainty, the defense discouraged Hopper from talking with anyone before taking the stand. But Hopper stood by his earlier account of the sighting, much to the chagrin of Kenneth Coleman and his assistant, Chuck Easley, who naturally tried their best to discredit him on cross-examination. "I felt like I was badgered up there," Timmy Hopper later told me. "Easley tried to twist my testimony around so the jury would somehow forget what I was saying. I saw Steve Brown that night. It was that simple."

THE CASE FOR THE defense took a turn for the worse, however, when, on direct examination, Mike Miskelley revealed what many thought to be an unconvincing account of his activities on the afternoon of March 23, 1981. After dropping Steve off at the Bank of Falkner, Mike claimed he picked up his paycheck at Griffin's Grocery, bought some gas, then turned around and headed *back out* Highway 370 toward Benton County to pick up a six-pack of Budweiser he had bought from a local bootlegger. It was stashed in the woods less than a mile from the site where Steve's remains were discovered. Miskelley testified that he opened up a beer, but it was too warm to drink. He put the beer in the car and headed toward home. Then he tossed the sack of beer in an old junk pickup truck about three hundred yards from his house. Mike testified that he and Luckett later went out to the site of the abandoned truck, and that the beer was still there with cobwebs on the sack. Luckett conceded that Mike's last-minute maneuvering to pick up the beer stash was "a drive I wish he hadn't made," but insisted his client's explanation was the correct and truthful one.

The State, however, offered several witnesses who testified that they saw Mike driving back from Benton County at an extremely high rate of speed. They said he was driving recklessly. Miskelley claimed he was driving fast because he had lost track of time and wanted to return before his father got home. Of course, the State argued that Mike was speeding home from the scene of the crime in the Benton County woods.

MAGGIE BIGGERS JONES'S testimony would be the centerpiece for the prosecution. She was the star witness, the "prosecutrix," as Luckett called her. "Her statement was the crucial, pivotal thing," agreed District Attorney Kenneth Coleman, reviewing the trial in a recent interview. "Everything else was just window dressing. In that sense the case was quite simple; it all boiled down to whether those twelve men and women on the jury believed her or not."

So when she finally climbed to the witness stand on the third day, all eyes were watching:

> . . . Mike said he would tell me on his deathbed. . . . He said he would go to hell. Then, one day on the phone, he said he had something to tell me. I told him to tell me what it was. I told him if he didn't tell me, that I would hate him. . . .
>
> He told me [the next day, in the high school auditorium] that he did this for me. He thought Steve was coming between me and him. He done it for a four-letter word called L-O-V-E. He said he had gotten mad Sunday and went and dug a hole. . . . He talked Steve into going hunting with him on Monday. He said that they got to the woods. Mike seen the hole that he had dug the Sunday before, and he knew he had to do what he come to do. . . .

Maggie's voice broke with emotion at this point, and she began to cry. The Browns also began to weep, and then a wave of tears swept back through the audience.

Most of the crowd was shocked by Maggie's testimony, for her earlier accusation of Mike had never been openly revealed or reported in the papers. Many people were hearing the details for the first time. Maggie continued:

He said that he turned his head and pulled the trigger, and he turned around. He said Steve took a step and he took another one and went to his knees and just looked at him, and Steve mumbled something, and he gradually fell to the ground.

I just wanted to know more. I asked him how it looked, and he said it didn't look bad. He said that he leaned up against a tree and cried. He said he loved Steve, but he loved me more. He said that it only took one. Said it hit him behind the left ear. He touched my head where. I asked him did he have blood in his blond hair, and he said, "Yeah. He didn't look bad; he just had a little blood running out his nose." He said he buried him. He said Steve was heavy. He said that he put the gun with him. I asked him how did he cover up the thing to keep it from being seen, and he said he used the shovel to cover it up, and that's all he told me that day.

LUCKETT CALLED Maggie Biggers's testimony an "outright lie." In a direct examination of Miskelley on the stand, Luckett drew out a different version of this "confession." Mike testified that he once offered a "false" admission in a kind of "flippant," offhand manner. He maintained that Maggie continually nagged him for weeks, imploring him to tell her the "real story." He said she prodded him every day until her suggestions "finally got on my nerves." He said she threatened to "hate me if I didn't tell her the truth." Then one day during class Maggie said, "You killed him, didn't you? You killed Stevie."

Miskelley said he decided to go along with her so "she'd get off my back."

"Sure, Maggie," he whispered, "I done it."

"You buried him, didn't you?"

"Sure, Maggie."

"After the disappearance," Luckett argued in chambers, "Maggie started continually badgering him, harassing him, causing herself to be a nuisance to him, picking on him, trying to get him to say something or admit things to her when she would suggest answers. Then it turned,

Your Honor, into more of a coercive-type affair where she would tell him she wasn't going to love him and this sort of thing if he didn't talk to her, and she would use the sex bribe, in a sense, against Mike Miskelley repeatedly, and then she'd go out with him and they'd have sex again and then she'd start going to work on him again. . . ."

AFTER THE PROSECUTION rested its case on the third day, Luckett directed most of his energies toward an attack on Maggie's credibility. Maggie maintained that after Mike "confessed" in May of 1981, she broke off all romantic relations with him. She said they were simply friends after this. It would be unseemly, of course, for her to admit before the Falkner residents that for months she had privately dated and engaged in sexual relations with the very person whom she now publicly claimed was the murderer of her former boyfriend. Luckett tried to show that this was precisely what Maggie had done.

First, the defense attorney produced several love notes that Maggie had written to Mike when they were seniors at Falkner High School—during the 1981–82 school year. Some of them she copied out of old poetry books; others she composed herself, including the one she titled, "My Endless Love." There was this piece of doggerel, for example, written in Maggie's flowery hand on a folded sheet of erasable bond with torn edges:

> *The violet loves the sunny bank,*
> *The cowslip loves the lea,*
> *The scarlet creeper loves the elm,*
> *But I love only thee.*
> > *Love ya, Maggie!*

After Luckett asked her to identify the notes, Maggie reluctantly acknowledged that she had authored them.

Next, Luckett called Lawrence Jay Roberts to the stand. Roberts had been Mike's boss at the Sonic Drive-In during the summer of 1981. Roberts testified that Mike and Maggie met privately at his apartment in Ripley many times. He said he even gave Mike a set of keys so the couple could have a place to rendezvous without their disapproving parents suspecting anything. "They were lovers," Roberts testified. "I mean, most all of us knew it."

During his cross-examination of Maggie, Luckett finally broached the subject of her relationship with Mike during the crucial period *after* the alleged confession.

Q: Were you unfriendly [with Mike] because of what you say he told you in May of 1981?

A: He was my friend.

Q: In spite of the fact that you say he told you that he killed Steve Brown, whom you loved?

A: Well, I told him he was my friend. I done a lot of things that I didn't want to do. . . .

Q: You loved Mike, didn't you?

A: I told him I did.

Q: But did you really?

A: No, sir.

Q: How long did this go on, where you were telling him you loved him and yet really didn't?

A: A long time.

Q: Were you just fooling him?

A: Well, I wanted to win his trust back. He didn't trust me after I had done told what he had told me the first time. He didn't trust me.

Part of Luckett's strategy was to portray Maggie as a femme fatale, in his words, "a little-kid dreamer who reads teen magazines, watches soap operas, and fantasizes that boys would go out killing people for her." Luckett sought to show that Maggie was a restless romantic with a long list of boyfriends. Luckett showed that, apart from her secret meetings with Miskelley, Maggie was "preengaged" to Steve Brown in July of 1980; that she was engaged to a man named Junior Carpenter around Christmas of 1981; that she eloped with a third man named Ronnie Bobo to escape "family problems" later in 1981 and sought a civil marriage in Alabama. (The justice of the peace there denied them a license because Maggie was a minor. He then notified the Biggerses, who authorized a juvenile officer to pick her up.) Thereafter, Maggie started dating a fourth man, Jack Jones, whom she married in November of 1982.

Much of this evidence would have been hot news for the audience and jury alike, but most of it was presented in chambers, out of public hearing. Judge Brown consistently sustained the prosecutor's objections to Luckett's cross-examination of Maggie regarding her alleged promiscuity, her relations with Mike, and her love notes. This was the kind of conversation that went on in chambers during much of the trial:

DEFENSE COUNSEL: "Your Honor, there are a lot of questions I want to ask this witness pertaining to matters that took place after this disappearance. . . ."

THE COURT: "What is the nature of the things that you want to ask her about?"

DEFENSE COUNSEL: "Well, going out with Mike Miskelley, sexual intercourse with him, various places they went, secret meetings, notes written, all of which she has denied in statements to us. . . ."

DISTRICT ATTORNEY: "You're talking about things that are totally irrelevant, immaterial."

DEFENSE COUNSEL: "Your Honor, I don't believe so. I think they are very probative. The State is trying to paint a case of a fight over a girl, and we're trying to show that she had other interests as well. . . ."

THE COURT: "Well, I don't see where the sexual life of someone has any probative value whatsoever. It's nothing but an assassination of her character. . . . I'm going to sustain the objection on the basis of this sex thing. . . . You're going to stay out of the sex business."

DEFENSE COUNSEL: ". . . They put this girl on the witness stand who appears to be the Virgin Mary and who says she loved Steve Brown and says she's just friends with Mike Miskelley. But these love poems don't say that to me. I think the jury has a right to look at these poems that she gave to him. The court can see by reading through these verses . . . that they [weren't] just friends."

FINALLY, ON THE FIFTH DAY, it came time for the attorneys to present their closing arguments. Luckett maintained that the State had failed to prove beyond a reasonable doubt that Steve Brown died of criminal agency. He argued that Maggie was motivated out of a kind of romantic delusion to create a fictitious fight between the two boys over her love. As for her seeming foreknowledge about the general location of the bullet wound, Luckett dismissed it as "a lucky guess."

Kenneth Coleman, on the other hand, stressed in very direct language that jealousy had led Mike to plan and execute the murder of Steve Brown in the Benton County woods. He claimed the entire case rested on the authenticity of Maggie Biggers's pivotal statement given back in May of 1981, particularly her knowledge of the path of the bullet. And all along, Coleman emphasized Maggie's willingness to endure public derision in order to bring the defendant to justice. "None of the elements of this crime are dependent on circumstantial evidence," he argued. "We have, in this case, the statement of Maggie Biggers Jones that just keeps this case from being a circumstantial evidence case. Every element of this crime is covered by her statement."

Coleman then waved Steve's rifle in front of the jury. "Mike Miskelley took this rifle and killed Steve Brown," he told the jurors. "You must not let him go free."

LATE IN THE AFTERNOON of March 26, Judge Brown had to ask the crowd to clear the aisle so the twelve jury members could shuffle back to the jury room, where they would decide the fate of Mike Miskelley. It was a bright spring day in Ashland, and sunshine was streaming through the tall windows. The crowd sweltered in the moist heat of the hall. Bill Luckett loosened his tie and leaned over the rail of the outside balcony to escape the stuffiness. The inside warmth radiated from the open windows into the crisp air.

The crowd waited only fifty-five minutes for the verdict. A silence fell over what at times had been an unruly audience, as if now for the first time they were beginning to understand the seriousness of it all. The high ceiling echoed with the sibilance of discreet conversation; there were whispered reassurances, a last-minute hug, a muted cough, the cries of an infant.

At 4:45 P.M. the door opened, and the eight-man, four-woman jury filed out. One of the members, Tate Peeler, who functioned as foreman, handed the verdict over to Maurine Bain, the county clerk. Her voice quavered as she read: "We, the jury, find the defendant, Mike Miskelley, guilty of murder."

Many in the audience gasped. All twelve of the jurors believed Mike Miskelley had killed Steve Brown. Several women, including Ann Miskelley, broke down in tears. There was no outburst of approval from the audience, only a hush of solemnity and restrained emotion. Mike sat in silence, stifling his reaction so completely that many who were convinced of his innocence said they suddenly changed their minds. "If he was innocent," remembers Maurine Bain, "he was the coolest cucumber I ever saw."

"I swear to God, I showed more emotion when I heard the verdict than that boy," Judge Brown told me when I met with him at his Calhoun City home. "He looked like a Mongoloid up there. Something must have snapped in his mind. Mentally, he didn't believe he did it. He had detached himself so completely from it, he didn't even wince. It was as if the verdict applied to someone else. His demeanor on the witness stand was not convincing of his innocence. If I were innocent, I'd look that jury in their eyes. I'd plead and beg and cry. They're humans, you know. They have feelings. If you show some emotion, a jury will help you out. Especially when you're going up against a girl like that one was. You know, a friend of mine leaned over to me after the trial was over, and told me, said, 'That little ol' girl ain't worth killing for.'"

Judge Brown read the sentence: "It's the duty of the court, under the laws of the State of Mississippi, to sentence you to serve the remainder of your natural life in an institution to be designated by the Board of Corrections. You'll be in the hands of the sheriff."

⋆　　⋆　　⋆

THE CITIZENS OF FALKNER lingered at the Benton County Courthouse to contemplate the significance of the linen that had been aired over the last five days. Mike Miskelley became an inmate at the Benton County Jail within an hour.

"I don't think we can ever forget the hurt," Steve's father told a reporter for the *Commercial Appeal* just after the trial. "But being able to get justice done makes it possible to have a positive outlook. We've gone through it for two years. We feel sorry for the Miskelley family for what they will be going through."

While Miskelley was adjusting to life as a convicted murderer inside the Ashland jail, the uproar over the trial grew in intensity all over Benton and Tippah counties. The verdict shocked half the community. Many suspected the trial was somehow rigged. Some residents felt Mike had been convicted on circumstantial evidence offered by one emotional young woman in a dramatic courtroom setting with a jury tainted by too much publicity. Others held that law enforcement officials had fired all their ammunition at the first and most convenient target—without bothering to explore other possibilities—to satisfy the witch-hunt mentality prevailing in Falkner.

Many of these doubts were captured in a letter that a woman named Janice R. White wrote in April of 1983 to the Ripley *Southern Sentinel*, entitled, "Is This Justice?"

That young man would have had to produce the person responsible for the crime in order to prove his innocence to those so prejudiced against him. . . . There are just too many unanswered questions for this to be let go . . . one set of suspicions prevailed over the other, and this, dear people, is terrifying. . . . For some, I'm afraid this trial became an arena for vengeance against an atrocious crime where "someone" must be punished.

The evening after her letter appeared, Janice White received an anonymous phone call. The caller hung on the line without saying a word. Soon she was receiving harassing calls every day. These calls continued for about two weeks, culminating on May 8, the day Janice White went to work and discovered that her heating and air-conditioning business—Tippah Refrigeration—had been burned to the ground. Her insurance company's investigator and the local fire marshal determined that it was a case of arson. They said the fire was ignited by gasoline.

Janice White stopped receiving anonymous phone calls that day.

WHEN I MET WITH HIM, Mike Miskelley was twenty years old. He had been confined to the Benton County Jail in Ashland for thirty-three months, where he spent his time polishing patrol cars and doing a little paperwork for the justice court clerk. Over time, he had become friendly with the deputies and with the sheriff. He and a fellow inmate had planted and harvested an impressive vegetable garden on a plot of land behind the jailhouse. He enrolled in a correspondence course on Mississippi criminal law to learn the mechanics of the court system that sentenced him to life behind bars—and has so far cost his family some $29,000 in legal expenses.

His most immediate fear was that he would be sent away to the Mississippi prison farm in Parchman, an overcrowded compound with a rather dismal reputation for violence and homosexuality. But he said he was confident his luck would turn. "I haven't cried yet," he said. "The day I cry will be the day I give up."

There were no visible scars in Miskelley's personality—only a kind of slow-burning frustration over the plodding pace of the court system. He seemed lighthearted at times, extroverted, whimsical, like the old class clown of Falkner High. Recently he consulted a doctor about his stomach pains. He discovered that he had developed an ulcer.

Some of the citizens of Ashland have criticized Benton County Sheriff E. P. "Pat" Gresham for allowing Miskelley to serve out his sentence in such casual and agreeable surroundings as the Benton County Jail, where his friends and relatives visit regularly, and the clerks and deputies pass the time with horseplay worthy of *The Dukes of Hazzard*. More than one person has suggested that Mike (many people in Ashland still refer to him as "the little redheaded bastard") ought to be sent away immediately to Parchman, where he'll get the treatment he deserves.

"I ain't bitter at nobody," he told me, "except Maggie, of course. You know, I've burned all my pictures of her since the trial."

I had to ask him, if he's innocent, why did he continue to remain involved with the girl who had called him a murderer? Miskelley apparently had asked himself the same question. "I don't know why I ever got mixed up with her," he said. "It was something about her, something about that big, big smile and those legs. Gosh, everybody was kind of crazy about her, I reckon. In Falkner, a girl like that can win things."

And what if his appeal is successful? Miskelley put down the Coke bottle in his hand and shrugged his shoulders. "Some people say, you know, 'You ought to get out of Mississippi.' But I don't have plans to leave Mississippi. This state's not so bad. It's the people who run it."

THOUGH THE TRAGEDY of Steve Brown's death still divides this rural community—and doubts linger in the aftermath of the Miskelley trial—the observable life of Falkner, Mississippi, continues from season to season with only slight variations in detail. The deer hunters in their orange caps and camouflage jumpsuits still sit in the Falkner Café, sipping warm coffee between stories. The farm machinery continues to rust in the fields. Wisps from the cotton harvest litter some of the roadside ditches, blending softly with the glaze of an early-morning frost. Over at Dale Biggers's place, the hillside awakens with the shrill crowing of a hundred gamecocks.

Pete Crum, who lost his bid for reelection as county sheriff, now works for Hill Brothers Construction Company of Tippah County. Wayne Miskelley is still a contract electrician; he's currently working on a project in Georgia. Timmy Hopper now attends Northeast Mississippi Junior College. Maggie Biggers Jones has been driving every morning to work in Blue Mountain, at the IMC plant there that manufactures kitty litter.

In the evening, the Falkner water tower shimmers in the orange radiance of a harvest moon. The Future Farmers of America gather around the ag shop after school as Dwight Brown outlines his strategies for winning a regional contest next month. The Falkner Eagles, their black-and-gold uniforms stained with red dirt, huddle over the last patch of dead grass by the end zone, in the shadows of the stadium lights on a crisp autumn night, as the cheerleaders yell to the crowd:

> We've got eagle power
> It's the greatest power on this earth
> Sometimes we're up, up
> Sometimes we're down, down
> But our feet are always on the ground
> Together we stand, stand
> Divided we fall, fall
> We're gonna fight till we do it all!

—1985

Postscript: The case of State of Mississippi v. Michael Wayne Miskelley *was appealed all the way to the Mississippi Supreme Court, which ruled, in a November 1985 opinion, that Miskelley had been "unduly restricted" in his lawyer's cross-examination of the state's star witness, Maggie Biggers, and that he should thus be accorded a new trial. "In our jurisprudence," wrote presiding justice Roy Noble Lee for the court, "cross-examination of a witness is a valuable right which may not be infringed upon or bridled."*

Miskelley was released on bond and prepared for a new trial. He hired another lawyer named Alvin Binder, a prominent defense attorney from Jackson who had represented Wayne Williams in the case of the Atlanta child murders. Binder succeeded in getting a change of venue, and the new trial was held in Batesville, Mississippi, several hundred miles from Falkner. During the first few days, the trial seemed to be going in his favor, but on the morning before he was scheduled to testify, Miskelley became agitated and scared. "I been living under this hell for six years," Miskelley told Binder that morning. "I got to find a way out. Is it too late to work out a deal?"

That morning Miskelley pled guilty to the reduced charge of "manslaughter in the heat of passion." The state sentenced him to ten years in prison, minus the three years he had already served.

When I asked Miskelley why he copped a plea so late in the process, in the midst of a retrial that was, by all accounts, going extremely well, he only said, "I was tired of fighting." He was suddenly seized with a premonition that the trial would turn against him. "It was like a dose of bad medicine you know is coming," he told me.

Alvin Binder seemed shocked and dismayed by his client's eleventh-hour reversal. "Well," he said to me, "I guess that is the stuff of life."

Miskelley served three years in Parchman prison and was released on good behavior. He lives in a small town in Mississippi with his wife and children.

AMERICANS ABROAD

Baked

HERE THEY COME NOW, the quitters. Hobbling into camp in the desert twilight, wincing, tears pooling in their eyes. Moving forward, just barely, in a solemn, arthritic procession. The bandaged. The damned. The quitters.

Some walk sideways, others backward, others on the toe-tips of their Nikes—searching for gaits that won't aggravate the blisters deep inside their gauzed feet. One runner from America is in so much agony that a friend has to carry him into camp. Another, a blind racer, his red-tipped cane tapping the ground, is led by a badly limping friend. A soldier from England staggers by: "I couldn't stop crying all night, mate. It was bloody awful!" The sun plinks out as abruptly as a heat lamp as it disappears behind a bulwark of dunes, and in the sanguinary light, they keep coming, this dirty straggle of gimps: the weak carrying the halt, the lame leading the blind.

On the announcement board in the center of camp, the French racing commissionaire has stapled a list of all the runners who've dropped out of the Marathon des Sables as of late afternoon, on the fourth day of this grim scramble across 142 miles of the Moroccan Sahara. The roster has now bloomed to more than three dozen after today's forty-seven-mile slog, the longest and most infernal of the race's six stages.

These casualties are the result of heat exhaustion, severe dehydration, or that Saharan specialty, personal psychodrama. The Gallic penchant for tragic diction deepens the humiliation: *Abandons*, the official list proclaims for all to see, and then, in Nixonian English: *Quitters*.

Organizers of the annual Marathon des Sables (Marathon of the Sands) tout it as "the world's toughest footrace," and who's going to argue? Founded in 1986, it was the brainchild of Patrick Bauer, a former concert promoter from Troyes, France, who two years earlier had walked across two hundred miles of the Algerian Sahara. Afterward, in a brilliant stroke of sadocommercialism, he decided to share the pain with others. Considered one of the first modern adventure races, the Marathon des Sables requires running more than five consecutive marathons in a single week, in 120-degree heat. But mileage alone doesn't begin to describe its hardships. It's seven days of sand devils, camel carcasses, and wheeling vultures, an event so frankly ominous that the entry form tacks on what it calls a "corpse repatriation fee." (Miraculously, only one participant has perished in the race's thirteen-year history, a Frenchman in his early twenties who expired on the sands in 1988 after suffering a massive heart attack.)

In recent years the Marathon des Sables has become increasingly popular among American runners. I had flown to Marrakech with a large contingent of the American runners, and had fallen in with them before the race. There were a few Olympian marathoners and scads of wiry triathletes. There were ex-marines and paratroopers and ripply-stomached cops. They were all members of the Tribe of the Human Sinew, with their buzz cuts and Vaselined thighs. They had made it a semiprofession, moving from one event like this to the next—the Western States, the Raid Gauloises, the Southern Traverse, the Bad-water 100, the Eco-Challenge, the Iron Man. All year long, it seemed, they traveled the circuit of pain. These sorts of superhuman endurance events had become a huge growth industry, especially in the United States and Europe. I was intrigued with the idea that people all across America seemed to be increasingly drawn to a kind of synthetic suffering. They were crossing oceans in bathtubs and pogo-sticking up mountains, at great risk to their health and sanity, enduring enormous hardships just so they could be "first." Was this pathology, I wondered, or the essence of ruddy good health?

The Marathon des Sables is an event that pushes the notion of synthetic suffering to its logical conclusion. As the participants run, then march, then crawl, and finally hallucinate their way across the bleached solitudes, they're required to carry all their own supplies: food, flashlight, sleeping bag, compass, knife, snakebite kit, distress flare, salt tablets, whistle, and, inexplicably, ten safety pins. Only water is provided, at the miserly rate of nine liters per day. Outside assistance of any kind is forbidden, unless a runner is lucky enough to collapse from sunstroke, in which case he is treated to a complimentary IV and a chopper ride back to camp—only to find his name then pitilessly displayed with those of the other malingerers and dropouts.

In the Marathon des Sables, however, malingering has its virtues, and foremost among them is fine dining. In an effort to keep their pack weight down, the racers eat extremely low on the hog: military MREs, Ramen noodles, *boeuf de* Mountain House. At night, they sullenly spoon their freeze-dried gruel and nod off, sleeping nine to a tent in a dark, tattered encampment reminiscent of *Spartacus*.

But once they elect to withdraw, the runners are allowed to crawl under the checkered tape that separates their squalid township from the more genteel wing of camp and break bread with the rest of us—marathon officials, journalists, medics, and other prosperous followers of the race. For us, the dining has been sublime. Desert? What desert? Each evening we've lounged on Berber carpets in billowy dining tents, listening to jazz and supping on foie gras, ratatouille, chocolate mousse, lamb tagine, even paella, and always with our choice of cold lager or a decent cabernet. At times, when the wind is blowing in a cruel direction, the savory smells of our dinner waft over to the Spartacans, teasing their nostrils.

The racers who dropped out after today's forty-seven-mile crucible are soon to join our happy crew. But wait, not so fast—before they can reach the steaming smorgasbord, they first must shamble past us as we lounge like emperors at our low tables. It's a dreadful promenade to have to make, a walk of shame, and as I watch them lurching into our midst, I almost feel a stab of pity. I feel especially bad for some of the American friends I'd gotten to know in Marrakech who seemed so full of hope then but now are so beaten down. Then, as I dig into my crème brûlée, I remind myself of a salient fact: These people paid $5,000 to come out here, on their vacations no less, to suffer like this. An ordeal is what they wanted. An ordeal is what they got. And in their agony, I feel certain, they're having the time of their lives.

AT DAWN ON THE OPENING DAY of the race, as the sun pops up bright but not yet brutal over the ruler-straight horizon, a crew of Berber hired hands collects trash and dismantles camp, stopping at one point to kneel in the direction of Mecca. A baby scorpion skitters out from a bedroll. Tied to a nearby tent is a bleating lamb, soon to be kabob. We're encamped near a little sand flea of a village called Timganine, a nine-hour Land Rover trip across the snowy Atlas Mountains from Marrakech. The start of the race is still a few hours off, but the runners are already stretching, checking their hydration systems, taking sober last inventories of their backpacks to see what else can be jettisoned. Walking up and down the long rows of black burlap tents is a little like skimming the dial of a shortwave radio—a snippet of German, a little Swedish, a few lines of Chinese, lots of nasally American English, some Irish brogue. But primarily French. Most of the race officials, and about a third of the 495 participants, are French. From top to bottom the event has a heavy Gallic flavor, with a certain high romanticism about the "meaning" of the desert that's at once quaint and insufferable.

As the runners continue their nervous fussing—downing salt tablets, attaching race numbers, taping up their backs and nipples to lessen chafing—I'm drawn to an oasis of serenity. Maurice Daubard, a sixty-eight-year-old Frenchman of fiercely proud bearing, is folded in the lotus position, meditating. A tall, wizened figure with cold gray eyes, Daubard hails from Moulins, where he's a famous ascetic, a practitioner of sundry martial arts, and a yogi. For years he's been plunging himself into freezing rivers or sitting in a tub of ice for hours, breathing deeply, inuring his will. Extreme cold, you might say, is his medium.

So what's he doing here, I ask him, in the furnace of the Earth?

He scrutinizes me. "I have learned to master the cold," he says. "Now I must master the heat." Daubard is ready for a change of pain-venue.

But why? What's the point of suffering? Daubard makes a tiny purse-lipped exhalation. "Suffering," he says, "is everywhere. It is the human condition. Yet suffering has much to teach. I am not a runner. I am missing one lung, from boyhood tuberculosis. But I will make it to the finish line. You will see. Every cell of my body has been conditioned for this race."

Daubard is unique in his clarity of purpose. Not many contestants are willing to admit they've come to the Sahara expressly to torture themselves down to the cellular level. Asked on their entry forms, *Why do you participate?* the racers assembled here convey motivations that range from the strange to the salacious.

"Because this is the mother of all events."

"The longest way is the shortest one."

"Because this is the desert."

"I'm looking for myself."

"To fly my soul."

A Frenchman: "Bread is the food of body, adventure is the food of mind."

An American: "To be all that I can be."

An Italian: "Behind the sand dunes, you can meet wonderful girls."

An Englishman: "Because I am mad."

Indeed, this race may be the ultimate gauntlet for those who possess the flagellant gene. We have a blind man from France who likes to box. We have an American running with a prosthetic leg. We have a group of seven American runners who've hatched an extraordinary plan for later this year to run seven marathons on seven continents in seven days, riding to each on a masseuse-equipped Learjet. We have an American entrepreneur who is now deeply involved in promoting a similar marathon across the Gobi Desert. There's a guy from Britain who's been conditioning himself by running on a treadmill in a sauna. There's the Sicilian cop, Mauro Prosperi, an Olympic modern pentathlete who got seriously lost in a sandstorm while running the Marathon des Sables four years ago. For nine days Prosperi wandered the desert eating raw bats and sucking wet wipes. Eventually he turned up in Algeria, two hundred kilometers off course, thirty pounds lighter, and on the verge of liver failure.

"It was a very bad and terrible experience," Prosperi tells me, fingering the gold chain on his bare chest. "And yet it was a great one." So now he's going to try again. "I am a competitor," he proclaims, "and I love the desert."

With the start approaching, the runners turn to their race maps. Only yesterday were they handed these all-important "Road Books," detailing each day's route. According to the Road Book, today's run will be short, a mere warm-up jaunt of fifteen miles. It won't be without its hardships, however. "In the event of a serious sandstorm," the Road Book says, "do not panic. Don't use your flare gun. NO HEROICS, PLEASE."

Perhaps it was this portentous language that has pushed Alan Syder, a British runner from Norwich, over the edge. Even before the starter's gun goes off, Syder becomes the event's first quitter. "This race just gets the better of you," is all he can say before hitching a ride back to Marrakech. Syder dropped out of the 1996 race, too, after only four days of running. For him, the Marathon des Sables is a cruel chimera, a thing he can neither seize nor entirely let go of.

The gothic atmospherics don't affect everyone. American Keith Baker looks downright blithe. A computer technician from New Mexico, Baker is affixing a pair of gaiters to his shoes to keep out the sand. A set of three white balls nestles at his side. "Running for days gets to be too dull," he says. "So I like to jog and juggle at the same time. I'm a *joggler*."

Everywhere, the skinny marathoners and ultrarunners stretch. But there also are schlubs in our midst—stout *volk*walkers curious to see if they can survive this thing. "I'm three or four bowling balls overweight," says Bob Benorden, a big, pale NASA computer programmer from Houston. "I haven't trained for this. I have no idea what to bring

in my backpack. I'm kind of winging it, if you want to know the truth."
He shrugs. "So I'll just walk the whole way."

Shouldering his elephantine pack, he strides purposefully to the start gate, which is now thronged with racers. A few Tuareg musicians are playing flutes and goatskin fiddles while two hired nomads stage a mock swordfight with ornamental sabers.

Patrick Bauer hops to the roof of a Land Rover, brandishes a microphone, and begins the long countdown. The Spaniards start singing football songs. The Italians perform Hail Marys. The Japanese become silent and grave.

Bauer yells, *"Trois ... deux ... un ... allez!"* Then they're off, screaming hordes in Supplex sunblock shirts and Foreign Legion hats, stumbling into the heat shimmer and out across the mighty ergs and oueds of the Sahara. Somewhere in the middle of the pack, just above the dusty stampede, three balls dance in the air.

WHATEVER THE MARATHON DES SABLES is, it's not a spectator sport. The Saharan backdrops can be striking, to be sure, but mostly this is an internalized event, the story of wills overriding the vetoes of feet. Yet it draws journalists from around the world—the BBC, French news crews, and a large number of American magazines, including *Soldier of Fortune*. We dutifully follow the race in Land Rovers, gawking at the runners, admiring their constitutions, happy that it's them out there and not us. At times we feel like voyeurs, watching a very slow and tedious car wreck.

For hours and days the great exodus carries on, moving with mirthless conviction under the not-so-sheltering sky. The race is making a jagged easterly crease across the brow of the Sahara, passing close to the disputed border with Algeria. Along the way the runners march over ridges the size of battleships and down indistinguishable corrugated dunes. They tread through dried-up lakebeds, dried-up riverbeds, and oases that seem on the verge of drying up. They hump across features with names like Takkourt n' Takouit, Afrou n' Tounalhazam, Atkounamass, D'lfert, Ahassia. One gets the impression after a while that these names are merely for effect, to amuse the mapmakers. This is no place for people, so why bother with nomenclature? This is geology without biology—deadscape. After the long column of runners threads through it, one imagines that this terrain may never see human trespass again.

Looking at a map, I can see that there are a few villages scattered about here, hidden in shaded oases or along the occasional green wadi. But we never seem to encounter them. A contingent of stone-faced Moroccan soldiers is traveling with us—our own security detail—though it's not clear who or what they're protecting us against. Carpet salesmen? White-slave abductors? We're the biggest village around, and largely self-sufficient, an enormous boa inching across the desert. Since our first night's bivouac, we haven't had contact with any locals, except for an old Berber man who wandered by on a mangy burro and blinked at us in disbelief. In a sense, this race is so insulated from Saharan culture, it could be run anywhere that's hot and spare and isolated—on 495 treadmills, say, in 495 saunas.

On the third day, while we're waiting for the racers to arrive at our checkpoint, I climb to the top of Mount Tibert, a thousand-foot spine of black granite that erupts from the sand about forty-five miles into the course. It's the race's first real obstacle. Somehow the runners will have to get themselves up and over this brutally steep escarpment, following a narrow, sandy path that leads through a pass. From Tibert's rocky summit, I can look back for miles and see the remnants of our tabernacle city. A curl of black smoke rises from a pyre of camp garbage.

Now I also can see the column of runners heading this way, a long, steady march of fire ants stretching out over fifteen miles or more. It's a vista at once comical and profound, all these grunting, numbered forms inching across the void, following splotches of fluorescent paint slopped onto the rocks.

From this vantage, it becomes a little easier to appreciate the race's aesthetic, to begin to see why the American runners with whom I've become friends often use words like "purifying" and "cathartic" to describe the allure of these sorts of races. Name the climate and longitude, and someone somewhere is surely running a race through it. Antarctica is not too cold. The Andes are not too high. How about Greenland? Greenland sounds hostile. Greenland sounds good.

But of all the hostile climes in which to race, I can't imagine any-place that beats the Sahara for reducing the experience to such stark fundamentals. The epic blond monotony of the terrain drives the mind back on itself. There's nothing to distract. Everything is stripped, essential. And what does a person think about when his interior and exterior landscapes are so reduced? Over the past few days I've been asking my American friends this, and the answer has been always the same: "I think about the next step." They seem to take comfort in such simplicity. For most of them, reaching the finish line is less an act of athleticism than of faith—faith in the ritual of marching, faith that completion will redeem all hardships along the way.

As the line of racers draws nearer, the silence of the desert is punc-tured by the steady *kwoish-kwoish* of water bottles sloshing. Mauro Pros-peri, the Sicilian cop, eventually limps by, in obvious pain. He's stubbed a toe so severely that he's torn off the nail. At the next checkpoint he'll have to drop out. I spot Bob Benorden, the mule from Houston, his eyes fixed on his feet. Behind him, among the stragglers, I hear someone singing: "I once was lost, but now am found, was blind, but now I see."

ON THE FOURTH DAY COMES THE KILLER: the diabolical double-marathon stage that will produce so many *abandons*. When we drive over the route in the glare of forenoon, my impression of the race shifts from "this is nuts" to "surely people will die." The distances between checkpoints seem chasmic, and somewhere along the way, the mood of the landscape appears to change from austere indifference to out-and-out menace.

It seems almost impossible that people could run in this oven, but the heat isn't fazing the race leaders. In the vanguard are a pack of dauntless Italians, two Moroccans, a respectable number of Americans, and a Russian named Andrei Derksen who trains in the blazing heat of Siberia and has won the Marathon des Sables three times. All lope along easily.

About ten miles into the route, however, travail begins. I spot Mau-rice Daubard, the ice-water mystic, and he's in sorry shape, barefoot, limping, his shoes slung over his shoulders. Stoic that he is, he tries not to let on. "I feel stronger with every step," he assures me. "I am one with the earth. The desert is my teacher now."

We stop at a checkpoint that, with a rare nod toward mercy, has been set up in a shady grove of tamarisk trees. The race, especially today's stage, is taking its toll, and the casualties are streaming into the MASH unit. A Frenchman is delirious. A guy from Hong Kong has a gruesome case of crotch burn. Others are being treated for sprained ankles, exhaustion, a fractured wrist, and an all-too-common condition that might be described as "heel tartare."

Bauer drives up, wearing Ray-Bans and a natty vest proclaiming him *Directeur de Course*. He mixes amiably with the runners, grimacing at the IVs and the lanced blisters, but he's an affable torturer: he doesn't have the stomach for their suffering. He gives the runners a thumbs-up, says *"Bon chance!"* and drives off in a cloud of dust.

We head on to the next bivouac site, not expecting the leaders to come in for hours, not expecting too many runners to come in at all. I swing by the bulletin board, where the race officials have tacked up dozens of e-mail messages from the runners' friends and family members—most of them, it seems, from America. *You are an awesome piece of machinery. You must actually like this stuff! Next time choose something a little shorter. Love, Debra.*

Relaxing in my tent, I am just beginning to doze off when there's an unexpected eruption of shouting and applause. Dashing outside, I behold an amazing sight: Mohamed and Lahcen Ahansal, two brothers from Morocco, are sprinting—*sprinting*—into camp, weeping with joy, holding hands as they cross the day's finish line. The Ahansals have done something almost eerie. They've covered forty-seven desert miles in six hours and ten minutes, in 120-degree heat, with rucksacks on their backs. The mood around camp is one of stunned awe. It seems we've witnessed the birth of some new athletic creature, a mutant with a different sort of writing, different feet, Prestone coursing through its veins. The Ahansals, who were born and raised in Zagora, a Berber town of fifteen thousand people not far from here, are now thirty-five minutes ahead of their nearest competition for the day, and about thirty minutes ahead overall.

While the Ahansals accept congratulations and sip their water ration, other runners trickle in, a lonely procession that drags on well into the night. The racers have until nightfall tomorrow to finish this stage before they're disqualified. But the longer they're out there, the slower they go, and the slower they go, the more they bake.

Around midafternoon on the race's only rest day, I walk over to meet the Ahansals, who are in a tent on the far side of the bivouac. Conditions in the runners' encampment have deteriorated by now from bad to deplorable. Flies swarm over bandaged feet. Runners claw through their rucksacks, ditching tomorrow's food, trading an empty stomach for a lighter pack. "Give you a mac-and-cheese for a Marlboro," somebody says.

Against this backdrop, the Ahansals look like boulevardiers, carefree and rested. Mohamed even went out on a little joy run this morning, taking in the scenery. Lahcen somehow has found the energy for courtship. He's putting the moves on Anke Molkenthin, a statuesque German runner who's in fifth place among the women—despite a fractured arm. As in any tiny village, the rumors are flying.

The brothers' success wasn't unanticipated, but no one expected them to be quite so dominant. Lahcen, at twenty-eight, is returning champion, having last year dethroned Russia's Andrei Derksen. During most of the year, Lahcen works in his family's palm groves, shinnying up trees, collecting dates. His rucksack is full of the things, the Berber equivalent of the PowerBar. But it's younger brother Mohamed, twenty-five, who's in the lead, with a cumulative time of 12:48:46, about three minutes ahead of Lahcen. He's a soft-spoken man who makes a living leading tourists into the Atlas Mountains. There's no tradition of running in Berber culture; there is, if anything, an anti-tradition. Around here, running is considered just about the stupidest thing you can do. "When we were little boys," Mohamed says, "we used to take off running across the sand. People would laugh. They would say, 'There they go, the crazy brothers.'"

On the other hand, the crazy brothers are within two days of reaping almost unimaginable rewards. The first-place purse here is about $5,000, second place $2,500, in a land where the average person earns maybe $1,200 a year. The Ahansals, I realize—perhaps alone among the racers—have no doubt whatsoever about what this race means for them. "At the souk," Mohamed tells me when I ask why he and his brother started to run at all, "our friends would try to persuade us to steal pieces of fruit. They knew no one could catch us. It is good, you see, to be fast."

THE FINISH LINE has been erected in the town square of Rissani, a warren of mud and concrete pitched on the edge of the world's largest palm grove, the Oases du Ziz. As Tuareg music blares, the king of Morocco scowls down from a portrait set on an easel. Our army escort is setting up barricades and wielding billy clubs, keeping the street urchins at bay.

Sipping mint tea, I mill among the quitters. There are plenty. Yesterday, during the penultimate and relatively puny twenty-six-mile stage, dozens of runners succumbed to accrued wear and tear. One racer took off at the gun, paced three steps, and fell face-first into the sand.

To my dismay, Bob Benorden was also among yesterday's casualties. "I was coughing up something that I don't know *what* it was," he says as we wait for the leaders. Worried medics started an IV. Then they gave him another. And another after that. Rejuvenated, Bob stood up, swaying only a bit, and prepared to reenter the race. "But it turns out they have this rule," he explains sadly. "Two IVs and you're out."

Still, Bob has already put down his deposit for next year's race. "I think I've figured this thing out," he says cheerfully. "I've just got to work on my hydration system."

There's a sudden eruption of cheers from the home crowd, and Mohamed Ahansal comes dashing in, his face burning with impish good cheer. He's covered the 142 miles of the Marathon des Sables in a cumulative time of sixteen hours, twenty-two minutes. Accepting his medal from Bauer, he vaults up to the bandstand, where he waves the red flag of Morocco and performs handstands and backflips. Big brother Lahcen comes speeding in twelve minutes later.

Then the rest start trickling in, their eyes pooling with tears, faces lit with ecstasy, the unquitters. Keith Baker, the American joggler, crosses the line with his three balls tossed in the air. Over the course of several hours, two hundred, three hundred, four hundred cross the finish line, a total of 432 out of the original 495. The runners accept their medals. They scream. They dance and they cry. But mostly they stare with beatific expressions, the proud, dazed look of communicants who've braved the pilgrimage to its redemptive end.

A few feet away from the main square, however, one runner's mood is black. Mauro Prosperi still can't believe he had to exit the race because of something so measly as a mangled toenail. The desert, it seems, has beaten him yet again, this time not with high drama—wandering lost in the wastelands—but with the banal. Prosperi has the perfect response: "In the autumn," he says, "I will run the entire length of the Sahara, five thousand kilometers, from the Atlantic Ocean to the Valley of the Kings." It's pain inflation. If seven days in the desert defeat you, try one hundred instead. He stares at the far dunes, anxious, I suspect, to get started.

The race winds down, the last dogged finishers plod across the line. A familiar, silver-maned figure catches my eye. Maurice! I didn't see him finish, and I feared he had joined the ranks of the quitters. But here he is now, the sixty-eight-year-old, one-lunged yogi, folded again into the lotus position, savoring a can of Coke. I want to commune with him, ask whether the desert taught him what he hoped it would, but he looks unapproachable in his moment of triumph. He's a million miles away, immersed in a tub of ice.

—1997

This Is Not the Place

Veracruz State, Mexico

NEAR THE TOWN of Palmyra, New York, rising over cornfields and dairy farms and the dark green thread of the Erie Canal, is a glacially formed monadnock known as the Hill Cumorah. It's too small to qualify as a mountain, but in its context Cumorah is an arresting sight, wildly out of scale with the somnolent farm country of New York's Finger Lakes region. At the hill's summit is an American flag, an asphalt pathway lined with pink rosebushes, and a golden statue of the angel Moroni, from the Book of Mormon.

I had come to this distinctive landmark one muggy evening in mid-July to watch the largest outdoor play in America, the Hill Cumorah Pageant, a two-hour spectacle that features a cast of over six hundred people. It's a kind of passion play that's been held in a grass field at the base of the hill every July for sixty-one years. When I arrived, an immense proscenium had been erected, and orchestral music was pouring through concert speakers. A crowd estimated at slightly more than ten thousand people had turned out for this, the seventh and final performance of the pageant. Along the edges of the field, hundreds of families were splayed out on blankets enjoying the cool air of twilight. Ruritans were selling hamburgers and personal pizzas, and cast members in biblical attire—deerskin robes, leather sandals, and long false beards—were ushering late arrivals to the last empty rows of plastic seats in the rear. Then the sun went down, and in a blaze of trumpets and laser lights swirling through smoke, the 627 actors gathered on the stage.

The Hill Cumorah Pageant tells the tale, in a drastically distilled form, of the Book of Mormon. The play traces the family history of the Nephites, a tribe of Jews who leave Jerusalem around 500 B.C., journey on foot across the desert, and then set sail for a promised land. They faithfully drift across the ocean, *Kon-Tiki* fashion, and, after many disasters at sea, come to light somewhere on American shores. Once established in the New World, the Nephites build impressive cities of stone and do remarkable work with agriculture and metallurgy, when they're not battling their chief adversaries, a crude band of Indians called the Lamanites, who wear antlers and feathered headdresses and look vaguely like the Aztecs. Christ makes a brief appearance in America, and there are wilderness wanderings, cataclysmic storms, even a volcanic eruption, with plumes of steam and potato flakes to simulate ash. The story ends with a great battle on the Hill Cumorah in which the Nephites are finally exterminated by the Lamanites. After the dust settles, only one Nephite remains: Moroni, son of the supreme commander, Mormon. It is Moroni's solemn duty to take the ancient records, engraved on a set of golden plates, and bury them in the hill so that someone, one day, will learn the true story of America's lost tribe of Hebrews.

As a coda to the play, the story jumps forward some fourteen hundred years to 1823. The spotlights are trained on a young man climbing high along the west face of the Hill Cumorah, while celestial strains of the Mormon Tabernacle Choir seep from the concert speakers. He kneels while the angel Moroni points to the spot where the golden plates are buried. The young man is the prophet Joseph Smith, and the record he removes from this hallowed ground is the Book of Mormon.

After the pageant I met a cast member, Sister Spencer from Michigan, a vivacious woman in her mid-forties who was stationed at the base of the statue of Moroni to answer any questions people might have about the import of the play.

"Whatever happened to the golden plates?" I asked her. "Are they in a museum somewhere?"

"No, they were returned to the angel Moroni, probably reburied somewhere," Sister Spencer said. "There are individuals in the church who would like to find them. But God will reveal them only when and if He wants to."

"Where did all of these events take place?" I asked her. "The wars, the civilizations?"

"Well," Sister Spencer said, "Joseph found the plates here; we know that. But we're not sure abut the rest of it. The scholars are now saying it all happened in southern Mexico."

"In Mexico?" I asked.

"That's what the experts at BYU are saying—Mexico, Central America. The Mayans and all those people down there. Those wonderful ruins."

This geographical leap seemed to me an implausible new wrinkle in an already implausible saga, but Sister Spencer's statement about the scholars at Brigham Young University, I would discover, was correct. The prevailing view within Mormon intellectual circles is that the primary action in the Book of Mormon did nct, in fact, happen in upstate New York, but in Mesoamerica. During the past half century, the Church of Jesus Christ of Latter-Day Saints has been quietly attempting to prove this new theory. Over the years, the church and wealthy Mormon benefactors have sunk what is conservatively estimated to be $10 million into archaeological research all across Central America in what may be the most ambitious hunt for a vanished civilization since Schliemann's search for Troy.

Much of the excavation work has been the stuff of scrupulous scholarship carried out under the auspices of Brigham Young University and, in particular, the Mormon-funded New World Archaeological Foundation, based in San Cristobal, Chiapas. Created in the early 1950s by a former FBI agent named Thomas Stuart Ferguson, the foundation initially concentrated its work on the preclassic period, roughly 600 B.C. to A.D. 300, which, not coincidentally, corresponds to Book of Mormon times. Yet the foundation has hired many non-Mormon scholars over the years and has published its findings without a whiff of religious bias.

Yet over the years southern Mexico has also seen a procession of Mormon cranks and amateurs nursing hopes of discovering the tomb of Nephi or the lost city of Zarahemla. Along the edges of legitimate, Mormon-financed archaeology, one finds a colorful demimonde, one that has turned out a steady crop of grainy videos and specious books written in the sweeping style of Erich von Däniken's *Chariots of the Gods?* A number of resourceful travel operators from Utah have capitalized on the trend, leading Mormons on "Holy Land" package tours to the ruins of Mexico, running advertisements in the *Salt Lake Tribune* and the *Deseret News*. Hundreds of Mormons make these freelance trips each year, packing into sour-smelling buses, wielding machetes and metal detectors and occasionally an archaeologist's trowel. With neither academic credentials nor official permits allowing them to go digging for relics, they bushwhack through the rain forests and savannas of Central America on the scent of lost Semitic civilizations.

MAINSTREAM ARCHAEOLOGISTS have scoffed at the church's long and, for the most part, discreet involvement with Mesoamerican archaeology—calling the Mormon theories patently absurd, procedurally flawed, even racist. The Smithsonian's National Museum of Natural History and the National Geographic Society have been so besieged with inquiries from enthusiastic Mormons over the years that both institutions have had to issue formal disclaimers stating that the Book of Mormon is not a historical text and that no evidence points to the existence of a Jewish civilization in ancient America. Perhaps the most outspoken critic of Mormon archaeology has been Yale University's Michael D. Coe, one of the world's preeminent scholars of the Olmec and the Maya. The author of the best-selling book *Breaking the Maya Code*, Coe says there's not "a whit of evidence that the Nephites ever existed. The whole enterprise is complete rot, root and branch. It's so racist it hurts. It fits right into the nineteenth-century American idea that only a white man could have built cities and temples, that

American Indians didn't have the brains or the wherewithal to create their own civilization."

Today, the ten-million-member Church of Jesus Christ of Latter-Day Saints is generally considered the fastest-growing denomination in the Western Hemisphere, especially among the Indian populations of South and Central America whose ancestors built the cities and temples that have so intrigued Mormon scholars. This is no accident, of course; the church has spent considerable money and effort proselytizing among the present-day Maya and other natives of the region, with church literature sometimes suggesting that the ancient Mexican god Quetzalcoatl was actually the triumphant Jesus Christ visiting the New World as depicted in the Book. Church missionaries often float the notion that American Indians are direct descendants of Book of Mormon peoples and are thus blessed with a sacred lineage.

Mormonism, in a sense, was born out of an inspired act of archaeology, Smith's stirring claim of having unearthed the golden plates. To this day, the Book of Mormon remains a sacred text with a unique status, in the sense that its value and weight, its purchase on the imagination of the convert, crucially depend upon its acceptance as an authentic artifact of archaeology, a written work that is historically accurate and even testable. From its opening page, the Book of Mormon presents itself not as a sacred allegory but as the record of an extinct race of Hebrews who lived and sweated and died on real American soil. The events in the book *had* to have happened, and somewhere on these shores, or the book is a fraud. Joseph Smith understood that any people with the sophistication of the Nephites surely would have left tangible traces of their civilization behind—a Hebrew inscription, a metal sword, a ruined temple mailed in jungle vine—and he always said that excavation work would eventually vindicate everything printed in the book.

But over the past fifty years, as Mormon scholars have begun to apply the techniques of modern archaeology, the search has only grown more complex, more desperate, more discouraging. Adherents of other faiths and sects have of course encountered similar problems when the astringent of science has been applied to their most cherished beliefs. The fields of geology and paleontology, for example, do little to substantiate the truncated time line of the creationists—quite the contrary. Despite the painstaking efforts of numerous Christian archaeologists, not a shred of evidence has yet appeared that suggests the presence of Noah's ark on Mount Ararat in Turkey. For years, India and Nepal have been engaged in a rancorous and ultimately futile archaeological rivalry to resolve the ancient debate over which of the two countries was the true native land of Siddhartha (the Buddha).

Then again, the Book of Mormon does pose unique problems for the empirical-minded reader—most fundamental, the problem of a wholly hypothetical geography. A Holy Land archaeologist can set up a dig in Jericho or Bethlehem and know with reasonable certainty that at least the location is about right. But a Mormon archaeologist is forced to work from a map constructed entirely from guesswork: none of the book's place-names match up with present-day sites, and the Americas lack the continuity of culture and language that one finds in Israel.

As archaeological digs throughout the Americas have increased our knowledge of ancient civilizations and led to such advances as the cracking of the Mayan hieroglyphic code, Mormondom has also been forced to confront the problem of evidence. What happens when the ground refuses to cooperate, when the soil fails to yield what the faith insists is there? For many Mormons, it's been a perilous quest, and more than a few who have ventured too far down the path have come back with their convictions in tatters, despairing at the lack of hard proof, wondering why the square pegs of belief won't fit into the round holes of the targeted terra firma.

JOSEPH SMITH WAS A RANGY young farmer when he began the two-year task of translating the Book of Mormon, "An Account Written by the Hand of Mormon upon Plates Taken from the Plates of Nephi." These golden plates, Smith said, were inscribed in an obscure hieroglyphic language called "Reformed Egyptian." A long and densely written epic that Mark Twain later described as "chloroform in print," the Book of Mormon was published in 1830. Shortly thereafter, a new religious sect was born, the Church of Jesus Christ of Latter-

Day Saints. Smith and his followers moved west to Kirtland, Ohio, then west again, to the Illinois banks of the Mississippi River, where a little city called Nauvoo rose from the canebrake, with Smith as general, mayor, newspaper editor, social chairman, lodge wizard, and beloved prophet. He improvised his own little satellite world, his own frontier phratry, out on the edge of America. He took thirty wives. He commanded what was then the second-largest standing army in the United States. He steamed up and down the Mississippi in his private stern-wheeler. He held grand feasts, dances, and wrestling matches. Smith was the life of his own party, following his passions right up until the end.

His most consuming passion, however, was for the American landscape itself—its ghosts and artifacts, the aboriginal prehistory of the New World, the puzzle of where the American Indians originated. In his youth, Smith had poked around the backwoods of New England as a "money digger," hunting for buried treasure that he said had been left by ancient civilizations. Throughout his life, he was fascinated by Indian mounds and liked to spin intricate romances about who built them, and why. "Joseph would occasionally give us some of the most amusing recitals that could be imagined," the prophet's mother, Lucy Smith, once recalled. "He would describe the ancient inhabitants of this continent, their dress, mode of traveling, and the animals upon which they rode; their cities, their buildings, with every particular; their mode of warfare; and also their religious worship. This he would do with as much ease, seemingly, as if he had spent his whole life with them."

When news of the stunning Mayan ruins at Palenque reached the United States in 1841 with the publication of John Lloyd Stephens's *Incidents of Travel in Central America, Chiapas, and Yucatan,* Smith speculated that the Maya must have been Book of Mormon peoples. At one point he enthusiastically stated that the Palenque ruins were "among the mighty works of the Nephites." A Nauvoo newspaper article later attributed to Smith went on to suggest, "It will not be a bad plan to compare Mr. Stephens's ruined cities with those in the Book of Mormon."

By that time, however, Smith was already enmeshed in more pressing plots—his run for the U.S. presidency in 1842, controversies arising from the church's views on polygamy, and mounting squabbles with state and federal authorities. Then in 1844, at the age of thirty-nine, Smith was murdered by a lynch mob at a jailhouse in Carthage, Illinois, where he had been temporarily imprisoned on conspiracy charges. Several years later, the church began the exodus west under the stern gaze of Brigham Young, a stout man who proved to be a shrewd institution-builder. Upon seeing the parched country around the Great Salt Lake, Young is said to have solemnly proclaimed, "This is the place!"

For the next hundred years, the church rarely revisited the question of just where in the New World the Nephites were supposed to have lived. The book offered few clues. The place-names that cropped up in the text—Desolation, Manti, Shemlon, Bountiful—matched up with neither ancient Indian nor modern American geography, and the descriptions and coordinates were vague at best. The book spoke of a "Land Northward," which the church fathers generally guessed to be North America, a "Land Southward" (South America?), and a "Land of Many Waters" (the Great Lakes?). Given these parameters, the faithful were left to assume that the action in the book had taken place in both North *and* South America, though mostly around upstate New York (especially the great Nephite-Lamanite battle depicted at the end), since that's where Smith had excavated the plates.

But within the anthropology department at Brigham Young University, another geographic paradigm began to evolve about fifty years ago. The more precisely scholars like BYU anthropologist M. Wells Jakeman studied the text, the more they realized that the action was, in fact, limited to an area of just a few hundred square miles. And the more they tried to superimpose the Book's mountains, rivers, oceans, weather, estimated travel times, and other characteristics over the physical landscapes of the Americas, the more apparent it became that wherever those few hundred square miles were, they certainly weren't anywhere near upstate New York.

When they boiled it down, what Mormon scholars were looking for was a "narrow neck of land," as the Book calls it, an isthmus set in a tropical climate (the text makes no mention of cold weather or snow) and surrounded by terrain known to have supported ancient peoples of sophisticated means—written language, masonry, astronomy, metal-working skills, and so forth. It eventually dawned on the scholars that they were throwing a dart at only one place, the same beguiling turf that Joseph Smith had speculated on from afar more than a century before: Mesoamerica, home of the Maya, the Olmec, the Toltec, the Zapotec, the Aztec, and other advanced civilizations of antiquity. After much study, Mormon scholars narrowed their focus to an area that encompassed slices of Guatemala and Honduras, and parts of the Mexican states of Veracruz, Tabasco, Oaxaca, and Chiapas.

"Book of Mormon Lands," they called it.

IF THERE IS a "headquarters" for Mormondom's interest in ancient Mesoamerica, it is a private nonprofit think tank called the Foundation for Ancient Research and Mormon Studies (FARMS). Housed on the BYU campus and handsomely endowed by the university and by faithful donors such as Mormon technobaron Alan Ashton (who founded the WordPerfect Corporation), FARMS is an energetic outfit that promotes all sorts of abstruse scholarship and research junkets of a vaguely cloak-and-daggerish nature. When I first called FARMS, for example, I was told that several FARMS researchers had proposed conducting "aerial reconnaissance missions" over southern Mexico to look for undiscovered ruin sites using the same "ground-penetrating radar technology," developed at BYU, that the U.S. military used to peer into Saddam Hussein's bunkers in 1991. Here, prochurch scholars write spirited disquisitions on themes related to the antiquity of the Book of Mormon and publish apologetic books and pamphlets at an impressive clip. It's a kind of all-purpose clearinghouse, the place inquisitive Mormons turn to for answers when critics raise nettlesome questions about the ancient provenance of the book or the apparent paucity of archaeological evidence for Nephite civilization.

When I dropped by FARMS on a bitterly cold and gusty winter day, I was led down the hall and introduced to the venerable white-haired theoretician sometimes referred to as the Thomas Aquinas of ancient Mormon studies—a tall, thin, precise gentleman in his mid-seventies named John L. Sorenson. A former chairman of BYU's anthropology department, Sorenson is a full-time scholar at FARMS and the author of numerous books, including the definitive work on the subject, *An Ancient American Setting for the Book of Mormon*. Personally involved in nearly every debate of consequence in the field for the past half century, Sorenson is one of the principal architects of the notion that the action of the Book of Mormon occurred in Mesoamerica.

Ushered into his office, I found Sorenson leaning against a map of Mexico, absorbed in thought as he peered out his window at a winter storm sailing in fast from the alkali flats to the west. Once I sat down he snapped from his reverie, like a maestro satisfied that the crowd was now sufficiently hushed.

"You know," he began, "I've never asked the question, '*Did* the events in the Book of Mormon happen?' I was born and raised in the church, and so for me this is beyond doubt. The question I've asked over fifty years of scholarship is, '*How* did they happen?' Where did these people live, what were they like, what did they eat? I am very interested in establishing the book's historicity. This is supposed to be the authentic record of a dead people. It won't suffice to say that Joseph Smith merely wrote it to impart a few spiritual truths. If it were ever conclusively demonstrated that Smith simply made it up, I don't know whether the church could survive."

Driven by this sense of geographical certainty, and possessed of a polymath's grasp of interdisciplinary detail, John Sorenson has spent the better part of his life hunkered in libraries, examining all sorts of arcane topics: linguistic cognates, ancient seeds of grain, comparisons of intestinal parasites, the possible resemblance of a specific Mayan glyph to a specific Hebrew character, the insufficiency of the Bering Strait land-bridge theory to explain how *all* Native Americans arrived in the New World. Listening to Sorenson tick off these baroque lines of inquiry, I felt as though I were in the presence of a first-rate mind that had long since become inured to the stalemates and disappointments of a bedeviling scavenger hunt. "I've been at this for over a half century," he said, "and believe me, I have ways of managing the data reasonably so that I can take into account every apparent problem and contradiction in the book."

The problems and contradictions in the book are legion, in fact, and dealing with them has kept Sorenson and his colleagues ceaselessly busy. Take the problem of elephants, to raise one prominent example. The book mentions elephants several times, and yet as far as we know there weren't any elephants in Central America. This issue leads down a trail littered with imponderables: Could it be an error in translation? Could a woolly mammoth qualify as an elephant? Did mammoths ever exist in Central America, and at a time contemporaneous with Book of Mormon peoples? (So far, the evidence is no.) Should the church dispatch archaeologists to Mexico to hunt for mastodon bones?

The Book of Mormon describes dozens of other species of animals and domesticated plants that have yet to turn up in any pre-Columbian Mesoamerican excavations, including horses, asses, bulls, goats, oxen, sheep, barley, grapes, olives, figs, and wheat. This is not to mention all the inanimate objects: coins, functional wheels, metal swords, brass armor, chariots, carriages, glass, chains, golden plates.

The cumulative effect of all these minute examples would seem to deal a deathblow to the whole enterprise of Mormon archaeology. Yet BYU scholars like Sorensen have found all sorts of exotic rationales to circumnavigate these issues. Sorenson has gone so far as to postulate that the book may have been referring to a tapir or a deer when Joseph Smith copied down the word "horse," although on the face of it, the idea of soldiers riding tapirs into battle seems ludicrously impractical. Sorenson has also suggested in his books and essays that the "chariots" referred to in the book weren't what *we* think of as chariots, but some considerably more primitive conveyance without wheels more akin to a sled or a sledge, or even a nuptial bed.

Other Mormon scholars have been less willing to trowel over these apparent inconsistencies. In at least one public forum, BYU archaeologist Ray Matheny has been surprisingly blunt about the serious dilemmas posed by these glaring holes in the archaeological record. "I'd say this is a fairly king-sized problem," Matheny observed at a tape-recorded symposium in 1984 in Salt Lake City. "Mormons, in particular, have been grasping at straws for a very long time, trying to thread together all of these little esoteric finds that are out of context. If I were doing it cold, I would say in evaluating the Book of Mormon that it had no place in the New World whatsoever. It just doesn't seem to fit anything that I have been taught in my discipline in anthropology. It seems like these are anachronisms." Matheny concluded his talk with a sockdolager: "As an archaeologist," he said, "what [can] I say . . . that might be positive for the Book of Mormon? Well, really very little."

With John Sorenson's elastic style of argumentation setting the overall tone, there is about FARMS a dizzying buzz of intellectual energy, with scholars investigating every imaginable cranny of inquiry, from hermeneutics to meteorology, from animal husbandry to the prevailing currents of the oceans. Yale's Michael Coe likes to talk about what he calls "the fallacy of misplaced concreteness," the tendency among Mormon theorists like Sorenson to keep the discussion trained on all sorts of extraneous subtopics (like tapirs and nuptial beds) while avoiding what is most obvious: that Joseph Smith probably meant "horse" when he wrote down the word "horse," and that all the archaeology in the world is not likely to change the fact that horses as we know them weren't around until the Spaniards arrived on American shores.

"They're always going after the nitty-gritty things," Coe told me. "Let's look at this specific hill. Let's look at that specific tree. It's exhausting to follow all these mind-numbing leads. It keeps the focus off the fact that it's all in the service of a completely phony history. Where are the languages? Where are the cities? Where are the artifacts? Look here, they'll say. Here's an elephant. Well, that's fine, but elephants were wiped out in the New World around 8000 B.C. by hunters. *There were no elephants!*"

"This is a very, very lonely line of work," Sorenson told me, running a hand through his thinning hair. "Non-Mormon archaeologists and anthropologists don't want to have anything to do with us. Still, Mesoamerica is such a wide-open field, with so many complexities and conundrums. Only one one-hundredth of one percent of the material has been excavated. And so I have complete faith that over time, the answers are going to rise up out of the forest carpet . . . like wild mushrooms."

★ ★ ★

IT WAS JOHN SORENSON who put me in touch with a group of young Mormon financial consultants from Salt Lake City about to embark on their own two-week archaeological junket in southern Mexico. Merrill Chandler, Steve Paige, and Jayson Orvis were close friends and business partners, all in their mid-thirties. They were heading down to survey a number of impressive ruins, from Monte Alban to Palenque to Chiapa de Corzo. I met them on a paintball field on the outskirts of Salt Lake City, where they held a weekly battle, and after the skirmish was over, they asked me to accompany them on their trip. I would be the fourth and only non-Mormon member of their "expedition," which was a bit of an overstatement, since they were without government permits and knew virtually nothing about the discipline of Mesoamerican archaeology. They called me "the gentile."

A few weeks later we were renting a VW bus at the airport in Mexico City and heading for points south. We looped through the foggy, pine-forested highlands of Chiapas, still seething with its Zapatista rebellion. We met with dirty-nailed Mormon archaeologists in San Cristobal, nosed around in caves, and took a dory up the Rio Grijalva, thought to be the holy river "Sidon" that figures prominently in the Book of Mormon.

The primary target of our trip, however, was the Olmec country along the Gulf Coast of Veracruz State. After much searching, John Sorenson has postulated that a certain mountain along the coastal plains of Veracruz called Cerro El Vigia is the "most likely candidate" for the Hill Cumorah of the Book of Mormon. (As fantastic as it may seem, Sorenson actually argues that there were *two* Cumorahs: one in Mexico where the great battle took place, and where Moroni buried a longer, unexpurgated version of the golden Nephite records; and the one near Palmyra, New York, where Moroni eventually buried a condensed version of the plates after lugging them on an epic trek of several thousand miles). Cerro El Vigia is the nub of a long dormant volcano, hanging over pastures of Brahman cattle and sugarcane fields. My comrades' plan was to climb Cerro El Vigia—"the sacred mountain," they called it—with shovels and sifting crates to look around for evidence of the battle that may or may not have taken place there fourteen centuries ago.

Steve was an anxious, flaxen-haired chili-pepper fanatic whose mind constantly raced with pet conjectures fed by topo maps and dog-eared Mormon archaeology books. Jayson, on the other hand, was soft-spoken, skeptical, his deep brown eyes pooling with doubts about the advisability of the trip. "I can't help wondering where this all leads," he had confided in me. "I guess my logical requirements are more stringent."

It was Merrill who would turn out to be the natural leader of our expedition. Brash, fearless, a large guy with a knack for accelerating the plot of whatever situation in which he happened to find himself, Merrill had been dreaming about this trip for years, and his expectations were sky-high. "We're not here just to eat some tacos," Merrill had told me as he climbed aboard our rental bus in Mexico City. "We're all stalwart members. This is our Holy Land tour."

The night before our planned "assault" on the hallowed mountain, we stopped off in the nearby lakeside hamlet of Catemaco, a town famous all over Veracruz as an annual gathering place for witches and warlocks. We ordered a paella dinner at an outdoor restaurant and began to discuss the great Nephite-Lamanite battle on the Hill Cumorah. Merrill read to us from Mormon 6:7: "All my people had fallen; and their flesh, and bones, and blood lay upon the face of the earth, being left by the hands of those who slew them to molder upon the land, and to crumble and to return to their mother earth."

"It was a bloodbath," said Steve. "Hundreds of thousands of Nephite corpses. Any battle that big, there's bound to be local legends."

"Exactly," said Merrill. "So what we need to do is find the head *brujo* of Catemaco and plumb his knowledge of the folklore around here. They say his name is Apolinar. Supposed to be the most famous one in Veracruz State. He lives just down the street here, at Hidalgo number twenty."

We eventually found the house, just off the *zócalo*, and studied the little sign out front—APOLINAR GUEIXPAL SEBA, BOTANICA Y CIENCIAS OCULTAS. Merrill rapped on the massive oak gate. After a long wait, the hinges creaked open, and there stood Apolinar himself. He was a frightening sight, a Hispanic version of Alice Cooper, attired in black leather pants and a black leather vest draped over luridly tattooed pectorals. He seemed unhappy to see us, as if we'd just interrupted something—the weekly infanticide, perhaps. But when Merrill paid him something in advance for his services, Apolinar reluctantly led us back to his lair, a room crowded with jarred elixirs and dried insects and the mingled fragrances of a dozen incense sticks.

"So may I help you in finding a loved one?" Apolinar's eyes glinted in the thin light of a votive candle. "Or are you ill?"

"No, *gracias*," said Merrill, who speaks fluent Spanish from his days as a missionary in Guatemala in the late 1980s. "We are Mormons. We've come from Utah, in the United States, to learn about Cerro El Vigia."

Apolinar regarded us in silence for a long moment, and said, "Ah, El Vigia. It is a magical place."

"Magical in what way?" Merrill asked.

"There are so many legends. It is said that there was once a fierce and bloody battle."

"A *what?*" Merrill said, his interest quickening.

"*Sí*, it is an old, old story," Apolinar went on. "Hundreds and thousands fell. It is believed that their ghosts are still up there, swirling in the mist."

Merrill was hungry for more. "In this battle you speak of—who was doing the fighting?"

"I cannot say more. It is a belief we do not like to discuss. But, if you must know more, well . . . it is said that there is a book buried up on the mountain."

Merrill was beside himself. A book? Buried in the hill? This is precisely what the Mormons believe—and I could sense that Apolinar knew it. He'd doubtless heard the story of the Mormon interest in Cerro El Vigia before, and he'd seen those squads of clean-cut missionaries all suited up and knocking on doors around town. I suspected he was preying on Merrill's hopes a little, just for kicks.

Apolinar could have been Lucifer himself, but Merrill seemed buoyed by everything the *brujo* had said. After we left Apolinar's place, Merrill drove us toward Cerro El Vigia, which was faintly visible in the moonlight, a dim swell of basalt scarved in fog. Merrill said he'd made up his mind to buy a little hacienda in the town of Santiago Tuxtla so he could come down from Utah on a regular basis to live near the sacred mountain. Now, as he beheld its presence, there was a look of misty awe in his eyes, the same devout look I'd seen on the faces of the Mormon pilgrims up in Palmyra, New York. It was the sentimental gaze of ancestral longing, the yearning for a kind of motherland. Only this was a motherland based on literary constructs and anthropological speculation rather than on bloodlines, a theoretical motherland thrice removed, with Hebrew ancestors said to be related to American descendants through an Egyptian-language text purportedly unearthed over 150 years ago by a young farmer nearly three thousand miles north of here. It was a nostalgia, in other words, that had to travel through a fabulous, labyrinthine circuit before it could be felt.

IT'S DOUBTFUL that any Latter-Day Saint has ever felt this sense of sentimental kinship with the Nephites as vividly as the late Thomas Stuart Ferguson, an attorney and former FBI agent who, from the early 1950s to the 1970s, was more or less the godfather of Mormon archaeology. Born in Pocatello, Idaho, and educated at Berkeley, Ferguson was a vigorous, headstrong man who believed with absolute certainty that excavations in Mexico would one day vindicate the Mormon faith. In the late 1940s, flush with excitement over the new Mesoamerican parameters that had been staked out by BYU scholars, Ferguson personally tromped through the jungles of Chiapas hunting for suitable candidates for Nephite ruins.

One of his comrades on those early freelance expeditions to Mexico and Guatemala was his friend J. Willard Marriott, the Mormon hotel magnate. In one letter, Marriott recalls, "We spent several months together in Mexico looking at the ruins and studying the Book of Mormon archaeology. I have never known anyone who was more devoted to that kind of research than was Tom."

Another of Ferguson's traveling companions to Mexico was John Sorenson, who was then a young anthropology Ph.D. candidate. "Tom was a lawyer, first, last, and always," Sorenson told me. "He had no training in archaeology. To him, things had to be *proven*. He wanted to hit the jackpot, to find a chariot or a Hebrew inscription or something. He was betting everything on a pull at the slot machine. Ferguson's view was, the Book of Mormon talks about horses, there should be figurines showing horses. So everywhere he went, his first question to campesinos was 'Seen any figurines of horses?' Tom felt like he had to have something moderately spectacular to sell to the church. No archaeologist had ever systematically looked at Chiapas before, so we took a Jeep up there and looked around." The results were impressive: Sorenson and Ferguson were able to identify some seventy potential sites in less than two weeks of traveling.

In 1952, Ferguson formed the New World Archaeological Foundation and then set about soliciting funding from the church and from well-to-do Mormon benefactors. The following year, the church quietly presented the foundation with an initial grant of $15,000, with a much larger sum of $200,000 to be given in 1955. Ferguson was shrewd enough to realize that if his quest were to succeed, he must hire objective, non-Mormon scholars, and he lured some of the most prominent names in the field, including Gordon Ekholm, who later became curator of American archaeology at New York's Museum of Natural History, and A. V. Kidder, the grand old man of American archaeology. From the outset, Ferguson stipulated that the NWAF "would not discuss direct connections with the Book of Mormon, but rather [would] allow the work to stand exclusively on its scholarly merits."

"Let the evidence from the ground speak for itself," Ferguson declared, "and let the chips fall where they may."

The NWAF set up its first large dig at Chiapa de Corzo, and the site proved a fabulous trove for studying the formative preclassic period. Ferguson was ecstatic. "The importance of the work carried out this past season cannot be overestimated," he wrote in a letter to the first presidency of the church. "I know, and I know it without doubt and without wavering, that we are standing at the doorway of a great Book of Mormon era."

In October of 1957, NWAF archaeologists dug up a cylinder seal from a site at Chiapa de Corzo that caused immediate excitement. The seal was inscribed with an unusual-looking ornamental design that, to Ferguson's eyes at least, resembled Egyptian hieroglyphics. In May of the following year, he sent a photograph of the seal to an eminent Egyptologist at Johns Hopkins University named Dr. William F.

Albright. Without prompting from Ferguson, Albright examined the photograph and, in a letter, stated that the cylinder seal contained "several clearly recognizable Egyptian hieroglyphs." Although other Egyptologists would later dispute Albright's assessment, Ferguson was overjoyed, believing with heart and soul that this was the first piece of incontrovertible proof of the Nephites. "In my personal opinion," he wrote in a moment of religious abandon, "[Albright's finding] will ultimately prove to have been one of the most important announcements ever made."

THE RUTTED DIRT road on the back side of Cerro El Vigia winds through green jungle, past the tin-sided shacks of campesinos, and eventually peters out on the high, wind-scrubbed flanks, where thousands of enormous basalt boulders are spread over the golden grass like caviar on toast. These are the lava fields that provided the raw material for the colossal Olmec busts—some of which weigh more than ten tons—that now squat in town squares along the Veracruz coast. How they managed to drag these immense rocks from the mountains is one of the many riddles that surround the Olmecs, who died out around 400 B.C. and are generally considered the progenitors of all other advanced civilizations in Mexico.

Steve, Jayson, and I were standing amid this boulder field, while Merrill held a compass in his hand and surveyed the landscape like a commanding general, envisioning the battle lines as they must have looked during the great Nephite-Lamanite engagement. We had been up here all day, wandering through a maze of impressive petroglyphs. It was dusk now, and Mexican free-tailed bats swooped down at us, attracted to the bugs that were attracted to our headlamps. Down in the valley, the first lights of Santiago Tuxtla gave off a skim-milk blue.

In the gathering darkness, a campesino named Carlisto pointed out a long, slender boulder lying in the scrub. On its underside, he said, there was rumored to be an elaborate carving that dated back to Olmec times. Apparently it had fallen over years ago like a pillar at Stonehenge, and no one had ever bothered to right it.

Merrill stood there considering the capsized monolith. He brushed his hand over the hard, pebbly surface and scanned it with his flashlight.

Maybe, Carlisto politely suggested, we would like to come back tomorrow morning and have a better look?

"I say we turn it over right now!" Merrill replied, and as if to emphasize his point, he shined his flashlight in our faces. "We've got plenty of manpower here," he added, nodding at the dozen or so friends and relatives of Carlisto, who'd gathered to see what the commotion was about.

Presently, all of us assumed our places around the rock and started building up a rhythm of shoves, tossing in stone chocks after each heave while Merrill used a large log as a prying lever. Soon we could see a piece of the underside, but it was caked in dirt and hard to make out.

"Maybe it's a horse," Steve said, hopefully.

With one last push, the boulder tipped forward and tumbled downhill. Twenty yards below us, it rolled to a stop in a cloud of dust. We all scurried over to it. There was just enough juice left in Merrill's flashlight to limn the outlines: a round lobe here. Another lobe over there. A long shaft that culminated in . . .

The campesinos couldn't contain their laughter. It was impossible to ignore the obvious. After an exercise that only hinted at the hernias and slipped discs the Olmecs must have suffered as they hauled their titanic rocks to the coast, we had succeeded in unearthing what must be one of the more magnificent stone phalluses in the New World.

"What does this mean for the Book of Mormon?" asked Steve.

"It doesn't mean jack!" Merrill replied, laughing for a while with the others. Then, as the campesinos wandered back to their shacks for the night, Merrill lingered in silence by the monolith, catching his breath, wondering whether this was, in fact, the place.

DESPITE TOM FERGUSON'S nearly effervescent zeal, the New World Archaeological Foundation managed to hold fast to its original pledge to keep Mormonism out of its scholarship, and over the years it developed an international reputation for first-class work. This had much to do with the efforts of Gareth Lowe, the meticulous Mormon archaeologist who served as the foundation's director for thirty years. "We were always dealing with a tension between doing good scholarship and just digging for Mormonism," recalls Lowe, who is now retired and living in Tucson, Arizona. "The church would tell people in the congregation, Relax, we have people down there who're investigating things. Just hold tight. They're on the case. But when I went down there, I realized I was very green and wide-eyed. I decided early on that we might never find anything that proves the Book of Mormon. But by doing good science, at least we could make a contribution. There was almost nothing known about these early cultures."

I asked Lowe whether, after all those years of digging under the auspices of the church, he was still a faithful Mormon. He paused thoughtfully for a long moment and then replied, somewhat gingerly, "Well, my wife still is."

Yale's Michael Coe worked with Gareth Lowe and other NWAF scholars in the fifties, sixties, and seventies, and says he has "nothing but absolute admiration" for their work. "They did the first really long-term, large-scale work on the preclassic in Mesoamerica, and they published it all. And by and large, their Mormonism never came through. Occasionally they'd get these dopes out of Utah who'd arrive with metal detectors and earphones and march around their sites trying to find the plates of gold. But the foundation's scholars always made sure they got on the plane and went back home. What's amazing is that they were able to do this kind of scholarship within the context of what is essentially a totalitarian organization."

By the early 1970s, surveying all of the foundation's notable findings, Thomas Ferguson began to assemble the case for the Book's ancient origins. Other than the "Egyptian" cylinder seal, the NWAF excavators had found nothing that seemed to authenticate the Mormon faith. Ferguson grew increasingly alarmed by this lack of progress. In a letter dated June 5, 1972, he would write, "I sincerely anticipated that Book of Mormon cities would be positively identified within ten years—and time has proved me wrong."

What began merely as a mild suspicion would become an inexorable undertow of doubt. In 1975 Ferguson wrote a twenty-nine-page paper analyzing the case for Mormon archaeology. Entitled "Written Symposium on Book-of-Mormon Geography," it had all the hallmarks of a legal brief. Under the heading, "Evidence supporting the existence of these forms of animal life in the regions proposed," he ticked off: "Ass: None. Bull: None. Calf: None. Cattle: None. Cow: None. Goat: None. Horse: None. Ox: None. Sheep: None. Sow: None. Elephant: None . . ."

In this same legalistic fashion, Ferguson surveyed the long list of plants and artifacts that pose similar problems for the Book of Mormon: barley, figs, grapes, wheat, bellows, brass breastplates, chains, copper, gold, iron, mining ore, plowshares, silver, metal swords, metal hilts, engraving, steel carriages, carts, chariots, glass. The evidence for their existence in pre-Columbian Mesoamerica, he succinctly summarized, was "zero."

Eventually Ferguson, the indefatigable apostle and founder of Mormon archaeology, came to the anguished conclusion that Joseph Smith had simply invented the Book of Mormon out of whole cloth. He pronounced Mormonism a "myth fraternity," and slipped into a profound spiritual crisis that lasted until his death, of a heart attack, in 1983. "You can't set Book of Mormon geography down anywhere," he wrote in 1976, "because it is fictional and will never meet the requirements of the dirt-archaeology. What is in the ground will never conform to what is in The Book." And in another letter: "I have been spoofed by Joseph Smith."

DESPITE THE CURRENT of doubt within liberal Mormon intellectual circles, and despite its own patriarch's profound disenchantment, the New World Archaeological Foundation lives on today. It's a small, dedicated outfit based in San Cristobal, Chiapas, with a tiny staff of archaeologists still quietly digging in the dirt of southern Mexico. When I stopped by to visit the foundation, I was greeted by archaeologist Ron Lowe, Gareth Lowe's son, who gave me a tour of the musty offices and examining rooms, with topo maps on the walls and countless portfolio drawers filled with carefully cataloged potsherds and artifacts. The foundation's budget has been scaled back, perhaps because the church leaders saw in Ferguson's story a cautionary tale about the perils of using science to "prove" the historical origins of the faith, and perhaps because so little had been found to pique the faithful's interest. The scaleback came in the mid-1990s, shortly after the foundation staff was embroiled in an embarrassing sex scandal: one of the senior Mormon archaeologists was formally accused of sleeping with the underage daughter of the NWAF cook, and this allegation led to a number of firings and a wholesale rethinking of the foundation's mission.

Still, Brigham Young University remains committed to funding the NWAF, and its current director, the respected Mesoamericanist and BYU professor John Clark, has pursued a cautious course of serious, no-nonsense archaeology.

"Everybody still believes we've got this secret agenda to validate the Book of Mormon, and it makes my life very difficult," Clark told me. "The problem is, we have these so-called Book of Mormon tours, we have a lot of people running around trying to find Nephi's tomb. I get very nervous about people knowing more than they can possibly know. Archaeological data in the hands of the wrong person scares the heck out of me."

Clark spoke with all the concentrated caution of a high-wire artist. I could sense that he'd had much practice negotiating the fine line that's strung between the faith that sustains him, the university that pays him, and the scholarly discipline that gives him professional respect. He said he wished Mormon archaeology, as a subject, would go away. Yet it was more than mere coincidence that of all the regions of the world, he'd chosen ancient Mesoamerica as the place to sink in his trowel and stake his career for Brigham Young University. It was as though the ghost of Joseph Smith were perched on his shoulder, pointing enthusiastically at maps and continents, suggesting places to dig for the ultimate treasure. Clark did his best to tune him out, but the founder's ghost was such a steady distraction, proposing such quixotic goose chases, spinning such fanciful diversions, that it was virtually impossible to ignore his presence, try as one might.

"Look," Clark finally said, "I'm just trying to be a professional archaeologist. To me, the Book of Mormon has the feel of an ancient document, and any problems are problems of translation. I believe it did happen someplace. I just don't know where. But I, for one, can live with the uncertainty."

—1999

Baruch

I WAS FEELING APPREHENSIVE the afternoon I took the bus out of Jerusalem and headed north through the hills into the heart of the *intifada*. I wondered what I'd say to my old friend Bruce. I hadn't seen him in ten years. In that time our lives had drifted far apart. He'd left his life in America behind and adopted a new country, a new language, even a new version of his name. Bruce had become *Baruch*, and he had recast himself as a Zionist pioneer in a settlement on the West Bank, living on disputed land that Israel had won during the 1967 war.

My bus pulled up to a road sign that said, BET EL, which means "House of God." This was said to be the ancient Biblical site where Jacob, sleeping on pillows of stone, dreamed he saw a ladder reaching to heaven. As I stepped off, a young man with a sunbaked face flashed a familiar smile as he called out my name.

Baruch was driving an old Volvo dented by stones thrown by Palestinians who lived nearby. Through the window I could see an Uzi lying across the passenger seat, a weapon absolutely necessary for his survival whenever he drove around here. "It's a different life I've got here," Baruch told me. "A *very* different life."

While some of the seeds of Bruce's metamorphosis had already taken root in high school, I still found it hard to believe my old friend had taken this path. Bruce and I had grown up in Memphis, he a conservative Jew, I a rainy-day Presbyterian. We'd played soccer together and prowled the blues clubs by the river. The Bruce I'd known in high school was a class clown with wild, frizzy hair and a bad eye that, because of a detached retina, sometimes wandered as though it had a will of its own. He was interesting and tolerant, a fierce arguer for fairness. As the editor of our school's literary magazine, he had shown, almost to a fault, an intense appreciation for all possible viewpoints. With generosity and zest, he introduced me to the rudiments of the Jewish faith. He went off to college in Massachusetts, and I'd heard that he became a prominent leader in a national Jewish youth organization. Gradually we lost touch with one another.

Ten years later, I was traveling for a month in Egypt and Israel. I was staying with an old college friend in the endlessly extraordinary city of Jerusalem, and somehow I got hold of Bruce's phone number. I decided to pay him a visit.

I had to marvel at how good he looked now. Nine years in the Mideast sun had turned his skin a deep bronze, and his hair was clipped short beneath his yarmulke. Baruch looked like he belonged here, like he'd found his place in the world. At twenty-eight, Baruch was the father of four children, and he spent much of the day studying the Torah.

He was excited as he led me on a tour of the settlement, which was clean and new and heavily subsidized by the Israeli government. Its various apartments and utility buildings felt as though they'd shot up overnight from the bleached countryside, like desert blooms. Baruch showed me a workshop where settlers cut and polished industrial diamonds for a living. He introduced me to his Sephardic wife, Anat, who seemed lovely but solemn and spoke little or no English. She was pregnant with their fifth child. Baruch admonished me in so many words not to shake her hand or touch her, as was the custom. He showed me an excavation site where American archaeologists had been sifting the ancient tells. Baruch pointed out that, among other things, the archaeologists had found evidence that Jews preceded Arabs here.

Later, we paused to speak with a group of Israeli soldiers watching over a Palestinian village that was astonishingly close. Baruch thanked one of the soldiers for his hard work and gave him a piece of home-baked cake to eat. As we looked down at the Arab lights and cooking fires that speckled the valley, we could hear dogs barking and pots rattling and the wails of infants in the crisp dry air. During the Gulf War, the settlers at Bet El could hear the refugees cheering crazily from their rooftops as Saddam's Scud missiles struck Tel Aviv. For every Baruch there were ten or twenty young Omars and Abduls across the way, refusing to countenance the legitimacy of any Jewish state, and thirsting always for vengeance. They grew more radical by the minute, dreaming of killing not only the Israelis, but also the Americans, who, in their minds, smiled on the whole situation from afar. I realized that Baruch and his villagers couldn't live at Bet El without the Israeli military constantly keeping an eye on things and clamping down on the resistance. Here, settlers and soldiers went hand in hand.

"Those people over there," I said. "Do they have a right to be there?"

"No, absolutely not," Baruch said adamantly.

"Why?"

"Because we were here first," he said. Baruch went on to give me a Biblical geography lesson about the lands of ancient Judea and Samaria and why the scriptures and traditions of the Jewish faith validate his proposition that the Hebrews belong here. "These lands," he said, "are the Biblical heartland of the Jewish people."

I tried to reason with Baruch, for in high school he had always savored logic. The archaeologists might "prove" that Jews occupied this particular piece of real estate first, but they could always dig deeper and find even older civilizations—Phoenician, Philistine, Hittite, Canaanite, whatever. In any case, Arabs have lived hereabouts for centuries, and they weren't going to leave now. Their hatreds were only going to fester, and their grievances, real and imagined, would predictably assume more violent incarnations. I was neither a Biblical scholar nor an archaeologist, but the political situation here seemed more than obvious. You didn't have to side with the Palestinians to see that each new house the settlers built was another nail, a very calculated nail, in the coffin of the international peace process. "If you ask me," I said, "you're here to inflame the situation. You're here to preempt any future possibility of peace."

Baruch did not exactly disagree. "This land is ours. We want them *out*. We're not here to argue. By occupying this land, we're creating a fact." Then he locked his eyes on me, and, with perfect confidence, said, "It's a law of Euclidean geometry that two points cannot occupy the same space. That's the situation here. It's our claim of sovereignty, or theirs."

The conversation soon dwindled into awkward silence. There was nothing more that could be said. In a few short minutes, we'd worked our way down to that most venerable formula for bloodshed, which is little more than a baseline sentiment of tribal survival, a sentiment beyond the reach of reason: *Us or them*.

Our visit lasted only a few hours. Always generous, he treated me to dinner, and we caught up on things, talking about old friends and old times, anything but politics. I glanced at my watch and realized I had to go if I wanted to catch the last bus to Jerusalem. Bruce dropped me off at the bus stop and waited while I got on board. When I turned to look back, he was standing with a machine gun slung over his shoulder with all the focused vigilance of a frontiersman defending his family from hostile Indians. And for a moment I saw Baruch in the tradition of the American pioneer, in the proud and defiant tradition that encourages one to change his name, change his home, change his identity, and freely push into the wilderness despite all dangers and obstacles. But for certain inconvenient realities that marred the picture, Baruch would, like the settlers of the American West, seem nearly heroic.

I thanked him for his hospitality and said, "It's good to see you, Bruce." For some reason, I couldn't call him Baruch. He smiled and turned away, and I added, "Be careful."

On the ride back to Jerusalem, his reference to geometry kept turning in my mind. *Two points cannot occupy the same space*. Bruce and I had spent many nights studying geometry together back in high school. He loved axioms, I remember, and he'd get this amazing grin on his face whenever he had nailed a particularly trying proof, shouting "Q.E.D!" I found it somehow terrifying to hear him conjuring up our old schoolboy lessons in this way. On some level, I envied him his certitude, the disciplined and even courageous conviction that gave direction to his choices. As a more or less typical American not long out of college, restless and probably a little spoiled, I didn't believe in anything with such clarity of faith. I knew that he had done a lot of hard thinking and had made a lot of sacrifices to get where he was now. His was not an easy life, and he was taking daily risks in the face of danger, both for himself and his growing family. Indeed, Baruch had lost several friends to the senseless acts of Palestinian terrorists. I worried for his safety.

But I did not know this Baruch. This Baruch infuriated me. It was disconcerting to see such a likable old friend finding fulfillment in such a baldly provocative life. It seemed to me that Baruch, and settlers like him, had made themselves a large part of the problem in the greater conflict of Palestine and Israel—a tragedy to which my own country is intimately and even financially connected, a tragedy that reaches out far beyond the tiny settlement of Bet El to enrage the world. Baruch and his fellow pioneers may have had many good reasons to be here— to practice their faith, to raise their families, to commune with the ancient desert—but in the end they were nothing so much as agitants, insinuating themselves into an already delicate situation and intensifying its urgent complexities. They could live their particular life just about anywhere but deliberately chose to be here in perhaps the world's most contested spot. Baruch didn't look at it this way, but he was perpetuating a cycle of heartache by his daily presence in a place that was not his native home, a place to which he'd traveled halfway around the world to stake a settler's claim.

Bruce would always be my friend; Baruch I would find forever incomprehensible.

The bus rolled south through the hilly desert, which glittered, here and there, with other shiny new West Bank settlements, each one as incongruous, as obstinate, as the next: huddles of light against the dry darkness, hard seeds of black hope.

—1992

Ghosts of Bataan

Luzon Island, The Philippines

"WELL, IT BRINGS BACK A LOT OF MEMORIES," Malcolm Amos told me in a soft, gravelly voice. "I don't know whether it's good for my system to be here. Because there are no good memories in this place."

Amos and I were walking down the long rows of graves in the American Cemetery in Manila—a kind of tropical version of Arlington National—where seventeen thousand American soldiers who died all across the Pacific lie buried beneath mango trees and riots of bougainvillea. Amos, a World War II veteran and former POW from a small town in Iowa, clutched a homemade walking stick he'd fashioned from bamboo. An amiable man in his late seventies, with downy white hair peeking from beneath his feed cap, he stopped from time to time to study the names.

I shook my head with a kind of dull incomprehension typical of my generation, I think, whenever we confront the magnitude of the losses suffered by those who fought in the Second World War. The Manila cemetery seemed to sprawl forever, the white crucifixes warping in the heat waves. There were names without bodies and bodies without names: Marble walls listed thousands of men presumed or known to be dead for whom no physical traces were ever found, while thousands of headstones marked recovered remains whose identities "are known only to God."

Amos, who had spent three years slaving in a prison camp sixty miles north of here, gazed abstractedly at the crosses. He said, "So many got sick and died, or were shot and bayoneted by the Japanese. I was one of the lucky ones, I guess."

Amos and about a dozen other World War II veterans had come to the Philippines with their families because they wanted to see the old battlegrounds and sites of their captivity. There are, we all must know by now, no good wars. But for men like Amos and his comrades, this war was decidedly, monumentally, bad. For these American veterans, coming back here to the Philippines is like revisiting the scene of a catastrophe, a landscape of wreckage and loss. On a sweltering day in May, these proud "ghosts of Bataan," hobbling on sore feet racked with residual neuropathies from the beriberi they suffered during their vitamin-starved captivity, had come to lay a wreath for their fallen comrades in the white marble chapel on the grounds. In all, it's estimated that more than ten thousand Americans perished in the Philippines—during the siege of Bataan and Corregidor, on the forced prisoner evacuation known as the Bataan Death March, in the Japanese-run POW camps, on ill-fated transport ships bound for Japan, or during General Douglas MacArthur's long, bloody retaking of the archipelago. As a whole, the American experience in the Philippines was one of the blackest chapters of our military history. For men like Amos, the experience isn't entirely finished. It may never be.

Staring at the carpet of crosses, Amos shook his head, a peculiar smile of disgust forming on his face. "I made it back, though," he said, as if to reassure himself. "I made it back."

"Why do you think that was?" I asked him.

He clutched his cane a little tighter. "I don't know," he replied. "By the grace of God, maybe?"

He was emphatic about framing his answer as a question.

★　★　★

IT WAS OFTEN SAID after the war that all the men of Bataan could expect to go to heaven because they'd already served their time in hell. The great trial they lived through was truly one of our national nightmares. These men suffered enough for a hundred lifetimes. They endured three years of gratuitous and often surreal mistreatment that, as they've come to the end of their lives, they still can't fully understand. They're old men now, but sometimes they still wake up in the night, sweaty and scared, tormented by visions.

The trip was arranged by an interesting outfit based in Sausalito called Valor Tours, which leads group excursions to the battlefields of the Pacific. America's infatuation with the subject of World War II had become something of a trend with unmistakable business implications, but at the same time it was a genuine phenomenon, fueled as it was by an increasingly desperate awareness that fathers and brothers and uncles everywhere were dying off without having told their stories. In addition to the Bataan vets and their families, there were a number of intense history buffs on our trip, people who simply couldn't get enough of the great saga of the U.S. disaster in the Philippines, the American Thermopylae. We visited prison camps, battlefields, naval stations, monuments, and memorials. We tramped over the island fortress of Corregidor and explored the old Spanish dungeons inside Manila's Intramuros. We spent a lot of time in a slightly dilapidated VFW hall, meeting old American soldiers who'd never left the Philippines after all these years. We stayed in the famed Manila Hotel, where General MacArthur once kept a penthouse office.

Every morning we awoke at "oh-six-hundred" and climbed aboard the bus for what amounted to a rolling World War II seminar. The Bataan vets seemed to pride themselves on rising before everyone else, often well before dawn. They were "the Greatest," as Brokaw says, but they were also, I'm quite sure, the Earliest Generation.

ON DECEMBER 8, 1941, swarms of Japanese planes took off from Formosa in thick fog, vectored across the South China Sea, and struck nearly every major American installation on Luzon—airfields, shipyards, depots, warehouses. Even though word of Pearl Harbor had reached them, the Americans in the Philippines seemed incapable of believing that the war was truly on. Because of a series of bad decisions and communications errors on the part of the American command, as well as several turns of incredibly bad luck, the Japanese Zeros caught much of the American Far East Air Force on the ground at Clark Field north of Manila, parked wingtip to wingtip and refueling. In a matter of hours, the United States had lost control of the skies.

Part of the American failure to respond can be blamed on an incredulity rooted in simple racism: the reputedly inferior Japanese military wasn't supposed to be an authentic threat. One of the men on our trip, a former tank radio operator named James Bogart, recalled the blasé mentality of the times. "We didn't really expect the Japanese to have the audacity to attack the all-powerful United States," Bogart told me. "We had heard that the Japanese were nearsighted and night-blind—and that they couldn't fly planes worth a flip." December 8 disabused Bogart of a host of misconceptions.

By Christmas, Washington had already come to regard the Philippines as a lost cause. President Roosevelt decided to concentrate American resources primarily in the European theater rather than attempt to fight an all-out war on two distant fronts. At odds with the emerging master strategy for winning the war, the remote outpost on Luzon lay doomed. In a particularly chilling phrase that later was to become famous, War Secretary Henry Stimson remarked, "There are times when men have to die."

The defense of the Philippines, our first great battle of World War II, would last four agonizing months. After the initial aerial attack, General MacArthur quickly retreated from Manila to the peninsula of Bataan, which, with its roadless jungles and steep volcanic headlands jutting out into Manila Bay, was better suited than the capital for a protracted defensive war. The men were stranded on this little neck of jungle, their backs against the sea. One Japanese officer likened the American predicament on Bataan to that of "a cat entering a sack." The men were forced to fight on rations of a thousand calories a day, with rusty, antiquated equipment that dated back, in some cases, to the Spanish-American War. They fought valiantly as their food and ammunition ran out. When defeat became certain, MacArthur was evacuated to Australia to build a new army. His ill-equipped, malnourished, malarial troops held the peninsula as long as they could. On April 9, 1942, they capitulated to the Japanese 14th Imperial Army. It was the largest surrender in American history.

"Bataan was sort of another Alamo, with certain variations to it," said Richard Gordon, a retired army major who fought with the 31st Infantry on Bataan's front lines. A stalwart eighty-year-old man with crisply etched memories of his ordeal, Gordon was one of the veterans who accompanied us on our trip back to the Philippines. "You put men out here to do battle with a far superior enemy. And you don't support them. When that happens you're throwing men's lives away. We were told, 'Hang on, hold out, help is on the way!' And after a while we began to give up on these little propaganda sheets that told us these things. We're stuck out here. We have an Uncle Sam somewhere. We just don't see him—in any form." Starving in their foxholes, feeling abandoned by their country, the men of Bataan took to singing a chant that would become their company slogan, a chant that they recite even today: "We're the battling bastards of Bataan, no mama, no papa, no Uncle Sam . . . and nobody gives a damn."

I spent several days with Gordon and his comrades on the Bataan Peninsula. In the port town of Marivales, hundreds of Filipinos came out to greet our entourage. As we stepped off our chartered boat, the locals draped sampaguita flower garlands around our necks and, their cheeks braided with tears, welcomed their brothers-in-arms back to the province of Bataan. We revisited the sites around Mount Samat, where some of the fiercest battles took place, where the tattered jungles had smoked and raged after nearly four months of continual fighting. The men recalled the desperation of their doomed defense, the sweaty camaraderie, the relentless shelling. But more than anything else, they seemed to remember the sharp burn of hunger. Near the end, they were forced to venture into the jungles and scavenge for wild game.

"Anything that was moving was ours," said Gordon's friend and fellow infantryman Humphrey O'Leary. "Water buffalo, monkeys, pythons, iguanas, parrots, snails. We were reduced to a situation where we would eat anything. It was that bad."

In March of 1942, when General MacArthur was ordered to leave the Philippines, the troops began to understand the magnitude of their predicament. "All of us could see we were going down the tubes," recalled Jim Bogart. "No army can fight a war when they're starving like we were. If I'd been asked to make a charge, I couldn't have done it. I had malaria and dysentery, and I'd already lost forty pounds. We couldn't believe we'd been completely abandoned."

Finally, the Filipino-American men surrendered. The Japanese force-marched them sixty-five miles north to a temporary enclosure called Camp O'Donnell. The prisoners were in no condition to walk, but the Japanese prodded them along anyway; if a man couldn't keep pace, he was shot, bayoneted, or beheaded. In the end, more than six hundred Americans and as many as five thousand Filipinos are believed to have died during the plodding atrocity that came to be known as the Bataan Death March.

WE HAD TRAVELED TO LUZON, in part, to trace the winding route of the March, through the rice paddies and cane fields of the Bataan Peninsula. As our chartered tour bus crept up the main coastal road, past the drowsy barrios of Cabcaben, Limay, and Balanga and the malachite-green slopes of Mount Samat, it was impossible for me to imagine the gloom and devastation that had hung over this place in April of 1942. The veterans stared intently out the windows as half-remembered vistas spooled by them, the air-conditioned coach comfortably gliding over the same terrain that had taken them, as captives, so many horrifying days to stumble across.

One incident on the Death March remained particularly vivid in Richard Gordon's mind. A young American soldier was lying by the side of the road, alive but in the throes of a malaria attack. A Japanese tank came down the road. At the last second, the tank driver, seized by a cruel whimsy, deliberately swerved and crushed the ailing American. The next tank in the column went over the man's limp body a second time, leaving it pressed flat into the pavement as though it had been steamrolled. "You stand there watching a human being flattened, well, that sticks in your mind forever," Gordon said over lunch one day in one of the Bataan barrios. "It was deliberate murder. He was nice, easy prey, just lying there. I'll never forget that sight. I'll go to my grave wondering how people can be that inhumane."

Yet the Death March was only the beginning of the long ordeal. In the prison camps, they slaved and starved. They buried legions of their comrades because their guards denied them even the most basic of medicines. They saw friends tortured and beheaded. We visited the site of one of the camps, Cabanatuan. It had been the largest American POW camp ever established on foreign soil, with as many as nine thousand men living there at one time. Today it's just a clearing in flat rice country, with a discreet white marble memorial listing the names of the nearly three thousand men who perished there. The morning we stopped by, water buffalo dozed in their wallows in the surrounding paddies. Children raked newly harvested rice along the shoulders of the road. A range of notched mountains, the Sierra Madre, clawed at the hazy sky. The young Filipinos in the neighboring village didn't quite know what to make of our procession of mostly elderly American tourists in Rockports and floppy hats, squinting in the sun, pointing at things that weren't even there.

Once, Malcolm Amos saw nine of his fellow prisoners shot because one man had tried to escape. The men dug their own pit, then knelt by the edge for the executioner to shoot them, one by one, in the back of the head, dropping them into their shared grave. On another occasion, Amos saw an American tortured by the camp guards. They stuck a tube in his mouth and turned on the hose until the water pressure filled up his stomach. "Then they jumped on his abdomen," Amos said, wincing with palpable disgust, "until his innards was just torn all to pieces."

"For three years, we were always living on the edge here," Richard Gordon said, "wondering what they were going to do to us, where the next beating would come from. I don't think there's a man who went through that experience who doesn't have some sort of psychological scarring—that certainly includes me. It takes a permanent bite out of you."

*   *   *

IT HAS BEEN SAID THAT BATAAN was a "dress rehearsal" for Vietnam. Certainly the experience there offered important lessons (about military preparedness, overextension, and commitment) that the planners in Vietnam seem generally to have ignored. As in Vietnam, the Bataan men found themselves fighting against an extremely foreign enemy in unfamiliar jungles of tropical Asia, waging a battle that seemed destined to fail. And as with Vietnam soldiers, the men of Bataan had to return home with a certain unspoken stigma, the awkward status of having "lost." Many of the syndromes and illnesses that have come to be associated with Vietnam veterans were suffered twenty-five years earlier by the American captives of the Japanese: nightmares and night sweats, bouts of profound depression, various mysterious symptoms that VA hospital doctors were reluctant to diagnose and treat, and all the hallmarks of post-traumatic stress disorder (although it was not then dignified with a name).

Fred Baldassarre, an industrial engineer from Hayward, California, was all too familiar with these symptoms. Baldassarre is the son of a now-deceased Bataan veteran, and he had come on this trip, in part, to understand some of the peculiarities in his father's character. "I don't ever recall him not fighting that war," Baldassarre told me one afternoon over San Miguel beers in Cabanatuan City. "He couldn't stop fighting it. The war was always in his head—like ambient noise. He was probably the most affectionate human being I've ever met, but at the same time he was prone to these incredible rages of temper. He would just snap. He was a very tough guy, but certain things would make him bawl like a baby. When I was draft age during the Vietnam War, he would get hysterical when the little envelopes came from the draft board. He would plead with me, 'Don't go.' He was willing to do anything to help me become a draft dodger. He'd say, 'You have to trust me on this. You don't want to go to war.' He just flat-out told me, 'I've served enough for both of us. You don't have to go.'"

Malcolm Amos's daughter, Lanae Hagen, recalled very similar experiences growing up in Iowa. "When I was a kid you could always tell when Dad was in one of his moods," she said. "We'd wake up in the morning, and his mattress would be on the floor. We'd find the radio out in the yard. Sometime during the night, he had thrown it out the window, broken the glass. He didn't even know he'd done it. My mom had to have her own bedroom. We knew that we just had to leave him alone when he'd get in one of his moods. 'Cause there was no dealing with him."

Another child of a Bataan veteran who accompanied us was Charlie Wyatt, a businessman from Houston. For Wyatt's father, the war manifested itself in a ritual. "Every week Dad would go down for a haircut, and he'd always get a manicure," Wyatt told me. "I think that he was trying to rid himself of all physical traces of what he went through in the camps. You see, the Japanese had pulled out all of his nails once. If he could look at his hands and see that they were clean and free and nice-looking, well, he was trying to push that to the back of his mind. Then all of a sudden something would happen. He'd be thinking of the pain he'd been through and then boom—he'd black out. We had no idea when it would occur next. Once it happened while he was driving a car. He was taking me to school and all of a sudden— boom!—we're in a ditch, smashed into a tree, and my head's up against the windshield."

More than anything, the veterans remember the experience of starvation. Lanae Hagen said that her father was quite nearly obsessed with the subject of food his entire adult life. "Food is very important to him," she told me. "In prison camp he and his buddies made a pact. When they got out of there, they were going to buy a grocery store and fill it full of food and lock the door and never come out. That's pretty much what he did—he ended up owning a grocery store in Iowa after the war. And even now, late in life, he still has this thing about surrounding himself with food. He buys cookies and hides them all over the place, the most crappy-tasting cookies that you could think of, just so that we won't eat them, so he'd have them all to himself. His own little stash."

In prison camp, the men often called themselves "ghosts." Not only did they look like ghosts after three years of captivity, but they felt as though they'd been forgotten by the land of the living—and by their own country. One can make the case that, in terms of scope and duration, their ordeal exceeded anything suffered by our armed forces in any other conflict throughout our history.

Given all the trials they had to endure, it's remarkable that any of them survived at all. In a way, I came to think of the men with whom I was traveling as the ultimate survivors, supreme beaters of the odds. Not only had they lived through the misery of a four-month siege, an infamous forced march, and three years in prison camps, they'd also somehow survived the tricky reimmersion into American society (so many of their comrades had died during those first few years—of depression, alcoholism, and various combinations of residual illnesses). And then these men had managed to get through fifty-five years of living to reach the unthinkable: a ripe old age.

Throughout our trip, I was continually amazed at how stoic they were. They had accepted their lot with enormous stores of grace. Each man had his own set of strengths that saw him through his ordeal— love of family, faith in God, a prodigious sense of humor. True, they all had scars, little quirks of prejudice. They refused to buy Japanese cars, refused to throw rice at their own daughters' weddings. But most of them had learned not to hate the Japanese people, because they understood that, as one of them put it, "the hate consumes you."

It is a common trait of the survivor to find something positive in the midst of an experience of great tragedy. Near the end of the trip, I asked Humphrey O'Leary if he had gained anything from all his suffering—an insight perhaps, a kernel of wisdom.

"You know," he said, "a man can adapt himself to anything. His natural resources, his instincts, will always come through. You'd be surprised how your mind can work when you're in a fix!"

O'Leary chuckled quietly to himself. Then he fixed me with a penetrating stare. "Never underestimate a person," he said. "This is something I learned. It takes a lot to kill a man if he doesn't want to be killed."

—2001

AMERICAN OBSESSIONS

Chasing the White Witch

Las Vegas, Nevada

WES PHILLIPS is a prodigious Buddha of a man in his mid-forties, with a monkish buzz cut, a neatly trimmed goatee, and a large, curdy forehead. He's sitting in the living room of his New Mexico house, right in the sweet spot, frowning slightly as he listens to his $100,000 sound system, which now is playing the strains of an old-time gospel quartet, the Fairfield Four. To the average person, the music spilling into the room would seem absolutely crystalline, almost indistinguishable from a live performance. But something is bothering Phillips. Something doesn't sound quite right. His pale blue eyes, enlarged behind his thick glasses, steadily scan the room for offenders—a patch of bare tile, perhaps, a cable that's on the fritz, anything that might be soiling the signal.

The equipment-review editor of the world's largest and most influential high-end audio magazine, *Stereophile,* Phillips is the sort of guy who writes long and sometimes densely footnoted articles that begin with sentences like "My relationship with digital has been a stormy one." Here in this adobe bunker crowded with six thousand records and three thousand CDs, here where the products of so many makers of stereo components have been either exalted or sacrificed on the altar of his exacting taste, Phillips projects an air of power precisely wielded.

He's cool, punctilious, sacerdotal, quietly nibbling a whiskey-filled Jack Daniel's chocolate. He wears black sweatpants, a black sweatshirt, black Adidas sandals. In his left hand he clutches his black remote control. With his right he strokes his black cat.

The stereo arrayed before us is his very own reference system, a room-dominating sprawl of metallic decks, snaking cords, pulsing tubes, and long lustrous banks of switches and buttons. It's a house-sitter's nightmare, a forbidding assemblage of space-age alloys, exotic woods, and pure unobtainium. Among Phillips's components: a Krell KPS 20 i/1 CD player ($8,000, ballpark), a Linn Sondek LP-12 turntable ($7,000), an Ayre K1 preamp ($6,000), and two Krell Audio Standard power amps ($35,000 a pair), which are parked like twin anvils on the floor and are equipped with blinking monitors that show the precise level of current the system is drawing from the wall, second by second. Linking everything up are networked MIT interconnects and speaker cables worth some $30,000. And then there are all the little tweaks: the power-purifying devices, the antijitter boxes, all designed to remove the last gremlins of noise pollution lurking in the circuitry.

It's an absolutely bitching stereo, to be sure, but not especially extravagant by the standards of the eighty thousand readers of *Stereophile*. "I know plenty of people," says Phillips, "who would not consider this a particularly refined system. They'd wish to . . . how shall we put it? . . . take it a whole lot further."

This month, Phillips will be reviewing the new Martin-Logan SL3 electrostatic speakers ($3,500 a pair retail), and he has just now assembled them in his listening room. For Phillips, setting up a pair of speakers for review isn't just a matter of plugging them in—it's an elaborate installation process that takes the better part of a week. He approaches a product review as if it were some sort of genetic experiment, building in all sorts of painstaking controls.

To prepare for his Martin-Logan review, Phillips has spent the past week "treating" the room, making a few last-minute acoustic improvements. Like, for example, the $3,500 worth of upholstered towers, called tube traps, that he's been placing in strategic crannies about the house. One of the current rages in high end, tube traps are designed to either reflect or absorb sound, depending on their placement, so that in theory a room can be "fine-tuned" for optimal highs, lows, and midrange. "Sound is like flowing water," Phillips says. "Wherever there's any sort of hard edge in a room, you tend to get eddies." Now, with what amounts to an acoustic forest growing in his living room, eddies are no longer a problem. "The tube traps are powerful tools," Phillips says. "We managed to break up the pressure zones. We've lopped off some of the highs and some of the lows, and what's left in the middle is really quite palatable."

No, what's bugging Phillips is something else entirely, something that seems to be emanating from the speakers themselves. Suddenly he's seized by an idea. He disappears for a moment, then comes back with a mason's level and places it on one of the speakers. The little swimming bubble bobs slightly to the left. Horrors! One of the Martin-Logans is listing!

Phillips gets down on all fours and makes a microscopic adjustments to the speaker's legs so that it stands exactly true. "You'd be surprised what a difference this makes," he says.

The gospel music plays on for a while. It sounds wonderful, but really no different than before—at least not to an uneducated ear.

"You see," Phillips says, "everything has come into focus."

It has?

"All the veils have dropped away, and now you can truly see the music. It's like looking through a fairly clean window and then taking the Windex to it and getting rid of that last bit of smudge that's obscuring what you're trying to see."

Phillips returns to the sweet spot and smiles. He nibbles another Jack Daniel's chocolate, a tiny compartment of sour mash bursting in his mouth. Beside him, his black cat purrs.

IT WAS THE GREEK PHILOSOPHER Zeno who postulated that if you halved the distance between point A and point B, then halved it again, and then again, ad infinitum, you'd never reach point B. You'd keep getting closer and closer, but with each halving, your progress would grow incrementally smaller. You'd never reach your goal.

That isn't a bad description for what's happening in the world of high-end audio. Everyone afflicted with extreme audiophilia seems to be pursuing the same goal, a goal sometimes referred to as sonic truth: to create a reproduction of the "original event" (i.e., a live musical performance) so accurately that it's impossible to tell one from the other. To remove all "artifacts" and "parasitic characteristics." To reconstruct the full "soundstage." To achieve "halographic presentation," so that the oboes can be visualized over here, the violas over there, the timpani rumbling in the rear. Over the past fifty years or so, quantum improvements in stereophonics have halved, and halved again, and halved again, this fundamental sonic gulf. Today, if you have a few grand to spend on some well-chosen equipment, you can sit in your own living-room sweet spot and listen to music that's pretty damn close to the original event.

But after you cross, say, the $5,000 threshold, the increments of improvement grow smaller and smaller, and the stereophile is forced to shell out more and more money to achieve less and less enhancement. He enters the realm of permanent upgrade and perpetual tweak, buying to the limits of his platinum-card ceiling or his spousal-acceptance factor, whichever comes first. He has to have the latest antijitter box and those new dissonance-reducing ebony pucks from Japan. Like oenophiles and transcendental poets, he begins to speak the glossolalia of the smitten, forever trying to describe the indescribable. He finds himself "chasing the white witch," as stereophiles sometimes describe their restless search for sensory perfection, for a pure signal in the din of the world.

Stereophile sits in an enviable position at the crossroads of high-end fanaticism. Founded in 1962 by an eccentric Philadelphia audiophile named J. Gordon Holt, it has since been taken over by Larry Archibald, a Harvard-educated former Mercedes-Benz mechanic. Packed with music reviews, artist profiles, a carbolic letters section, and equipment reports often illustrated with charts and graphs of NASA-level complexity, the magazine comes richly larded with ads from such obscure companies as Mondial Designs Limited, Voce Dolce, Eiger Sound Philosophy, and MBL of America.

Stereophile's readership is 98 percent male, a figure that pretty well sums up the gender realities of the entire high-end industry. The high end is one of the last remaining bastions of male exclusivity, with a testosterone-laden ethos that filters down to the stark chrome-and-leather atmospherics of high-end salons. "You walk into most high-end hi-fi shops," says Phillips, who once worked as a salesman at a well-known emporium in Manhattan, "and they might as well have a sign on the door that says, GIRLS KEEP OUT. It's like an elite club, and if you don't have our chromosome structure, well, you don't belong."

Apart from music aficionados and technogeeks, Phillips notes, the high end also attracts a certain kind of buyer who's not only male but reflexively macho in his purchases. "There are a lot of different schools within the high end," he says. "One of them is the Big Dick School. There are people who're just after the biggest, baddest systems they can find. You know, mine is definitely bigger than yours."

"IT'S NOT FAIR to call them speakers, really," Phil Jones says, sizing up his companion behemoths parked in a mood-lit Las Vegas hotel suite. "They're more like acoustic weapons. I mean, they'll crush you. They're extreme in every possible way."

Jones is a New Hampshire–based high-end audio engineer, one of the best in the world, and definitely a proponent of the "mine goes to eleven" philosophy. The president of Platinum Audio, he is talking about the prototype of his newest invention, the Air Pulse 3.1, a sculpted horn-design speaker that's all the buzz among audiophiles at the 1997 Consumer Electronics Show. Jones and his fellow high-enders are encamped at a modern suites hotel called the Alexis Park, forming what amounts to a posher, nerdier suburb of the larger, ninety-thousand-person CES convention. A few thousand designers, manufacturers, dealers, and installers have been spending the past few days trundling from room to room to room, inspecting the latest advances in amps, preamps, interconnects, turntables, CD players, noise conditioners, and room-tuning equipment. But they keep circling back around to suite 2600, Jones's suite, to eye the Air Pulse 3.1. They whisper and hubbub among themselves—

"Excellent diffusion."

"Superb horn propagation."

"An almost imperceptible noise floor."

Jones chose this year's CES to unveil the Air Pulse 3.1, a speaker design that he has been obsessing over for twenty years. He put the finishing touches on these monsters just two days ago and then had them FedExed here from his design laboratory in New Hampshire. They're beautiful, elephantine masses of wood with deep-throated horns that appear somehow simultaneously futuristic and retro. They're six feet high, three feet wide, four feet deep. They weigh nine hundred pounds apiece. The sinuous, intricately baffled cabinets are crafted from fine mahogany, maple, and birch, every inch varnished and buffed to perfection. "They're a statement piece," Jones says, gazing over at his brainchildren, which just now are tamely seeping strains of cool-school jazz.

"They're designed for a forty-foot-by-forty-foot listening room," Jones continues. "In this little suite, they're like a Lamborghini that's stuck in Tokyo traffic. They look sweet, but when you really crank them up, you wouldn't even want to be in the same room with them. It's kind of sad, you know. Their owner will never know their true capability."

Outside, the pinkish twilight has given way to the neon and sodium-vapor glow of the casinos. Suite 2600 is packed with so many curious aficionados that one of the Platinum Audio executives has had to lock the door for fear of breaking the fire codes. Now people are pressing their noses against the windows, tweed-jacketed sound druids who look as if they've been rejected from Studio 54.

The price tag, the price tag! Everyone is dancing around the subject, but they want to know: What will Jones be asking for the Air Pulse, retail? "We spared no cost," Jones assures his admirers. "I mean, with each cabinet you're looking at over $1,200 *in glue alone!* We were tired of having to live in a world of compromise. So with this speaker, our only constraints were 'Can you get it through the door? Can you fit it in the room?'" Then Jones ducks into the back room to meet with a potential buyer from Hong Kong.

So the issue remains: What about the price? Finally someone discreetly pops the question to the other Platinum executives in the room. "Considerably into the six figures," replies Jones's chief financial officer, a beetle-browed bald guy in a sport coat and a bow tie. "We'll probably price them right at $150,000. They will unquestionably be the most expensive speakers ever manufactured in world history." He's beaming.

I look around the room and see that nobody is batting an eye—just lots of sophisticated nods, adroit goatee stroking. A young man in a silk scarf who calls himself "the installer to the stars" in Hollywood is kneeling at the foot of one of the Air Pulses, paying silent homage. A couple of dark-suited businessmen from Kuala Lumpur covetously rub the curved acres of burnished wood. To them, a hundred fifty thou for a couple of babies like these seems perfectly reasonable. In fact, Andrew Singer, owner of Manhattan's premier high-end shop, Sound by Singer, will later tell me, "They're ridiculously underpriced—that's way too cheap! You're talking about what could be the best speaker ever made. Phil Jones has done the impossible—he's made a horn-loaded speaker sit up and behave! Even if they were priced at a quarter mil, I know plenty of decisive buyers out there who have the vision to say, 'Yeah, I want 'em. Wrap 'em up.'"

JUST DOWNSTAIRS from the Air Pulse demonstration, a smaller, quieter coterie of audiophiles are chasing the white witch. Rafael Rodriguez, an anxious salesman from a Southern California cable-manufacturing company called Synergistic Research, has set up a comparison test. In this test, Rodriguez hopes to prove once and for all that his cables are the best in the world. To take his test, he has assembled a number of the luminaries of the high end, including *Stereophile*'s Larry Archibald and Wes Phillips. Parked in straight-backed chairs by some potted plants, the two men do their best to work up the interest, but their minds are numb and their feet swollen from four groaning days of Vegas suite hopping.

Rodriguez and his crew couldn't be more enthused. They're piping in classical music on a fantastic stereo system that's now hooked with a competitor's speaker cables. Rodriguez gives me the color commentary, explaining what the signal really sounds like when it's coming through these obviously inferior cables: "It's just spitty and awful. It's not orderly. It's like a junked-up closet. You don't even want to go in there."

Rodriguez then switches the system over to play the same piece of music through Synergistic's $900 Resolution Reference copper-matrix conductor cables. "Hear how everything has opened up? Hear how orderly everything is? These cables are for the person who says, 'I want reality, and I want it in my home.'"

After the cut of music is over, there's a long, pregnant pause. Rodriguez trolls the room for reactions.

Oh, yes.

Impressive resolution.

Quite dramatic.

Then Larry Archibald, a big, amiable guy with a bald pate, clears his throat. "I'm not hearing a difference," he says flatly. "Nope. Not hearing it at all. Or if I am, they're just not differences that are important to me."

Incredulous stares from Rodriguez. Stifled gasps from the other listeners. The emperor has no clothes. Larry Archibald, august publisher of the high end's bible, has just told a roomful of distinguished audiophiles, in a loud and emphatic voice, that he *can't hear the difference!*

A few hours later, Rodriguez has already improvised an explanation for Archibald's little faux pas. "You know," he says, "it's pretty well known within the industry that Larry is . . . well . . . I don't know how to delicately put this. *He's losing his hearing!* His ears are going! It's a sad, sad thing, really. All of us in the industry are concerned for him. But that's old age for you. The ears are always the first to go!"

—1997

Sisters of the Bowl

Kissimmee, Florida

TO GET TO OUR WORLD, I head south out of Orlando on the Orange Blossom Trail, past the outlet malls and the strip joints and the Gatorland Zoo, until I come to a white pavilion surrounded by water fountains and cypress swamps. When I arrive, the parking lot is packed with thousands of nearly identical minivans with bumper stickers that say, WHEN I WORK, IT'S A PARTY, or GO AHEAD, MAKE MY DAY—THROW A PARTY, or I'M A PARTY MACHINE, or I DON'T BELIEVE IN THE TWO-PARTY SYSTEM—TWO PARTIES A WEEK JUST ISN'T ENOUGH.

This particular August, Our World's auditorium is filled with helium balloons and snappy tunes by the Tijuana Brass. A mirrored disco ball sprays shards of light over a crowd of two thousand hysterical women: Valley moms with beehives. Corn-fed hausfraus with thick ankles shoved into high-heeled shoes. New age Southern belles seeking self-esteem. A smiling army of Carol Merrills and Vanna Whites. Tri Delta sorority girls in color-coordinated suits and pumps, impossibly together, impossibly precise. Our Ladies of Containment, Sisters of the Bowl.

The women are squirming in their seats, shaking pompons, forming human "London Bridges" in the aisles for their friends to march under. Others parade across the stage holding placards from their local distributorships—or "ships," as they're called in the parlance of Tupperware Home Parties.

SOUTHBAY PARTY SALES SAYS HELLO TO OUR WORLD!

THE ANGELS ARE HERE!!

FIESTA PARTY SALES

The women are growing restless. They want to see "product"—the unveiling of the season's new merchandise—and they will not be denied. "Give us product!" they demand. "Product *now*!"

Near the stage, forty-five ladies from Pinnacle Party Sales, a distributorship in Rockville, Maryland, are bouncing arm in arm to the music. Pinnacle has much to celebrate this year: they've had a record-breaker summer, thanks in large part to a hot streak by their perennial top seller, Sheila Looney. A jolly forty-seven-year-old redhead from Bowie, Maryland, Looney manages a sales unit called the "Looney Tunes." Last year she made "Top Category" and is ranked number fifty-six in the nation in personal party sales.

Tupperware, Looney says, is the best way to combat what she calls "kitchen chaos." Back home in Maryland, her kitchen is a triumph of Teutonic orderliness. In her refrigerator, the sealed modules of Tupperware are stacked in their manifold sizes and shapes, ensuring that no juices or gravies will ever mingle by accident.

This week Looney has won loads of awards, including a new dining room set. A trail of ribbons reaches to her knee. "We have a high energy level," Looney boasts. "We get very excited. It's like being in camp all year long. And we make money doing it! And prizes! And trips! We're always running into people who say they can't understand why we're having so much fun. They're asking, 'What is the deal?' They look very perplexed."

Over the years, Looney has won eight company cars. Her latest one, a Lumina minivan, is parked in the Tupperware lot. "My trophy on wheels," she says, beaming. "We have the best car plan in the direct selling industry. See, I didn't have to sell ten thousand Mary Kay lipsticks to get it! And it doesn't come in pink!"

Looney and her husband, Bob, drove down from Maryland. Bob, a carpet and flooring salesman, has accompanied Sheila to many of the rallies and seminars this week, but today he told Sheila that if he heard another motivational talk his "brain was going to explode."

The chanting has grown louder: "PRODUCT, PRODUCT, PRODUCT!"

"New products always excite us," Looney explains. "When I get home the hostesses are going to be calling me up. These people are truly Tupperholics. They want *new, new, new!*"

Standing at center stage is Gaylin Olson, a swarthy young exec with smoothed-back hair and a Pepsodent smile. As president of sales, Olson is the Bert Parks of Tupperware: the emcee and keeper of the harem. The women call him by his first name. "Isn't he wonderful?" Looney burbles. "He's not some far-off executive. You can *talk* to him. Gaylin's a Tupper child, you know. His mom sold Tupperware. So does his sister! He's one of us!"

Gaylin is wearing a *Ghostbusters* getup with a plastic orange flamethrower holstered to his side. He holds a wireless microphone in his hand. "We're going to recognize you like we've never recognized you before!" he promises. "There's lots of deserving people out there who really SOCKED it to us this year. Boy, you've really wowed us! You've broken ALL the records! You're moving your way to GREATER levels of success. It's such a privilege to be a part of this great family. I feel one heart beating in this room right now, and it's called . . . *Tupperware!*"

"Product! Product! Product!"

Gaylin: "What's that? You wanna see WHAT?"

"PRODUCT!! PRODUCT!! PRODUCT *NOW!!*"

Gaylin: "Okay, okay. You want product? Are we going to show you some product! We're VERY excited about this new item and we want to share it with each and every one of you today. Because you're SPE-CIAL people. Because you're TUPPER people. Get ready, folks! Hold on to your seats. 'Cause we're going to show you a WHOLE NEW LINE of Tupperware that we just know you're going to love! This is a company of DREAMS! So close your eyes and DREAM with us! We want you all to say hello to the NEW . . ."

. . . drumroll . . .

"... sixteen-piece ..."

... screams, squeals, gasps ...

"....TABLETOP LINE!!!!"

"Way to go Tupperware! Way to go!"

A projector flashes a misty image on an overhead screen—the soft pastel bowls and plates pictured alongside fresh fruit spritzed with tiny beads of moisture. The Tijuana Brass pours out louder than ever.

Gaylin: "You *like* it! It's BY FAR the best material in the world, and it's EXTREMELY scratch resistant!"

"Sock it to me, Tupperware!"

Gaylin: "It's made of plastic but it looks like the finest china IN THE WORLD! And it comes in Desert Peach, a color so rich that Donald Trump picked it as the base color at one of his Atlantic City hotels."

Now Gaylin is passing out free samples of the new Tabletop Line, fresh from the factory in Hemingway, South Carolina. Thousands of the brightly wrapped packages circulate through the crowd. The ladies frantically rip the wrappers off, tear at the cardboard boxes. In a few minutes, the auditorium is strewn with ribbon and plasticware parts. They juggle the lids, balance the plates on their heads, dangle spoons from their noses.

"Love that Tupperware! Love that Tupperware!"

Gaylin: "There's NOTHING that Tupperware can't do! We've designed a mug that's not for sissies. Can you feel that? Just FEEL the heft! And see, that's a man-sized cereal bowl. This is some VERY special plastic!"

The Harem is satisfied. The Tupperware spirit is gathering in the crowd and suddenly everyone is singing the company anthem. Sheila Looney and her colleagues from Pinnacle Party Sales sing along, and most of them do the accompanying hand signals that everyone in Our World knows by rote—

I've got that Tup-per feeling up in my head,
Deep in my heart,
Down in my toes,
I've got that Tup-per feeling all over me,

All over me
To stay!

EVERY SUMMER FOR FORTY YEARS, Tupperware Home Parties has assembled its metaphorical family for an emotional sales rally called the "Jubilee." It is one of the largest corporate reunions in the world, an elaborate pageant of treasure hunts, musical skits, and car giveaways that costs the company upward of $4 million a year. More than ten thousand salesladies come for the three-day event. Attendance is so large that the company can't accommodate them all at once, so the ladies arrive in five successive waves over a two-week period. "It's our way of thanking the sales force for a job well done," Gaylin Olson explains. "They all go home with something—gifts, prizes, vehicles. We're totally committed to them. We have to show a lot of enthusiasm up there. At Jubilee, we set the emotional tone for the whole year."

The ladies flock here from all over the globe to wash themselves in the spirit of "Our World," as they call their far-flung business sorority. They attend candlelit induction ceremonies. They stay up late at night in their Orlando hotel rooms for pillow fights and wine-and-cheese parties. But there is also work to attend to at the Jubilee. Each morning the women lug their bulging spiral notebooks to seminars entitled "How to Increase Your Party Average" or "Friend Finding for the Holidays," where accomplished salesladies share their wisdom:

". . . Smiling changes the whole sound of your voice. Put a mirror in front of you during phone interviews to make sure you're always smiling."

". . . If your Tupperware gets smelly, stuff the container with newspaper and place it in your freezer overnight. The carbon in the newspaper will draw out the odors."

". . . Always remember that our chief competitor isn't Rubbermaid. It's that gal who says, 'That's good enough! Let it spoil a little!'"

The Kissimmee headquarters is the sentimental home of Our World, and it exerts a powerful pull. The three-pavilion facility was designed by Edward Durell Stone, architect of the Kennedy Center in

Washington. Its brightly lit corridors are spick-and-span, and the toilet water in the company bathrooms is kept a refreshing Ty-D-Bol blue. Outside the main building is a thousand-acre park of manicured gardens and meandering trails where pilgrims go on inspirational walks. Japanese footbridges cross palmy lagoons where blue herons stand vigil. Everything on the grounds is labeled and has a "the" in front of it: The Wishing Well. The Opportuni-Tree. The Friendship Fountain. The Walk of Fame.

But the most remarkable attraction at the Tupperware headquarters is a million-dollar permanent art exhibit called the Museum of Historic Containers. It traces mankind's struggle against spoilage in all its grim forms. The tour begins with an Egyptian earthenware jar from 4000 B.C. and proceeds more or less chronologically, displaying objets d'art from the Babylonians, the Greeks and Romans, the Incas, and so on. There are containers made of shells, reeds, and horns. There are compotes, cruets, ewers, urns, tankards, and Delftware bowls.

Having seen the history of containment, visitors are then invited to gaze upon its future. The tour moves to a second room filled with the latest runs from the Tupperware factory. The products are neatly arranged on the display tables. Modular Mates. Servalier Bowls. Super Crisp-It Containers. The wisdom of six thousand years has led human civilization *directly to this room*. For a few moments the visitor can hold a little piece of victory—the triumph over the microbe and the cockroach and the mold spore: the paragon of packages.

WELCOME TO A LAND OF FANTASY, the sign greets the incoming pilgrims at the company headquarters. "Welcome to Your Over-the-Rainbow Jubilee!"

This year's Jubilee is based on an Oz theme. The company has decorated the grounds with an eighty-foot-high rainbow made of 64,000 Tupperware seals in bright colors, each seal autographed by a different salesperson from around the world.

The Oz theme is apt, for as a businessman, the late Earl Silas Tupper, the company founder, was not unlike the Wizard. Cranky, paranoid, flustered around people, leery of unions, Tupper ran his company from the shadows. He cultivated an image of quiet, unapproachable omnipotence. He was president, general manager, treasurer, and sole stockholder. From a dark office in his Massachusetts plant, he followed the minutest details. In his later years, he carried around a black box which held, he claimed, his "greatest invention ever," but he refused to open it. He was obsessed with quality control and constantly worried that competitors were stealing his patents or attempting to sabotage his company.

Tupper hated to attend sales conferences; all those squealing women upset him. Few Tupperware salesladies ever met him or even knew what he looked like. Tupper was more interested in things than people. He came alive when asked to explain the process of making the molds, the chemical principles involved, the machinery of extrusion and lamination, the injectors and vegetable dyes. Tupper's hyperactive mind was forever looking for ways to shave off waste. Once when Tupper was wheeled into an operating room for surgery, the doctor found him scribbling notes on how to improve the gurney he was lying on.

Tupper was a self-taught chemical engineer who formed his own plastics company in the mid-1940s and worked as an independent "custom molder" for DuPont. At the time, plastic was still a new and vaguely frightening material. It looked bad, it smelled bad, and it was slimy. It also had a tendency to split.

Earl Tupper was bullish on one substance in particular: polyethylene. Working out of a brick plant in Farnumsville, Massachusetts, he kept fiddling with his polymers and monomers until he found a way to purify the stuff, to make it tough and yet pliant: a substance that would remember its own shape. He made it tasteless, odorless, greaseless— not to mention pretty. He called his refined substance "Poly-T."

In 1945 his first product appeared in the stores: the seven-ounce Bell Tumbler. It was perfect. It was so perfect that he gave it a lifetime guarantee. Among Tupper's first customers was the director of a Massachusetts mental institution, who found plasticware far superior to the noisy aluminum cups and plates the hospital had been using. He marveled that the only way his patients could damage Tupperware was by "persistent chewing."

Tupper then loosed his engineer's mind on the spatial economics of the American icebox. In the late 1940s, most containers for refrigerators were made of ceramic, glass, or enameled metal. They took up too much space and were prone to chipping and breakage. A plastic bowl could work wonders in the refrigerator, Tupper thought. The trick was to devise a secure lid. In 1947 he found the answer: a double-grooved lip that worked like a paint-can lid in reverse. The patented "burpable" seal made its debut later that year in the Wonderlier Bowl, which is still featured in the company catalogs.

That same year, 1947, a divorcée from Dearborn, Michigan, named Brownie Wise got a new set of Tupper's Wonder Bowls as a gift. She didn't know what to make of them at first. "It took me three days to figure out how they worked," she recalls. Her baptism in plastic came a few days later. "I was putting one of the bowls in the refrigerator, and I dropped it on the floor. I said, 'Can you beat that?' It *bounced*!"

Wise was a perky woman with razor-sharp business instincts and prematurely gray hair clipped in a "poodle" cut. She was precisely the salesperson Earl Tupper needed. Wise understood that the home was the logical place to sell Tupper's bowls—a nonthreatening environment in which she could explain the seal and the burp and the delightful unsliminess of Poly-T. "It was a demonstrator's dream," she said in a rare personal interview in 1987. "There was a classical shape to the bowls, but they needed active demonstration. You could show how it would fit in the empty spaces in your refrigerator. It was full of action!"

Within a year, Wise had twenty dealers working for her distributorship and was moving more plasticware than anyone in the nation. Tupper was impressed. "You talk a lot and everybody listens," he told her. "How about helping me build a company?" He put Wise in charge of the entire sales division and set her up in a palatial headquarters in the vacant swamplands south of Orlando.

For eight years, Wise was the reigning queen of Tupperland. She spun a corporate confection of hugs and tears and sorority high jinks. She made the cover of *BusinessWeek* in 1954. *Cosmopolitan* called her "Florida's Most Amazing Business Woman." Nicknamed "Sunshine Cinderella," Wise wore white gloves and frilly hats and drove a pink convertible with green leather upholstery. Her office at Tupperware headquarters had three telephones and was as big as a basketball court.

She lived in a Spanish-style villa with an indoor swimming pool and owned an island covered in citrus groves in the middle of Lake Tohopekaliga.

Wise understood the art of motivation. She was given to uttering inspirational bromides. "Think as big as a house!" she'd say, or "Put hop in your hope!" Wise knew how to use props for dramatic effect. She carried around an ugly blob of plastic that she dubbed "Poly" (she claimed it was the first piece of polyethylene that Earl Tupper ever saw). At conventions she'd ask her salesladies to close their eyes, rub Poly, and make a wish.

Wise's den-mother optimism spread like a contagion. For thousands of women, Tupperware became a form of secular faith. Anna Tate, a retired Tupperware distributor in Gaithersburg, Maryland, still has vivid memories of Wise's speeches. "People were spellbound. She gave people faith in themselves, which is a magical quality. She inspired women to attempt things that they never thought they could do." Tate remembers a business trip Wise once made to St. Louis. More than 150 Tupperware salesladies greeted her at the airport, and someone rolled out a red carpet. "These women acted like bobby-soxers waiting for Sinatra. It was hero worship!"

The hero worship sometimes took odd forms. At a 1952 sales meeting in New York, Wise invited a woman to the podium and asked her to select a prize from a huge assortment of gifts piled on the stage. "Choose anything you like," the woman was told, "anything at all."

"In that case," the woman answered, "I'll take the dress Brownie is wearing."

Wise promptly repaired to her hotel room, removed her outfit, and emerged with a fresh change of clothes. Thereafter, winning Brownie's clothing became an established tradition at Tupperware gatherings. She would attend rallies in $150 dresses and $35 hats, knowing that every thread—petticoats included—would be given away as prizes.

To facilitate the annual orgy of giving at the Jubilees, Wise knew that the Tupperware headquarters had to be a mecca of enchantment, a dollhouse world that would draw the women back. Wise had a silver pattern designed for the company and gave place settings away as prizes. She commissioned a noted horticulturist to raise a breed of

"Tupperware" roses (at night when the ladies returned to their hotel rooms they would find fresh Tupperware roses lying on their pillows). She created a lake called "Poly Pond" and "christened" it by tossing in a Tupperware container filled with polyethylene pellets. Anyone who dipped her hands in its waters would enjoy good luck all year. "There's an alligator in there, too," Wise warned the salesladies, "for dealers who don't work!"

For all her shenanigans, Wise was gravely serious about the company's public image and had little tolerance for people who found Tupperware funny. Once the company's public relations firm called Wise to say that it had succeeded in getting Tupperware written into a script on the *I Love Lucy* show. As Wise remembers it, "I said, 'Oh, no!' I did not want anyone to make fun of Tupperware. One wrong word could throw the whole thing off. Lucy was going to have a Tupperware party at her home. I said, 'It won't help us. I won't allow it.' I was just afraid it would end up with a Tupperware bowl upside down on Ricky's head."

Dour New Englander that he was, Earl Tupper took a dim view of all of Wise's corporate tomfoolery. He didn't like the way she had turned his company into a sorority house and was worried that Tupperware Home Parties had become a one-woman show. The disdain was mutual. "I could not say I liked Tupper as a person," she says. "I don't think I even knew him as a person. He was the most impersonal person I ever met. I never once called him 'Earl.' It was always 'Mr. Tupper.' The man was a stone wall."

Wise says that one day in early 1958 Tupper stormed into her office and coolly informed her that he was selling the company to an as yet unnamed corporation; he presented it to her as a *fait accompli*. She quickly got the message: Tupper was firing her. "It was very well thought out, apparently," Wise told me when I spoke to her by phone (she was in her late seventies and living in Kissimmee). "I asked him, 'Is that it?' And he said, 'Yes, that's it. It's already been decided.' I got up and walked out and never came back."

Later that year, Tupper sold the company to Rexall Drugs for a reported $9 million. Tupperware had grown too unwieldy for him to manage alone. He gave away most of his millions to the Smithsonian Institution and spent his last years living as a hermit in Costa Rica. He claimed he'd invented a revolutionary new container that would render his patented "burping" bowl obsolete, but it never materialized. He died of a heart attack in 1983 and was buried near San José. It is often asked, but the answer is no: he wasn't interred in Tupperware.

INSIDE THE HOUSE AT 13102 Broadmore, deep in the coves and cul-de-sacs of Silver Spring, Maryland, eight women are gathered around the beveled-glass coffee table nibbling hors d'oeuvres from one of those sectioned trays with the molded dip well in the center and the little triangular compartments that prevent the carrot sticks from trespassing on the kiwi.

Tonight's hostess, Patty Betz, is a cosmetology teacher and mother of two. Muffin the miniature Maltese is digging tunnels in the wall-to-wall carpeting. A video game called *Gauntlet* is parked in the dining room, a permanent piece of the furniture. "It's awesome," one of the neighborhood kids raves. "You can't die!"

Through the pandemonium, Sheila Looney remains calm. She is wearing a white lab coat with a gold-plated name tag. "Let's play a little word-association game," she suggests. "See if you can think of a food item that starts with the first letter of your name."

Leia picks "lasagna."

Santha goes with "sweet potatoes."

Mary Carol: "M&M cookies."

And so on. With games like this, Looney claims she can master twenty names without error. "And people love to hear their names called out!"

Now Looney is ready to get down to business. On the dining room table, in the shadow of *Gauntlet*, the products are stacked and nested. "*This* is your salad bowl," Looney begins, holding it high so all can see. "It's a really pretty piece. It isn't *just* a salad bowl. It can be a cake dish. And the dome top can be turned upside down and used as a pedestal for a punch bowl. See? And it's a great place to keep your fruit. The dome top creates a little hothouse effect in there. It'll ripen your bananas in no time! Isn't that marvelous!"

Looney then points out a little-known distinction about Tupperware lids; only the round seals, she says, are actually burpable. "If it's round, you make the sound," Looney explains. "If it's square, it keeps the air."

Another distinction: Tupperware gatherings like this one aren't actually called "parties" anymore. Too goofy-sounding. Too home-makerish. The marketing people who ponder these matters down at Tupperware headquarters have been toying with a more contemporary term for years. Now it's official; parties are known as "classes."

Sheila Looney elucidates. "To come to a Tupperware gathering, a mother has to leave the kids at home with the father. She can't very well say, 'Oh, by the way, honey, I'm going to a party.' But if she says, 'I'm going to a class,' well, that sounds more impressive. It takes on a whole new psychological look. She's going to *learn* something."

By whatever name, the Tupperware party has proven a surprisingly resilient ritual of commerce. After forty years of choreographed camp, the party retains a mysterious appeal, blurring the lines between work and play. Every 2.7 seconds another Tupperware party starts some-where in the world. Business school professors have scratched their heads in bewilderment at the whole strange dance. The party plan runs on irrational principles that can't easily be parsed into graphs and charts for a Harvard case study; the obstacle of the party puts psycho-logical distance between the product and the buyers. They can't just have a Tupperware bowl. They have to seek it out. They have to *want* it. And in the wanting, they think of other, deeper wants. So many shapes to choose from, and so many colors. Why should they chase a dill pickle around in a clumsy jar full of brine when it could be neatly lodged in a Pick-A-Deli canister? What bright, accessible, compart-mentalized worlds their kitchens could be, if only . . . When their turn finally comes to kneel at the Tupperware altar, they positively crave it. They must have it! And once they have it, they keep wanting more.

Looney has come tonight to spread a new environmental message. Tupperware, the company that buys more than one billion pounds of polyethylene pellets a year, is going green. The manufacturing plant is now melting down the little uglies that come out of the mold wrong and is recycling them into a new line of large-size storage containers.

"They come in this pretty forest-green color," Looney demonstrates, "to remind you of the ecology."

But the most dramatic development in Tupperland, Looney announces, is a new generation of cookware that promises to do for the American microwave what Modular Mates did for the refrigerator. A few years ago the Tupperware technicians took a look around and realized that 85 percent of all American homes had microwaves. But Americans were microwaving Neanderthals, practically roasting their meat on a stick. They were guessing at the times and zap strengths, sizzling the outside of their chicken while leaving embarrassing cores of frozen meat on the inside. This was not good. This was inefficient.

So the Tupperware technicians invented "Tupperwave."

Tupperwave is a complete cooking system for the Micro Age. It features a "stack cooker" that allows you to microwave three separate dishes simultaneously. You can cook a square meal for six in under twenty-five minutes. All you have to do is follow the recipes and plug in your food groups according to the simple tier system. Error-free nuclear food science, cooking by numbers. "It's marvelous!" Looney gushes. "The dish on top has your most concentrated heat. That's where your raw vegetables go. In the middle is your entrée. And on the bottom is your most delicate heat. That's where you're going to have your rice. It takes the mystery out of microwaving."

In fact, Looney proclaims, a sample meal is baking in the kitchen right now. "Can you smell the apples cooking?"

Ten minutes later, the meal emerges from the microwave, the three piping hot dishes flawlessly presented in their separate compartments: fluffy rice, tender chicken with broccoli, and sweet apples. "Doesn't that look appetizing?"

By the end of the evening, Looney has sold close to $300 in merchandise and dated two more "classes." The new stack cooker has been a hit. Santha (a.k.a. "sweet potatoes") has already placed her order. Truth be told, Santha has been a Tupperware backslider in recent years. She hasn't bought any in almost a decade. She has resorted to twisty ties and Ziploc bags and Saran Wrap. She has let things spoil. She knows that at forty-two dollars, the stack cooker is the most expensive item in the catalog. But tonight she's got the Tupper feeling. "Other things wear away," Santha says. "But Tupperware goes on and on."

ON THE LAST NIGHT OF JUBILEE, a nearly full moon rises over the cypress swamps at Tupperware headquarters. It's time for the Wave-Off, the final farewell to the ladies as they depart for home.

The Tupperware executives are standing on a platform in front of Building A, dressed in *Wizard of Oz* costumes—Dorothy, the Tin Man, the Cowardly Lion, the Scarecrow, and Gaylin Olson as the Wizard. Red floodlights illuminate the colonnade behind them, and the Friendship Fountain sprays a fine mist over the scene. The giant rainbow made of 64,000 Tupperware lids arches across the sky.

A thousand vans are lined up bumper-to-bumper along the Orange Blossom Trail, a mile-long procession of headlights boring through the humid Florida night. Sheila Looney has packed all her awards into the Lumina for the long trip back to Maryland. Now she is waiting in her van with her husband, Bob, at the wheel, as parking assistants direct the procession with fluorescent airport beacons.

One by one the vans roll by the platform. The women throw open their side doors and energetically wave at the Oz characters. "Thank you!" they cry, some of them snapping off pictures. "We love you!"

"So long, Tupperfriends," the executives call back, squinting in the glare of the flashbulbs. "Come back!"

"We love you, Gaylin!"

"Thanks for sharing!"

"You really socked it to us!"

The column of vans files out of the Tupperware driveway and turns north toward Orlando and the Gatorland Zoo, primed for another invasion of America.

"So long, Our World! See you next year!"

Gaylin Olson heaves a momentary sigh of relief, but he knows this is no time to relax. Tomorrow morning another wave of two thousand salesladies will be arriving, and they will want to see Product.

—1991

Webster's Children

MOSTLY I REMEMBER THE FEAR, the gasping, white-knuckled, adrenaline-soaked fear. It was in one of those experimental schools of the early seventies, with the monochrome beige carpeting and the huge "open classroom" designed by some Marxist architect whose aim was to drown the individual voice in a sea of adolescent noise. The entire seventh and eighth grades were gathered in the auditorium. The hot, moist chamber hung with doom. Mr. Springfield, the principal, hovered over me, clutching a word list.

There were only two of us left standing. Me and Doug McCown, I believe it was. Mr. Springfield kept throwing words at us like an evil one-eyed pitcher.

Filament . . .

Godsend . . .

Sacrilegious . . .

Suffocate . . .

Tuxedo . . .

I was in the seventh grade. I had on bell-bottom corduroy Levi's and a Lacoste shirt. I wore Earth Shoes. I was a mess.

My teachers had impressed upon me the gravity of the situation. If I won this contest, I could compete in the city spelling bee, sponsored by our own Scripps Howard newspaper, the *Memphis Commercial Appeal.* And if I won that, I could take a trip to the national event in Washington, D.C. I could shake President Nixon's hand and check out the museums. I would be the school's ambassador. I'd even get on TV.

But it was more than that. Winning this event could be the first step in a brilliant career. It was sort of like the inverse of the "single puff of marijuana inevitably leads to heroin" gateway theory: You learn to spell, and then, in the next frame, you're an astronaut or an Olympic stud pole-vaulting across the front of the Wheaties box.

If you want to know, I was a pretty hot little speller. I liked words, and I liked letters, and I was well acquainted with the vagaries of the "schwa." My teachers were counting on me.

But then I peered into the auditorium and saw Ted and Tom and Bob and Steve (the cool guys had monosyllabic names). I sensed by the aloof way that Ted & Co. regarded me as I squirmed on the stage that this was a highly uncool scene I was partaking in, and that I had better find a way to extricate myself.

Mr. Springfield stepped to the mound and fired another one. "Parachute," he declared. Ah, an easy one, I thought. Doug gave it his best shot: "P-a-r-i-c-h-u-t-e!" An honest effort, but alas: *DING!*

My turn. "Parachute," Mr. Springfield repeated. All eyes were on me. The room fell into silence. My teachers seemed to egg me on, but Ted and Bob only glowered. I stared down at the little smiling alligator on my shirt and pondered my future.

THE 240 SPELLERS who descended on Washington for the 1991 Scripps Howard National Spelling Bee would have scoffed at a little gnat of a word like "parachute." For three days I sat in the Presidential Ballroom of the Capital Hilton watching terrified, metal-mouthed pre-pubescents as they made quick work of such words as "tjaele," "caoutchouc," and "mesoprosopic." They were practically professionals, well versed in Latin, Greek, and Sanskrit roots. The best ones had full-time coaches.

They came here from forty-eight states, plus Mexico, Puerto Rico, Guam, and the Virgin Islands, to take part in "the Armageddon of

Orthography." The prodigies, most of them seventh- and eighth-graders, had boned up on "Words of the Champions," a daunting list of some 3,200 mind-benders put out each year by the Scripps Howard spelling bee staff. In the center of the ballroom, upon a mighty throne lit by glittering chandeliers, sat the silent umpire: Webster's Unabridged Third International Dictionary, a book with the heft of an anvil. One by one, the contestants shambled to the microphone with huge numbered placards hung around their necks. The master of ceremonies, an owl-eyed and extremely well-enunciated man named Alex Cameron, would present a word of up to twenty-odd syllables derived from the international scientific vocabulary or Hindi-Urdu. I could hear the speller's brain muscles flexing as he or she stalled for time. *Will you please use it in a sentence? Can I have a definition? Does it have a homonym?*

Some of the contestants broke down in tears, and one even threw up. Each fought valiantly, but in due course, after two days of elimination—*DING!* Finally, after a pressure-cooker finale, a new Queen of Spelldom was crowned: Joanne Lagatta, from Madison, Wisconsin, clinching her victory with the word "antipyretic."

To the Scripps Howard spelling bee staff in Cincinnati, it's a given that spelling should form the core of one's education. A tight crew composed largely of former spelling champs, the staff is zealously protective of the bee's reputation, and quite secretive about its internal workings. The staffers insist that it is strictly an "educational event," and are liable to go ballistic if you suggest, as I did once, that the bee is, in part, a promotional gimmick for the Scripps Howard newspaper chain.

When I visited the Scripps Howard headquarters, high up in an Art Deco skyscraper in downtown Cincinnati, I was invited to examine the bee archives. Shortly after I sat down, the lady who'd long been in charge of the National Spelling Bee, an apparently humorless schoolmarm named Mrs. Miller, who looked precisely like you'd think the protector of this vital national institution would look, emerged from her office and gave me the third degree about what I was "up to." Looking up from the yellowed news clips, I could immediately tell that she had it in for me. Mrs. Miller had me pegged as the worst kind of writer, *a satirist.* "I was invited up," I explained. "One of your staff members said it was okay."

"Well, it's *not* okay," she said, arms akimbo, and stormed down the hall.

A few minutes later one of the bright-eyed staffers interrupted me. "I'm sorry," she said. "Mrs. Miller has asked me to escort you from the building. We need to go now."

"Are you . . . throwing me out?"

"If you don't cooperate, we'll be forced to call the police."

In fact, the National Spelling Bee did originate as a promotional gimmick. In 1925 the Bingham family, publishers of the *Louisville Courier-Journal,* sponsored the first National Spelling Bee in Washington as part of a bitter circulation war with a rival Louisville newspaper. The first contest was held in an auditorium at the Smithsonian and had only nine contestants. Frank Neuhauser, then an eleven-year-old from Louisville, won on the word "gladiolus." He received $500 in gold pieces and got to shake the hand of President Calvin Coolidge. When Neuhauser's victory train pulled into the Louisville station, the townsfolk welcomed him with bouquets of gladioluses. I met Mr. Neuhauser in his Washington law offices. A sweet and eminently sensible patent attorney in his late seventies, he seemed to think the bee had gotten way out of hand. "Nowadays the words are just too big," Neuhauser said. "I couldn't even get through the first round."

Scripps Howard bought the rights to the event in 1941, and has been hosting it ever since. Over the years, the bee has produced no Pulitzer Prize–winning authors, no PEN-Faulkner nominees, no Nobel laureates in literature. In fact, most of the bee winners have tended to gravitate toward science and engineering fields. According to a Scripps Howard newsletter, spelling champs have gone on to be secretaries, waitresses, doctors, lawyers, and fashion designers. One of the champs was arrested in 1971 after he "blew his nose on the American flag during a Vietnam War demonstration."

There have been moments of high heroism at the bees, such as the time in 1983, when thirteen-year-old Andrew Flosdorf of Fonda, New York, found he could not spell a lie. Flosdorf removed himself from the bee by confessing that the judges had misheard him when they thought he had spelled the word "echolalia" correctly. He exited the stage with a standing ovation and a clear conscience, later explaining: "I didn't want to feel like slime."

THE VALUE OF ORTHOGRAPHY has been debated throughout American history. Some have noted that many of the English language's greatest writers have been horribly inconsistent spellers—Chaucer, Milton, and Walt Whitman, to name but a few. Others point out that "proper" spelling is a relatively recent concept inspired by priggish lexicographers. Speaking at a Hartford spelling bee in 1875, Mark Twain bemoaned what he called a "spelling epidemic" that had swept the country. "I don't see any use in spelling a word right, and never did. We might as well make all clothes alike and cook all dishes alike. Sameness is tiresome. Variety is pleasing." William James concurred: "Isn't it abominable that everybody is expected to spell in the same way? Let us get a dozen influential persons each to spell after his own fashion and so break this tyranny."

On the other hand, English mavens and self-appointed custodians of culture have insisted that a standardized orthography is one of the pillars on which our language and ultimately all public discourse rest. Go soft on spelling, and there goes the empire. For some, the ability to spell is even a kind of class litmus test. In Philip Roth's *Portnoy's Complaint,* the protagonist kills a budding romance when he discovers that his inamorata can't spell.

We have our own capricious tongue to blame for the existence of spelling bees. If English made any sense, if it followed steadfast rules of phonetics, if it didn't have such a titanic vocabulary, our orthography would pose no great challenge. It is, of course, English's greedy appetite for "loan words" that makes it such a rich and yeasty language. Lexicographers estimate that 80 percent of the English vocabulary is foreign derived, from such varied sources as Danish, Latin, Greek, Swedish, Hebrew, Arabic, Bengali, and Native American tongues. The Oxford English Dictionary lists some 500,000 entries. By contrast, the German vocabulary has only 185,000 words; French, a paltry 100,000.

Perhaps the greatest single headache in English spelling is the schwa, or "uh" sound (which, it should be noted, is the same sound that we make when we can't spell a word). All five of our vowels, working singly or in various dark cabals, are capable of producing the "uh" sound: *a*go, *a*gent, san*i*ty, compl*y*, foc*u*s. Word experts say that fully half of all errors in spelling involve the dreaded schwa. Two other oft-cited menaces are the "f" sound, which can be spelled f, ff, ph, gh, and pf, and the "sh" sound, for which there are at least thirteen possible spellings: sh, s, ss, sio, ssio, tio, cio, c, sci, ch, sch, chs, and psh.

Over the ages, idealists have tried to rid English orthography of these and other offenders. The most ardent proponents of simplified spelling have included Ben Franklin, Noah Webster, Andrew Carnegie, George Bernard Shaw, and President Theodore Roosevelt, who once demanded that the Government Printing Office adopt a list of some three hundred phonetic spellings—including dropt, chast, thru, and thoroly. But the Washington wits made sport of his pet project, and the movement soon fizzled.

The last major campaign for spelling reform was waged by the *Chicago Tribune*, whose owner, Joseph Medill, once called conventional spelling "a tyranny of absurdities that fill our schoolhouses with misery and keep millions of English-speaking people in lifelong bondage to the unabridged dictionary." In 1934, his grandson, Col. Robert McCormick, ordered the *Tribune* to adopt a list of more than eighty simplified spellings, to wit: jax, lether, hocky, burocracy, crum, dialog, hefer, tho, trafic, fantom, and frate. But the paper surrendered in 1975 after too many advertisers complained that the new orthography was bad for business. Years later, a sign in the *Tribune's* freight elevator still offered testimony to the failed crusade: FRATE ONLY.

THE TRADITION OF THE SPELLING bee is much larger than Scripps Howard and its twenty newspapers, of course. It's a venerable custom in America—older than baseball, older than basketball, older than the Boy Scouts. The ghosts of history breeze in and out of those long lists of words. Spelling bees are a form of folk theater dating back to the one-room schoolhouses and Grange halls of our pioneer past.

There is something unmistakably American about the spectacle. In the 1820s, a precocious Horace Greeley burned up the town halls of New Hampshire with his spelling prowess. The young Dwight Eisenhower also served his time on the spelling circuit, but stumbled over the word "syzygy." Blockhead Charlie Brown made it to the National Spelling Bee but choked on "beagle."

Noah Webster, the spiritual father of the spelling bee, would probably grimace at the horrors that routinely crop up in "Words of the Champions": spinescent, realschule, scytodepsic, palynology, mackereler, ngege, dorsiferous, ferraiolone, immiserization, fanchonette, tessitura. How do these words get picked? What diabolical processes conspire to bring these monsters up from the ocean depths of the dictionary?

To answer these questions, I consulted the word panel, a group of professional language sleuths who prepare the word lists for the national bee. One of the word panelists is an editor of Merriam-Webster dictionaries in Springfield, Massachusetts. Others are editors associated with Chicago-based Encyclopaedia Britannica. "We're word mavens," boasted sometime panelist Anita Wolf. "We're acutely aware of the subtle differences between words. A lot of obscure journals on language pass over our desks." The word panelists put in hundreds of painstaking hours researching the list. They clandestinely show up at the National Spelling Bee each May to witness firsthand the misery they have wrought. Their identities are kept a tight secret, partly out of fear of reprisals from irate parents. As Wolf pointed out, "It would be hard to explain to a parent who's having a conniption fit how we arrived at some of our words."

Word panelist Jim Lowe conceded that the final rounds at the national bee are composed of words "that would never occur in any conversation." But Lowe seemed unconcerned about this. "I look for challenges in spelling. What the word means is largely unimportant to me."

Many of the words reflect the personal tastes of the panelists. "I read a lot of botany," explained Wolf, "so I stick in a lot of plant words." And for some reason, foreign foods and dishes often crop up. "One year we had about twelve different kinds of pasta," she recalled.

Despite the random tastes of the panelists, there is method in their madness. Among their criteria:

- No corporate trademarks.
- No capitalized words or formal names.
- No words with apostrophes or diacritical marks.
- No words that appeared in last year's bee.
- And no words that may sound vaguely dirty or embarrassing, such as "asinine," or "phocomelia." As word panelist Jim Carnes explained: "Words or definitions that may elicit an undesirable reaction in a bunch of thirteen-year-olds are automatically removed."

But why all the impossibly difficult words? The word panelists pointed out that the spelling bee is both a contest and a public entertainment. There can be only one victor. In the space of two days, more than two hundred contestants must be eliminated, and $64 words are the handiest method of dispatch. It may not seem fair, but that's show business. "Frankly, I'm not interested in finding out who the best speller is," said Alex Cameron, an English professor at the University of Dayton and the official bee pronouncer. "I'm interested in finding a winner."

Cameron noted that if Scripps Howard merely wanted to find the best young speller in the land, its staff would prepare a written test and thereby remove the element of luck. But that, of course, would be boring. J. Quitman Stephens, a ponytailed staffer who is a former spelling champion from Marshall, Texas, put it this way: "Who would want to come to Washington and take a test? You can stay in class and take a test. But this makes learning look glamorous. You get to stand up onstage. People all over the United States are watching you. There's all this attention. You are pampered like a king. Your are treated like what you are—a champion."

Still, even staunch defenders of the national bee worry that over the past decade the event has become truly arcane. "The bee is not an amateur competition anymore," argues Wolf. "There are kids out there now who are more interested in being champions than in losing gracefully." The late Jim Wagner, a Scripps Howard executive who ran the bee for nearly two decades, lamented that it had become "a torture test." "I don't believe in using a word solely for the purpose of eliminating a contestant," Wagner told me. "You know, some word for a rare ant in Madagascar, or an endangered species of fish that is found at the bottom of the Indian Ocean."

IF WE MUST NAME NAMES, we can lay some of the blame for English's orthographic confusion on a certain printer named William Caxton. It was Caxton who introduced the printing press to London in 1476. Before him, it never occurred to anyone that there should be a uniform orthography. Caxton noted that words were spelled differently from one shire to the next: People spelled according to their regional dialects. His chosen spellings reflected the English he heard in the streets of London. "Caxton helped to fix the language on the page before its writers and teachers had reached a consensus." note Robert McCrum, William Cran, and Robert MacNeil in *The Story of English*. "It is to this that English owes some of its chaotic and exasperating spelling conventions."

Caxton's legacy was further complicated by Shakespeare, who played fast and loose with his spellings, and often invented words out of whole cloth. "[Shakespeare's] spellings," explain McCrum et al., "were enshrined in the First Folio and are responsible for the chaos of modern English."

When Noah Webster arrived on the scene two centuries later, he took one sidelong glance at the chaos and went to work setting it straight. A Calvinist lawyer from Hartford, Webster had no tolerance for untidiness of any kind. The man who came to be known as "the Schoolmaster of the Republic" produced numerous textbooks and dictionaries, but his most popular and perhaps most influential text was the *Blue Back Speller,* which sold more than 70 million copies during his lifetime. This slender volume did much to streamline American spelling and purge the language of certain Britishisms that Webster found odious (defence, mould, fibre, theatre, honour). The speller was in use for more than a century, and became a basic text in the frontier schools of America. One writer at the time spoke in awe of Webster's "battalions of words which make his spelling-book pages look like spiritual armies marching against ignorance."

Webster is generally credited with popularizing the custom of the "spelldown." Webster insisted that students shouldn't even attempt to learn to read until they had fully mastered orthography; such secondary concerns as the meaning or connotation of words should come later. Webster's mission was to fashion a federal language that would be spelled and pronounced the same in every region of the country. He sought to stamp out all local dialects, particularly the Southern drawl, which he found highly distasteful. "Great efforts should be taken," he implored the young republic's schoolteachers, "to make pupils open the teeth and give a full clear sound to every syllable." His spelling book, he said, was "calculated to destroy the various false dialects in pronunciation in the several states . . . and render the pronunciation of the language accurate and uniform."

By the early 1800s, spelling bees had become a popular form of evening recreation in the American hinterlands for children and adults alike. Competition could be stiff. One Indiana woman noted in her diary in the 1830s: "Towards the close of the evening, when difficult and unusual words are chosen to confound the small number who still keep the floor, it is scarcely less than painful."

Spelling bees became a national craze following the publication of an 1871 Western dialect novel, *The Hoosier Schoolmaster,* by Edward Eggleston. The novel celebrated the spelling champions of Flat Creek, Indiana, where children "loved spelling for its own sake, and who, smelling the battle from afar, came to try their skill." By 1875, thanks largely to Eggleston's book, spelling had become, according to a *London Times* reporter, the "prevailing infatuation in America."

*   *   *

IF INDIANA WAS THE NATION'S HOTBED of orthography in the 1870s, today it's Colorado, home of the Denver Spelling Junta. Over the years, El Paso, Pittsburgh, and Seattle have won their share of titles, but the Denver bee has led the pack, producing six national winners and numerous runners-up since 1925. When asked to explain this curious fact a few years ago, Roy Romer, then the governor of Colorado, speculated: "Maybe it has something to do with the radiation coming from Rocky Flats," the state's infamous nuclear facility.

Part of the reason for Colorado's hegemony is that the *Rocky Mountain News,* a large Scripps Howard daily in Denver, sponsors a rigorous statewide contest that is reputed to be even more of a crucible than the national bee. And the paper has done much to glamorize its spelling champs over the years. "When I got back from Washington, I felt like one of the Broncos," 1979 National Spelling Bee winner Katie Kerwin told me. "I was a state hero. I'd go to gas stations and there'd be placards everywhere saying, 'Congratulations, Katie!'"

Not coincidentally, Denver also boasts some of the best spelling coaches in the land. Perhaps the most celebrated of these is Florence Bailly, a gimlet-eyed, middle-aged freelance instructor who has coached three National Spelling Bee winners, including her son, and countless regional champions over the years. Bailly chooses her pupils with the same discrimination that an Olympic figure-skating coach uses in sizing up the next promising young athlete. Students have been known to camp out on her doorstep and plead with her to take them on. "I only accept one at a time," Bailly told me when I dropped by her house in Denver. "I insist on having them for at least two years. I have them study about forty thousand words. They become almost obsessed with it. They cannot stop. They're like little sponges. It's all they want to do. When they leave me, I want them married to that dictionary."

Bailly, who drills her students in Latin and Greek roots and dictionary skills, believes that spelling should be taught not as an exercise in memorization but as a broad course in English etymology. "While it's true that rote learning can win a spelling bee," she said, "what's the point of spelling like a parrot? What a pitiful waste of time! You might as well ask them to memorize the phone book."

The year before, Bailly's eighth-grade entry, Jennifer Phillips, finished fifth at the national bee.

"Who's your understudy this year?" I asked.

Bailly drew an ominous face. "Her name is Julie Vogel," she said. "A seventh-grader. She has greatness in her, I think."

"So you think she'll win?"

"Let's just say this. She's a very significant threat."

"THE WORD," Mr. Springfield reiterated, "is parachute." His eyebrows were arched, his lips pursed in a reptilian smile.

"Parachute?" I asked for good measure.

"Yes, parachute," he assured me.

"Par . . . a . . . chute," I said, plumbing the murky mysteries of the word. "Hmmm."

"Please proceed," Mr. Springfield demanded, glancing at his watch.

"P-a-r-a . . . " I spelled haltingly. I heard titters from the audience, a gasp, a cough.

I was too scared to look up, but I could feel the weight of Ted's and Bob's stares. My palms grew sweaty. My feet quivered in my Earth Shoes. I was quite certain that I hated Mr. Noah Webster. I knew how to spell "parachute," but I wanted out.

". . . s-h-o-o-t," I blurted.

DING!

Doug went on to win the spelling bee, and for all I know, he's now an astronaut. Later that day, I ran into Ted & Co. in the hall. I expected high fives, but to my surprise, I found that they were sore at me. "You idiot!" Ted said. "We were rooting for you, but you blew it! You could have at least lost on a hard word! Anybody can spell 'parachute'!"

—1992

At Home in a Fake Place

Santa Fe, New Mexico

THE MAN IN THE WHITE truck was cranking up the hill, coming for us. We could hear his big diesel engine, the gears grinding angrily as he wound up the rutted gravel road toward our new house. He was a county inspector, a member of the dreaded architectural police, on an official errand. He nosed ominously into our driveway, and stepped out. The high desert soil crunched beneath his boots. He was a wiry, swarthy-skinned man in jeans. His long black ponytail swung as he walked toward us, accompanied by an officious-looking male assistant gripping a clipboard.

It took only a quick glance at our house for the inspector to make his determination. "You are in violation of the codes of the Santa Fe Special Mountain Review ordinance," he said. His tone was grave.

Santa Fe is world famous for its architectural rigor, of course, its strict regulations governing construction, its niggardly palette of acceptable earth tones. Like a handful of other historically obsessed places across the country—Cape Cod, the French Quarter, San Juan Capistrano, Charleston, Mendocino—Santa Fe is a town that strenuously bears down on its residents to achieve a certain uniformity of appearance. Even out in the county, far from the city's especially rigid historic district, the Look is enforced by peer pressure, by neighborhood covenant, and sometimes by law. But after nearly ten years of living here, I had never met one of the mythic enforcers of the Style Council. Certainly I never imagined one would pay *me* a visit.

Simply put, the newly remodeled 1977 house we'd just bought was *too tall*. The previous owner apparently didn't get a proper permit. We were now informed that our house lay a mere eight feet within something called the Mountain Special Review District, an all-or-nothing line of demarcation that requires residents to observe a raft of building restrictions as long as a chile ristra.

What would we have to do to comply? Well, the top of the house would basically have to be lopped off. We would be required to rip away the entire roof, which was made of a sage-green metal, an apparently contraband substance in the Santa Fe foothills. And after that, we could be forced to put in a comprehensive gray-water system and outfit every room of the house with fire sprinklers. All of which could cost a hundred grand, maybe more.

I thought I detected a twinkle in his eye and a spring in his step as the inspector strode back to his truck and rumbled down the road, on the scent of other architectural infractions.

My wife and I watched in shock as his dust cloud dissipated over the road. We had always thought of ourselves as architecturally correct. We despised the monstrosities that had been built high above town by yodeling Gatsbys with too much turquoise and too little taste. We had laughed derisively when Shirley MacLaine's proposed mountaintop Shangri-la had been voted down by the town fathers (though perhaps she'll get her way in another life).

Surely the house we'd bought was *not* one of those out-of-scale ridgetop castles—was it? It was a twenty-five-year-old, single-story home, screened by mature piñons and cottonwoods, and not visible from anywhere in town. We had immediately set about making it workable as a family house. Like all home construction projects, it soon became a mind-numbing, bank-expunging process, and a substantial marital irritant. What we hadn't counted on was this added layer of vexation— contending with narrow interpretations of the architectural code.

From the outset, my love of Santa Fe has been, in large part, architectural. With so much generic prefabrication cluttering the modern

American landscape, I'm grateful to have ended up in a town that concerns itself with its own physical history and cares, to an almost neurotic degree, about how it looks. I'm far from being smitten by the preposterous lengths to which the Santa Fe style gets taken in the messy reality of the commercial vernacular—the faux-dobe Office Max, the faux-dobe Burger King, even the faux-dobe Cheeks topless bar and adjacent porn shop. But there is something extraordinary here, a cumulative effect that's the result of generations of uncommonly careful planning, a fragile quality that could be easily wrecked with a few ill-considered buildings.

Suddenly, however, I was one of the Philistines.

The business about lopping off the top of our house wasn't an idle threat. We had heard of numerous examples of buildings being reworked to satisfy the punctilious requirements of the style. Around town, one can see dozens of handsome old structures originally made of stone, brick, shingle, board-and-batten, or clapboard—important historic buildings, many of them, though not rendered in the Santa Fe style—that have been troweled over with brown stucco to make them conform. A few years ago, on Artist Road, the inspectors had deemed a certain new house to be in violation. Driving by the place on the way to the ski basin, I couldn't see anything wrong with it; it looked much like the other Pueblo Revival estates stacked up the hillside. But make no mistake: this house was a miscreant. It was three feet too tall. Someone had spray-painted a dotted line across the top where the new roof had to go, as though following cutting directions for a cereal box top. I could only imagine the costs involved in truncating an entire building. And now we were looking at doing the same thing.

WHEN I FIRST CAME HERE IN 1994 to take a job at a magazine, I had no particular notion of making New Mexico my permanent home. My opinion about Santa Fe evolved in three specific layers of assimilation. Initially, and for the first full year or so, I was struck with the usual dumb enchantment many people seem to feel when they experience this high and dry old capital, so different from the balance of North America. The tang of piñon smoke in moldering adobe courtyards, yellow slash of cottonwoods along the acequia, sunbeams slanting through thunderstorm virga rolling in from Navajo country: few are immune to this town's formidable charms. I wasn't.

People here speak incessantly, annoyingly, about "the Light." It's said that the light here has an ineffable quality—golden, celestial, magical—the result of some combination of high altitude, southern latitude, and the bone-dryness of the air. I was skeptical of its specialness, but when I came here I sensed it immediately. It was in mid-September, after the summer monsoons had tapered off, and the skies were sharpened with a new clarity. Along the low road to Taos, the Hatch chile vendors were roasting freshly harvested peppers in enormous tumbling contraptions, issuing a carbon haze over the countryside. In the morning, I could look up and see a fuzz along the upper reaches of the southern Rockies—the first snow dustings of the season. And below the soft white line, threading like a neon necklace through the ponderosa forests, were the vast stands of aspen.

My second reaction to Santa Fe, after the novelty wore off, was one of alienation. It fully hit me that this city was a lot of things I didn't like—a tourist trap, a New Age mecca, a retirement haven for the filthy rich. I began to loathe the sight of bleached cow skulls, dream catchers, concho belts, and drawling doofuses in long sheepskin coats and cowboy hats who'd never been anywhere near a horse. The downtown seemed to have lost much of the frowzy authenticity it once apparently had. The astronomical cost of real estate had displaced many of the old Spanish families, and their ancestral adobe compounds had turned at a furious clip into art galleries, aromatherapy boutiques, and high-colonics spas. Having been declared one of the world's "spiritual meridians" (by whom I'm not too sure), Santa Fe had become a magnet for a truly remarkable cross-section of questing individuals from the rest of America—Hollywood wellness junkies, eccentric art dealers with a taste for the occult, Ultimate Frisbee–playing trustafarians, Texas billionaire widows willing to give anything a try. Just as every third person in Washington is a lawyer, every other Santa Fean seemed to be a transmedium, or an empath, or a vivation professional. The ads in the weekly alternative paper, the *Reporter*, conveyed it well: "I am a lawyer-mediator who specializes in self-empowerment and holistic divorce." "My special gift is transformational breathwork and somato-emotional release." "I am a certified rebirther who sidelines in deep tissue massage." "With the psychic surgery techniques of the Reverend Jonna Corti, no actual blood or tissue is removed."

AFTER A WHILE, I also grew weary of the Santa Fe architectural style, one of the things that had first entranced me. It seemed to me the tradition needed a shot in the arm. I found it odd that Santa Fe, an art capital full of renegades and free spirits, should be so blandly conformist in this one area of endeavor. I began to miss a little of the unpredictable clutter of those "ordinary" cities back east that had grown haphazardly and without a concerted look in mind. I came to agree with Robert Leonard Reid, who in his engaging collection of essays, *America, New Mexico,* declared the style "enfeebling, as homogeneous gene pools are enfeebling. It is incestuous and oppressive. Most of all it is boring."

Santa Fe's architectural persnicketiness felt all the more odd when one considered where it was. In New Mexico, one of the most fiercely independent-minded swaths of the United States, a man's double-wide is his castle, and if you happen to wander onto that man's property, he's likely to have an impressive cache of automatic weapons he'd like to show you. After scores of films and books about the state's most famous citizen, Billy the Kid, New Mexico is practically national shorthand for cowboy impetuousness and just plain anarchy.

(Scene from a Peckinpah Western that was never made: Billy the Kid is holed up in his new Pueblo style house in Santa Fe, surrounded by a posse of concerned citizens from the review board. "Billy, this residence is not regulation!" they say.

"Sorry, boys!" Billy says, poking his Winchester out one of the windows. "I will not accept pebble-dash stucco! And I'll paint my house any damn color I want!")

In fact, Santa Fe was once a much more architecturally eclectic city. The town's Spanish Pueblo tradition has venerable roots, of course, but the craze in its current ubiquity didn't begin in earnest until 1912, the year New Mexico achieved statehood. The town's aesthetic elite, under the aegis of the Museum of New Mexico, realized that Santa Fe's best hope for a prosperous future lay in tourism. And what tourists seemed to want for a backdrop was the spell of old adobe architecture without intrusion from the modern world. The civic planners gave the town a catchy new name, "the City Different," and drew up codes for all future building. Principally, they took their cue from nearby Indian pueblos—Taos and Acoma, in particular—while blending in Spanish-Moorish and American Territorial elements to forge a romantic style that was relentlessly low, squat, and beige.

As architectural historian Chris Wilson has slyly pointed out in his perceptive and controversial book, *The Myth of Santa Fe,* this effort, at its core, was not a preservation movement, but rather a selective decoration project by fiat, a scheme of singular ambition to achieve atmospheric conformity in the once Wild West. All other modes of construction were decreed non grata, even though dozens of other fine architectural traditions—Queen Anne, Federal, Tudor, Prairie, Mission, Arts & Crafts bungalow, to name a few—were in evidence around the city. The Santa Fe style was, as Wilson posits it in an intriguing oxymoron, "an invented tradition."

Invented or not, the tourists got the traditional look they wanted. With the building of new Pueblo Revival hotels, museums, and curio shops, the style took hold and never let go. By midcentury it had become a determined civic creed. "Relying as we do upon the tourist dollar," the daily *New Mexican* stressed in a 1956 editorial, "Santa Fe cannot afford to allow even occasional architectural misfits to slip by."

When I moved to Santa Fe in the mid-nineties, during the lingering hangover of the Reagan-era boom, the style had become an international signature, a shorthand that conveyed not only an architectural effect but a whole horsey, bolo-tied, hot-peppered way of life. The Look was so entrenched, and the Style Councillors so single-minded in their pursuit of it, that many architects around town virtually gave up on the prospect of novel design. There were only so many possible variations on the theme. The obligatory portal here, exposed vigas there, kiva fireplace in the corner, canales poking through the flat-roofed parapet: What was the point of originality? An architect might as well design by numbers and phone in the blueprints.

More and more, this adopted home felt like an artificial place, a theme park whipped up for Indian masqueraders and spiritual cowboys, where even the doghouses were made of adobe. Fanta Se. Pseudo Fe. Santa Fake. It was the name of a look, a dream, a fashion, a cologne, a cuisine, an SUV. But I wasn't sure it was a town.

THEN AN UNEXPECTED THING, or rather series of things, happened. Before I even realized it, I began to put down roots here, in a thousand little ways. My wife and I had children, they made friends, we made friends with their parents. Life happened. As all city dwellers do, we found our haunts and hideaways—an Italian restaurant, a third-generation barbershop, a market with fine cheap wine, the butcher who sells good local lamb. We kept meeting the most unusual people. Like Munson, a genteel sculptress who shapes enormous stumps of wood with a Stihl chain saw. Jack, the white-bearded environmentalist, one of the original Monkey Wrench Gang, who told me about the day he buried his dearly departed friend Ed Abbey deep in the Sonoran desert. And the filmmaker Jenniphr Goodman, who a few years ago wrote and directed a widely distributed independent film, *The Tao of Steve*, which captures much of Santa Fe's casual, quirky charm.

With this process of assimilation came my third (and, I believe, permanent) impression of Santa Fe—an ever-ripening understanding that this is an extraordinary outpost of North American civilization. Beneath the stucco of tourism lies a fascinating, tolerant, laid-back Western town. The more I traveled, the more I came to appreciate this funky old place, for its physical and intellectual openness, for its modest size, for its relative lack of smog-spewing traffic, for its always interesting climate, and above all, for the sense it constantly gives of space and possibility stretching to the horizons. Santa Fe's greatness lies in the peculiar creative wattage of a place that has none of the usual attributes of a real city: It isn't a harbor, a river port, a college town, or a manufacturing hub. There is precious little industry here, and (one of the little-discussed advantages of the desert) not enough water to encourage much development of any kind. Santa Fe isn't even the railroad junction people have long imagined it is—the Atchison, Topeka, and Santa Fe Railroad actually came through here on a spur. Even today, the station lies some fifteen miles south, in the tiny town of Lamy.

So what is Santa Fe, then? Historically, it's always been an end-of-the-line kind of place: the end of the Camino Real, the end of the Santa Fe Trail, the northern end of the desert, the western end of the prairie, the southern end of the Rockies. People who gravitate to Santa Fe—artists, chaos theorists, photographers, chefs, and psychics—often tend to be the sort of people who could live most anywhere but choose to live here because they've found inspiration, or solace, or even amusement in looking at the United States of America from what seems like a long way away. For living here does at times feel like living on an island surrounded not by the seas but by vast oceans of land. We're in America, but somehow separate from it. We're our own little cyst, a dusty enclave of semiexpats who thrive on living at the end of the line.

And the tourists? One eventually makes a pact with the tourists, for it soon becomes obvious they're the ones who make everything else possible—the restaurants, lectures, concerts, and films, the opera and the art. Yes, the Texans in their large bus-tour groups can be most annoying, but one learns they are people too, many of them, with feelings and needs and other humanlike qualities. Anyway, Santa Fe can no more bad-mouth tourists than Gloucester can bad-mouth codfish. Without them, we would merely be an unusually old hick town with good breakfast burritos and an adobe Dairy Queen.

One also makes a pact with the color beige. There's not a city anywhere in America that blends so seamlessly with its natural environs—and that is due, in large part, to the ubiquitous color of dirt. Look down upon Santa Fe from the top of Atalaya Mountain and you can scarcely believe there's a town of 75,000 souls, so camouflaged and dug-in are the jumbled compounds of the city.

It would be a good dynamic for Santa Fe if the architectural aperture opened just a little, and if the stylistic gatekeepers recognized the city's true heritage of richly varied construction by accepting, even *encouraging*, a slightly wider variety of hues, traditions, and motifs. What the hell—the birds wouldn't fly backward, and the tourists would keep on coming.

But I've made my peace with Santa Fe style. You have to if you're going to live here and stay sane. The thing is, it's a style that works. As I've come to consider not the individual look of the individual buildings, but rather their aggregate effect, I've seen the wisdom of low, squat, and beige. The Santa Fe style isn't so much an architecture, I now realize, as an antiarchitecture, an unobtrusiveness of construction that gives the whole Sangre de Cristo Mountain landscape—and what a landscape!—first billing.

Which is precisely why we have the Mountain Special Review District, and inspectors who come knocking on the doors of unsuspecting homeowners up in the foothills. The mountains matter here.

However, my wife and I were relieved to discover, after some tense hours of investigation down at the county land use office, that the inspectors were mistaken. Our home wasn't improperly permitted, after all. It wasn't in violation because, although it had been recently remodeled, the house was originally built before the codes were in place and was thus grandfathered in. However, one of our proposed additions has since been narrowly denied. As I write this we have months and months of legalistic hearings to look forward to, justifying our existences before various boards of architectural Torquemadas. If we're lucky, we'll get a "variance," which apparently is about as hard to get in Santa Fe as an apology from the IRS.

We're told our odds of success are limited, but I have it on good authority we're going to prevail. How do I know? My channeler told me.

—2002

AMERICA, POST 9/11

Points of Impact

New York, New York

WHEN RONNIE CLIFFORD FIRST WENT TO the psychologist in October 2001, he presented his case as an enormous engineering project. Here are the problems, he said, here are the elements and fractures and stress points: now put me back together again. Ronnie used the metaphor deliberately, for he was trained as an architect and well versed in the principles of structural engineering and computerized design. For decades he had made his living understanding why buildings stand.

The therapist, a specialist in post-traumatic stress syndrome, accepted the engineering project, and the two men went to work, six hours a week. "I was in pieces, just falling apart," Ronnie says in the lilt of his native Ireland. "I was having intense dreams. I couldn't get out of the building. I was there every night, trying to get out of the place. I would jerk myself awake, exhausted, in shock. Weird things were happening, bizarre things. I was seeing the number eleven popping up everywhere, in all kinds of places—like the towers themselves, the way they rose in the sky like an eleven. And whenever I got in the shower, I would constantly scrub my feet, just scrub and scrub, like there was something dirty down there and I had to get it off."

Ronnie had to shut off the television, had to retreat from the world.

Everywhere he turned, there it was, an image, a reference, a reminder. Even his friends and well-wishers started to annoy him. The consoling phone calls, the well-meaning e-mails, the sympathy cards—he wanted it all to stop.

Ronnie drives his dark green Jaguar around the historic town of Glen Ridge, the New Jersey neighborhood where he lives and works. It's a rooted place of rambling mansions and shops set in a quilt of woody suburbs seventeen crow-miles from Manhattan. Ronnie lives with his wife, Brigid, and their daughter, Monica, in a charmingly fusty shingle-style house built in the 1920s, with hardwood floors, windows warped by time, and a garage out back that was once a livery stable. The vintage gaslights that grace the streets never turn off. "Day and night—they're always on," he notes with amusement, but also with the air of someone who values permanence and tradition.

Ronnie is a solid, fair-skinned man with thinning red hair, thick fingers, and freckled arms. His eyes are blue and warm, and squinch into crow's-feet whenever he laughs or smiles. Because he didn't leave his family farm in Cork and head for America until he was twenty-seven, his accent is strong and mellifluous. He is forty-seven years old but sounds like a boy when he talks, his voice high-pitched and keen with wonder at life's trick connections, evidence of design in the seemingly random. He is attentive to the strange atmospherics that seemed to well up around 9/11, all the little coincidences, real or imagined, not to mention the strange numerology of the day. "Something higher was at work," he suggests. "When I look at all the things that happened to me and my family that day, I realize that you couldn't design an algorithm to put all these events together."

Over a salmon pasta at his favorite Italian restaurant in Montclair, where the waiters all know him, he asks me, thoughtfully, almost in a whisper, "Have you ever had anyone close to you die?"

My father, I say. He had a heart attack in his car and smashed into a telephone pole.

"Well, it would be like if someone said to you, Hey, guess what, your dad died. Your dad died. Your dad died. There's a car. There's a telephone pole. A little reminder. Every day, every hour, somebody opens it up in your face. Somewhere along the way, I realized, my God, it's never fricking ending, is it?"

THAT MORNING, BEFORE DAWN, RONNIE woke up almost giddy with excitement. There had been a big thunderstorm the night before, with major power outages across northern New Jersey. The storms had swept to the east and cleared the atmosphere, leaving everything tingly and cool. Ronnie put on a blue business suit and a yellow silk tie. He'd bought them special for this day. He wanted to look sharp for a business meeting—"the meeting of all meetings," as Brigid would later call it—that he had scheduled with a group of Chicago software executives. The stakes were high; if all went well, the meeting would profoundly change Ronnie's business life, launching him into a specialized niche of the Internet that involves using the World Wide Web to train employees of large companies. Ronnie's little sister, Ruth, whom he always called on for fashion advice, had helped him pick out the suit and was especially keen on the yellow tie. "You always want to stand out," she'd told him emphatically a few days before.

The meeting was supposed to take place at the Marriott Marquis in Times Square, but early that morning Ronnie received a phone call and was told there'd been a last-minute change. They were meeting at the World Trade Center Marriott instead. Ronnie kissed Brigid good-bye, and then took the commuter train to Hoboken. Then, because he realized he had time to spare, he decided to board the ferry. The Hudson air was bracing, and the rippled water caught crescents of the morning light as the sun climbed behind the vivid ramparts of Manhattan. "The city was breathtaking," Ronnie says. "Before a meeting, it's always important to feel good, and I felt great."

Ronnie disembarked from the ferry and walked past Cesar Pelli's Winter Garden complex, then strolled along the waterfront with his leather bag slung over his shoulder. He was killing time, steeling himself for his meeting while drinking in the views. When he went to architecture school in Boston in the seventies, the Yamasaki towers were widely considered a joke, "the boxes that the Chrysler and

Empire State buildings came in." But just three days before, Ronnie had been sailing in Long Island Sound and had taken in the vista of the Trade Towers with unexpected fondness. "They were out of place and overbuilt," he says. "But they would grow on you."

Around 8:45 he walked into the lobby of the Marriott, which was connected to the north tower by a revolving door. He checked his yellow silk tie in a mirror and took a deep breath, preparing himself to take the elevator up. Then he felt a massive explosion, followed several seconds later by a kind of reverberation, a strange warping effect that Ronnie describes as "the harmonic tolerances of a building that's shaking like a tuning fork." Baffled, Ronnie peered through the revolving door into the lobby of the north tower. He could see it was filling with black haze. People were scurrying to escape what had become an "incredible hurricane of flying debris."

Yet Ronnie remained untouched. It was as though the revolving door were a glass portal to another realm, a world of chaos and soot just inches away. The Marriott lobby was calm, the marble surfaces polished and antiseptic. For a few seconds, the two adjacent worlds did not meet.

Then the revolving door turned with a suctioning sound followed by a sudden burst of hot wind, and out came a mannequin of the future. A woman, naked, dazed, her arms outstretched, her hands swollen and blistered beyond recognition. She was so badly burned Ronnie had no idea what race she was or how old she might be. She clawed the air with long warped fingernails turned porcelain white. Her skin was black and glistening red. The zipper of what was once a sweater had melted into her chest, as though it were the zipper to her own body. The woman's hair was singed to a crisp steel wool, and her barrette was pressed into the back of her head. Her blackened eyes were welded shut. With her, in the warm gust of the revolving door, came a pungent odor, the smell of kerosene or paraffin, Ronnie thought.

Then the mannequin became a person, moaning in agony, crying for help. Ronnie had little idea what had happened to her, or where exactly she had come from, but he knew that whoever she was, she was his responsibility now. He had no emergency medical training and scarcely knew what to do. He sat her down on the marble floor, then dashed into the bathroom and poured cool water into a clean black polyethylene garbage bag that he found. He ran back outside and gently dribbled the contents over her body.

Then he sat down on the puddled floor and tried to comfort her. Despite her condition, she was lucid. He took out a pen and notepad from his leather bag and jotted down the information as she talked. Her name was Jennieann Maffeo. She was an Italian-American woman from Brooklyn, unmarried, forty years old. She worked for PaineWebber. She was an asthmatic, she said, and had an extreme intolerance to latex. She could not adequately describe what had happened to her. She was standing next to a man she knew outside the north tower, waiting for a bus, when she heard an explosion above. In a dubious effort to protect them from falling debris, a security guard herded everyone inside the north tower lobby. Suddenly, Jennieann told Ronnie, something bright and intensely hot enveloped her, a vapor. She thought it had dropped down the elevator shaft. She was worried about the man next to her. Surely he was dead, she feared.

Periodically Ronnie yelled for a medic, but no one came. He and Jennieann were lost in a surging crowd. People were streaming through the revolving doors now and scattering everywhere in panic. Ronnie didn't know what to say. His new suit was soaking wet, and wisps of dead skin clung to it. He sat close to Jennieann, but didn't think he should hold her, for he feared that the germs on his hands would cause an infection that could be fatal. He thought about his headstrong sister, Ruth, and wondered what she would do in this situation. A trained cosmetician, she had once run a day spa in Boston. She had made health, particularly skin health, her professional and personal concern. She often used to refer to the skin as "the largest organ of the body." She knew what vitamins to take, what salves to daub on cuts and burns, and she always coached Ronnie to take care of his skin. She would have known what to do.

Jennieann turned to Ronnie. "Sacred heart of Jesus, pray for me," she said.

Ronnie, who'd grown up Catholic in Ireland, knew a few prayers. "Yes, let's do," he said, "just to pass the time."

Sitting in a pool of water, alone in the swirling stampede, he whispered the Lord's Prayer in her ear.

*   *   *

SILVION RAMSUNDAR CREAKS IN HIS BLACK leather sofa, a television remote clutched in his hand, as the jets from Kennedy Airport whistle overhead. The relentless background keen of the planes has grown so nerve-racking that he and his wife, Nimmi, have considered moving from their home, which is in South Ozone Park, Queens—infelicitously situated beneath the main flight path for the JFK airliners. Silvion touches the bandaged wound on his left shoulder and says, "I hear them all the time, all the time. I can't stand it. Tools of destruction, that's all I can think about. They remind me."

It's not as though Silvion could ever forget, nor that he ever truly wants to, not entirely. He is a head-on sort of person, and he's made confrontation a part of his recovery. In his living room, nailed to the wall for any visitor to see, in a place that he can never ignore in the casual comings and goings of his daily life, is a framed pair of photographs of the Trade Towers; a before-and-after shot. In the top picture, the metallic duolith gleams in the sun; in the bottom there is only the smoky void.

"It's part of my history," he says, in a tone that seems to acknowledge that some people might find the photographs, hung where they are, to be perhaps too bluntly front-and-center. "I don't ever want to forget the towers. If you want to know who I am you have to understand that. I worked in them for ten years Everything that I have in my life happened during the years when I was working there—I bought my first house, my first car, met my wife, had my daughter. Every morning I woke up and got on the A train to downtown Manhattan and there they stood. Two massive brutes sticking out and saying, Here we are."

Silvion is a genial man in his mid-thirties. He's an intensely practical person who, like many denizens of the financial world, does not succumb easily to melodrama. He speaks in the brogue of Queens, where he has lived most of his life. But he's a native of Guyana, born of Indian parents who moved to New York City seeking a better life when he was a young boy. His mother is a devout Muslim, his father Hindu.

His black hair is cropped short, his skin a deep bronze. A long, fresh scar tracks across his jawline.

"I try not to let it consume me," Silvion tells me. "I've almost displaced the fact that I was there, as though it happened to somebody else." As he talks, the tang of curry drifts from Nimmi's kitchen. Their five-year-old daughter, Mariah, wriggles in his lap, taking care not to touch his left side.

Above us, the planes keep circling. The Ramsundars can't help thinking about crashes, especially after the October plane that plummeted only a few miles from here in the Rockaways. That disaster was declared a "catastrophic mechanical failure" caused by wake turbulence, but the Ramsundars have their doubts.

Nimmi, a tall, slender woman who is also a Guyanan of Indian descent, emerges from the kitchen holding a bowl of homemade pepper sauce. She says calmly, "Every time a plane passes overhead, we sit and listen and pray, Just let it pass over our heads. Don't let it land on top of our house."

THE MORNING SKY swelled with paper, a glittering bulge of confetti. Silvion watched the cloud floating down and wondered what it was. It looked beautiful against the sharp September blue, a trillion motes dancing in the fair light. Silvion was standing on the forty-fourth floor of the south tower, in the sky lobby café, waiting in the cashier's line with a Danish and a cup of coffee. He was making small talk with Christine Sasser, a friend from his office. He heard a thud of some kind and thought someone back in the kitchen had dropped a large stockpot. Now he was studying the strange plume of ticker tape that was enveloping the other tower. Bewildered, he squinted out the window for a moment, then proceeded toward the cashier.

Silvion rode the escalator with Christine up to the lounge on the forty-fifth floor, where televisions were blaring. While he sipped his coffee, a news show reported that a small commuter plane had crashed into the north tower. Peering out the window, Silvion couldn't see anything. A voice broke over the Port Authority intercom and announced in a neutral voice: "There is a fire in the north tower. Firemen are on the scene. Do not worry. The south tower is secure. You may return to your offices."

Silvion and Christine decided to go back up. How much damage could a commuter plane do? They were expecting an active market and wanted to get started on their day. They worked for a division of Fuji Bank called Mizuho Capital Markets, which deals with interest rate derivatives.

At approximately 8:50, they pushed the UP button for the express elevator. Their office was on the eightieth floor.

The thirty-six-floor ascent required two separate elevator rides, the first one to the seventy-eighth, and then a second, shorter one to the eightieth. The doors slid open, and Silvion and Christine walked into their office, only to learn that it had been almost entirely evacuated. Only three security guards, and a few of the firm's high-level Japanese executives, remained. Silvion found Charles, a security guard he'd been friendly with for years.

"Where's everybody?" he asked. "It's just a commuter plane."

"No, no, it's *big*," Charles answered. "An airliner. Look."

Silvion walked around to the far side of the office and gasped. The steel corduroy skin of the north tower was pried open.

From there he had a good view of where the plane hit. It was a huge gash with flames pouring out. Black smoke tendriled through the building's metal grid. Silvion and Christine looked almost straight across at the fire. Then they saw a man emerge from the hole. He was standing at the edge, looking down, wide-eyed with fright. "I wanted to throw him a rope or something," Silvion says. "I was wondering, What's this guy going to do? I was watching his actions. It was hard to tell whether he was young or old, or what he looked like, because of all the smoke and the soot. But I knew he was in trouble, that the heat must have been incredible. I had to stop and watch. It was mesmerizing."

Then the man jumped. Silvion watched him drop all the way down to the ground. "It took me a second," says Silvion, "to realize that I had just watched somebody die."

Once he registered the magnitude of the damage across the way,

Silvion pleaded with Charles, "Are you guys leaving? C'mon, let's get out of here!"

"In a few minutes," Charles replied. "We've got to check up on the place."

Silvion and Christine rode the elevator back down to seventy-eight. The sky lobby was congested with more than a hundred people, all anxiously waiting for the express cars, tapping their feet, cutting nervous jokes. They lingered for what seemed like a long time but was probably only a few minutes. Christine tried to make a call from her cell phone but couldn't get a signal. Silvion nervously fingered his briefcase and said, "This elevator had better come soon or else we'll have to take the stairs."

A few seconds later, at 9:06 A.M., Silvion glimpsed a brilliant flash of milky light out of the corner of his left eye. There was a boom and a terrific concussion of air: The wing of the United Airlines jet had penetrated his floor and cut its way into the concrete core. The entire wall to his immediate left ripped open, and a pressure wave hurled him twenty feet across the lobby.

As he tumbled through the air, he felt debris striking and piercing his body. He landed on his back and struck his head. His briefcase was tossed in the opposite direction, never to be seen again. The ceiling was caving in, and a miscellany of tiles, Sheetrock, and pipes landed on him. Silvion could smell what he later learned was jet fuel, and could see fires all around him. The sky lobby was seething with smoke, and it was growing hot.

Silvion wasn't sure if he could move. He could barely feel his legs. He had cuts everywhere. He was bleeding from his ears, and there was a long laceration across his jaw, with the skin hanging loosely from his chin. He was having trouble breathing. Something hard and sharp had embedded itself in his upper chest, and the wound was pulsing dark blood, a red coin growing on his chest. His left arm dangled lifelessly.

Silvion lay dazed for a few moments, not knowing what to do. He had no idea what had happened. The only thing he could imagine was that an explosion from the other tower had somehow carried over and ignited the south tower, a kind of echo effect. He studied his wound long enough to ascertain that whatever had entered his body was significant, about the size of a deck of cards, large enough to "open up a pretty big hole." He could neither lift his arm nor move his shoulder. Nerves and muscles had been severed. He felt certain that his arm was broken—and possibly his collarbone. He was worried that the projectile had struck a major artery, or possibly a ventricle of his heart.

Then he realized that a person was lying across his legs. He sat upright and, with a bit of a struggle, rolled the man off of him. When he turned over, Silvion looked at his sodden face and knew that he was dead.

"AT A CERTAIN POINT," Will Jimeno says, "your house becomes your prison." Will sits at his dining room table, next to his gun rack, gazing at a deer in his backyard. Ever since he got out of the hospital in late November, Will has sat here, day after day—a cop under a kind of house arrest. The view never changes. The TV blares. The deer doesn't move.

In fact, the deer isn't real. It's a rubberized decoy that Will keeps for bow-hunting practice. The fake buck is startlingly lifelike, though, enough to fool my eye for a moment as it stares back at us with its hard blank orbs, a creature comically out of place next to the barbecue grill and other suburban detritus on the back porch. "I love the shooting sports," Will says. "But if I take an animal, I do it with my crossbow." Ordinarily, Will would spend much of the fall in a deer stand somewhere in the pine barrens of New Jersey, slathered in Camo Scent. But this year he missed the season entirely. For three months he lay in a hospital, anesthetized, his veins coursing with blood thinner. "Next year," he vows. "Maybe next year."

Will lives in Clifton, New Jersey, in a modest boxy house clad in green fiberglass siding. As we talk, his wife, Allison, bathes their newborn in the kitchen sink, while their older daughter, Bianca, watches *Sponge Bob Square Pants* in the other room. Will is a burly man with a full, round face and black hair cut in a military buzz. He was born in Colombia but moved to America when he was two and grew up in nearby

Hackensack. Before he became a cop for the Port Authority of New York and New Jersey, Will served four years as a gunner's mate in the navy, pulling four deployments in the Pacific on a ship that carried attack helicopters.

Will is suffering from a painful condition known as "compartment syndrome," which was caused by the extreme trauma of his injuries. His left leg is bound in a formidable-looking brace, and various crutches and walkers are strewn about the house. He wears a Port Authority Police Department T-shirt, black gym shorts, and a pair of hospital-issue circulation hose. "Aren't those lovely?" he says darkly. "They come in two different colors—black and nude."

Today it's nude. The hose are pulled up nearly to his knees and are designed to press firmly on the skin, to prevent swelling by stimulating circulation. "I guess I'm used to them now," he says, "but shit, they sure are ugly."

Will has occasional bouts of depression and despair, but by and large he's been optimistic. He's had to keep busy, and staying busy has been a godsend. His days have been taken up with physical conditioning—an exhaustive regimen of treadmills, flexes, weights, hydrotherapy, and stretches. He had eight surgeries, including elaborate skin-graft procedures and extensive reconstructive operations to repair the damage to his nerves and muscles, but his leg is still a mess. "It swells up like it's got a mind of its own," Will says. "I'll wear a brace the rest of my life, but I will walk again—I'm determined."

Will motions for me to come a little closer. He turns his left knee outward and shows me the leg. "It's getting a lot better," he assures me. His knee is badly swollen, and the thigh is a blue-green swirl of bruises and ruptured blood vessels. The skin along much of his leg is cross-hatched with scars from his stitches, and all the hair has been shaved off. In his thigh there is a strange-looking orifice of surgically removed flesh, a ropy-skinned hole that's deep and large enough to accept a cork. "For draining," is all he says, and I don't press him further.

On Will's face I see an iron determination to put the best face on things, and a certain resignation, the stoic look of someone still young who has begun to accept the limitations and indignities of his condition while feeling stabs of incredulity that this really is the new him. If there once had been a macho aspect to his personality—proud hunter, sailor, cop—it has been humbled.

Will has had to keep his efforts so intensely focused on the physical that he hasn't had time or inclination to dwell on the psychological. The proportions of the tragedy still tax his imagination. The Port Authority lost more police officers that day than any American police force has ever lost on any single day. Thirty-seven PAPD officers died, along with thirty-eight Port Authority employees. Many of them were his dear friends. Will says, "I don't think I've internalized it, and I'm not sure I ever will. I think it's still setting in. I can't believe my friends are gone. Every day I sit here and I ponder on it. The only thing I take from it is this: life's short. What these people did makes no sense. I still can't believe I'm alive. To live through all that happened down there—it was the definition of a miracle."

WILL WAS WORKING OUTSIDE the Port Authority bus terminal that morning, a rookie cop working what's called the "image post," policing the rush-hour crowds with his Mace and his 9mm Smith & Wesson holstered at his side, when he saw the shadow of a low-flying plane pass over Forty-second Street. A few minutes later he received an alarm over his radio—an airliner had crashed into the World Trade Center. Immediately Will and a crew of six other officers boarded a Port Authority bus and tore through Midtown toward the tip of Manhattan.

When the bus pulled up in front of the towers on Vesey Street, Will was aghast at what he saw. The site was coated in a fine gray talc and strewn with miscellaneous chunks of metal and busted concrete. The carcasses of cars and buses smoldered along Vesey Street. There were dead squirrels, dead sparrows, dead pigeons, their demise brought about by an uncertain agent. The torched husk of an airplane part was stuck like a harpoon into the side of a building. People lay on the sidewalk, drenched in blood, some of them in neck braces, with medics at their sides.

Senior officers, Port Authority men Will knew and respected, were looking up at the north tower with tears in their horrified eyes. Most of the Port Authority policemen refused to believe the plane crash was an accident; they suspected this was a terrorist situation right from the start. Ever since the 1993 WTC bombing, the Port Authority had been an agency understandably steeped in extreme paranoia. As Port Authority property, the World Trade Center was theirs to protect, and they were trained to be suspicious. "As soon as we pulled up to the site, we knew we were at war, that this was a combat situation," Will says.

Even on the ground, Will could smell the jet fuel. From his years in the navy, he was well acquainted with its sharp, acrid stench, and he knew something about how intensely hot jet fuel burned. He was skeptical of the firemen on the street who insisted that they could climb up into the building and fight the fire by conventional means. Will says, "What I knew from the navy was that water won't cut it—you can't put out jet fuel without foam."

While fussing with his equipment, Will kept hearing explosions, one every few seconds, a ragged beat of concussions thudding up and down the street that sounded almost like fireworks. Finally he turned around to look: they were human bodies, dropping from above, exploding on impact. They sent up aerosol clouds of blood and left large divots in the sidewalk. The ground became littered with shorn body parts and random scatterings of personal effects—watches, high-heeled shoes, coins, a briefcase, Palm Pilots. Will forced himself to look up and finally understood the dreadful truth—that these people were jumping deliberately, that the heat was pushing them out. "I've heard experts say they were dead before they hit the ground," Will says, shaking his head. "But that's not true. I saw them. You could tell—they were conscious to the very end. They saw what was coming."

Sgt. John McLoughlin, a Port Authority veteran who knew every inch and rivet of the buildings, asked for four volunteers to accompany him into the north tower and start rescuing victims. Will raised his hand. The group quickly assembled. The five men were preparing to venture into the north tower when the second crash came, the United Airlines plane slicing into the south tower. The Port Authority's suspicions had played out. If there had been any doubts before, there were none now—this was definitely a terrorist attack. Because of the direct frontal angle of the impact, this second explosion was much more massive than the first. The shock wave worked its way down the building, like a thrum in a bell.

Even so, Will and his four comrades gathered their helmets and their hatchets and their Scott Air-Paks and pressed into the concourse of the World Trade Center.

RONNIE CLIFFORD was still whispering the Lord's Prayer in Jennieann Maffeo's ear when the second plane hit. The whole edifice rumbled and groaned and swayed; then the floor beneath him buckled hideously and seemed to raise him off his feet. Pieces of the building were falling all around him, and people were running in panic. Ronnie knew then that they absolutely must get out.

"Jennieann," he said. "Can you stand up?"

"I'll try," she answered feebly.

"We've got to get you out of here," he said as he helped her to her feet.

Ronnie removed his new suit coat and threw it over Jennieann's front so that she wouldn't have to walk out of the building naked. A nurse who worked for the Marriott hotel arrived with a bottle of oxygen and a mask, which she held over Jennieann's mouth as they shuffled across the hotel's crowded lobby. Drawing closer to the door, Ronnie saw that the exit was extremely congested, and realized that it might take a long time for them to get out. While they were waiting, he heard someone say, "A plane hit the tower," and then someone else said, "A second plane hit the other tower," which was the first time he had an inkling of what had happened. "I thought, my God, who have we pissed off this much?" he says. "Who's responsible for this?"

Ronnie was growing more and more frustrated and alarmed. The exiting crowds weren't moving fast enough through the bottleneck at the door. Jennieann was in excruciating pain. He had to get her to a hospital. Finally Ronnie held her arm and pushed impatiently through the throngs.

"Out of our way!" he screamed in a voice he did not know he had. "Make way, make way!"

When the people turned and looked, they instantly shrank in horror. Suddenly Ronnie and Jennieann were able to file straight out the door, as though the waters were parting before them. "They were shocked and disgusted—they couldn't get away from us fast enough," Ronnie says. "It was like I was taking Frankenstein out of the building."

When they emerged on the street, the scene was, as Ronnie puts it, "total carnage—burning cars, shattered glass, blood on the streets, and these incredible noises, these thudding and thumping sounds." Ronnie looked up and saw two men skydiving out of the building, going down face-first with a kind of gusto, it seemed, as though they had vowed not to die in poor form. Then he saw a lady plummeting, clutching her purse. "I keep thinking about that purse," he says. "I can't get the image out of my head. Why, through all that, was she worried about her purse?"

Even in her state, even with the chaos and horror all around, Jennieann was sufficiently aware to be self-conscious about her nakedness. Ronnie understood that his blue suit coat wasn't enough. Then, seemingly out of nowhere, a huge man who apparently worked for one of the Marriott restaurants appeared with a clean white tablecloth and gently wrapped it around Jennieann. It was as though he had foreseen Jennieann's predicament and spontaneously found a solution. The man smiled at her and helped Ronnie get her down the steps.

A fireman was standing on the street corner next to Ronnie and Jennieann. He grimaced sharply at the burning buildings, which seemed to be breaking apart. Ronnie could hear the sound of them cooking, the sound of rivets popping, glass shattering under pressure, the sighs steel girders make when they bend. Then suddenly, with wild gesticulations, the fireman screamed at the milling crowds: "Run, run, run! I'm telling you, just run and don't look back."

"Can you run, Jennieann?" Ronnie asked.

"I think so," she said. She looked at her feet. The rubber platforms of what had once been her running shoes were melted to her soles.

"Let's try then," Ronnie said. He took her arm, and in a tentative, shuffling gait, they started running.

* * *

ON THE SEVENTY-EIGHTH FLOOR of the south tower, now an upheaval of fire and fuel-splattered wreckage, Silvion Ramsundar tried to shake off the shock. The heat was intense, and flames were engulfing the corridors. Across the building, where the explosion had come from, Silvion could see an aperture of daylight. "I was just laying there, thinking, Is it over? Am I going to die right here? What happened just now?" He peered through the thickening smoke and realized that the majority of the hundred or so people who, like him, had been waiting for the elevator were now dead. At least they weren't moving.

Silvion scanned the lobby for his friend Christine and, to his relief, spotted her thirty feet away, stunned and injured but still alive. She had sustained lacerations along her arms from blasted shards of glass and metal, and her left ankle was bleeding profusely from a deep cut. Christine was having difficulty seeing through the haze. She nudged the man lying next to her, thinking he was Silvion. The person didn't move.

Silvion managed to stand. Picking his way among the dead and injured bodies, he hobbled over to Christine. She sat up and slowly registered his presence. She saw the red stain blooming on his white shirt and said with a new sense of alarm, "You're bleeding bad."

"I'm okay," he replied. "I think I can move. How about you?"

Christine nodded and struggled to her feet. Realizing that they had only minutes to escape before the smoke would overwhelm them, Silvion remembered that there was a stairwell somewhere near the elevator bank. He and Christine fumbled along the wall for a door. Although he couldn't see it, Silvion grabbed what felt like a handle with his right hand. He gave it a jerk, but it wouldn't turn.

Now the black smoke was so dense along the ceiling, they had to creep on the floor. Not far from the first door, they found another. Silvion gave it a try, and this time the latch turned. The heavy fire door swayed open—it was the emergency stairwell he'd been looking for. The stairway was hot but relatively clear of smoke. Silvion brightened for a moment, then hesitated. He wasn't sure he could make seventy-eight floors. His condition was worsening. His breathing was shallow and labored, and he was growing weak.

For a brief moment, Silvion gazed back through the smoke of the sky lobby. He heard choking, coughing, the cries of the injured. Seventy-five bodies, perhaps more, lay in a tangle on the fumy floor. He thought about his friend Charles, the office security guard two floors up, and realized he must be dead now.

In daydreams and reveries, Silvion can still summon the sight of the sky lobby with sickening vividness. It bothers him, not only the horror, but the sheer randomness of it. "There was only one quadrant on that floor that was safe from the plane, and it happened to be where I was standing," he tells me. "I didn't get the brunt of it. If I'd been standing ten feet to my left, I wouldn't be sitting here."

Silvion turned back toward the stairs. He leaned against Christine, and they began walking down in the harsh sodium glare of the emergency lights, on steps that were brightly marked with fluorescent tape. Silvion and Christine settled into a pace that was comfortable for him, stopping occasionally so that he might catch his breath. As they descended, more and more people filled the stairwell. Some were hyperventilating and removing articles of clothing in response to the heat. Occasionally Silvion would have to step around people who were obviously out of shape and could go no further; they sat on steps slick with sprinkler water, trying to catch their breath. "I often wonder if they ever made it out, those people," Silvion says. "I hope so. But I doubt it."

Somewhere in the high sixties, Silvion reached a landing that was obstructed by a massive beam. Two large men struggled with it and managed to shift it just enough so that the file of evacuees could crawl through. Silvion slipped between the girder and the floor, and then he and Christine resumed their descent.

As they walked, people could see that Silvion was critically injured. His face was pallid, and he had "a faraway look in his eyes," as one witness, Doug Brown, put it. Brown applied his handkerchief to the wound as a compress. Later, a woman removed her slip and cinched it around Silvion's shoulder to stanch the blood. They kept walking, counting down the floors. The throbbing in his clavicle was powerful and sharp, but his adrenaline flow somehow kept him from fully registering the pain. Probably he was in shock.

Silvion kept his mind fixed on the floor numbers and tried as best he could not to consider his wound.

*   *   *

WILL JIMENO and his Port Authority comrades were down in the concourse, not far from a Gap store, at a point almost equidistant from the two towers—and just beneath the famous bronze globe, the signature sculpture that was designed to symbolize world peace through world trade. The concourse level was ordinarily a bustling shopping mall, a city of commerce set at the feet of the two giants. But that morning the stores were desolate and strewn with broken glass, and the tile floors ran cold with firefighters' water.

Their sole mission, Sgt. John McLoughlin told them, was to extricate people—fighting fires or salvaging property was a moot concern now. They opened up an equipment locker and rummaged for rescue gear: flashlights, crowbars, extraction tools, gloves, first-aid kits, and self-contained breathing apparatuses known as Scott Air-Paks. Tuned to Port Authority frequencies, their radios blew a gale of staticky screams.

In the group of five cops was a veteran named Chris Amoroso, and two other rookies, Dominick Pezzulo and Antonio Rodrigues. Pezzulo and Rodrigues were close buddies of Will's, having all graduated in the same police academy class. Thirty-five years old, Dom Pezzulo was a funny Italian from the Bronx, a weight lifter who, Will says, was "built like Jean-Claude Van Damme." He had a beautiful wife and two kids, and loved to fish for blues in Long Island Sound. Rodrigues, whom everyone called "A-Rod," was a colorful bald guy with a thick Portuguese accent. A gifted artist who'd studied to be an aeronautical engineer, A-Rod was always sketching caricatures of the other PAPD cops. "Dom and A-Rod were cutups, both of them," Will says fondly, showing me their pictures. "They could make you laugh."

The younger men had great confidence in their sergeant, John McLoughlin. A highly decorated veteran of the department, McLoughlin was a tall, resolute Irishman who had won a medal for his valor in the evacuation during the 1993 Trade Center bombing. He'd later helped redesign the building's emergency plans. The men never questioned McLoughlin's judgment. Will says. "If he asked me tomorrow, I'd follow him into that building all over again."

The five men tossed the paraphernalia into a rolling canvas laundry cart and then hustled toward the freight elevator. They prepared themselves for going up into the heat of the north tower.

RONNIE CLIFFORD and Jennieann Maffeo, running from the buildings along the West Side Highway, found an ambulance beside a green knoll in Battery Park. He spirited her, still wrapped in a Marriott table linen, into the hands of the medics and gave them the notes he'd scribbled earlier that described her vital facts and medical allergies. As the ambulance took off for the Cornell Burn Center, Ronnie said with all the hopefulness he could summon, "You'll be okay, Jennieann."

He called Brigid, his wife, from a nearby pay phone. "I'm all right," he told her, in a voice that she would later describe as "close to panic." She was watching CNN. There was a long pause as he tried to think of what else to say. "I've just gone through something terrible," he said, struggling for composure. "I'm alive. I'm okay. I love you."

Ronnie hung up and tried to get his bearings. His suit and tie, he realized, smelled of fuel and charred flesh. He turned around to look again at the towers. The infernos were raging even more fiercely than before. People were still occasionally leaping from above, while firemen were gathering in large numbers and marching into the buildings.

He called his sister Ruth's cell phone but couldn't get through. The signal was dead. He knew Ruth would be worried about him. She lived beside a lighthouse on Long Island Sound in an old mansion near New London, Connecticut. But then he remembered that she wouldn't be home. She was on a trip to Los Angeles to take her four-year-old daughter, Juliana, to Disneyland and to attend a seminar led by the best-selling self-help author Deepak Chopra. Like Ronnie, Ruth was a devoted Catholic, but she also had an affinity for what he called "alternative paths." Her best friend, Paige Hackels, was joining Ruth and Juliana on the trip. They were in California now, he guessed. Whatever Ruth was doing, he hoped to God she wasn't watching CNN.

Ronnie wasn't sure what to do next. He felt he ought to go back in and try to help more people evacuate the building, or volunteer at one of the hospitals. Then he thought about Monica, his daughter. He remembered that it was her birthday. They'd planned to have a celebratory dinner that night. Ronnie says, "I thought my getting home alive would be the best present I could give her." Monica was turning eleven.

SILVION RAMSUNDAR and his friend Christine shuffled out of the south tower around 9:50 A.M. After walking through the concourse and taking the escalator up to the ground level, Silvion emerged into the glare of the street, a blood-caked wraith dusted in gray flour. The EMS workers went to work on him immediately. His left lung was collapsed, his pulse was faint, he'd lost a dangerous amount of blood, he was seriously dehydrated, and he was in shock. A photographer for one of the New York tabloids snapped his picture, a portrait that would become one of the more hideous images of the day. His wound had become unbearable. "My body sort of relaxed," Silvion says. "I had a sense of relief—okay, I made it, seventy-eight floors. And that's when the pain really kicked in."

It was only when Silvion was hurtling toward St. Vincent's hospital in the ambulance that he learned what had happened. "A *second* plane?" he quizzed the driver, incredulous. His mind reeled at the implications. The plane had struck his very floor; the gas he'd smelled was jet fuel. The first plane crash couldn't have been an accident. We were at war. He was struggling to absorb this fabulous train of bad news, when the morphine began to take over.

RONALD CLIFFORD boarded the ferry to Hoboken, reversing his course from earlier that morning. The ferry operators were in emergency mode. They weren't even bothering with tickets; they were simply ushering aboard as many passengers as they could. During the surreal ride across the Hudson, Ronnie stood on the stern of the boat and watched the buildings burn. His begrimed jacket was slung over his shoulder, a sordid memento of a business meeting that was not to be.

Then, at 9:59, just as he reached the creosote piers of New Jersey, the south tower collapsed. In a terrific, thunderous implosion, the eleven became a one.

WILL JIMENO was directly beneath it all. Within seconds, Will and his four comrades were assaulted by tile, marble, and a hail of glass shards. There was a tremendous snarling roar that Will could feel more than he could hear, "an undescribable noise, like something impossibly huge was coming." Sergeant McLoughlin pointed toward a safe place, the shaft of a freight elevator. They scarcely had time to dash behind the pillar of concrete when the south tower came down on them. Will momentarily lost track of everyone else. He ran until the world became dark and close and his body could no longer move.

He may have been unconscious for a while, but he doesn't think so. He couldn't catch his breath. He was hacking and spluttering in a cloud of pulverized concrete, a cloud so thick he couldn't see. It felt as though someone had poured hot sand down his throat. His left leg was pinned by something large and ponderous, like a block of stone. He felt sure he'd broken his femur. It felt as though the weight of the towers was bearing down on his thigh. He was coated in a fine dust, a puree of insulation, Sheetrock, fabrics, fibers, papers, paints, plastics, wiring— the mingled grounds of the modern world. The dust got in his ears, in his lungs, in his mouth; it suffused everything.

Even now, six months later, Will can smell it. It's not a bad odor, but it's distinctive and unforgettable. Says Will, "It's the smell of World Trade Center; that's all it is."

Finally the cloud began to dissipate, and a tiny shaft of light slanted in from a hole in the heap of debris. Will couldn't see the sky, but the aperture provided just enough filtered light for him to make out forms and shapes. It took Will a few minutes to discern the situation. He was in what amounted to a tiny cave, trapped by a pillar of concrete, which was a piece of the elevator shaft he'd hidden behind. Various fires flickered in pockets and folds all about him. His radio was out of reach.

Will called for Pezzulo. "Dom—you all right?"

"Yeah," he said. "I'm here." Pezzulo was also pinned by blocks of rubble. He lay only a few feet away from Will. Once the dust settled a little more, they could see each other.

They heard McLoughlin stirring somewhere in a void below. The sergeant was gasping in pain, but he said he was okay. He was trapped in a fetal position. McLoughlin couldn't see a thing; nor could the other men see him. By the sound of things, the sergeant was in worse shape than Will. "Somebody relieve the pressure!" McLoughlin yelled. "I can't stand it."

"A-Rod? Chris?" Will called out for the two others, Rodrigues and Amoroso, but got no response. "After a few minutes, we knew they were no longer with us," Will says.

Then they were assailed by a horrible chirping sound, incessant and shrill, like a dozen car alarms going off: it was the Scott Air-Paks, the self-contained breathing apparatuses. The men hadn't had time to put them on, but they were stashed in their backpacks. An Air-Pak has an attached motion detector; if its wearer doesn't move within one minute, an alarm is triggered. The signal is designed to be incredibly harsh and loud so that rescuers might locate a fallen comrade. But now so many Scotts were sounding off all around the World Trade Center, there was little hope of locating anyone. The alarms were, in effect, canceling each other out by their sheer numbers. It sounded like a field of crickets.

RONNIE CLIFFORD took the commuter train home from Hoboken. Next to him sat a lady who was already deep into a bottle of booze. The cars were overcrowded and chaotic, with people on their cell phones crying to their spouses and loved ones. Someone nearby had a Black-Berry, a wireless Internet device, and was receiving chilling updates over the tiny liquid crystal screen. *Another one's hit the Pentagon. Another one's gone down in Pennsylvania. Another one's heading for the White House.*

As the train hummed and clacked west toward home, Ronnie's thoughts drifted back to Jennieann. His heart went out to her. It seemed to him that she had saved his life, just as he had saved hers. If he had remained in that building much longer, dallying, perhaps helping other people, he'd be buried now. If those horrified crowds in the lobby hadn't instantly made way for them like they did, he might still be trapped. In the queer way fate had worked, Jennieann had been his ticket out of there. He prayed for God to spare her.

In the months that followed, he would dream repeatedly of Jennieann. He would be in the Trade Center, holding her hand, consoling her. They kept searching in vain for a way out. The building was locked up as though it were a prison, as though it had malice of its own. Every night he'd dream the same dream. He'd wake up exhausted, suffocating, terrified. One night, though, the details of the dream would change slightly. He was with his sister, Ruth, holding her hand, trying to find the way out. Only the building was some old stone castle back in the Ireland of their youth. It was dark and wet, like a dungeon. Ruth was impeccably dressed as she always was, in autumn colors, wearing a beautiful tweed coat, her long red hair flowing. He and Ruth kept searching for the way out. Then he realized that the arches of the dungeon had become the steel gothic arches at the base of the World Trade Center, the distinctive ornamental mesh that would remain standing long after the buildings had collapsed.

APPROXIMATELY A HALF HOUR after the south tower fell on Will Jimeno and his friends, Dominick Pezzulo managed to free himself from the rubble. He thought he might crawl toward the hole and seek help, but instead he decided to attempt to liberate Will. He dug with his bare hands, because he didn't have any tools. Although it soon became apparent that the cause was hopeless, Pezzulo persisted, clawing at the debris, struggling with blocks of concrete ten times his size. The Scotts continued to chirp relentlessly.

Then Will heard another noise—another rumble in the distance, like the mounting wrath of a volcano.

"Dom," Will said. "Something big's coming."

Spooked by the sound, Pezzulo backed up a few feet and braced himself for another collapse. "Oh, my God," Will said, "here we go again." The north tower was coming down around them.

From above, a jagged block of concrete fell through the hole and penetrated their crawl space. Will watched as the slab struck Pezzulo and "laid him down like a rag doll."

Pezzulo withered in pain. He made a wisecrack to the sergeant, something about requesting permission to take a coffee break. But Pezzulo knew it was serious. He was losing a lot of blood. He turned to Will and said, "I love you, Will."

Will said, "I love you, buddy."

"Don't forget," Pezzulo added. "Don't forget I died trying to save you guys."

Then Pezzulo did something curious. He unholstered his 9mm sidearm, pointed it up toward the hole, and fired off a few rounds. Will says, "It was like a last-ditch effort, as if to say, We're down here, come find us."

Will watched as Pezzulo slumped back and gasped for air. His gun fell to his side.

John McLoughlin, unable to see anything down in his black hole, shouted through his pain, "What's going on up there?"

"Sarge—it's Dom. He's gone. I just saw him pass."

A TEAM OF PLASTIC SURGEONS at St. Vincent's sutured Silvion Ramsundar's chin back together. Then they went to work on his chest. The X-ray revealed that although no bones were broken, the piece of shrapnel was lodged dangerously close to his aorta. The doctors were worried that if they weren't extremely careful in removing the object, they could cause irreparable damage to the nerves in his shoulder, paralyzing his arm for life. Once they dug out the gobbet with their surgical tools and examined it under the bright lights of the operating table, the doctors decided it was part of an airplane, a shard of aluminum from the United Airlines flight that had crashed into his floor. Silvion wanted to keep it as a souvenir—a piece of world history once embedded in his body—but an FBI agent arrived with a Ziploc bag and told them to hand it over. He marked it, EVIDENCE, and carried the artifact away.

* * *

THE HOUSE IN GLEN RIDGE didn't look the same. When Ronnie Clifford arrived home in the late morning, he found that tree trimmers had cut down a noble old birch tree, a landmark of the neighborhood, in his front yard. It was inevitable—the tree was diseased and had to go, but he'd forgotten that this, of all times, was the scheduled day.

Ronnie embraced Brigid, and then climbed upstairs straightaway for a shower. More than anything else, he wanted to rinse away the residue of his unbelievable morning. At least he had his daughter's birthday party to look forward to. He paused to think about what this would mean for Monica as she grew up, to have turned eleven on the eleventh of September 2001, to have that black date as her birthday. Monica was across the street at the Glen Ridge middle school—innocent, for now, of what had transpired in the city.

Ronnie, it turned out, was innocent, too. He thought he'd escaped the tragedy's long reach. He had vaguely assumed it was only fair, after witnessing so much, after doing his part as a Good Samaritan, that he should sail away on the Hoboken ferry, unscathed. But then he received a piece of news by phone which, after a bit of work on the Internet, he would confirm. Among the ticketed passengers on American Airlines Flight 11, the first plane, the one that hit the north tower, was Paige Hackels, Ruth's best friend, and a close friend of his as well. A little later in the afternoon he was able to verify an even more devastating fact concerning the United Airlines flight, the second plane from Boston: Ruth and her four-year-old daughter, Juliana, had been on board.

Shortly thereafter, Ronnie's brothers called from Ireland. They'd watched the towers collapse on television and just wanted to make sure everything was okay. Ronnie was in pieces. "I'm fine," he said through the tears, "but I'm afraid we're in trouble."

Ronnie had somehow lost track of when Ruth and Juliana were supposed to fly to Los Angeles. He thought they'd gone out the day before. Paige had intended to fly with Ruth, but there'd been some kind of mix-up at Logan. One took American, the other United, but they both ended up in the hands of the hijackers, friends in separate missiles aimed for New York.

Ronnie tried to imagine Ruth's last moments on the plane. If there was even the remotest chance of negotiation, she would have been involved, he felt certain. Growing up she had always been the peacemaker, the conciliator, the only girl in a family of four quarrelsome boys. But reasoning with these men was probably out of the question. Most likely, Ronnie thought, she would have been sitting calmly in her seat as they banked dangerously low over the Hudson. And in the seconds before the plane hit, she would have been holding little Juliana, and singing a song in her ear.

WILL JIMENO AND SGT. McLOUGHLIN were the only ones left now. Amoroso, Rodrigues, and now Pezzulo were all dead. The two men waited for hours for something to happen. Occasionally fireballs floated down into the hole and landed beside them and then extinguished themselves in the wreckage. One of the fireballs must have landed near Pezzulo's Smith & Wesson and heated it up. Suddenly the gun went off, and Will could see bullets ricocheting in the hole. "I told Sarge, you're not going to believe this, we're getting shot at!"

They talked to each other a lot during the afternoon, the veteran sergeant and the rookie. They talked about their families, about life and death, about their lost comrades who lay buried about them. Both men were in agony, squirming helplessly under the intense pressure, their appendages swelling up. But they were lucid the whole time, never slipping into unconsciousness. Will had lost all feeling in his legs. With his one free hand, he tried to dig himself out using a spare magazine of his gun, to chip away at the concrete, but it was useless. All he could do was hope someone would come. Every couple of minutes, he would yell out "eight-thirteen!"——Port Authority code for "officer down." But as midday stretched into late afternoon, his calls began to lack enthusiasm.

Then, from the hole above, Will heard a voice. Someone was frantically shouting a name. *Are you down there? Are you down there?*

Will couldn't catch the name, but he shouted back——"Sergeant

McLoughlin and Officer Jimeno are here!" He was ecstatic. But then the voice left them and never returned.

This killed Will's spirits completely. He began to talk to himself, out loud, a steady stream of dire thoughts. He thought about Allison, his wife, who was eight months pregnant. He found a pen in his pocket and started to write her a note but couldn't make the pen work. "At that point I pretty much accepted death," Will says. "I asked God to please watch over Allison and my little four-year-old, and the new baby girl. I wanted to see the baby, just once. I just asked Him, when I'm in heaven, please, please, let me see her."

At around eight o'clock, Will was aroused by another voice. "United States Marine Corps, can anybody hear me?"

When Will yelled back, the marine said, "We can hear you; keep yelling."

Will cried, "Don't leave us. The last guy left us."

The marine peered into the hole and spotted Will. He said, "Kid, I'm not leaving you."

Soon the paramedics came, and firemen and NYPD cops and Port Authority officers, a long trail of men, harnessed to one another, clambering over the anthill. For three hours they dug and scraped and sawed, pulling away rebar, widening the hole. They used their bare hands. They used welding torches and buzz saws and the famed Hatch tool, the so-called "jaws of life." Finally they got to Will. They feared they would have to amputate his left leg, but finally they were able to budge the pillar just enough to slip him free.

Eventually they would get to McLoughlin, but first they had to pull Will from the hole. They slid him into a basket and started hauling him out. With the pressure now relieved, his leg suddenly ballooned and throbbed. "I was swollen up like the Michelin Man," Will says. "If anyone got too near it, I screamed at them."

At around eleven o'clock that night, thirteen hours after the south tower collapsed on him, Will emerged from the rubble. The emergency crews erupted in cheers. From the litter, Will looked around in amazement at the devastated site, a smoky panorama of harsh lights and humming generators and flickering welders' sparks.

"Where is everything?" he said.

One of the officers leaned over and said to him, "There's nothing left, kid. It's all gone."

MOSTLY, SILVION RAMSUNDAR MISSES the views. The way electrical storms scudded in from the Atlantic, the sunsets that went on forever, the way the morning sun lit up the clustered spires of lower Manhattan, the Statue of Liberty standing sentinel at his feet. He says, "I always loved watching the storms come in, being up there that high, seeing the clouds and the lightning at eye level. I'm going to miss those."

Silvion spent two weeks mending in the hospital, followed by months and months of physical therapy to restore his shoulder. The arm still tingles and throbs, and it bothers him in countless little ways. As he talks, he twists and flexes his arm. "They say it's never going to be a hundred percent," he notes, his face wrinkled in pain. "It gets all locked up. It annoys me that I can't pick Mariah up the way I used to, to take her up to bed. But they say, Just be grateful you can use your arm at all."

When he arrived home from the hospital, he didn't relive the incident, exactly, but he had a lot of bad dreams. He kept finding himself in terrifying situations—being trapped in a fire, smashing up his car, being chased by people who wished him harm. Then he started having anxiety attacks whenever he drove over a bridge in his Honda. Suddenly he would find himself gripping the steering wheel, a tightness in his chest. "I keep thinking that a plane's going to hit the bridge and we're going to go," he says. "It just pops in my head all of a sudden. I get really nervous and start slowing down. This feeling overwhelms me. It's something I have to work through."

The past few months, Silvion has logged some serious quality time with the family. Vacation in the Bahamas, doing chores, ceaseless trips to Home Depot. As we talk, there's a supply of interior molding piled on the living room floor—one of numerous home-improvement projects he's got going. Mostly he's been having a grand time since 9/11. Nimmi calls the past six months "our second honeymoon."

At the same time, Silvion says he's growing cabin-feverish. For ten years, work—intense work, at Wall Street speed—was his life. Nowadays he doesn't bother getting up until nine. "I went through a stretch where I felt useless," he says. "I'm ready to go back to work."

WHEN HE GOT to Bellevue Hospital, Will Jimeno was met by a green army of surgeons. He didn't understand why, with a tragedy of such mammoth proportions, he should get such solicitous treatment. He imagined the hospital must be filled with thousands upon thousands of cases. He didn't understand that, at this point, there were no other survivors. He was the survivor, he and his sergeant and a tiny handful of others who would be pulled out the next morning. They rolled him into the operating room and went to work. When they sucked out his lungs, the vacuum ticked and chattered with the steady sound of grit. At one point, Will actually saw a small rock sliding up through the tube.

The racking pressure of blood and backed-up fluids had built up so powerfully in his leg that when the doctors cut it open that night, the hospital walls splattered like a Jackson Pollock canvas. In seven days Will had eight operations. The doctors had to go back in repeatedly to excise the dead tissue. They worried about blood clots and aneurisms; they worried about kidney failure and lung failure and gangrene. They watched him like a hawk, because acute compartment syndrome could be fatally sly.

All those weeks in the hospital, Will thought about his comrades. He still does. Especially A-Rod and Dom. He can't get them out of his head. He's commiserated with their wives, described how brave they were in death. One day Will learned that the workers down at Ground Zero had located A-Rod's foot, and that very night he dreamed a vivid dream about him. They were down in the hole again, and A-Rod was pinned in the rubble next to him. Then he rose up out of the debris like some colossus, his big bald head covered in dust. A-Rod brushed himself off and looked right at Will with a wide smile. And then he said, in his thick Portuguese accent, "Maaaan, dat suuuucked!"

Sergeant John McLoughlin was released from the hospital in January, after some two dozen operations and a long stint on kidney dialysis. He's improving gradually. Every now and then, Will gives him a call. "Sarge's getting along okay," he says. "One day at a time. Like me, trying to get by. I tell him never to feel responsibility for their deaths, because I can speak for those guys. I tell him, 'If there was any sergeant we were going to follow, it was you.'"

Will has no idea where the rumor got started, the beautiful, fantastic rumor. In the hours after they were discovered in the rubble, Will and Sergeant McLoughlin became the subject of an incredible story that was repeated so often over the Internet that for a few days the national media reported it as confirmed fact: a Port Authority cop, in some accounts several, was said to have "ridden the wave" of debris down from the eightieth floor and survived with barely a scratch. It was the kind of legend that springs up in the chaos of a catastrophic event—a wildly untrue story that nonetheless reflects a true hope. All around the world, people were holding vigil, praying that more victims would be pulled alive from the ruins. If a man could ride down the mighty wave and live, then maybe there was still hope.

"I have no idea how that story got started," Will says. "But let me tell you something; you'd have to be Superman. When that building came down, it became a shredder."

Will keeps a photograph lying around the house, an eerie picture of Ground Zero on that first night. "See the angels?" Will asks me. The photograph is splotched with dozens and dozens of strange ghostly lights, hovering over the scene. Maybe they're merely the trail of flashlights captured in the blur of a long exposure, but it's true; they look exactly like angels, milky white—with wings, even. "Depends on your point of view, I guess," Will says. "I think that's their souls, the souls of all the ones that died, rising up to heaven."

Will was raised and schooled as a Catholic, and it has been Catholicism that's seen him through this. "I always believed in God," he says. "Before this happened, I always prayed to Him. And now I thank Him every day for allowing me to be here. I have moments where I'm not happy, where there's mental anguish. Maybe a year from now it'll hit me even more. But right now I'm doing pretty good. I'm at peace with this."

Will has decided to remain with the Port Authority Police Department. He didn't live through all this just to quit, he says. He's always wanted to be a police officer; it's in his blood. "I'm not going to be running after bad guys anymore, because I'm limited now, physically," he says. "But I'm definitely going back. You'll see; I'm going to be an integral part of the department."

Before 9/11, Will and Allison knew they were having a baby girl, but they had bickered over the name. Will wanted Rebecca. Allison wanted Olivia. When they found him in the rubble that night, he asked someone to get on a cell phone and call his wife and tell her to name the baby Olivia. "If I didn't make it," he says, "I didn't want her to feel guilty about going with the name she wanted."

Now Will is holding his newborn, a beautiful three-month-old with a full head of hair. She was born November 26, which is also Will's birthday. He was there at the hospital at Allison's side, crying in his wheelchair. Now he lifts her up and holds her high over his head and smiles up into her eyes. She smiles back.

Her name is Olivia.

SILVION RAMSUNDAR GREW UP in Guyana and in the West Indian neighborhoods of Queens, and Islam was always part of the texture of his life. For his mother, a devout Muslim, the events of 9/11 have been especially difficult. Silvion, for his part, can't decide what he believes. "There might be a God," he says, "there might not be. As long as you do good deeds, I believe good things will happen to you."

Working as an investment banker, as someone who made his living spinning the arcane calculus of derivatives, it's natural that Silvion should think of 9/11 primarily in economic terms. "People do what they do for money," he suggests. "Islam is just an excuse they use. But if these countries were in a better economic condition, if their leaders didn't keep all the money, the rest of the people wouldn't be using religion as a camouflage for their own doings. What you have now is very poor people who have nothing to live for. It all comes down to money."

In a very real sense, Silvion is Americanized, secularized, confirmed in the high church of pluralism and the mutual fund—the very things, of course, that make the terrorists burn. And yet one of the odd twists to the whole event, for him, is that because he is of Indian descent, dark skinned and raven haired, Silvion sometimes gets the look, the double take of suspicion. *Who are you, where are you from, what's hidden in your shoe?* "Yeah, I've gotten it," he says. "But you know what? It's justifiable. Until this threat is completely gone, I have to expect it. If people are going to profile me, fine. I'll be courteous and nice."

It's often a hallmark of the survivor personality to minimize the aftereffects of an ordeal; people seldom want to stick out as public curiosities, to be forever stamped with a residue of horror. Dwelling on it only deepens the stamp. Silvion refuses to construct his new life around the tragedy, refuses to believe his experiences are beyond what his own personal reserves and resources can handle. He relies on himself, and on his immediate family. He steers clear of shrinks, of twelve-step trauma sessions, of appearances on *Oprah*. He sits beneath his before-and-after diptych of the Trade Towers, and assures me, with a kind of provisional confidence, that he's okay.

"As time passes, I focus on other things," he says. "That's not to say that later on in life it's not going to come flooding back. You hear about people who've been to war and then much later on they start having dreams. That's something I do worry about. But support groups, therapists—that's not my style. I don't feel that I have a problem. Do I have suppressed feelings that I'm hiding? I don't know. I can't tell you yes; I can't tell you no. I know this is what's working for me right now. Being home, blocking it out, thinking about other things. Not feeling sorry for myself. I just try to say, You know what—there's thousands of people who didn't make it. I made it."

Silvion plans to return to work soon at Mizuho Capital Markets and get back into the derivatives game. He has one modest request, though. If he has a choice, he'd prefer not to work any higher than the thirtieth floor.

Silvion says with a wink, "I'm good at ground level."

LATER IN SEPTEMBER Ronnie Clifford went to visit Jennieann at the hospital. She was wrapped in gauze from head to toe, save for narrow slits for her eyes and her mouth. She'd been burned over 90 percent of her body. Although she was heavily sedated and could not talk, her sister said she seemed to be aware of visitors. Ronnie sat with Jennieann for a while, and urged her to be strong. Before he left, he placed his yellow silk tie on the pillow beside her, the tie he'd been wearing on the eleventh, the one Ruth had so strenuously coached him to wear. The tie was freshly laundered but still bore faint stains from the World Trade Center. Ronnie wasn't sure why this gesture had occurred to him. He just wanted for her to have something to remember him by. Something that stood out.

Ronnie received updates from the Maffeo family every week. Jennieann stayed in the hospital for forty days, drifting in and out of consciousness. The mounting infections, the multiple skin-graft operations, the side effects from her medications—it was all too much for her system. On October 21, she died of kidney failure. At the funeral, Ronnie embraced her father, a sweet elderly Italian man from Brooklyn. Mr. Maffeo took Ronnie's face into his hands and said, "Thank you for giving me my daughter."

The same day that Jennieann died, the Clifford family received a phone call from the recovery authorities. Workers down at Ground Zero had located Ruth's remains. The DNA comparison tests had produced a perfect match. "I don't know what they found, and I don't *want* to know," Ronnie says. Now he has a place picked out in Ireland, a secret place beside a river in Cork that was special to her. Soon Ronnie will make the trek to Ireland and sprinkle her ashes in the river.

"It's a little weird," he says. "Ruth and I had talked about death this summer. We discussed what it would be like and where we'd go. I still feel she hasn't left me. I used to call her, and the phone would be busy, and I'd find out she'd been calling me. When you're that close to someone, they're always there."

More than twelve hundred people showed up a week after 9/11 for the funeral of Ruth and Juliana. Ronnie organized a huge celebration afterward on Ruth's front lawn in Connecticut, a dinner party that carried a touch of the Irish wake tradition, with long, bittersweet remembrances and a Celtic bagpiper.

As soon as he got home from the funeral, Ronnie collapsed in exhaustion. "My emotions were swimming around," he says. He kept having visions of being trapped in a huge vault that was vibrating and pulsating, buckling and warping. He was a nervous wreck. One time

Monica and a friend were horsing around on the hardwood floor and made a sharp thumping sound. Ronnie flew off the handle, just completely lost it. All he could think of was falling bodies. The skydivers, the woman with her purse. He couldn't get the images out of his head.

Finally recognizing that the problem was "far greater than anything I could deal with," Ronnie went to a psychologist's office and filled out the evaluation forms. Doug, the therapist, sat back in his reclining chair and invited him to talk about his life. He asked Ronnie to keep a journal of his dream life. He brought him under a kind of mild hypnosis and had him relive every tiny detail—every sight and smell and sensation—of that horrible day. "I found that your mind can play a lot of tricks with you," says Ronnie. "Doug helped me to put it back together in logical order. To rebuild my capacity to understand what I'd been through."

The other part of Ronnie's recovery has involved sailing. He's been a sailor ever since he was a boy in Cork. It's always been a part of his life, not competitive sailing but just "mucking about" in the water. In recent years he's kept a twenty-six-foot fiberglass boat in a slip in the Bronx. "It's a bit of a tub," he says, "but it's good for cruising in the Sound." The first time he went out after September 11, it was as though he'd never been on the water before. He was unsteady, indecisive, skittish in the boat. He was reluctant to heel her over in strong wind. He was nervous about every little piece of the rigging. Whenever the boat made a shudder, his heart raced. At what seemed like his lowest moment ever, he found himself looking across the Sound, beholding the gap in the skyline.

When he first came to New York back in the early eighties, fresh from architecture school, he was in awe of skyscrapers. For him, they were the ultimate American expression; they captured the sense of sweep and possibility that had drawn him from Ireland in the first place. He took a job at the Housing Authority designing low-income dwellings. Often he would go up to Windows on the World during slow times and spread his blueprints on the table. For hours and hours, he'd look over the harbor and do his work.

Eventually he developed an expertise in modeling buildings on computers, and this led to an interest in designing databases. In his planned meeting at the Marriott on September 11, he was proposing to join forces with a group of computer software executives to start a brand-new company. But the meeting never happened, and the deal fizzled. Then something remarkable happened. A few months ago, he was approached by yet another software entrepreneur who asked him, out of the blue, if he wanted to own 50 percent of *his* company. It was exactly what he was planning to propose at the Marriott that morning, in his new blue suit and yellow silk tie. In other words, he ended up exactly where he wanted to be; he just took a long, circuitous route getting there. Now he's executive vice president of the company—Tradewind Net Access, it's called— and business is thriving beyond his wildest dreams. "Even in a recession, we're rockin'," he says with a buoyant laugh. "The next time you hear from me, maybe it'll be on the cover of *Fortune.*"

Sailing seemed to go along, hand in glove, with his good luck. As the weeks went on, he kept at it. Every weekend he was out there on the Sound, getting his confidence back. As the fall progressed the winds grew stronger and he found himself taking more and more risks. One day he was out in twenty-five-knot winds and he realized that he was smiling.

Even the hole in the skyline ceased to prey on him as it had before. He scarcely even noticed it.

Sitting in the library of his house in Glen Ridge, I ask Ronnie if he thinks he'll ever find meaning in September 11—the day his daughter turned eleven, the day his sister smashed into a building at the very moment he was reciting the Lord's Prayer into the ear of a horribly burned stranger. "Meaning?" he says, turning the word over in his mind. "It was so horrible, so horrid, so horrendous, there's got to be goodness afterward. To me, the Trade Towers represented good and evil. Positive and negative. Before and after. *Two ones.*"

Outside, in the broad daylight, the vintage gas lamps are burning up and down the street.

"For me," Ronnie says, "the meaning is the rest of my life."

—2001

Among the Kawasaki Republicans

Imperial Sand Dunes, California

"LET'S GO for a naaaat raaaad," Jess said, and so we did, five of us on five pieces of Japan's finest, zipping east from our campsite in fumy bursts toward the dunes.

Our posse disappeared into the crowds of vehicular pilgrims and roamed the desert night, plunging into bowls, fishtailing through gritty washes, and bouncing over the kidney-punishing corrugations of the sand highway. Never having been on a quad before, I was at once thrilled and alarmed by the squat little thing's insectile energy, its nervous, reedy-throated eagerness to respond. "You're gonna love the *parrr*," Jess had said, and he was right—so much force in your throttle hand.

We were in the midst of the dune system in southeastern California where Patton had trained his tank divisions for North Africa, and where later another general, Gen. George Lucas, had massed his troops for the filming of *The Return of the Jedi*. It is the largest sandbox on the continent, two hundred square miles of desolation whose very name connotes power and entitlement: the Imperial Sand Dunes.

Forty miles away, the eastern horizon glittered with the lights of Yuma, Arizona, a military town on the Colorado River, and the biggest city anywhere in this vast circumference of nothing. Yet we were in the middle of an even bigger city, a temporary constellation of encampments spread out over the desert in haphazard groupings whose population, all told, would later be estimated at 200,000 souls. They were the Kawasaki Republicans, a flag-waving, towelhead-hating, no-nonsense tribe of Made-in-Americans who had, nonetheless, long ago allowed an exception to Dai Nippon for the simple reason that her two-stroke and four-stroke engines were far and away the world's best.

On any holiday weekend from Halloween to Easter, the Imperial Dunes could be expected to attract impressive hordes. But we had come during the high holy days of the duner calendar, Thanksgiving week, when the wheeled mayhem raged day and night and stretched from the Mexican border for forty miles, to the mesquite and creosote wastelands in the east, and all the way to the Chocolate Mountains in the north, where the navy ran a gunnery range.

On tonight's night ride, Jess was leading our group to a place called Competition Hill, a notorious gathering spot hidden back in a cleft of dunes where, according to him, the mood at night was consistently one of "drunken ridiculousness."

Jess hails from my hometown of Santa Fe, and has been coming here to ride motorcycles and ATVs for nearly a decade. A mechanic by trade and primary instinct—"just a motorhead's what I am"—he is a calm, taciturn man of fifty-five, with crafty fingers callused from a lifetime spent fiddling with engines. Although a veteran of the scene, he was decidedly not one of the crazies.

As our posse rumbled east, we encountered more and more duners all trending more or less in the same direction—on motocross bikes, on Baja buggies, on trikes and turbocharged go-carts, in jacked-up four-by-four trucks, in $100,000 dragsters and customized sandrails. We were a libertarian vehicular army, composed of vintages and makes that would have made Patton wince, moving with jittery determination over the bulging oceans of sand.

Finally we crested a dune and there it was in all its sordid glory: Competition Hill, an imposing hump that was easily three hundred yards high and choked in a haze of spent nitro. A congregation of perhaps thirty thousand people raged at the base, while dragsters, in profligate drafts of fuel, gunned it up the hill like sperm swimming to an egg. Some of them made it, and those who didn't would slither down for another try. Many of the rigs were equipped with enormous "sand paddle" tires, which made the ground shake with a thluttery thump for a hundred yards. Some riders popped wheelies all the way up, while others applied too much throttle and flipped over backward—usually without medical incident.

Legions of spectators sat on their vehicles or in the beds of trucks, blasting their formidable stereos, swilling beers and Smirnoff coolers, while Bureau of Land Management officers nervously patrolled the outskirts. In the distance a magnesium bonfire—probably fueled by old mag wheels or a discarded transmission case—gave off an eerie molten glow.

High on the dune crests surrounding us, we could see the headlights from miscellaneous vehicles, looping erratically, penning a strange electric calligraphy over the sand. Even through our helmets, the sound was deafening—the mechanical grumbles and sighs, the great muffler flatulence, the anxious whine of two-stroke Yamaha engines, which, in ragged concert, sounded like the bleating of a thousand lambs going to slaughter.

"See what I mean—drunken ridiculousness," Jess yelled appreciatively over the din. "And so much *parrr!*"

That was really all anyone could say: there was a lot of power out on that sandhill, an obscene amount of it, a tanker's worth of fuel sucking through carburetors and going up in smoke.

As the United States of America steamed toward war with an oil-rich nation, under the aegis of its oil-business president from the oil state, we sat astride our high-revving Raptors and Banshees, 200,000 of us opening up the throttles on our Thanksgiving holiday. Because we had much to be thankful for. Because subsidized petroleum is a constitutional right for our God-given thrillcraft. Because we were a country of movers and users, the most powerful nation in the history of this blue carbon planet—and that power ran, nothing short and nothing less, on oil.

THE IMPERIAL DUNES, a vast domain watched over by the relatively laissez-faire Bureau of Land Management, has long been a proving ground for a certain irascible streak of Western individualism.

People came out here to do what they pleased, to shoot off their guns or squat for months at a time or start up the occasional crystal-meth lab. In the summertime, no one much cared to live in this austere, below-sea-level realm, where the Mojave and Sonoran deserts blend and the temperature regularly surpasses 125 degrees. But during the moderate winter months, the dunes beckoned as a playground for weekend off-roaders from the exploding metropolises of Phoenix, San Diego, and L.A. The dune buggy in large part evolved here in the 1950s, and in its long sandy tracks came a procession of other vehicles, each one more nimbly wide-ranging than the last, leading finally to the most impertinent beast of all, the modern all-terrain vehicle—scourge of mothers, naturists, and anyone with a love of quiet. The Imperial Dunes Recreation Area has become the ATV capital of the world, a national flashpoint where the concept of transportational freedom gets spun out to its wildest, weirdest edge.

Last year, the *Mad Max*-ian scene at the Imperial Dunes had spiraled to what BLM officials called "near-riot conditions." By the week's end, there had been a murder, two stabbings, two accidental deaths, seventy arrests, any number of brawls, and an attack on a ranger—not to mention 260 hospitalizations and more than fifteen hundred citations for everything from public nudity to staging unlawful pit bull fights. A *New York Times* headline had aptly called the Imperial Dunes "the most illegal place in America."

OUR CAMPSITE, AN ALUMINUM WARREN of some twenty thousand RVs parked near Highway 78 at a place called Glamis, was a loud, dusty place where rebel flags flew in abundance and hirsute vendors sold T-shirts bearing sunny messages like MADE IN AMERICA, TESTED IN JAPAN, LET'S GO NUKE AFGHANISTAN. Glamis calls itself the "Sand Toy Capital of the World." There isn't much to the place other than a kind of all-purpose commissary of corrugated tin called the Glamis Beach Store with an adjoining pizzeria, Mama Jeanie's, that boasts "coldest beer in the desert."

The road that Glamis is built along, California Route 78, is an important line of demarcation for the duner folk. Anything north of 78 is a protected wilderness area where off-roading is strictly forbidden. As I walked along the highway coming back from the Glamis Beach Store, I was struck by the contrast: On the left was a smoky vista of torched vehicles, discarded tires, expended glow sticks, engine belts, beer cans, crisscrossing tracks, and frenetic mechanical activity stretching to the horizon. On the right side of the road: pristine dunes, solitude, undisturbed washes fringed with smoke trees, palo verde, and desert buckwheat. If you walked out there a while, you might actually encounter what they call *wildlife*—a desert tortoise, perhaps, a kangaroo rat, a fringe-toed lizard.

The most controversial species in the whole Imperial Dunes tableau is the Peirson's milk-vetch, a homely member of the legume family whose pea pods rattle in the wind. A threatened species, the Peirson's milk-vetch has become the snail darter of the California desert; in recent years, various environmental groups have succeeded in closing off large sections of the dunes to protect this endangered flowering plant. The duners, led by the Arizona-based American Sand Association, have predictably countersued and loudly claimed that, on the contrary, the milk-vetch is neither so rare nor so fragile as to be much damaged by off-roading activity. Some duner spokespeople have suggested that off-roading is *good* for the milk vetch because it helps churn up the sand and spread the seeds.

In Glamis one morning, I met a young ATVer from Las Vegas who pretty much encapsulated the off-roaders' conventional wisdom on the matter. I asked him about the issue because he was wearing a T-shirt that proclaimed, FRIENDS DON'T LET FRIENDS BECOME ENVIRONMENTALISTS. He looked over at the wilderness area north of the road and said, "The milk-vetch isn't nothing but a weed they're using to keep the off-roaders out. It's an aesthetic issue—they don't like the way we play. But look out there. Who'd want to hike in that shit? This land is no good for anybody but us."

I walked the long rows of RV encampments around Glamis, dumbfounded by the massive investment in hardware and hauling equipment required to move the great fleets of toys to this remote barren of sand. People essentially brought their own rolling garages, and the tool geeks loved to show off their beautifully arranged socket wrenches and ratchet sets. For their own protection, campers typically parked in clusters of four or five families, drawing their RVs tightly together like circled wagons from the Wild West days to prevent some stray jackass from barreling through. We learned the hard way that we had to create a little DMZ of domestic safety for ourselves. My first night, I'd left a little gap in the perimeter behind my rental RV, and a dune buggy came blasting through our encampment at a good forty miles an hour, popping a wheelie as he sputtered past our fire.

People were perpetually getting hurt. The dusty thoroughfare in the Glamis campground was a freak show of casts, neck braces, stitches, busted teeth, arthritic limps, and ghastly scars. Everyone knew that if they kept riding long enough their time would come, but they didn't seem to care. Or if they did, they sublimated their caring in the form of a grim determinism. I could catch the general tone of it in the bumper-sticker slogans: IT DON'T HURT TILL THE BONE SHOWS. BRAKES ARE FOR WUSSIES. GET IN, SIT DOWN, SHUT UP, AND HOLD ON. The basic sentiment, repeated in innumerable ways, was, Go faster, don't look back, live in the moment, push the envelope, get what you can right now, and screw the other guy if he gets in the way. It's a message pounded into the younger generation at an astonishingly early age. All around the Glamis campground I kept seeing fathers counseling their young sons or daughters in the solemn rituals of riding ATVs. Four years old, three years old, it didn't matter: they could never be too young. I saw them all over the place, little urchins on miniature ATVs turning figure eights around campfires for their doting parents, bobbling in their seats because their little legs couldn't quite reach the footpads.

A FEW ROWS DOWN from our campsite, I met Ron Bridge, a thirty-year-old welder from Glendale, Arizona, who's widely known as "Captain." A burly, shaven-headed guy with intriguing facial hair and a pierced ear, Captain was a prime example of a certain happy breed I kept encountering at Imperial Dunes: the custom builder. From the tired husk of a 1977 Ford 4×4 pickup, Captain had created a magnificent monstrosity he called the Dinosaur Chaser. It was an open-air desert cruiser equipped with eight bucket seats and painted a garish yellow. Moonlighting in his shop, Captain had fashioned the entire body himself, welded a roll cage on it, and put on a new set of thirty-five-inch Super Swamper Bogger tires. The Dinosaur Chaser was a spirited brute, and Captain loved showing her off.

He fired up the big 460cc engine. I hopped in with a group of his friends, and we took off into the dunes with Eminem blaring on the stereo. They were old school buddies from Phoenix, most of them in their early twenties, who'd been partying all week in the dunes. Like Captain, everyone had a nickname—Velcro, Duck, Funk, Monda, Johnny Five, Roach.

The Dinosaur Chaser growled up and down the hills toward a place called Oldsmobile Hill. Every few hundred yards there would be another marooned beast that was sadly stuck in the sand. We pressed farther into the dunes, and then Captain spotted a steep, short hill that he wanted to jump. Half the crew hopped out, and Captain and I took the Dinosaur sailing. We kept at it for a half hour, launching ourselves in the air and coming down hard in a great clanking thud, until a sheet of metal came unriveted and waved crazily in the breeze.

Once I got far out into the dunes, away from the worst of the mayhem, I found that people were remarkably friendly, almost disarmingly so. It was as if just being out there qualified me as a member of the club. At one point I met a duner veteran named Dave Mleynek. He was a garrulous, forty-six-year-old mechanic with warm, sad eyes and a slight osteopathic discomfiture from the numerous mishaps he'd had in the desert. The guy had clearly taken some hard knocks, but he spoke of duning as a glorious addiction that was bigger than he was and couldn't be shaken. "Been coming out since the seventies," he said, "and it hasn't wore off its draw."

Mostly what Dave liked to do was pop wheelies. Ever since he was a kid, that was the thing that chiefly held his interest. He could keep a wheelie going for minutes at a time, on virtually any kind of terrain. "I don't mean to brag, but wheelies is sort of what I'm known for out here," he said, swelling up with just a little bit of pride.

Dave's vehicle of choice was the three-wheeler, probably the most dangerous of all dunecraft. Without prompting, he told me about his first accident, which occurred in 1978. He was out riding when he hit a "whoop-de-doo"—a washboard pattern of large bumps—and was bucked off his three-wheeler going fifty miles an hour. He wasn't wearing a helmet ("we never did in those days") and landed squarely on his face. "Just tore the inside of my mouth all to pieces," he recalled with a deep wince. "The stitches all come out and six months later I was still spitting out sand."

Dave chuckled in a melancholy sort of way and then went on to tell me about this year's broken collarbone and an incident he witnessed several years ago when his niece lost a lung in a buggy accident. His worst accident had happened only a year ago. He was out riding his 1985 350x Honda three-wheeler when he came upon a peculiarity of the desert known as a "witch's eye," an unexpected void or pit usually caused by a dust devil. "I rode down into that sucker and *wham*—compound tibia. My bone was just sticking out of my jeans." He hiked up his left pants leg and showed me an impressive, humpy scar. "When I got to the Yuma emergency room, they asked me if I had ever been hospitalized before. And I said, 'Boy, you sure do ask dumb questions around here.'"

ON MY LAST NIGHT in Glamis, a Sunday night, nearly all the hellion hordes had gone home, and in their absence I could hear the desert sighing in relief. Only a few campsites were still intact, their fires twinkling miles away like distant satellites in the black voids. The night was cool and crisp, and in the new dustless clarity I could see the stars for the first time all week.

That night I had fallen in with Tim Ramsey and Chris Hamlet, two brothers-in-law from Vista, California, whose campsite was directly across the Glamis wash from mine. Tim and Chris were both avid ATVers, but primarily they had come to the Imperial Dunes to promote an arresting new vehicle called the Patriot. Simply put, the Patriot was a miniaturized monster truck, a preposterous little runt that was an exact replica of a full-scale monster truck shrunk down to one-third the normal size. Andy's demonstration model was parked right beside us, and somehow it put a permanent smile on my face. Equipped with a fuel-injected Honda engine, four-wheel drive, and massive tires, this little Mini-Me of metal offered, according to the Patriot brochure, all of the "ground-pounding, adrenaline-charged features of the big boys' rigs . . . but at one-tenth the price."

All week long the Patriot had been the talk of Glamis. Andy had taken it up Competition Hill and the brute had performed magnificently. She made the summit without even breaking a sweat. I'd been watching the crowds milling around Andy's demo Patriot, scratching their heads in amazement. For understandable reasons, it seemed to be especially popular among midgets.

We were sitting around the campfire—Chris, Tim, and I, along with a die-hard dirt-biker from England named Jules—and as the evening wore on a fifth of Jack Daniel's materialized. We got to talking about the Patriot, and what could be done to spread the word about this strange, wonderful, Lilliputian truck. The Patriot, it seemed to me, was a vehicle whose day had fully arrived: a scaled-down ride for scaled-down times. Hunters and ranchers would love it, and it might even prove to have tactical applications for the military.

"Oh, that's already happening," Tim said matter-of-factly. "The emir of Kuwait just ordered a hundred of them."

I stared into the campfire and tried to imagine the army of the future, in which each foot soldier came equipped with his own personalized monster truck. But then something caught my eye. Off in the distance, almost to the horizon, a blaze was growing on an enormous expanse of sand. The flames curled in a huge circle that had to be three hundred yards in circumference.

"Gasoline fire," Chris said contemptuously. "They're just wasting fuel, the assholes."

We watched the flames build as the pyros, whoever they were, kept dumping more fuel. And then, just as it was starting to die off, another one erupted at another campsite a few miles off to the east. And then a third, toward the west. They were copycat blazes. Each camp was trying to outdo the previous one. It was a gross little game of consumption: on their final night in the Imperial Dunes, these people had nothing better to do than torch their last reserves of petrochemicals.

But then Andy and Chris got to thinking. "You know," Chris said, "we could do a lot better than those clowns."

We all nodded vigorously. Chris's wife, who was watching TV inside the trailer with their daughter, caught wind of what was happening; she didn't like the sound of it at all. There was some discussion of the fact that in his youth, Chris had been something of a pyrohead, and had once gotten into serious trouble starting an inferno in his suburban neighborhood.

But tonight Chris was adamant. We all were. Maybe it was the Jack and Coke talking. "Whatever we're going to do," I said, "let's do it *now.*"

Tim squeezed himself into the Patriot and cranked it up, its wee body humming incongruously on its massive knobby tires, shaking the ground around us. We grabbed some matches and a couple of five-gallon jerry cans of fuel and hopped on our quads. And then, with the Patriot leading the charge in a blaze of halogen lights, we shot across the rolling dunes of California, a gang of wastrels setting off to build a good fire.

–2003

Unembedded

Kuwait City, Kuwait

I BEGAN TO HAVE REAL DOUBTS about going through with my mission to "embed," as a journalist with the United States Marines, when a reporter raised the unexpected question, "What do I do if I barf inside my gas mask?"

The question was perfectly serious—nausea can be one of the first symptoms of a chemical attack—but the young lieutenant who was leading the seminar, on a tennis court at the Hilton Kuwait Resort, had obviously never been forced to consider this situational fine point. "That would be a problem," the lieutenant said. "If you vomit liquid, you'll just want to clear it by pushing this and blowing hard through that." He grasped his gas mask and fingered the outlet valve for all of us to see. "But if you've got spew chunks, they could clog the valve and you'd . . . well, you'd be a goner."

As I followed this conversation, I was wearing my own gas mask, breathing in its stale rubbery essence and trying to imagine how I would react in the Iraqi desert when the first chemical alarm sounded. There were approximately fifty journalists on the tennis court, hunched in little seminars of ten under the smiting Arabian sun. Through the salt haze to the east, we could see an aircraft carrier heaving in the blue-gray waters of the Persian Gulf. We were here to receive our "NBC training" (Nuclear, Biological, Chemical), and we had only moments ago been issued our masks, medicines, and charcoal-lined chemsuits in brown plastic garbage bags. The lieutenant insisted that we practice donning our masks until we could perform the procedure, eyes shut, in nine seconds or less. It should become part of our "muscle memory," he said. Out in the desert, an alarm would sound and we would hear, "Gas! Gas! Gas!"—the cry always going out in threes. "Your first instinct when you hear the alarm will be to get one last little breath," our instructor said, inhaling sharply. "But if we're in a cloud of nerve agent that's just what it'll be—your last breath."

If, after successfully securing the mask, we began to experience any of the telltale signs of nerve-agent poisoning—such as profuse drooling, a sudden intense headache, or a general confusion "about who you are"—we were immediately to medicate ourselves with the "autoinjectors" provided in our kits. I opened my bag and studied one of the little plastic syringes. It was filled with an antidote called atropine and equipped with a tightly coiled interior spring that was strong enough to plunge the needle through several layers of clothing and into the deep tissue of the thigh. In an emergency, we were supposed to hold the autoinjector firmly against our flanks for a good ten seconds, as the atropine slowly drained into our bloodstream.

For the rest of the seminar, as we practiced other unmentionables, I sat there on the tennis court, breathing thinly in my mask, wondering how our sad, tense world had come to this.

IT HAD BEEN A LONG, queasy week for the five hundred journalists waiting to embed with the U.S. armed forces in Kuwait. For many, including those who, like me, were scheduled to join up with the marines, there had been repeated scheduling delays and snafus that had pushed back by more than a week our promised rendezvous with the troops who were camped in undisclosed locations in the sandy wastelands near the Iraqi border. We were told to return to our various hotels, lie low, and wait for a phone call. For some, this extra week was a reprieve, but for most of us it was a curse, especially in a country without alcohol.

A paranoid, they say, is a person in possession of the facts. Maybe I was becoming paranoid, but the signals all around me were unsettling at best. The *Kuwait Times* was filled with stories on dirty bombs, suitcase bombs, smallpox, drone aircraft, Vx, sarin gas, and all the other nasty tricks that Saddam may or may not have planned for us. A crack team of NBC experts from the Czech Republic could be seen around town in their rubber suits, monitoring the air.

At restaurants and spontaneously arranged hotel parties around town, journalists spooked one another with biochemical ghost stories. We were going to be with the soldiers, experiencing whatever hardships and horrors were happening on the ground. I was finally coming to appreciate the weird, circular argument behind this conflict: The war's stated purpose was, in large part, to prove to the world that Saddam had weapons of mass destruction; if he really had them, and few doubted that he did, it seemed only logical to believe that he was going to use them, especially when cornered. The planned invasion was thus designed to root out the very weapons we hoped—and at the same time feared—that he possessed. And we journalists were coming along not only to witness any chemical nastiness that might ensue but also, presumably, to breathe it.

Yet there was about the whole embed process an ineluctable forward drive. Even those of us who entertained doubts about this war were forging ahead, despite our better instincts—because it was happening, because it was history, because it was bigger than all of us. With the embed program, the Department of Defense was embarking on a public-relations experiment of unprecedented size and scope. By the look of things the Pentagon truly wanted us to be right there on the battlefield, free and unfettered, reporting precisely what we saw. It was an ambitious arrangement that in some ways harkened back to the days of World War II, when war correspondents like John Hersey and Ernie Pyle roamed the battlefields in search of good stories.

Still, I had trouble fathoming why an administration that had shown no particular concern for world opinion in the previous months would go to such lengths to accommodate so many journalists. One military officer at the Hilton privately suggested an answer: "We want you here to document the gas and the other stuff Saddam has in his arsenal. If he has it, or, God forbid, uses it, the world's not going to believe the U.S. Army. But they'll believe you."

This, the more I thought about it, was not a very encouraging reason to be here. As the day of the embed drew closer, I began to feel like a lab rat, heading off for great chemical experiments.

For the most part, the embeds worked by luck of the draw. You were not told your exact slot until you got here, and you were pretty much stuck with it. My slot was one of the sexy ones—quite possibly the sexiest. I was to be with the Reconnaissance Battalion of the 1st Marine Division. First Recon was basically the front line. Wherever its men were was likely to be the most dangerous spot in the marine "battle space." As I milled among the other journalists—many of them hardened war correspondents and military geeks—I was repeatedly congratulated on my good fortune. They said things like "First Recon, aye, the able-bodied killers," "Lots of action," and "You're gonna get some real good stuff out there." One guy just raised his eyebrows and said, "You got a death wish?"

MY COVETED SLOT HAD BECOME available very late in the game, and I had a week to scurry onto a plane. I got my anthrax and smallpox vaccines, and took a course of typhoid pills. I got a dog tag, an Iridium satellite phone, and a Kevlar helmet and flak jacket. I double-checked my life insurance policy and hastily drew up a will. The last few days before I left home were beautiful and strange. Every detail seemed amplified, resonant, fateful—a stupid argument I had with my brother, the queer way my dog stared at me, the peace medallion my son's friend gave me to wear in the desert. When you're going to a place where dying is the whole point, you look for signs.

I kissed my wife and three young boys good-bye, and some forty hours later, found myself in the well-oiled kingdom of Kuwait. At my hotel, I quickly befriended some of the other embeds, and we compared omens. Evan Wright, a reporter for *Rolling Stone*, told me that his great-grandfather had been gassed in World War I, and had died of complications several years later. This family curse did not constitute a deterrent, however. Evan didn't seem especially creeped out by this war. "But there is one thing that bothers me about going into Iraq—*chemical mines*," he said, introducing a whole new threat I never even knew existed. "From what I've read, I'm pretty sure Saddam's got them."

Evan and I fell in with another reporter, Rex Bowman, with the *Richmond Times-Dispatch*. Rex said his wife had wept more than he'd expected when he left, and he was plenty terse now, but this was the assignment of his career. He had done a stint in the air force in Berlin listening to Russian radio transmissions, but he had never been remotely close to combat. "Although covering rural Appalachia as I do," he said, archly, "I've seen a whole lot of corpses."

It was Rex's forty-second birthday, and through a series of e-mails his wife back in Roanoke had secretly gotten the word to us about a certain Bowman family superstition that demands placing a surprise dollop of butter squarely on the nose of the birthday celebrant. During what we called our "last supper" at the Kuwait Hilton, it fell to me to carry out the odd ritual. "How did you know?" Rex said, momentarily shocked and laughing as he smeared the daub off his nose. "Can't really explain it. It's just something we've always done, for generations. For good luck."

THE LAST STRAW, for me, was a little session the marines held just before the embed buses were scheduled to take us away—a session, oddly enough, that was primarily designed to allay our fears about chemical attack. The seminar was run by a blunt, amicable jarhead, a Sergeant Parks, who launched right into a description of what might happen if we were "slimed" by a "snowstorm," the operative term for a toxic cloud in the new military parlance. Parks related how a victim of a chemical attack would lapse into intense, twitching convulsions, which he likened to "doing the funky chicken." The nerve agents could be hurled at us in any number of ways, he said: drone aircraft, short-range surface-to-surface missiles, Scuds, mortar shells, artillery rounds, even *chemical mines*. At that, I looked over at Evan, and his eyes widened. As a matter of policy, the armed forces were proceeding on the prudent assumption that every incoming round contained chemical agents until proved otherwise; consequently, we could expect to wear our chemsuits—which were cumbersome, clammy, and inordinately hot—most of the way to Baghdad. Parks then gave us color commentary on the effects of the various blistering agents that Saddam might use. "If you ingest mustard gas," he said, "it will cause horrible sores that will eat right through your esophagus." He said he'd seen photographs of skin blisters "as big as my hand." Then he amended the description: "Not just blisters, but blisters on top of blisters. Thing is, if you try to lance them they just keep on growing." Some blistering agents, he said, cause the skin to blow up in hideous cauliflowers of deformity. "This one victim's hand looked just like Jiffy Pop," Parks said.

That was quite enough for me. I stopped taking serious notes at this point, and simply wrote, in large, definitive letters, *We're fucked*. I knew then and there that I couldn't go through with this. Although I had nothing but respect for the United States Marines, I had not signed a contract and was, I'd almost forgotten, free to leave. This seemed like a good time.

I told Capt. Joe Plenzler, the marine in charge, "No offense, but I can't do this." And, as I did so, I was struck by an almost desperate desire to go back—not only back home to my wife and boys, but back in time, back to the days of bull markets and meaningful alliances and guiltless French wine. I resolved to join the coalition of the unwilling, and to cover the war in some other way, from some other vantage. I turned in my chemsuit, my atropine injectors, and my mask. I was immensely relieved to learn that it wasn't too late. I wished Capt. Plenzler Godspeed and good luck. An hour later, I saw the embed buses pull out of the Hilton's parking lot and chuff north, toward the Iraqi border.

A FEW DAYS LATER, I made my way to Doha, Qatar. The headquarters for the United States Central Command (CENTCOM) was hidden somewhere in this heretofore obscure and apparently not pronounceable nation. To get there, I ventured to a crushed-rock moonscape beyond Doha's outskirts until I came to a facility that looked like a maximum-security prison. PROVE YOUR IDENTITY, a sign said. It took a full hour to get past Jocko the bomb-sniffing dog and the X-ray machine and onto a shuttle bus, which made its way past a reef of concrete barriers and stopped outside a prefabricated metal warehouse. I opened the door and was assailed by blinding fluorescent light and a whoosh of refrigerated air.

This was the CENTCOM media center, decorated by a set-designer from Hollywood at a cost of more than $250,000. The briefing room was impressively appointed in metallic gray-blues, with digital clocks and maps and plasma screens. Something about the place reminded me of the movie, *Capricorn One,* in which NASA conspirators stage a "Mars landing" for world television inside a secret hangar placed incongruously in the remote desert.

The international media had come to Doha in droves because this was supposed to be the white-hot nerve center of the war. Once the hostilities got underway, however, two main points became apparent to us. The first was that momentous things really were happening here, somewhere on this surreal and sun-blasted American base. The second was that journalists weren't going to get anywhere near those momentous things. We had come all this way, mainly, to be with General Tommy Franks, who we all confidently assumed would be the voice and face of the war. But Tommy Franks was almost nowhere to be found. We couldn't see Tommy Franks. We couldn't talk to Tommy Franks. We couldn't breathe air in the room that Tommy Franks had been in, *yesterday.* With visible discomfort, the general did conduct maybe three briefings, but otherwise he seemed more than content to turn over the public dimension of the war to his subordinate generals. The problem was, we couldn't interview the subordinate generals, either. The CENTCOM media center, we soon learned, was a thoroughly sanitized and shut-off nodule of Army spin.

Franks's disregard for the media made him seem mysterious and likeably elusive. He was too busy running the war to emerge from his bunker and talk about it, and that was refreshing, even if it was frustrating for us. Franks was, as he himself liked to say, "no Norman Schwarzkopf." His style was strikingly different from the famously gabby master of ceremonies of the last Gulf War. Franks was a jowly, jug-eared man with basset-hound eyes, a high-test Texas drawl, and a disarmingly self-deprecating manner that showed itself in lines like "ahm 'fraid that's above my pay grade." He liked to stick to what he called "fact-based information," and tended to use certain stockphrases over and over again—his most groove-worn expression was "at a time and place of our own choosing." Franks was not a West Pointer, but a rather prosaic Army artilleryman who rose, slow and steady, through the ranks. Now he was a four-star general, the commander of the almighty CENTCOM, the man at the aegis of the campaigns in both Afghanistan and Iraq. It's doubtful there has ever been a general in American history who flexed so much power on the world stage but who, at the same time, seemed so utterly uninterested in his public persona. Generals of this caliber—Patton, MacArthur, Westmoreland, Schwarzkopf—have tended to be peacocks, people who rose by relentless ego, vanity, and charisma. Franks, it seemed, had none of it.

All of which proved exasperating to the news organizations that had come halfway round the world, at huge expense, to set up shop in this tiny little emirate. The star of the show wasn't a star, and what's more, he didn't want to be. Within a few days, Matt Lauer from the *Today Show* and George Stephanopoulos from *Good Morning America* had pulled out, and there began a mass media exodus. The word went out that CENTCOM was a drag if not a farce of an assignment, that no real information was attainable here that couldn't be gathered at the Pentagon, that it was all script and thinkspeak.

And Doha itself was an exceedingly strange city to be stuck in. With the discovery of the world's largest natural gas reserve, Qatar was on the fast track to becoming the richest nation, per capita, on earth. But compared to Kuwaitis, who have several generations of oil money under their belts, the Qataris seemed friendly, slow, and unsophisticated, the Beverly Hillbillies of the emirate states. Doha was a decent place, all in all, but achingly, oppressively dull. Most of the petroleum work was hired out to Texans, and everything else was done by coolies from Pakistan, Bangladesh, and Yemen, many of whom would toil their whole lives here without the slightest prospect of gaining citizenship. The Qataris themselves were what you might call *extremely* gainfully unemployed, and had almost nothing to do with their endless leisure time but go four-wheeling in the dunes, or dabble with sport falconry, or adventure shop. At the huge mall in Doha, phalanxes of shockingly rich Bedouins aimlessly roamed the air-conditioned thoroughfares in immaculate white robes with diamond cuff links, fidgeting with their worry beads, talking on gold-plated cell phones, and hunting for $50,000 Swiss watches.

Unlike Kuwait City, drinking was permitted in certain Doha establishments. My hotel, the Marriott, had a Mexican restaurant where a Filipina waitress in a sexy cowgirl getup went from table to table beseeching people to drink shots of tequila. Her trusty bottles of Cuervo were stashed at her waist in a double-holster, and she would periodically remove one and "fire" it at a promising-looking customer, pretending to blow smoke from its barrel before returning the bottle to its place. If you accepted her challenge, a mariachi band would rush over and blast intensely loud music right in your face. Everyone in the joint would turn and watch in rapt amazement as you threw back your shot. Then they would erupt in a sustained formal applause. This was a wild night in Doha.

Qatar is run by a corpulent, jolly, politically progressive, polygamist emir, Sheikh Hamad bin Khalifa al-Thani, a man whose iconoclastic embrace of modernity is exceeded only by his tolerance for contradiction. As a savvy alternative to creating his own defense forces, the emir had personally arranged for the American military to set up operations here. He was also responsible for bringing Al Jazeera to Qatar. The controversial Arabic-language news channel, which claims a viewership of more than 35 million people, is headquartered right in Doha. The emir is one of Al Jazeera's primary financial backers and remains its steady, if silent, champion. The channel flourishes in large part because the emir, in refreshing contrast to most leaders throughout the Arab world, actually believes in a free media.

QATAR'S HOMEGROWN TELEVISION network would become, often at cross-purposes with CENTCOM, the *other* great nodule of spin. At the war's outset, Al Jazeera was widely considered a rogue state among journalistic enterprises. Its decision to broadcast lurid footage of captured and apparently executed American soldiers caused a great stir at CENTCOM. Lieutenant General John Abizaid took the opportunity, during a briefing, to decry the "disgusting" images, scolding Al Jazeera's reporter, Omar al-Issawi: "I regard the showing of those pictures as absolutely unacceptable." Afterward, al-Issawi was philosophical. "Look, the General's reaction was perfectly understandable," he said. "Those were his boys. As a reporter for Al Jazeera, I have been harassed and threatened by intelligence agencies. This was pretty mild, actually."

As the war progressed, however, al-Issawi became something of a celebrity, emerging as one of the more eloquent and coolheaded commentators. At CENTCOM, Al Jazeera's office was located next to the briefing room on "Coalition Way" (all the hallways had semifacetious designations), and al-Issawi's reserved seat at briefings was in the front row, near the podium, next to CNN's. When al-Issawi raised his hand, Brigadier General Vincent Brooks almost always called on him, addressing him as "Omar."

"Slowly, people at CENTCOM are starting to realize that we're not the enemy," al-Issawi told me one morning as we made our way to a briefing. "We're not some insensitive monster bent on bashing America." Al-Issawi has a taut, lean build and the cautious air of a man who has weathered many controversies and covered many wars. Thirty-six years old, he is a Lebanese citizen who was born and raised in Kuwait and educated at colleges in Iowa and Virginia. He speaks in a determined, formal Sidney Poitier kind of English, his voice low and soft and mellowed by Marlboros. He wears desert khakis, suede boots, and an impressively pocketed correspondent's jacket, and often carries a stainless-steel thermos filled with viscous Turkish coffee. He collects silk textiles and fine kilims on his frequent travels as a foreign correspondent and likes to rocket around Doha in his new BMW M3, listening to heavy metal.

Al-Issawi parked his car in the stony lot outside CENTCOM, then inched through security. Inside the media center, al-Issawi was immediately accosted by well-wishers and back-slappers. "Omar—my man!" an Army officer said. "Caught you on Larry King again," a television producer said, with a wink. A reporter from *The Nation* told al-Issawi that he was becoming a favorite among female viewers back in America. "They say they can't decide which is more beautiful, your Arabic or your English," he said. Another CENTCOM journalist suggested, "You've risen to star status." Al-Issawi scowled. "Let's hope not," he replied. "They say the light from a star reaches us long after it has depleted its resources."

Al-Issawi got his start in broadcasting in 1987, as a deejay for an FM station in Beirut, spinning Led Zeppelin, Iron Maiden, and Pink Floyd tunes while war raged in the streets. In 1994, he moved to London to work for the BBC's Arabic World Service Television. He was sent to Yemen, Sudan, Afghanistan, and Bosnia, where he sustained a gunshot wound in the leg. (A BBC colleague was killed in the same attack.) When the BBC disbanded the Arabic station, in 1996, a nucleus of the staff, including al-Issawi, moved to Qatar to create Al Jazeera. Al-Issawi soon became one of Al Jazeera's most prominent correspondents and commentators. In 2000, he made an acclaimed fifteen-part documentary for Al Jazeera about the Lebanese war, which gave him new insights into the perils and complexities of occupying a war-torn country. Shortly before the war started, al-Issawi traveled to Iraq to conduct some interviews for a documentary that he's producing about the PLO. "I found Iraq one of the saddest, most stifling places on earth," he said. "It's the most brutal regime the world has seen since Stalin. I vowed I would never go back again until Saddam has been evicted from power."

One night, at the end of a long day at CENTCOM, al-Issawi retrieved his BMW and drove through the desert toward the fantastical modern skyline of Doha. He was bleary-eyed and looking forward to a Heineken. He put on a Black Sabbath CD—"post-Ozzy, I'm afraid." Very soon, he said, the war would be over, the CENTCOM hordes would go away, and only Al Jazeera would be left. Yet things would never be the same—not in Doha, not anywhere in the Middle East. "With this war, your country has set something in motion across the whole region," he said. "All Arab eyes will be watching to see what you do. It's a test, an experiment. Everything is uncertain. Everything except this: we can never go back."

—2003

First

Camp Pendleton, California

THE MARINE IS IMMACULATE. He stands at attention inside the embassy, with his polished sidearm glinting in its holster. He looks like a puppet, a perfect toy soldier. Nothing is out of place. The high and tight buzz cut, the dress blues, the blood stripe, the white-white gloves, the green braided fourragère tassel, the white cap with its chin strap so firmly cinched it cuts a groove in his skin.

The little boy stares up at the marine as though he's seen a ghost. "What's *that?*" he asks, and he points at the radiant creature.

His dad shushes him, his mom reminds him it's not nice to point. His older sister and younger brother are there, too. They are an American family from West Virginia, just off the plane. Groggy and jet-lagged, they're waiting to get their official identification badges. The boy is four years old, and he's come to live at the American embassy in Tehran, where his dad, a tradesman with the navy Seabees, has been posted as a security engineer.

The year is 1977. The shah is still in power, but the country is sliding fast into revolution. The family takes an apartment right on the grounds of the embassy, not far from where the marines stay. Every morning the little boy sees them coming and going. He watches them with his dark brown eyes. He studies their strange movements, asks them endless questions. He becomes their mascot. They pat him on the head and give him presents. They call him by his name—*Shane.*

One day the boy is swimming in the embassy pool with his parents. A couple of marines march briskly by, off to somewhere important. They cut familiar looks at him and smile. The boy's been living in Tehran for more than a week, but the fascination of the marines has yet to wear off. Something about them grabs him, the discipline in their posture, their splendid formality, their ready competence, their other-worldly air.

"Look," the boy says to his parents. "*That's* what I want to be." He says it with a resolve they'll never forget, a resolve they're not alto-gether comfortable with. And he points.

ON THE EARLY MORNING of Friday, March 21, 2003, the sandy plain of southern Iraq still holds the previous day's heat. Second Lt. Shane Childers stares at the flickering outlines of a vast oil pumping station, listening to the murmur of his radio. He rides standing in his amphibious assault vehicle, pointing out developments on the horizon, his Kevlar helmet bobbing high above the hatch in the desert air. Perched up there in his "track," as the unlovely twenty-ton marine assault vehi-cles are called, Childers presents a clear silhouette for any snipers who might be waiting in the darkness. It's a posture that worries some of his platoon mates, who at times think their lieutenant carries himself with a confidence that borders on the reckless—'like he thought he was Rom-mel or something," as one platoon mate will later put it.

Childers roars across the Rumaila oil fields in a large convoy—some two hundred men riding in several dozen tracks, Humvees, seven-ton trucks, and tanks. His lip bulges with Copenhagen as he alternately fidgets with a map and squints at the landscape. The country, what lit-tle Childers can see of it in the darkness, is flat and featureless and marked only by occasional pieces of derelict petroleum equipment half swallowed by the sand. Up ahead, trench oil fires burn in large arcs around the pump station complex, laying down a mantle of noxious smoke that has rendered his night-vision equipment useless.

Lieutenant Childers is a rangy, meticulous man quivering with energy. A graduate of the Citadel, he has a triathlete's build and smoldering, unibrowed eyes the color of bittersweet chocolate—"those crazy eyes," as one of his squad leaders describes them. He speaks in a steady staccato that, in accent, is a blend of West Virginia, Mississippi, California, Puerto Rico, Wyoming, the Carolinas, and all the other places he's lived in his thirty years—which is to say there's no discernible accent at all, only the resolutely American voice of the corps. Childers's face lights up with periodic explosions, with flares and antiaircraft tracers, and he seems happy—happy finally to be in the place where he's yearned most of his life to be, leading a platoon of United States Marines into combat in the opening hours of a major ground war.

Childers clutches his M-16 rifle. He's wearing a Kevlar flak jacket with slide-in ceramic plates and a load-bearing vest packed with ammunition. A lanyard Maglite flashlight is slung over his neck. He carries a compass, a GPS, two canteens, three radios, two smoke grenades, and two M-67 fragmentation grenades. On top of it all, he's sheathed in a charcoal-lined chemical suit that makes him sweat profusely. His gas mask dangles in its canvas creel at his side.

Childers's company—Alpha Company of the 5th Marines—has been given one of the first clear missions of the ground war. Their assignment is to secure a particularly important facility in the vast Rumaila oil fields, a complex marked on the map simply as *Pumping Station No. 2*. The station is enormous, fifteen hundred meters by fifteen hundred meters, an industrial labyrinth designed to squeeze crude from a nearby gas-oil separation plant east toward the port of Umm Qasr. According to the recon reports, an entire Iraqi brigade (more than a thousand men) has dug itself into the compound and is poised either to fight or to blow up the whole place.

Judging by all the fires, Childers fears that pump station number two may have already been sabotaged. In recent days, Coalition forces have gathered evidence indicating that Saddam's troops are indeed planning to destroy the oil fields. Among other things, trains bound directly for the Rumaila oil region have been transporting significant quantities of explosives.

Childers takes a long pull from the nozzle of his CamelBak hydration pack. As the commander of Alpha Company's second platoon, he is personally in charge of the fate and welfare of forty-two men, most of them kids, eighteen, nineteen, twenty years old. At Camp Pendleton, their base on the southern California coast, he's had the better part of a year to mold this particular group of grunts. Fifteen of them are squeezed inside his track right now, and Childers can sense that they're anxious about the coming battle. He gives them a pep talk, reminding them that they've spent weeks training on their objective. During the long stay in Kuwait, he'd had his men poring over satellite imagery of pump station number two, studying photographs provided by Predator drones, and attending seminars run by a petroleum-industry consultant. They even went so far as to construct a terrain model of the facility and rehearsed seizing the compound until the mission was rote. "We're ready," he'd written in a letter back to the States shortly before their departure. "Every day we just get harder and tighter, more disciplined."

Now Childers shouts over the rumble of the diesel engine: "You're good to go. You're the best fuckin' devil dogs in the One-five—I'm proud of you."

Childers's track idles with the other vehicles in the Alpha Company convoy, which is now aimed at the pumping station in an enormous diamond formation, poised for battle. He listens intently to his radio headset and waits for the signal to attack. His face is bathed in the luminous glow of his digital watch—a Finnish-made Suunto, with a built-in altimeter, barometer, temperature gauge, and compass.

At about three A.M. marine artillerymen unleash a barrage of mortars and rockets on the pumping station, a furious assault that lasts some twenty minutes. The muzzles of the artillery pieces have names crudely scrawled on them, grim monikers like "Shoot to Thrill" and "Population Control." Taking care not to hit assets of petrochemical infrastructure, they train their sights only on outlying buildings where recon intelligence indicates that the largest numbers of Iraqi soldiers are holed up.

A few minutes later, the signal comes, and the men of Alpha Company storm the complex. The metal ramps drop down from the tracks, and Childers and his platoon emerge on foot, fanning out over the vast, vaporous grids.

* * *

"HE WAS LIVING FOR THAT DAY," says Sgt. Bradley Nerad.
"Man, he was in it for this."

Sergeant Nerad sits in a debriefing room at Camp Pendleton, staring distractedly out the window onto the parade deck, where members
of the 5th Battalion march in tidy columns, preparing for a change-of-
command ceremony. A burly hoss from rural Wisconsin, Nerad is the
staff sergeant for Alpha Company's 2nd Platoon—Childers's unit. Like
all the other 5th marines, he's just returned from Iraq. Their belongings from the war are parked outside, crammed in stacking green metal
containers that have yet to be sorted. Many of the marines outside still
wear bandages and dressings from various gunfights in Iraq. Nerad and
his buddies are glad to be back in the embrace of California weather.
Even now, a cool finger of fog curls in from the Pacific and rolls over
the eucalyptus trees that line the barracks. It's late June, and the war is
technically over—or at least the president has declared a kind of victory. At Camp Pendleton, home of the "Fighting 5th," the most decorated regiment in marine history (whose unofficial motto is, "MAKE
PEACE OR DIE"), there is a sense of rebirth; this immense military preserve, pinned between the sprawls of Los Angeles and San Diego, stirs
with the triumphant sounds of long-absent war machines. Bright ban-
ners are draped over the gates, and the returning marines have been
greeted as heroes at the conclusion of a successful mission.

But the war isn't over, and everyone here knows it. American soldiers are still dying in Iraq at a steady snare-drum beat—dying in checkpoint ambushes, in sniper shootings, in suicide bombings, in drive-by
incidents too numerous and too messily ordinary to lodge in the public
memory except as a blur of low-grade despair. The headlines have
frayed into the mean little bulletins of occupation.

Nerad doesn't know what to make of the war now. Mostly he just
looks relieved to be home. He's worn out, sick of sand, and in dire need
of alcohol. Tomorrow he goes on leave, and will do what he can to forget the past four months.

Right now, Nerad wants to talk about his buddy Childers. As the
highest-ranking noncom in the platoon, Sergeant Nerad often butted

heads with the lieutenant. "He was zealous, I'd say *over*zealous," Nerad says, shaking his head and smiling. "Sometimes he wanted to work the platoon to death." But it's obvious Nerad loved Childers, and worried about him, like a brother. Childers was lonely, he says, in the way that the most intense marines are often lonely. Such was his devotion to the corps—to the ascetic purity of the jarhead existence, to the hard life of fitness, to all the marine protocols and nomenclature and lore—that there wasn't room for anything else.

"Marine, that was it," says Nerad. "That's the only thing he wanted. Girlfriends, a family, naw. He wouldn't go out drinking with the others and come back red-eyed. He'd be out driving around in his red Ranger pickup, buying stuff for his platoon at Home Depot—batteries, lumber, stupid stuff he thought they needed for their training. Then he'd just go home, to his apartment in San Clemente, and get a bottle of Johnnie Walker Black, and stay up all night, sipping scotch alone."

Childers liked to listen to NPR, or Johnny Cash records—sometimes he'd play along on the harmonica. He'd dig into one of the hundreds of technical military books on his shelf, titles like *The Art of the Rifle, Maneuver Warfare, Stormtroop Tactics*. As the night wore on, Nerad says, he'd "get to dreaming up shit to do with his platoon. He'd go online, looking stuff up. Sometimes he'd call and wake me up like at three in the morning, just to talk about some exercise he had in mind. He'd want to talk for hours."

Childers had enlisted in the marines when he was seventeen, as a headstrong high school senior from Saucier, Mississippi, a small humid Gulf Coast town along the Little Biloxi River. He completed his basic training at Parris Island, South Carolina, just in time to be shipped out for the Persian Gulf War (the duration of which he spent on a navy warship). After the war, he floated the Pacific and the Mediterranean on extended marine cruises, and spent several more years at North Carolina's Camp Lejeune, taking specialized courses such as jump school and training for night navigation. Then, like the toy soldiers who so transfixed him as a kid in Tehran, he earned a diplomatic post as a guard at the American embassy in Geneva. He escorted foreign VIPs around town, traveled to Paris for a high-level diplomatic conference, and took an avid interest in outdoor sports, spending his free time climbing and mountain biking in the Alps or whitewater rafting in France. A year later, he accepted a similar assignment at the embassy in Nairobi, where he climbed Mount Kenya, went on Serengeti safaris, and pursued an intense love affair with a beautiful young Israeli woman, Adi. He considered converting to Judaism, in part to please her family, and in part because the demands of the faith appealed to his sense of rigor. But ultimately his relationship with Adi fizzled.

At the late age of twenty-seven, Childers, then a sergeant, decided he wanted to become an officer. To do that, however, he knew he had to graduate from college, something no one in his immediate family had ever done. He qualified for a special program that landed him at the Citadel, South Carolina's venerable military academy. With the peculiarly focused ambition of a more mature student trying desperately to play catch-up, he consumed the experience whole. He made the dean's list and graduated in three years. He ran in numerous school triathlons and explored the Appalachian Trail on breaks and long weekends. Majoring in French, he was fluent by his graduation in 2002, having taken summer immersion courses in France, Cameroon, and at Middlebury College. Now a voracious reader—he especially liked military histories—he resumed life in the marines on an entirely different career track.

Childers had become what the marines call a "mustang," a special breed within the ranks. Mustangs are officers who earn their commissions much later in their careers but who, as a result of their grunt pedigree, often still act and perceive situations more like noncoms. Enlisted men say you can't get anything past a mustang, because he's already seen everything and knows all the tricks. Having gotten most of their carousing out of their systems, mustangs tend to be more serious than their younger officer counterparts. It's often said that mustangs have a total perspective that gives them a special confidence on the battlefield.

Certainly all this was true with Childers. But he could also be moody, Nerad says, and he had his moments of self-doubt. Sergeant Nerad remembers that when they were camped in Kuwait, Childers made a cryptic comment that concerned him a little. They were bivouacked in a huge tent city that the marine planners christened, with characteristic poetry, "Living Support Area Number Five." Childers had been occupying his downtime by playing softball, looking at *Maxim* magazines, ritualistically cleaning his rifle with a paintbrush, and reading a Robert Ludlum novel, *The Sigma Protocol*. Deprived of solid information from back in the States, the camp was rife with outlandish rumors—it was widely stated and believed, for example, that Jennifer Lopez had been murdered. Like everyone else, Childers was bored out of his mind much of the long stay in Kuwait, frustrated by the false warnings, the seemingly endless ramp-ups and rev-downs while the diplomats worked to no avail. "Several expected D days have come and gone," he'd written to his parents. "Everyone just wishes we could get it on—hate the waiting."

One day, Childers and Nerad were sitting around bullshitting, as they sometimes did, talking about what the war would be like, how it would all pan out. They wondered when they'd be crossing the LOD, or line of departure. Maybe their nerves were getting the better of them, but at one point Childers stared off into the distance and said, with an unfamiliar severity in his voice, "I probably won't come back."

Nerad looked at him funny. "Hey, c'mon."

"I don't know, man," Childers said. "I just don't think I'm coming home."

Nerad tried to reassure him. "You bet you are," he said. "The marines need you—you know too much."

Whatever it was, Childers couldn't shake the feeling. It lingered in the air for an uncomfortable moment; then he turned away and fixed his eyes on the desert.

LIEUTENANT CHILDERS AND HIS PLATOON COMB the burning outskirts of pumping station number two, looking for signs of life. The marines wield shotguns, SAWs, and M-16s and sweep flashlights over every recess of the compound. But for the steady background drone of various pumps, turbines, and generators, the site is eerily quiet. All the lights have been switched off. Throughout the complex are freshly dug foxholes, but the "brigade" of Iraqi troops appears to have vanished. The grounds are littered with American propaganda leaflets, presumably air-dropped days before, urging prompt surrender. Many of the buildings look as though they'd only recently been vacated. Burning candles sag in humps of glistening wax, and plates of half-eaten dinners are set out on tables. Bedding and prayer mats are tossed about in corners. In one building, the marines find a large portrait of Saddam Hussein glowering down at them.

Childers scurries over the site, with his radioman following him everywhere. Although he is ten to twelve years older than most of his platoon members, Childers is in impressive physical condition. Shortly before coming to Kuwait, he had climbed California's Mount Shasta, for the fourth time in his life. He's such a manic and tireless roamer that the marines call him "Ricochet Rabbit."

As the marines tighten their grip on the place and burrow deeper into the complex, a few Iraqi prisoners begin to offer themselves up in ones and twos. They emerge from crude underground bunkers with their hands up, waving grimy white rags, trembling in fear. Some wear green Iraqi army uniforms, while others have donned robes over their military garb, as though attempting to disguise themselves as noncombatants. Many seem to be civilians from nearby villages pressed into soldierhood.

Childers is having trouble getting a fix on the true lines of Iraqi authority, and how—or even *if*—they'd been planning to defend the place. It appears to him that the Iraqis were taken almost completely by surprise. He can see that the artillery barrage prior to their attack has taken a significant toll. Corpses are strewn about, and dozens of Iraqis lie moaning in pathways and by roadside ditches, clutching shrapnel wounds. On his radio headset, Childers calls in medical corpsmen to treat the wounded. He orders his marines to round up the unharmed prisoners and bind them in "zip-ties"—temporary hand-cuffs made of hard plastic.

Around dawn, Childers and his men spy a young Iraqi soldier emerging from his bunker. The man hops on an old motorcycle and takes off across the open desert. Several Alpha Company marines draw their M-16s on him. Bullets sputter in the sand. The man rides in a desperate zigzag pattern to dodge the fire, and for a few moments it looks as though he might get away. Finally, several hundred yards out, one of the rounds finds its target. The Iraqi man wobbles crazily and then is hurled over the handlebars, with the motorcycle tumbling in a cloud of dust. The marines are amazed to learn that he's still alive, even though the bullet that took him down entered the back of his head and exited from his jaw, blowing off much of his lower face.

In a few short hours, the assault on pump station number two is already winding down. Childers is ecstatic: his devil dogs have performed magnificently. The first mission in Iraq is shaping up to be an unqualified success, part of the larger preemptive action throughout the Rumaila region that military planners will later cite as one of the masterstrokes of the war. As the sun climbs over the sand flats to the east, the men of Alpha Company are in control of the enormous facility. They've collected scores of prisoners. Any plans Saddam Hussein may have had to sabotage this sector of Rumaila have been averted. And there has not been a single American casualty.

A GOLD STAR FROM THE AMERICAN LEGION hangs by the front door of the Wyoming ranch house. An old blue Toyota pickup is parked in the gravel driveway. The house is yellow, with a mushy green shingle roof. It sits on a rolling, wind-beaten piece of land that's nubbed with sage. In the distance, snow-dusted peaks erupt in every direction, an embarrassment of mountains: the McCullough Peaks, the Absarokas, the Bighorns, the Pryors, the Beartooths.

Joe Childers greets me at the door. He's a strapping, generous-spirited man with a bulbous nose and spiky gray hair. He wears a Carhartt jean jacket and muddy cowboy boots. A tire gauge rests in the pocket of his denim shirt.

In 1992, Childers retired from his life of far-flung travel with the Seabees, the proud fraternity of skilled mechanics and tradesmen who build and fix all there is to build and fix for the U.S. Navy. He did two stints in Vietnam and then bounced around to nearly every corner of the world—Midway, Okinawa, Puerto Rico, Paris, Madrid, Jamaica, the Central African Empire, to name a few—on various Seabee assignments. It was a fine career, affording a far better life for him and his family than had he continued working in the grim coal mines of his native West Virginia. Now he's a roustabout for a Wyoming oil company. "I got to eat," he says, by way of explanation.

Mostly, though, he likes to lose himself in the work of this 125-acre ranch. It's a few miles west of Powell, a small northwestern Wyoming town named after the famous explorer and geologist John Wesley Powell, who lost an arm in the Civil War. Joe has owned this beautiful, ragged spread for twelve years, and it's his true love. Irrigating his fields with canal water diverted from the Shoshone River, he grows alfalfa and silage corn, and raises Black Angus cows, donkeys, mules, and Belgian draft horses. An accomplished blacksmith, he spends a lot of time at barn sales and auctions, buying antique and often broken farm equipment which he may or may not ever mend into usefulness but can't pass up. The place looks like a museum from the Cyrus McCormick era. The carcasses of old agricultural implements—harrows, rakes, sickles, grain drills, yokes, and any number of horse-drawn plows—lay rusting everywhere. Roaming about all these various relics are cats, dozens of them.

How many you got? I ask.

He starts to count, then gives up. "I don't know—*lots*," he says with a chuckle. "Not many mice, though."

Joe grabs two Bud Lights from the fridge in the barn. "Boy, Shane sure loved this place," he says. "Whenever he was on leave, he'd come stay with us. He loved to go on long runs up there in those foothills. He'd just take off and be gone for hours. Last time he was here was around Christmas. We had a couple feet of snow. He hitched up the Belgians to the sleigh and took off across the fields. You should have seen him up there, driving 'em."

Shane was beginning to think seriously about other careers beyond the marines—lately he'd been talking a lot about becoming an FBI agent. But he also dreamed of buying land in Powell and making a go of things as a small-time rancher, like his dad. In one of his letters to his folks from Kuwait, he'd written, "I wouldn't do things any other way, but I really do think of getting out after this tour. Have other things to worry about right now though—Love you, Shane."

Shane's company had been preparing to go to Okinawa for its next deployment, but Joe wasn't surprised when he heard that Shane had been called up, at the last minute, to go to Iraq instead. The Childerses have had a curious and long-standing relationship with the Middle East, as though their familial fate keeps circling back on itself. Not only did Shane serve in the first Persian Gulf War, but as a Seabee, Joe worked various stints in the region, including Kuwait, Bahrain, Dar es Salaam, and, longest of all, Iran. Living in Tehran at the tumultuous end of the shah's reign, installing and fixing locks and wiring closed-circuit-television security cameras at the embassy, Joe witnessed first-hand the startling beginnings of America's toxic relationship with the Islamic world. Among his many side skills, Joe is a professional far-rier—an expert shoer and trimmer of horses' feet; to earn extra cash, he spent much of his free time traveling around Iran, all the way up to the Caspian Sea, often with little Shane in tow, caring for the pleasure horses and thoroughbreds of the shah's rich friends. "Shane always remembered Iran—they was his first memories of life," Joe says. "He used to love to tell people that he'd grown up there during the revolution. He kind of felt at home in that part of the world."

All around them, the country was unraveling. Nearly every day there were demonstrations or explosions or clouds of tear gas hanging over the city. In late 1978, when all nonessential personnel were told to leave, Judy and the children went home to West Virginia. In February of 1979, Joe, along with most of the diplomatic staff, was briefly held hostage by Islamic fundamentalists who took over the embassy, in a little-known precursor to the infamous hostage crisis that would shock Americans a few months later. "They stormed the gates and yanked down the American flag," Joe says, "They held us at gunpoint, and marched us over to the ambassador's residence. Outside the gates, Tehran was crumbling—shooting, looting, burning. Basically it was a war zone." This anti-Americanism was still so new to Joe that he didn't recognize the full fervor behind it. He says, "I guess I wasn't as scared as I should have been."

We wander inside, where Joe's wife, Judy, is busy sorting boxes of sales orders that arrived this morning from Avon. She is a short, sturdy, direct woman from Idaho Mormon country with a warm but cautious smile.

   We all sit down in the living room to watch the Kentucky Derby on a fuzzy television with rabbit-ear antennae. Judy produces several family albums. She shows me a picture of Shane riding a horse in Spain, another one of Shane at a formal embassy function in Nairobi with his Israeli girlfriend, Adi, stunning in her evening gown. "Here's one when he was just a little bud," Joe says. It was taken in Puerto Rico, where Joe had a Seabee job alongside the dry docks at Roosevelt Roads Naval Base. Shane is holding a palm frond that's three times his size. He looks at the camera with those smoldering brown eyes, eyes that seem to look through you and on toward some distant beckoning future. The image is slightly blurred, as though Shane is moving too fast for the camera.

   "He had a lot of go in him," Judy says. "It was sometimes hard to find a baby-sitter."

   In high school in Mississippi, Shane held himself to a demanding but wildly unpredictable sense of perfectionism. Like his dad, he was intensely interested in the way things worked and liked to take machinery apart, piece by piece. He argued a lot, especially with his mom, and could be insufferable when advancing his notions. He had a natural tendency to gravitate toward people who were older and smarter than he was, and he would ask them endless questions about the books they read or the steps they took to get where they were. He had a fierce intolerance for bullies of any kind, and did not hesitate to confront them. He played catcher in Little League. He hunted squirrels, fished for crappie and bream, fearlessly captured copperhead snakes, and roamed the backroads in his Mustang II. He was intense to the point of masochism about his physical conditioning, but was something of a loner, uninterested in most team sports. By his sophomore year, he was already molding himself to be a marine. He used to train himself silly, gulping down raw eggs, doing hundreds of sit-ups, running untold miles, and reading all the literature on the corps he could find. He signed up for an early entry program and never looked back. His sister would later joke to a newspaper reporter that she didn't know what the jarheads at boot camp could possibly teach him—by temperament and constitution, he was already a marine.

   "It was part of his destiny," Joe says, "ever since he saw those marines in Iran. And he knew from the start he wanted to be infantry, a grunt, getting the worm's-eye view. Because the grunt is the guts of the whole thing. Everything else is supporting *him*."

Judy serves up three enormous steaks, extra-rare, from their private herd. "You know," Joe says, carving into his meat, "I been around animals all my life. It's almost always true that if one in the litter's going to die, it's going to be the best one. Pigs, chickens, but especially horses and cows, that best one, you watch him, he's gonna up and die on you."

Joe stares vacantly out the window toward the alfalfa field, and chews.

THE DESERT SUN IS BRIGHT but not yet intensely hot. By 7:30, the trench fires around the pump station are slowly extinguishing themselves. The men of Alpha Company, raccoon-eyed from having worked all night, buzz with excitement over their successful action. They're now in "the consolidation phase" of the operation. What started as an assault has become defensive in nature: the marines are now simply holding what they've gained and policing the area for any remaining threats before turning over the entire facility to a unit of British soldiers and petroleum engineers, who will guard it indefinitely.

Then, a little after eight o'clock, an explosion shudders the complex: Corp. Benton Groce, from Alpha Company's weapons platoon, is searching one of the many outbuildings when he takes a fateful misstep and triggers a land mine. It is a "toe-popper" grenade, a small mine designed to disable more than to kill. The blast blows Groce's boot off and mangles his legs. He has two broken ankles, a fractured tibia and fibula, and numerous shrapnel wounds. Medical corpsmen stabilize him, and then radio for a CH-46 helicopter to come medevac him to Kuwait.

With Groce's injury, Alpha Company's confidence has been thoroughly rattled. They've been fearing the presence of land mines all along—parts of the Rumaila fields are known to be infested with them—but the incident has suddenly injected a measure of reality into what had begun to seem a war without repercussions. Now everyone's nerves are on edge. The marines step gingerly about the compound, trying to finish mopping up.

Around 8:30 A.M., the men of Lieutenant Childers's platoon make one last sweep of the area but fail to find any more prisoners. The complex appears to be flushed clean. Childers is satisfied that his platoon's immediate assignment has been fulfilled. He wants to bring the platoon together and conduct a debriefing. He yells to his scattered men, tells them to "collapse back to the vehicles!" The tracks are parked together along the side of the road to the east of the pumping station beneath a clump of scrubby desert trees. About a hundred yards away, a severed oil pipeline running parallel to the road exhales a continuous breath of fire and smoke.

"Collapse back to the tracks!" Childers announces again, this time giving the command to his squad leaders over his radio headset. "Roger that!" he hears back. The forty men of his platoon abandon their various searches and gradually emerge out in the open. They funnel toward the tracks and gather beneath the paltry shade of the trees to await Childers's next instructions.

Suddenly a tan Toyota pickup truck squeals around a concrete barricade and barrels toward the tracks. Most of the marines are turned away from the road, their backs to the truck, and it takes them a moment to pick up on the suspicious incongruity of the sound. Childers hears the revving engine and walks out into the road. He squints at it. The other marines are instantly nervous.

Most of the other marines of his platoon are partially hidden by a modest-sized berm that runs crossways to the road. But Lieutenant Childers is exposed. He crouches in the shoulder of the road, trying to assess what the truck is up to. He can't tell whether it's friend or foe. It looks like a harmless civilian vehicle, but for some reason it keeps on coming, accelerating to forty, fifty, sixty miles an hour, hurtling down the pump station road.

Childers knows something is amiss now. He stands up and switches his M-16 from safety to fire. The machine gunners up in the tracks are watching with growing concern, but the truck is too close for their fifty-caliber machine guns, which are useless close in: they can't draw down on their target quickly enough.

The truck races at seventy miles an hour. It's possible now for Childers to see that it's packed with six or seven people, some of them lying low in the bed. The truck is small and rough-sounding and pocked with dents, and while it's coming fast, it drives sluggishly, as though burdened with too much weight.

Childers raises his M-16 to fire, but the Toyota is right on him, no more than eight feet away. One of Childers's squad leaders, Corp. Jesse Odom, is crouching right next to him. For a split second, Odom locks eyes on the Iraqi driver. There is fear and desperation in the man's face, and also anger. At the last instant, the Toyota swerves toward them. Odom sees the barrel of a weapon peek from the driver's side window as the truck passes by. Then he sees the muzzle flashes and hears a stitch of automatic fire. In random stutters, the desert dust kicks up all around him.

CORPORAL JESSE ODOM IS a bright young jug-eared fellow with cropped strawberry-blond hair. He's from Easley, South Carolina, and speaks in a firm, earnest Southern voice. He stands at a chalkboard at Camp Pendleton, drawing a diagram of pump station two, marking it with vectors and cross-hatchings, trying to explain how a simple situation could slide so thoroughly out of control in a few seconds. Above us, attack helicopters streak across the Pendleton skies. The breeze whistling through the window is tangy with Pacific salt.

As Odom stares at the diagram, he wonders why he's alive—why the bullets spared his form in the road and found another. He's in his mid-twenties, and still having trouble grasping the caprices of the war from which he's just returned—unharmed, but not untouched.

"That truck, shit, I still don't know where it came from," he says. "Up till that point, I guess you could say we were kind of cocky. Damn, it pissed us off, shocked us. It made us keep our alert up—really, for the rest of the war."

Odom, like many of the marines, has come to view the first day of battle as a kind of encapsulized arc of the whole war—the electric speed and confidence with which they seized their objective, the almost eerie lack of initial opposition, the feared chemical counterattack that never came. Then there was the complicating sense in which the enemy they encountered was not to be regarded as an enemy but rather as a potential friend, a repressed victim of a bad regime, in a war not of conquest but of liberation. Finally, after the immediate mission was accomplished, the marines entered the far riskier and more difficult open-ended phase, the paranoid policework of occupation.

The incident at pumping station number two, Odom believes, was an ambush in reverse: the Iraqis in the Toyota, attempting to flee the pumping station complex, were startled to find the marines dug in by the roadside, and reflexively struck out with a spray of AK-47 fire as they tried to speed past the unexpected obstacle. Lieutenant Childers, like any good platoon commander, was in the center of things, at the point of maximum danger, looking out for his men.

"Childers, Goddammit, he was the best," Odom says. "Sometimes he got on my nerves. But I loved the man to death. He was like a second father to the platoon." Odom describes Childers as an uncompromising but inventive taskmaster. At Camp Pendleton, and at Twenty-nine Palms, where the marines did their final live-fire exercises before the war, Childers constantly devised new ways to torture the men of his platoon, to spice up the physical training regimen. "Once, he went out and bought this four-hundred-pound tire, like from a giant bulldozer or something. Then he made us haul it up First Sergeant's Hill, all of us just struggling with it to the top." Odom points out the window to the miserably steep hill, its shaggy grasses swirling in the ocean breeze. "Childers was always coming up with shit like that."

Odom takes a cell phone call from his girlfriend back in South Carolina. It's been six months since he's seen her, and he can't wait to go on leave. "Gotta go, baby," he says, and after he hangs up, he gets to talking about Childers's legendary troubles with women. He'd had a few girlfriends over the years, and was once briefly engaged to a woman named Leo, but somehow the relationships always went sour. In the end, his women failed to relate to the intensity of his drive, or to the self-loathing that burned in back of his striving for a perhaps unattainable perfection. "One time he actually said to me, 'Fuck girls. They're a waste of time. They just get in your way.' We were camped in Kuwait and I was expecting a letter from my girlfriend, but it didn't come.

Man, I was in bad shape. He said, 'Yeah, that happened to me during the Persian Gulf War. My girl never wrote me once.' He said there was a way you could diagram your life as a circle. At different points around the circle you had your career, your education, your family, your interests. He said there was one gap in his circle, one part that was missing."

Childers filled the gap with a relentless work ethic and a kind of old-fashioned zeal for the life of the corps. Living alone in his tiny apartment in San Clemente, he'd rise before dawn every morning and run ten miles before breakfast. He'd swim for miles in Pendleton's Olympic pool, or take his $3,000 road bike on long rides around the base. He was intensely interested in the nitty-gritty nuances of ballistics, and was constantly trying to perfect his aim or work out the bugs in the sights of his various weapons (he had a Colt .45 Titanium revolver that he was especially proud of). Childers loved Pendleton, this austere theme park with its obstacle courses, dive tanks, and rappelling platforms, its capillaries of jogging trails, even the infamous work yard up in the hills where they sentence "unmotivated" marines to smash rocks into gravel—the whole domain set in a rugged coastal wilderness, or at least what passes for wilderness, in Southern California. Childers hated jarheads who thought the marine corps owed them something. He was one of Pendleton's many hard, idealistic monks. Other than a punching bag and his guns and his long shelves of military books, he had few belongings to slow him down; the only sentimental souvenir he kept from his life of peripatetic striving was an impressive collection of coins from the hundred or so countries he'd visited in his thirty restless years.

Childers wasn't exactly a flag-waver; his allegiance was to something purer and more intense. He had certain self-sacrificial notions of what a marine, a true marine, should be. He was grounded in fierce principles of professionalism, and he believed in the rock-bed rightness of the mission at hand—to take out a peculiarly evil tyrant, to save the oil infrastructure that could help pay for the country's metamorphosis, to unfurl the flag of democracy in a bleak region of the world to which fate kept bringing him back. One day in Kuwait, Odom recalls, Childers told him, "'Make sure the marines in your squad know why they're here, and that they're doing the right thing.' In camp, he had read something in a newsmagazine that said, 'Nothing in Iraq is worth risking a single American life.' Well, that really pissed him off. He told me, 'There are things worth dying for. Make sure you tell your marines that.'"

WHEN CHILDERS ABSORBS the bullet, his body doesn't immediately register the impact. He has a puzzled expression, and he exhales in a groan. With his rifle still in his hands, he drops to his knees. Then he falls slightly forward, his helmet tapping the ground. He rolls sideways, and curls into a fetal position.

Odom crouches next to his lieutenant. He can see a small round hole in Childers's uniform, on his right side, just along the bottom of his Kevlar vest. The puncture is about the size of a large pea. Curiously, he can see no blood. Odom's not entirely sure what's happened. All he can see is that Childers is having trouble catching his breath. For a second he entertains the slim hope that maybe Childers has only had the wind knocked out of him. But then Odom peers into his lieutenant's eyes. They're staring off into space. His expression is vacant, the face hardly recognizable to Odom.

Childers struggles to say something. "I'm hit," is all he can moan. "In the gut."

Someone cries for a medic, "Corpsman up!"

The Toyota truck, with its drive-by shooter, has sailed by and is now some fifty yards down the pump station road, racing toward the east. The men "light up" on it. Marines like to say that if they take an enemy round, they reply with a hundred rounds. In a murderous staccato, a dozen or more weapons chowder the vehicle with bullets. Yet the truck keeps on accelerating.

Odom can see that Childers has stopped breathing. He decides not to wait for the corpsman to get there. Hurriedly, he bends down to give Childers mouth-to-mouth resuscitation. There is a trail of Copenhagen on Childers's lips, but Odom hardly notices. Without hesitation, he removes the plug of tobacco from his lieutenant's mouth, and breathes into him.

To his surprise, the CPR succeeds in reviving Childers. His eyes blink open. "Can't believe it," he mutters. "Can't believe I got shot."

The marines are still blasting away at the Toyota, drilling it with bullets. A hundred yards down the road, the truck veers sharply to the side and finally comes to a stop close to the billowing break in the oil line. One of the occupants dangles a white shirt out the window and waves it.

Sergeant Nerad, who has been watching in disbelief, is blind with fury. All he can say is, "Them bastards." He races over to see what's happened to his lieutenant.

Odom is still crouched over him. Tears well in Childers's eyes. Odom notices that Childers's pants leg is stained with piss. One of the navy medical corpsmen attached to 2nd Platoon, a young Filipino named Jeffery Calzado, arrives. Calzado hunkers with Odom and inspects the lieutenant. He can see immediately that Childers is in severe shock. His breathing is erratic, his blood pressure plummeting. His skin is cold, his face lax and expressionless. The hole in his abdomen is seeping only a tiny amount of blood. Calzado knows that a bloodless bullet wound is not a good sign, that the real bleeding is internal.

They decide to get Childers out of the road and move him somewhere safer. Odom cradles him and somehow hoists him over his shoulder. He hauls Childers back to the cluster of vehicles parked beneath the trees. Odom lays him down on the metal ramp of one of the tracks.

Other corpsmen stream over to help. They cut away Childers's clothes and equipment with shears, leaving him dressed only in shorts and the blouse of his NBC suit. Another corpsman, Noah Glanville, gives him a syrette of morphine for the pain. Calzado props his legs up and checks his vital signs, while Dr. Shelton Tapley administers an IV. When they examine the wound more closely, the corpsmen discover that it's actually *two* wounds: the bullet entered the abdomen, just to the right of his navel, and then cleanly exited from his left kidney.

It was a one-in-a-million shot, they decide. The bullet—most likely a .308-caliber round from an AK-47—hit a few millimeters below the ceramic plates of his Kevlar vest, possibly striking at the instant when

Childers was raising his weapon to fire, so that the vest was momentarily hiked up higher than usual. The bullet angled in such a way that it hit a major artery. Now Childers is hemorrhaging massively, but it's all internal.

While the medics work on him, the marines suddenly hear the sound of another car engine approaching. A white Land Cruiser, stuffed with seven Iraqi soldiers, charges down the same road, aiming right at them. Just as the Iraqis in the Toyota had done, they're attempting a fast break from the pumping station complex, but this time the machine gunners in the tracks are ready for them. The oncoming vehicle is clearly within their range, about two hundred meters away from their position. They swivel their big barrels and open up the fifty-caliber machine guns. With a deafening report, the enormous rounds tear into the Land Cruiser and shred it like foil. In a few seconds the SUV stops in its tracks, its body yawning with smoky holes. All seven Iraqis inside are either dead or seriously maimed. The interior of the vehicle is a hideous sight, strewn with body parts and slathered in gore. One of the Iraqi soldiers sits with his intestines flung out over his lap.

With Childers down, Staff Sergeant Nerad realizes that he is technically in charge of the platoon now. Mainly, his thoughts are with Childers, his eyes wide with worry. He's devastated to see his lieutenant like this. Nerad inspects Childers's M-16 and notices that although the trigger has been switched from "safety" to "fire," the weapon hasn't been discharged. The Toyota had come on so fast that Childers hadn't had time to get off a round.

Nerad watches his lieutenant struggling for his life. He urges Childers to stay strong and breathe, breathe, breathe. But at this point Nerad thinks Childers knows he's going to die. "There were tears in his eyes," Nerad says. "You get a wound like that, it floods you. He knew."

The medics recognize that the only hope of saving Childers now is to chopper him immediately to a hospital in Kuwait. The helicopter that was supposed to medevac Corporal Groce, the land-mine victim, still hasn't arrived, so the dispatcher puts in another request, this one issued with maximum urgency.

As the corpsmen continue to work on Childers, Odom stays at his side, stroking his face, talking to him gently. "You're the best platoon commander we coulda ever had," he says. "Stay calm, keep breathin' now."

But the life is ebbing from him. His eyes are dilated. His tongue hangs thickly. He moans softly and, in a barely audible voice, says to Odom, "It hurts."

His breathing has become shallow and labored, and now he is completely unresponsive. The corpsmen ask Odom to open Childers's mouth and insert a special plastic implement designed to facilitate breathing by keeping the air passages open. But it doesn't work; it only makes him gag. Childers is down to eight respirations per minute. Doc Tapley begins to administer CPR, but the lieutenant's breathing continues to slow down.

Meanwhile, two marines, Corp. Mike Cash and Corp. Brandon White, both of Alpha Company's Headquarters Platoon, creep up on the bullet-pitted Toyota pickup truck. Four Iraqi men, all of them badly shot up, emerge from the truck and raise their hands in surrender. Struggling with their wounds, they shamble across the road and are met by a none-too-sympathetic party of marines, who frisk them and bind them with zip-ties, then lead them over to a makeshift prisoner holding area that's been set up in a recently excavated pit. The Iraqis, terrified they're going to all be executed together, plead with the marines, crying, "No shoot, no shoot!"

Cash and White continue to study the Toyota truck. They can see that a few other Iraqis remain inside. One of them appears to be dead—or at least not moving—and a couple of others are too badly injured to walk under their own power. Cash skulks up a little closer and suddenly realizes that at least one Iraqi is still trying to hold out. The man is behaving suspiciously. He sits cross-legged in the back of the truck, stretching his torso forward to stay as low as possible. Every few seconds, he peeks over the rim of the truck bed, darting nervous looks at Cash and White.

Cash thinks he sees the barrel of a rifle winking in the morning light. He yells at the man in Arabic, tells him to throw over any weapons he may have and to raise his hands above his head. The Iraqi refuses, and keeps on "turkey-peeking," as Cash puts it, frantically popping his head up and down. Cash yells again in Arabic but gets no response. Finally he loses all patience. He sprints toward the vehicle and pumps eight rounds into the man.

The Iraqi slumps over, dead. In his lap is a loaded AK-47.

Cash and White peer into the truck bed and take a quick inventory: a radio, some maps, several AK-47s, a large duffel bag full of civilian clothes, and a fifty-gallon drum that sloshes with a putrid gruel of rice and sour tomatoes. The cab is strewn with glass shards and brass shell casings. Wet blood smears the seats and windows.

Two badly wounded Iraqis remain, one inside the cab, another splayed by the side of the road. Cash and White decide to leave them there. They inspect the Toyota for any remaining weapons, then hasten back across the road to where the marines are dug in.

A dozen or more Iraqi prisoners are concentrated inside the pit. Suddenly one of them becomes extremely agitated and emerges from the rest of the group, sobbing. The man glares at Cash with wild eyes and shrieks at him in fairly good English, "Hey, you, mister, you shot my brother!" He gestures toward the Toyota truck with the dead Iraqi in the back.

Cash wheels on him. "Yeah, I shot him. 'Cause your brother had a fucking AK-47 aimed at me!"

The marines can't believe that some of these prisoners are still alive. They're mangled, peppered with gunshot wounds. A young man has a hole in his lower back that's large enough to accommodate two fists. Another has been separated from a significant portion of his jaw and is missing his lips. Still another has been shot *nine times*. And yet these prisoners are still standing, talking, even smoking the cigarettes that their captors, softened somewhat by the Iraqis' pitiful appearance, have offered them. The marines are both sickened by the carnage and fascinated by the Iraqis' stoic and uncanny toughness. "These guys were either superhuman," an Alpha Company marine will later say, "or they were all jacked up on amphetamines."

Some of the marines think the medical corpsmen should deny treatment to the four injured Iraqis who climbed from the Toyota, and heated words are exchanged. Enraged and upset by the sight of their fallen comrade, their attitude toward the men who just shot Childers is, for now, *Let them suffer.* But cooler heads prevail, and eventually the corpsmen are allowed to work on the prisoners, irrigating and dressing their wounds, setting up IVs, injecting morphine for pain. "These guys were begging us to save them," says corpsman Gentry Lloyd, a medic who treated a number of the Iraqis. "We had a responsibility to treat them no matter what they'd done before."

By the ambulance track, meanwhile, Tapley and Glanville have worked on Childers continuously for nearly twenty minutes. He cannot breathe on his own. His pulse is faint and thready; then it fades altogether.

Nerad circles back to check on his lieutenant, but Tapley and Glanville shake their heads. "He's gone," Glanville says. Childers is still laid out on the ramp of the ambulance track, a pale and strangely bloodless corpse dressed in boxer shorts, his body marked by one perfect wound, left by one perfect bullet. The hood of his chemical suit has been draped over his head like a shroud.

Shortly after nine o'clock, a CH-46 helicopter descends upon the site in biting swirls of dust. The marines place Corporal Groce and Lieutenant Childers inside. Slowly the helicopter climbs over the smoldering grids of pump station number two and angles for Kuwait.

THE MARINE IS IMMACULATE. Lying in his open coffin, he looks like a puppet. Nothing is out of place. The high and tight buzz cut, the dress blues, the blood stripe, the white-white gloves, the green braided fourragère tassel. His parents stand over him, crying, holding each other. The face sags in the wrong places from dehydration, but no wounds are apparent. He looks a little darker and a little thinner than the son they remember. The body has flown in a steady westward arc from Kuwait to Germany to the National Military Mortuary in Dover, Delaware, and finally here, to a funeral home in Powell, Wyoming. A detail from Marine Casualty Assistance has come to make sure the remains are "presentable," and that everything is done according to protocol. His uniform is crowded with ribbons and medals, including a Purple Heart.

The Childerses stare and stare. They know it's their son lying before them, but they keep repeating his name aloud as though they're not absolutely sure, as though there's still some chance it's a mistake. Maybe he's still in Iraq, policing the sullen streets of Baghdad. Maybe he's still coming home with the others in his platoon once the long mission is through. Or maybe he's still there on the battleground, in the desert oil fields he helped save, in the first hours of the first full day of the ground war: first to cross over, first to accomplish his mission, first to die at the hands of the enemy.

For months Judy had been having dreams that she would lose one of her two sons. She'd wake up from the nightmare and try to ignore its import. She kept having motherly premonitions. "There was something eating at me, but I couldn't put my finger on what it was," she says. She recalled that the last time he was home, Shane had looked and looked at her, "like he was trying to tell me something."

The marine protocol person hands Judy a few of Shane's personal effects from Iraq. When she holds Shane's I.D. card and his watch—the high-tech Suunto digital he was so keen on—she is flooded with emotion; something about the hard specificity of the artifact drives home the reality for her. "He's really not coming back, is he?" she says, and she begins to cry.

And for just a little while longer, she and her husband hold each other and, staring at their radiant son, they wail, "Shane. Shane. Shane."

Lt. Shane Childers was declared the first combat death in the Iraq war, and was promoted, posthumously, to first lieutenant. He is buried in Crown Hill Cemetery in Powell, Wyoming.

On the war's fifth day, the men of Alpha Company killed three Iraqi men who refused to slow down as their truck approached a marine checkpoint along the Euphrates River; the Iraqis, it turned out, were unarmed civilians.

After they were stabilized, the Iraqi prisoners who killed Lieutenant Childers were evacuated by helicopter from Iraq. Since the Kuwaiti government forbids Iraqi soldiers from entering the country, even for treatment at an American field hospital, the prisoners were all taken to a navy hospital ship in the Gulf. According to a navy corpsman assigned to escort them, every one of them survived.

At the time of this writing, 324 American soldiers have died in Iraq.

—2003

Acknowledgments

ANY ANTHOLOGY that reaches back this many years and ranges over this many places will inevitably tax the author's memory of all the folks he has to thank.

This book could not have come about without the forbearance (not to mention the generous expense accounts) of a good number of inspiring editors who turned me loose on America. First and foremost, my brilliant editor at Anchor-Vintage, Andrew Miller, saw the possibility of this collection and deftly culled and shaped these pieces. Laura Hohnhold read everything with perspicuity and a mirthful eye.

Many of the chapters in this book first appeared in the pages of *Outside,* which after twenty-five years of publication remains one of the boldest and most adventurous journals around. Magazines are like sausages—you don't want to know how they're made—but the quality that sets *Outside* apart is its game and effervescent willingness to go anywhere and take on anything; I hope some of that spirit is captured in this book. There's no way for me to thank everyone at *Outside* who had a hand in conceiving and shaping (and fact-checking) these particular stories, but I must single out Hal Espen, Jay Stowe, Mark Bryant, Greg Cliburn, Gretchen Reynolds, Alex Heard, Nick Heil, John Galvin, and Michael Paterniti, as well as *Outside*'s always energetic publisher, Larry Burke.

I'm grateful also to a number of astute editors at other publications who helped hatch early incarnations of these stories, including Jim Conaway at *Preservation,* Nick Paumgarten at *The New Yorker,* Rick Woodward at *Double Take,* Jacob Weisberg and Andrew Sullivan at *The New Republic,* Margaret Low-Smith and Ellen Weiss at National Public Radio's *All Things Considered,* Dan Ferrara at *Worth,* Ken DeCell at *The Washingtonian,* Tim Sayles at *Mid-Atlantic Country,* Meg Guroff at *Modern Maturity,* and Linton Weeks, Rich Leiby, and Peter

Perle at *The Washington Post*. Also, special thanks to the sharp and resourceful editors at *Men's Journal*, especially Sid Evans, Tom Foster, Mark Cohen, David Willey, and Leslie Lewis. I'm eternally indebted to the feisty and ebullient Ken Neill at *Memphis*, who first published my work and who had enough faith to let me go outrageously long with the narrative, "A Murder in Falkner."

Several chapters in this book originally appeared, in slightly different form, in *Stomping Grounds* (William Morrow, 1992), and came to fruition in large part thanks to the vision and steadfast efforts of Joy Harris and Harvey Ginsberg.

Special thanks to Dottie and Walker Wilkerson, Camille Hewett, Amber Hoover, Alyssa Brandt, Mark Crosby, Robert Gordon, Andy Court, Edder Bennett, Jon Cohen, and my always amazing and entertaining boys, Griffin, Graham, and McCall. Finally, cosmic gratitude to my supremely cool agent, Mr. Sloan Harris, and to my partner in crime, Anne Goodwin Sides, who, in addition to reading everything in here with a careful radar, was my inseparable companion through every mile of this book. *Ienjoya!*